BLADE
OF THE IMMORTAL

The Gathering II

publisher
Mike Richardson

series editor
Mike Hansen

collection editor
Chris Warner

collection designer
Amy Arendts

art director
Mark Cox

English-language version produced by Studio Proteus for Dark Horse Comics, Inc.

BLADE OF THE IMMORTAL Vol. 9: THE GATHERING II
Blade of the Immortal © 2000, 2001 Hiroaki Samura. All rights reserved.
First published in Japan in 1997 and 1998 by Kodansha Ltd., Tokyo.
English translation rights arranged through Kodansha Ltd. New and
adapted artwork and text © 2000, 2001 by Studio Proteus and Dark
Horse Comics, Inc. All other material © 2001 Dark Horse Comics, Inc.
All rights reserved. No portion of this publication may be reproduced, in
any form or by any means, without the express written permission of the
copyright holders. Names, characters, places, and incidents featured in
this publication either are the product of the author's imagination or are
used fictitiously. Any resemblance to actual persons (living or dead),
events, institutions, or locales, without satiric intent, is coincidental. Dark
Horse Manga™ is a trademark of Dark Horse Comics, Inc. Dark Horse
Comics® is a trademark of Dark Horse Comics, Inc., registered in various
categories and countries. All rights reserved.

This volume collects issues fifty-one through
fifty-seven of the Dark Horse comic-book series,
Blade of the Immortal.

Published by
Dark Horse Manga
A division of Dark Horse Comics, Inc.
10956 SE Main Street
Milwaukie, OR 97222

darkhorse.com

To find a comics shop in your area, call the
Comic Shop Locator Service toll-free at 1-888-266-4226.

First edition: December 2001
ISBN: 1-56971-560-2

3 5 7 9 10 8 6 4

Printed in Canada

BLADE
OF THE IMMORTAL

art and story
HIROAKI SAMURA

translation
Dana Lewis & Toren Smith

lettering and retouch
Tomoko Saito

The Gathering II

TM
DARK HORSE MANGA™

ABOUT THE TRANSLATION

The Swastika

The main character in *Blade of the Immortal*, Manji, has taken the "crux gammata" as both his name and his personal symbol. This symbol is also known as the *swastika*, a name derived from the Sanskrit *svastika* (meaning "welfare," from *su* — "well" + *asti* "he is"). As a symbol of prosperity and good fortune, the swastika was widely used throughout the ancient world (for example, appearing often on Mesopotamian coinage), including North and South America and has been used in Japan as a symbol of Buddhism since ancient times. To be precise, the symbol generally used by Japanese Buddhists is the *sauvastika*, which moves in a counterclockwise direction and is called the *manji* in Japanese. The arms of the *swastika*, which point in a clockwise direction, are generally considered a solar symbol. It was this version (the *hakenkreuz*) that was perverted by the Nazis. The *sauvastika* generally stands for night, and often for magical practices. It is important that readers understand that the swastika has ancient and honorable origins, and it is those that apply to this story, which takes place in the 18th century [ca. 1782–3]. *There is no anti-Semitic or pro-Nazi meaning behind the use of the symbol in this story. Those meanings did not exist until after 1910.*

The Artwork

The creator of *Blade of the Immortal* requested that we make an effort to avoid mirror-imaging his artwork. Normally, Westernized manga are first copied in a mirror-image in order to facilitate the left-to-right reading of the pages. However, Mr. Samura decided that he would rather see his pages reversed via the technique of cutting up the panels and re-pasting them in reverse order. While we feel that this often leads to problems in panel-to-panel continuity, we place primary importance on the wishes of the creator. Therefore, most of *Blade of the Immortal* has been produced using the "cut and paste" technique. There are, of course, some sequences where it was impossible to do this, and mirror-imaged panels or pages were used.

The Sound Effects & Dialogue

Since some of Mr. Samura's sound effects are integral parts of the illustrations, we decided to leave those in their original Japanese. We hope readers will view the unretouched sound effects as essential portions of Mr. Samura's extraordinary artwork. In addition, Mr. Samura's treatment of dialogue is quite different from that featured in typical samurai manga and is considered to be one of the features that has made *Blade* such a hit in Japan. Mr. Samura has mixed a variety of linguistic styles in this fantasy story, with some characters speaking in the mannered style of old Japan while others speak as if they were street-corner punks from a bad area of modern-day Tokyo. The anachronistic slang used by some of the characters in the English translation reflects the unusual mix of speech patterns from the original Japanese text.

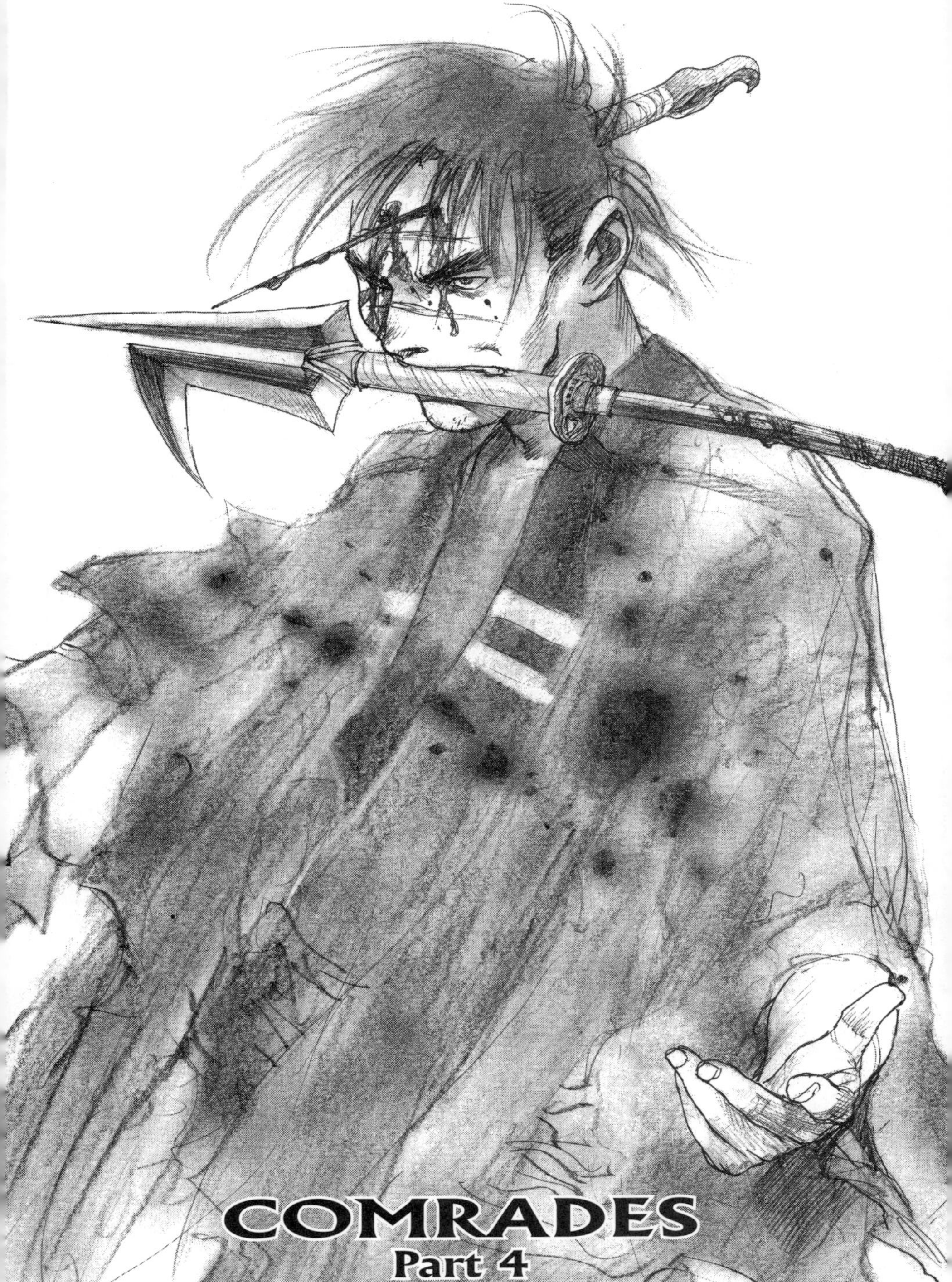

COMRADES
Part 4

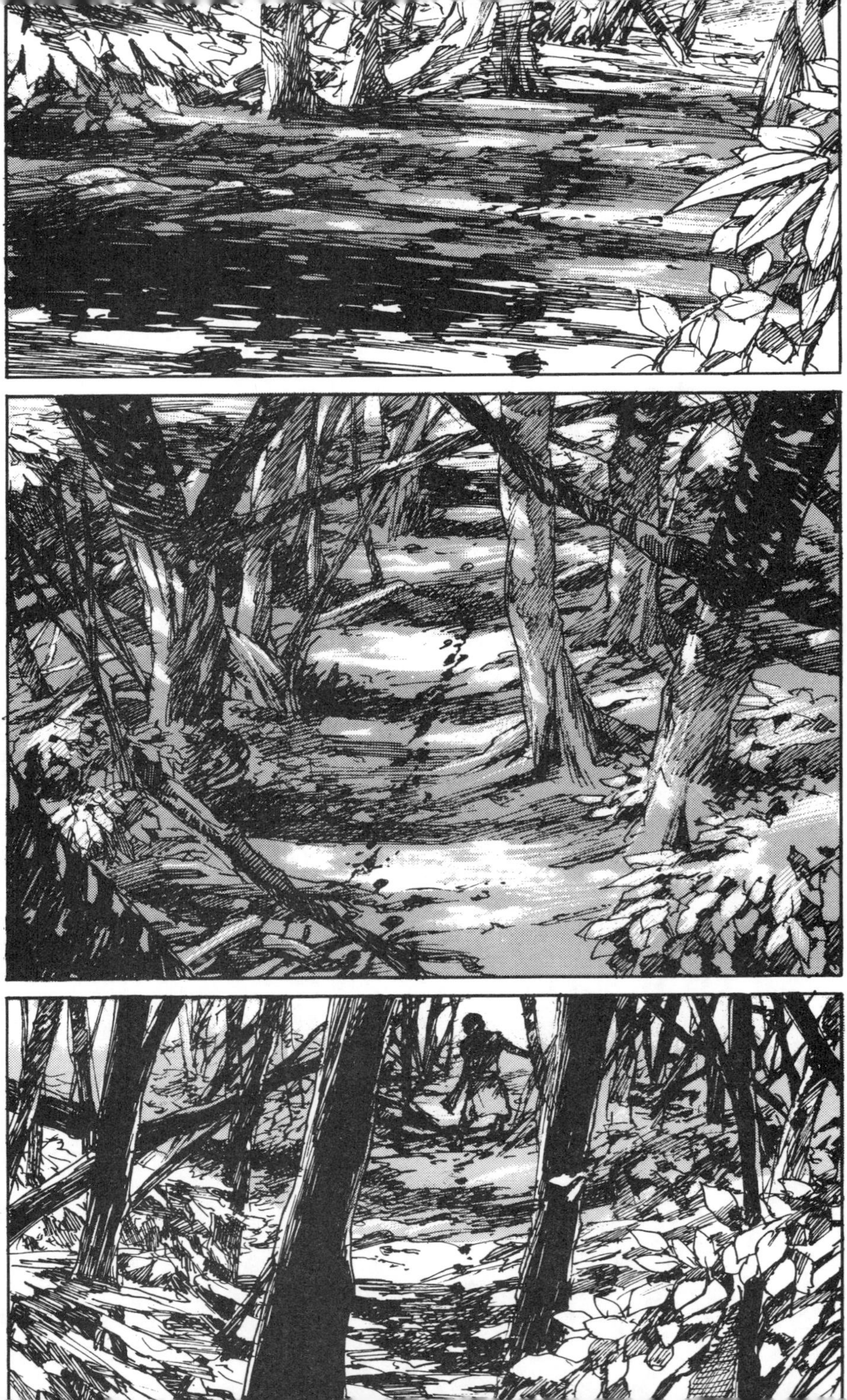

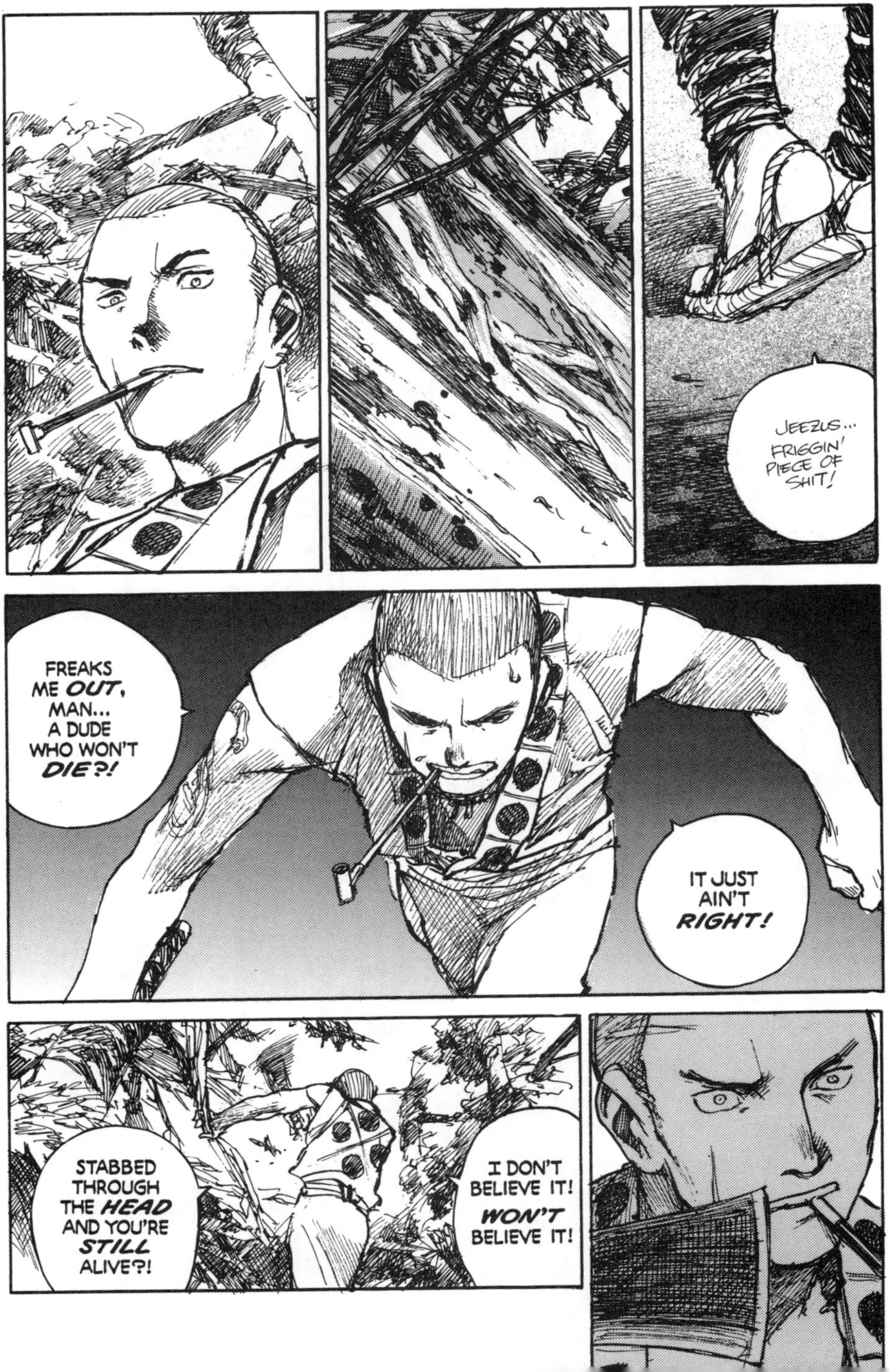
JEEZUS... FRIGGIN' PIECE OF SHIT!
FREAKS ME OUT, MAN... A DUDE WHO WON'T DIE?!
IT JUST AIN'T RIGHT!
STABBED THROUGH THE HEAD AND YOU'RE STILL ALIVE?!
I DON'T BELIEVE IT! WON'T BELIEVE IT!

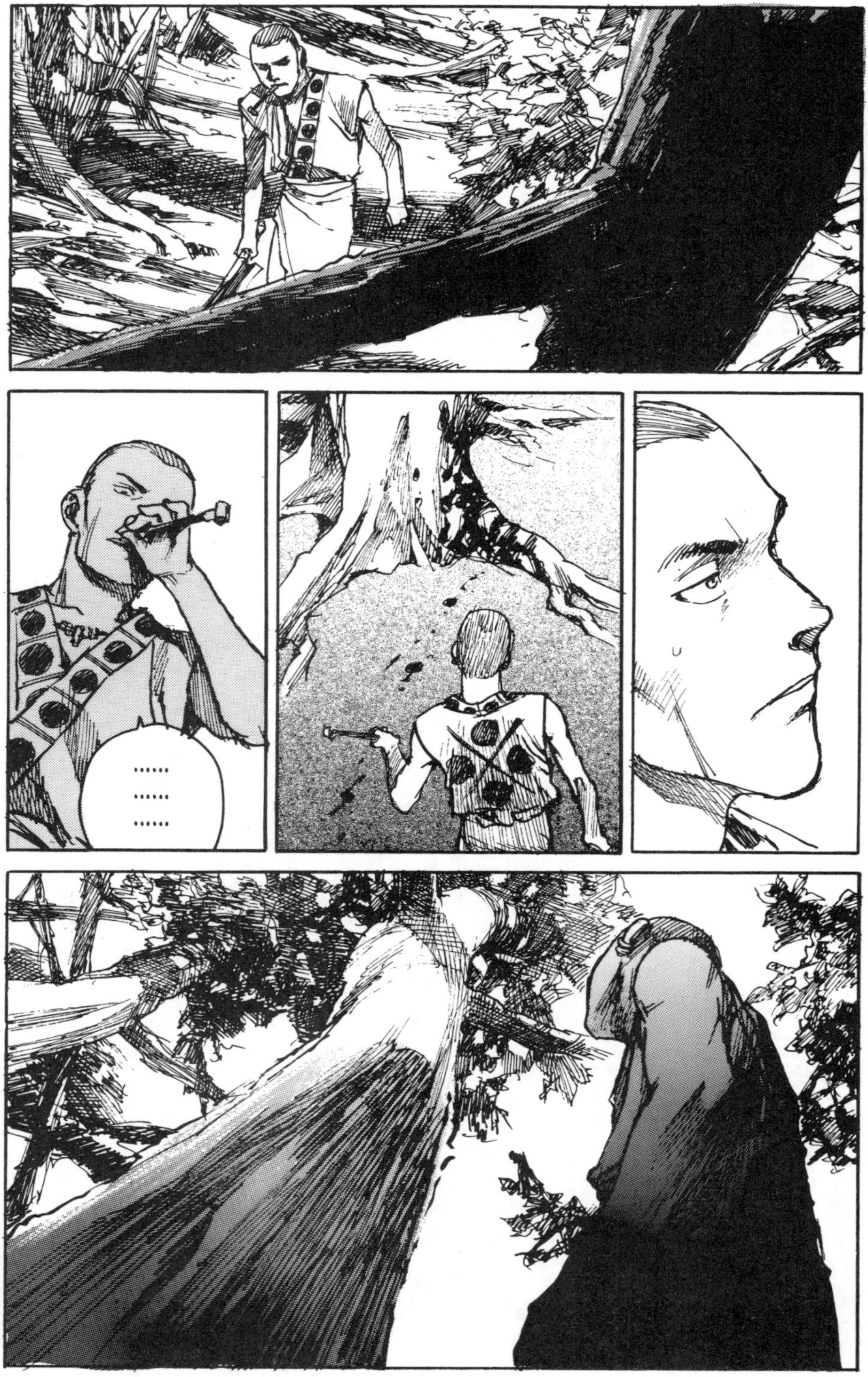
......
......
......

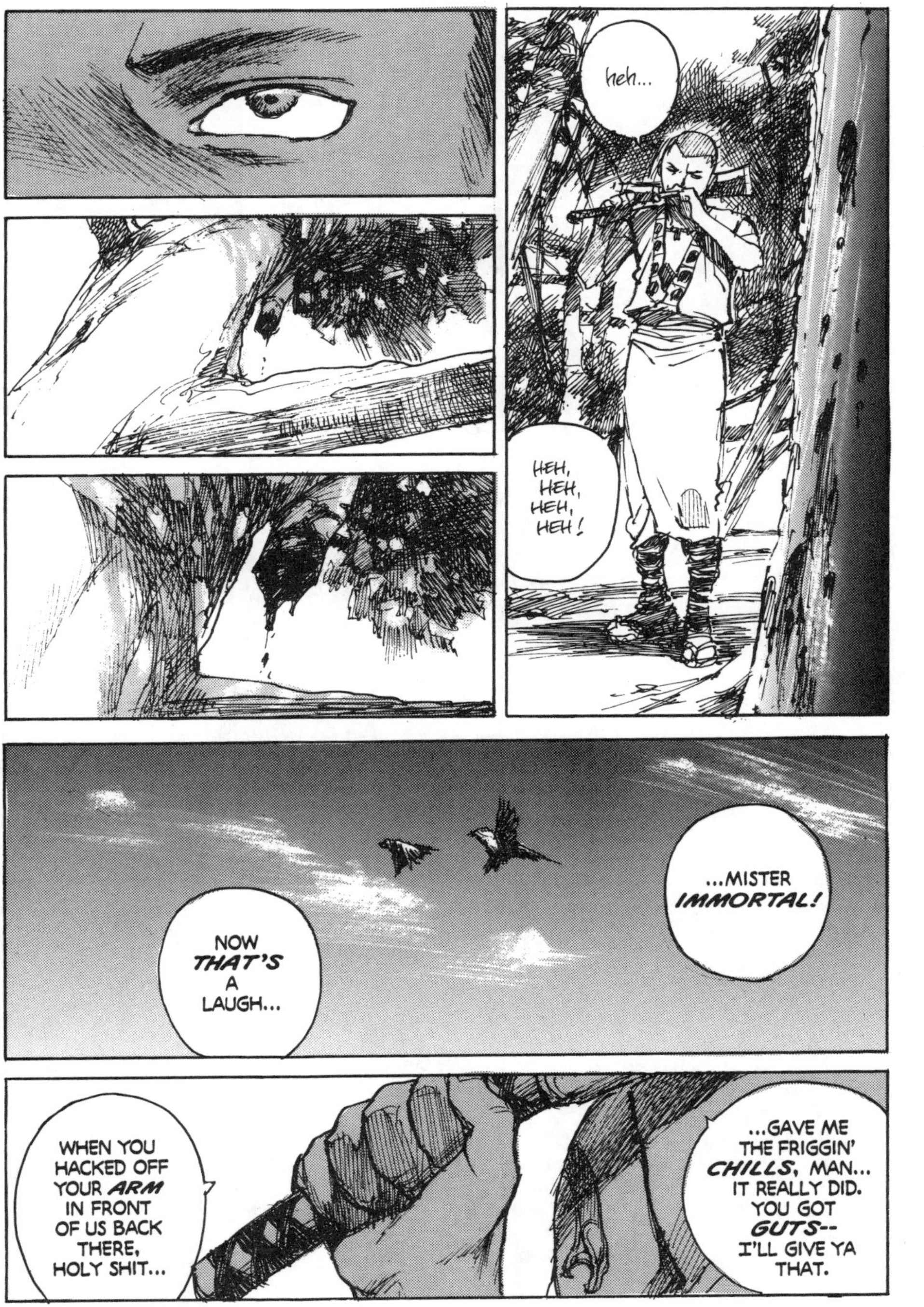
heh...
HEH, HEH, HEH, HEH!
NOW THAT'S A LAUGH...
...MISTER IMMORTAL!
WHEN YOU HACKED OFF YOUR ARM IN FRONT OF US BACK THERE, HOLY SHIT...
...GAVE ME THE FRIGGIN' CHILLS, MAN... IT REALLY DID. YOU GOT GUTS-- I'LL GIVE YA THAT.

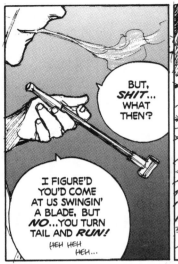

BUT, *SHIT...* WHAT THEN?

I FIGURE'D YOU'D COME AT US SWINGIN' A BLADE, BUT *NO*...YOU TURN TAIL AND *RUN!*

HEH HEH HEH...

NOT EXACTLY *SAMURAI* STUFF, DUDE!

IS THAT *IMMORTAL BOD* OF YOURS ALL YOU'VE GOT GOIN' FOR YA? *EH??*

KNCH

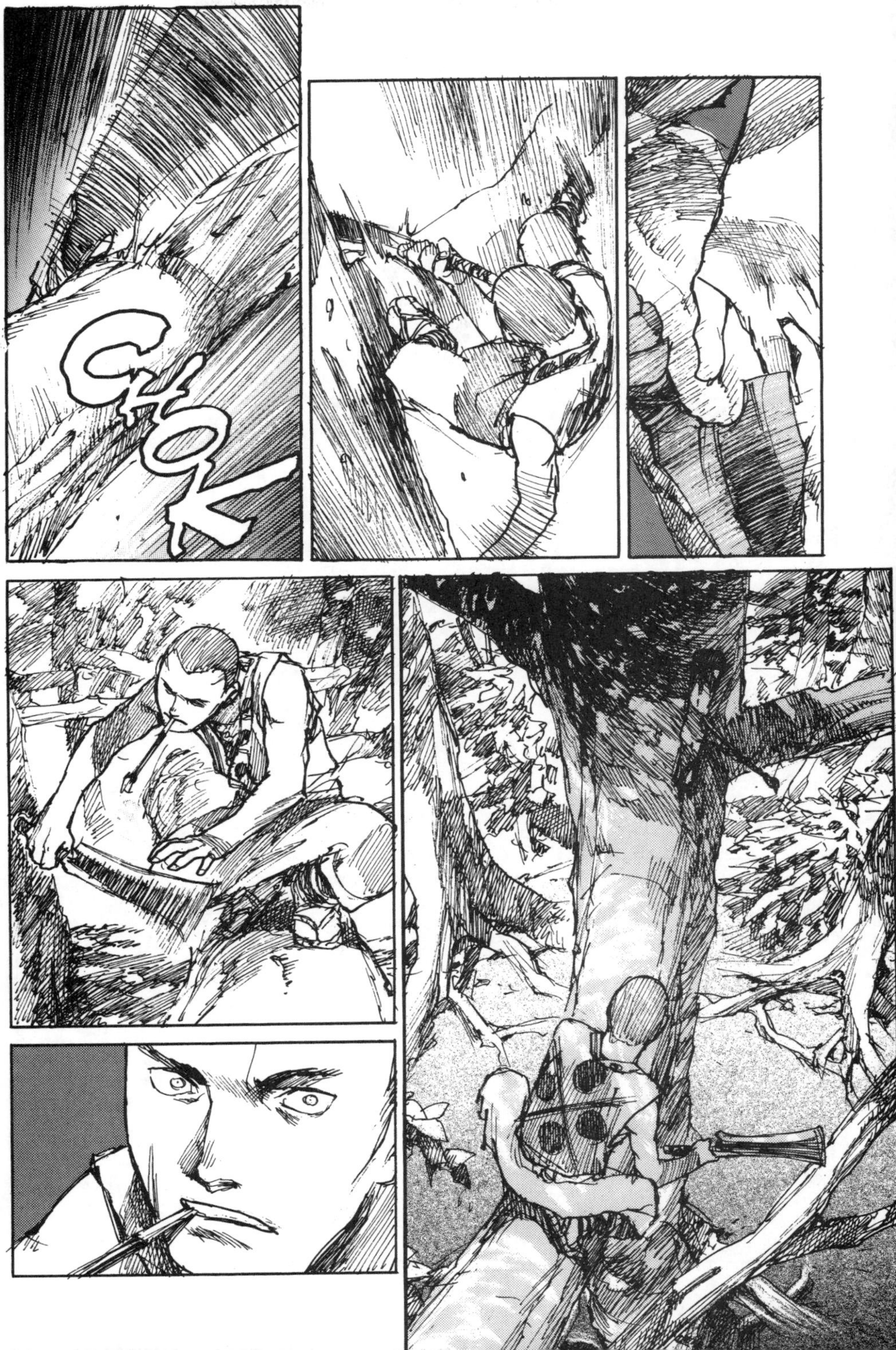
CHOK

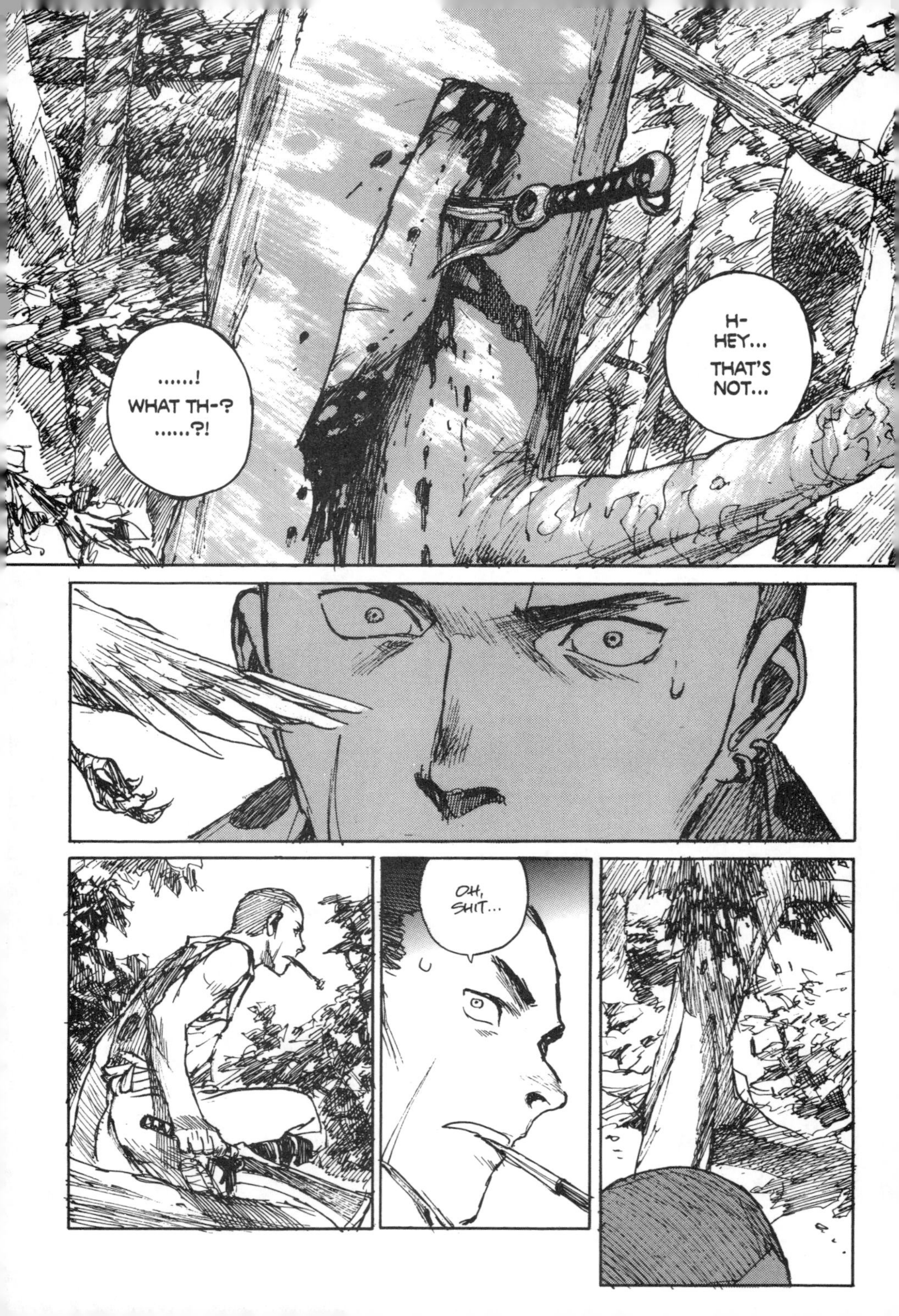
......! WHAT TH-? ......?!
H-HEY... THAT'S NOT...
OH, SHIT...

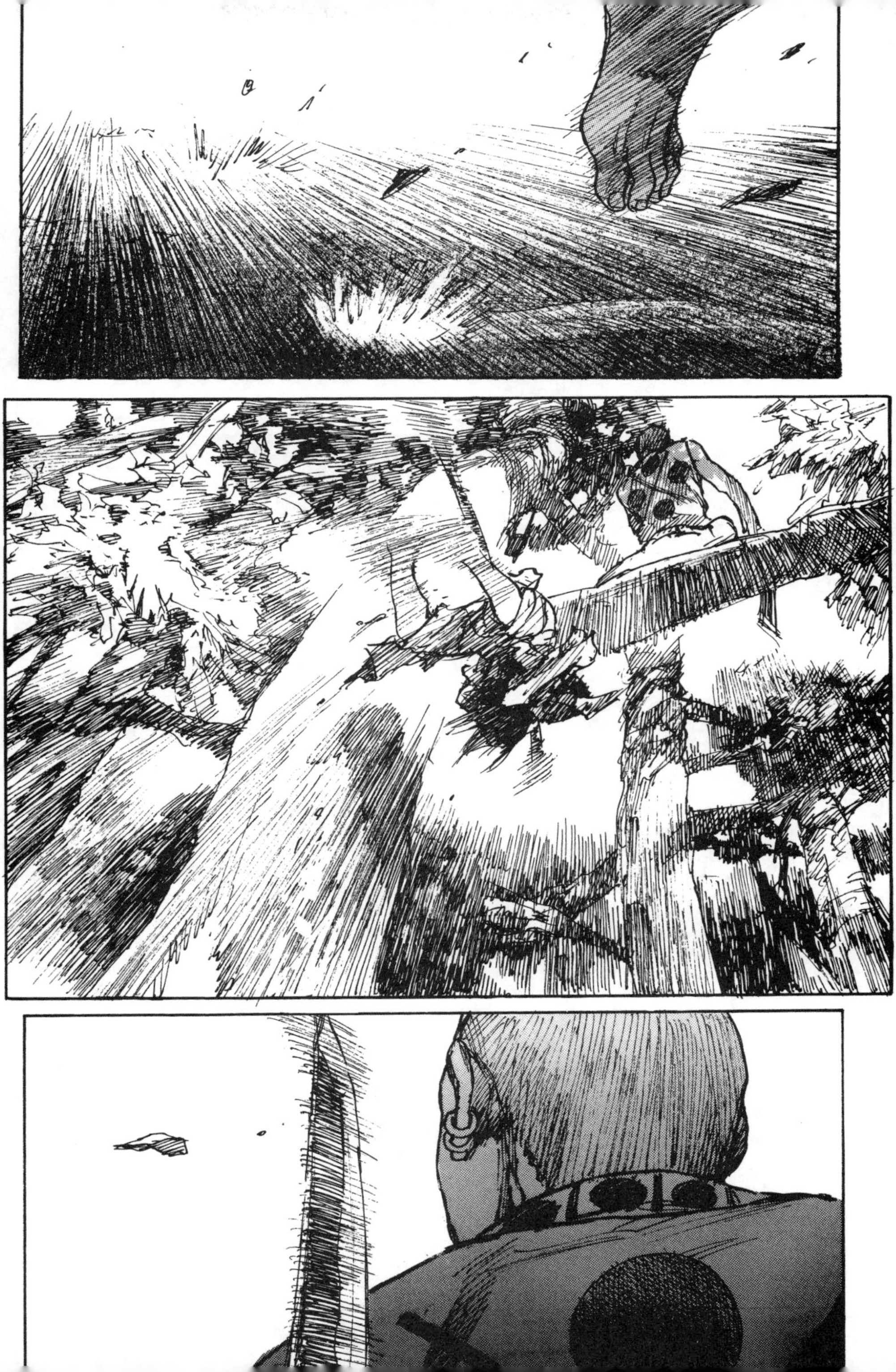

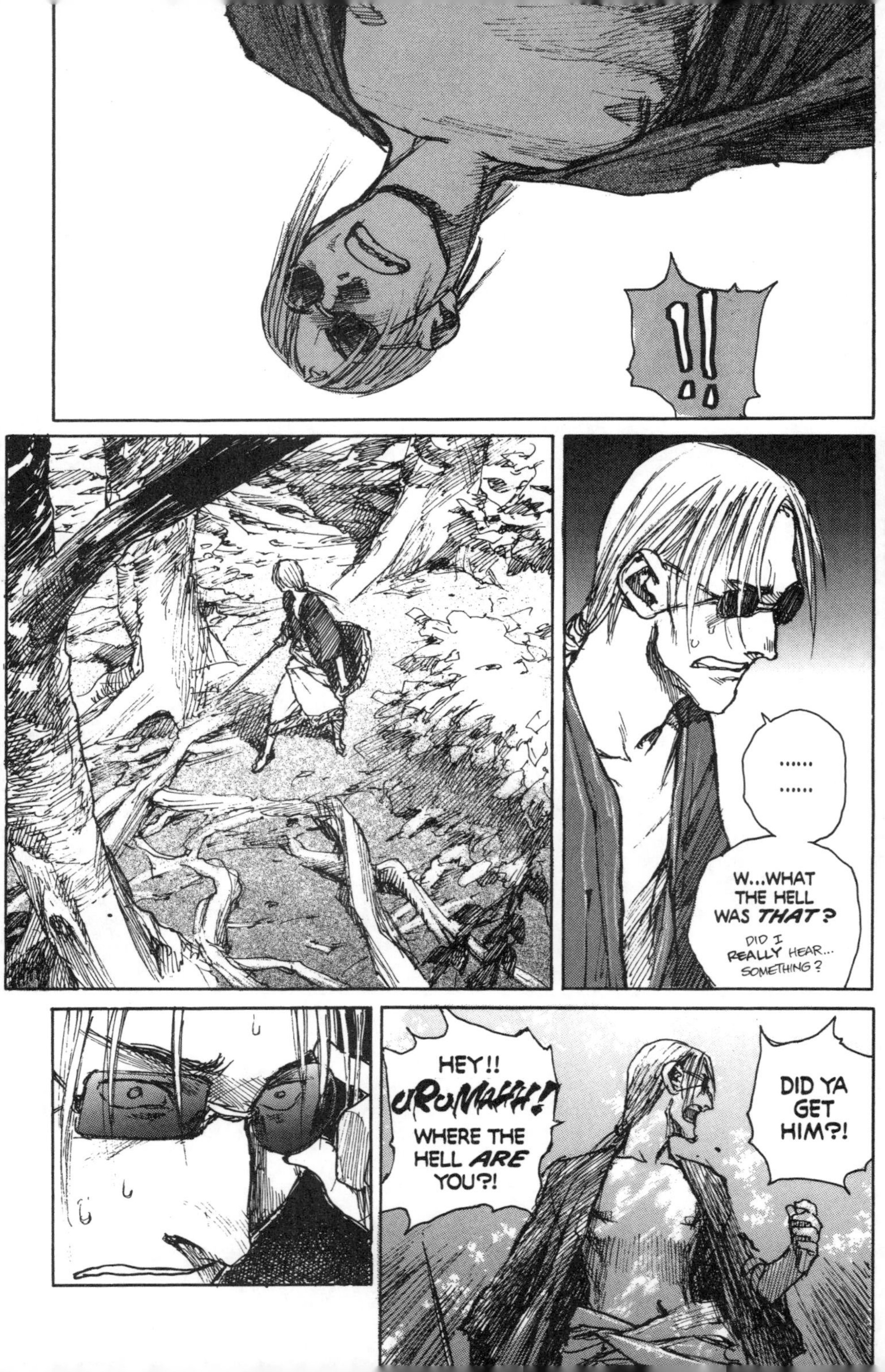
!!
......
......
W...WHAT THE HELL WAS THAT?
DID I REALLY HEAR... SOMETHING?
HEY!! URUMAHH! WHERE THE HELL ARE YOU?!
DID YA GET HIM?!

ANSWER ME, YOU USELESS *TURD!!*

IF I GOTTA CARRY MY OWN CRAP BACK TO EDO, I'M GONNA BE *PISSED!*

.....
.....
.....

THIS AIN'T *FUNNY*, DAMN IT... SHIT... WHO *CARES* IF HE'S FREAKIN' *IMMORTAL?!*

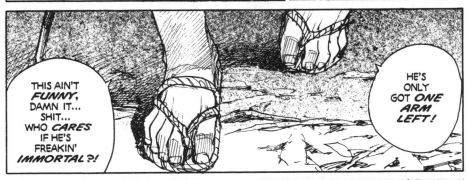

HE'S ONLY GOT *ONE ARM LEFT!*

IF YOU'RE GONNA BE A *LOSER*, URUMA, JUST KEEP IT TO WHEN YOU'RE GAMBLING WITH *ME*, OKAY, DUDE?

GOD *DAMN* IT!!

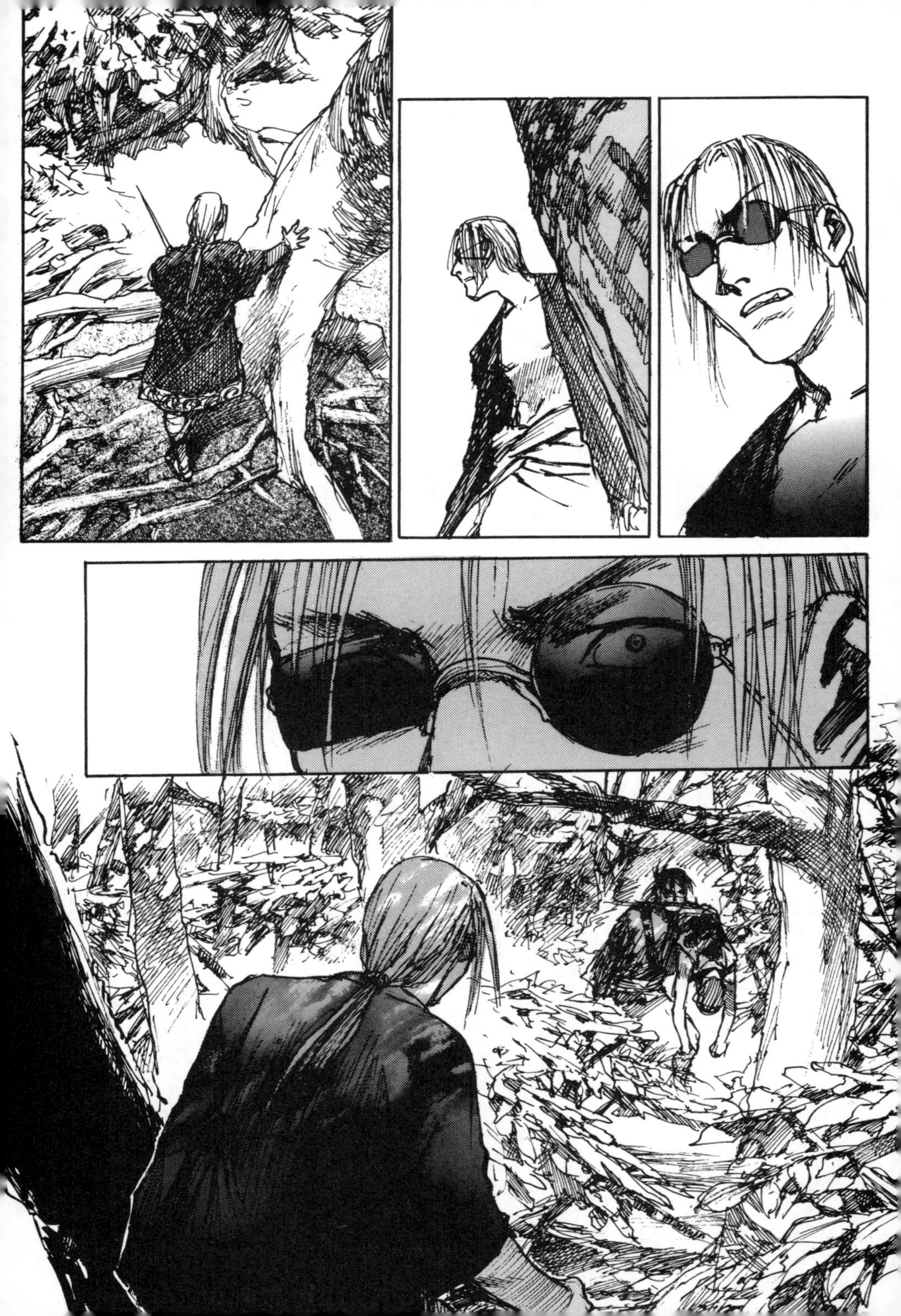

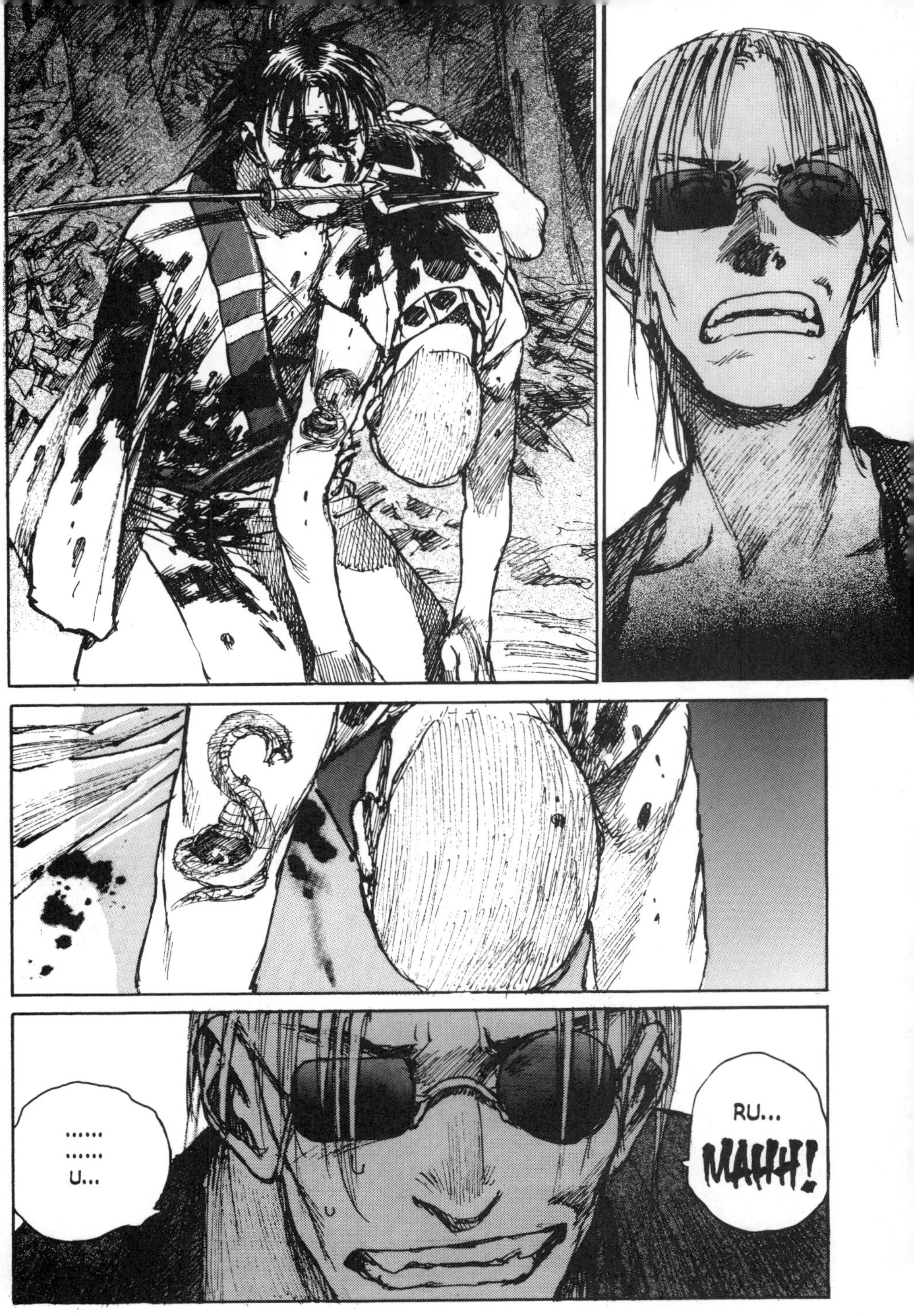
......
......
U...
RU...
MAHH!

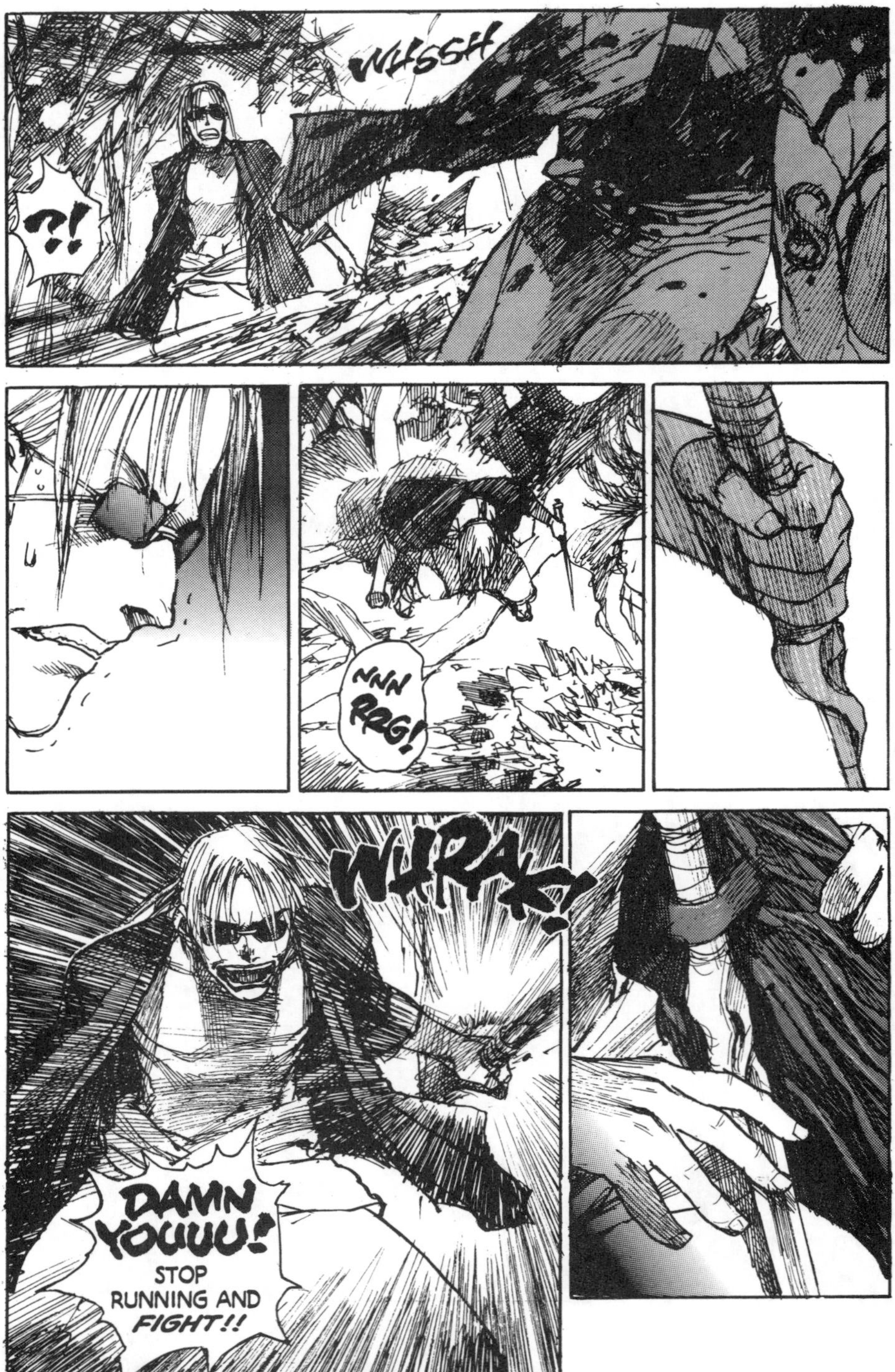
WHSSH
?!
NNN RRG!
WHAK!
DAMN YOUUU!
STOP RUNNING AND *FIGHT!!*

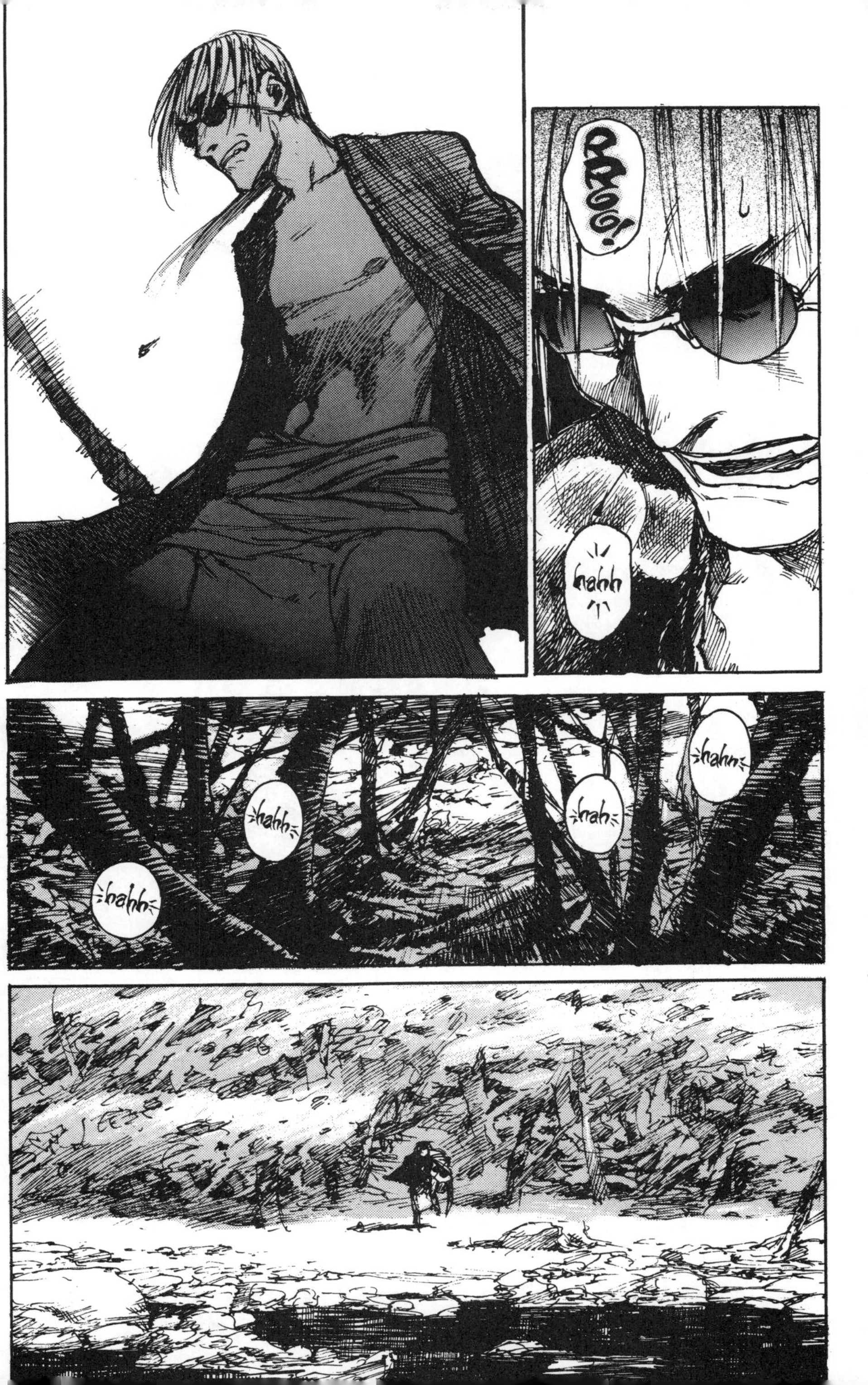
Ahgg!
hahh
hahh
hahh
hah
hahn

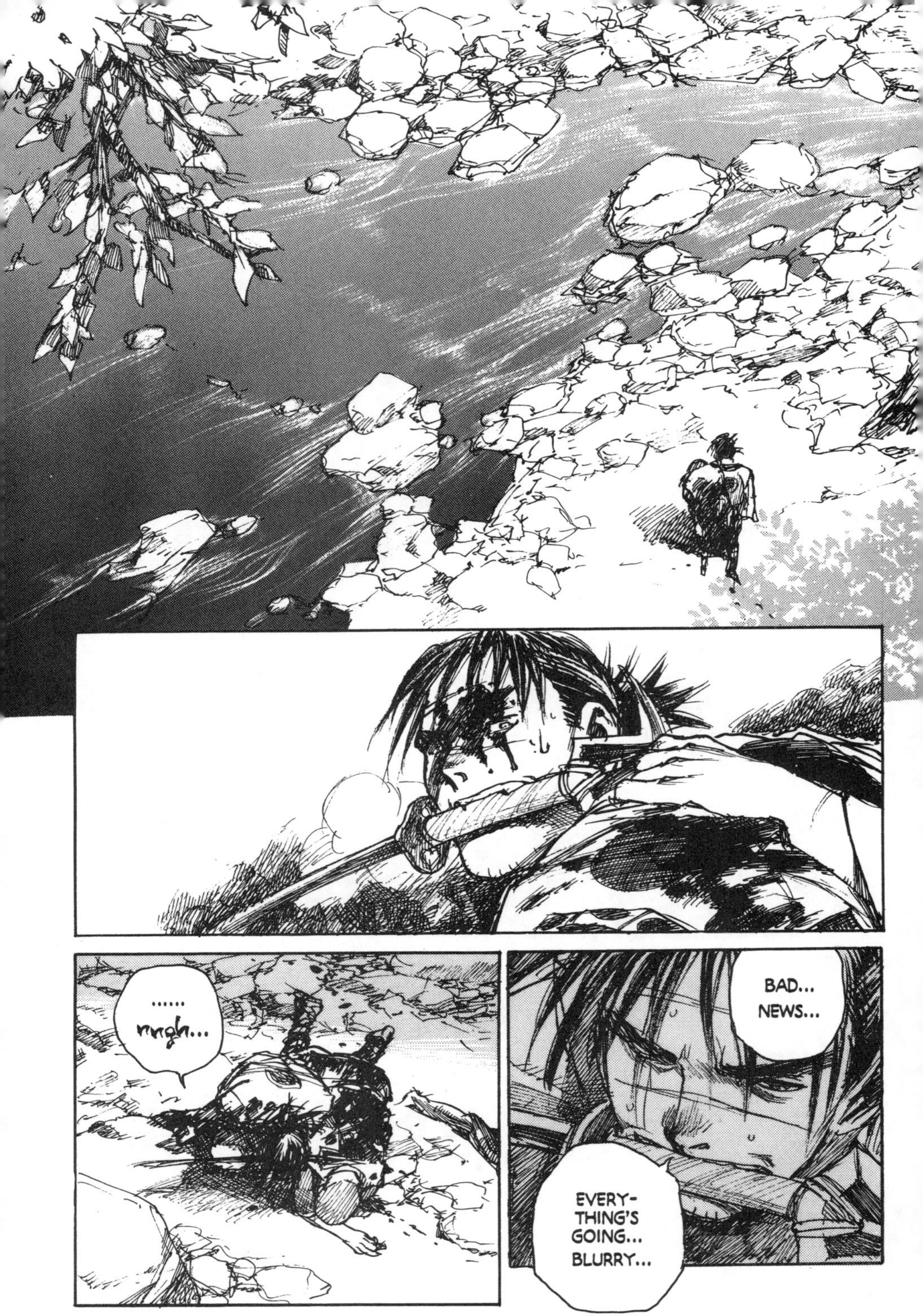

...... nngh...
BAD... NEWS...
EVERY-THING'S GOING... BLURRY...

KHNGF!
OWN!

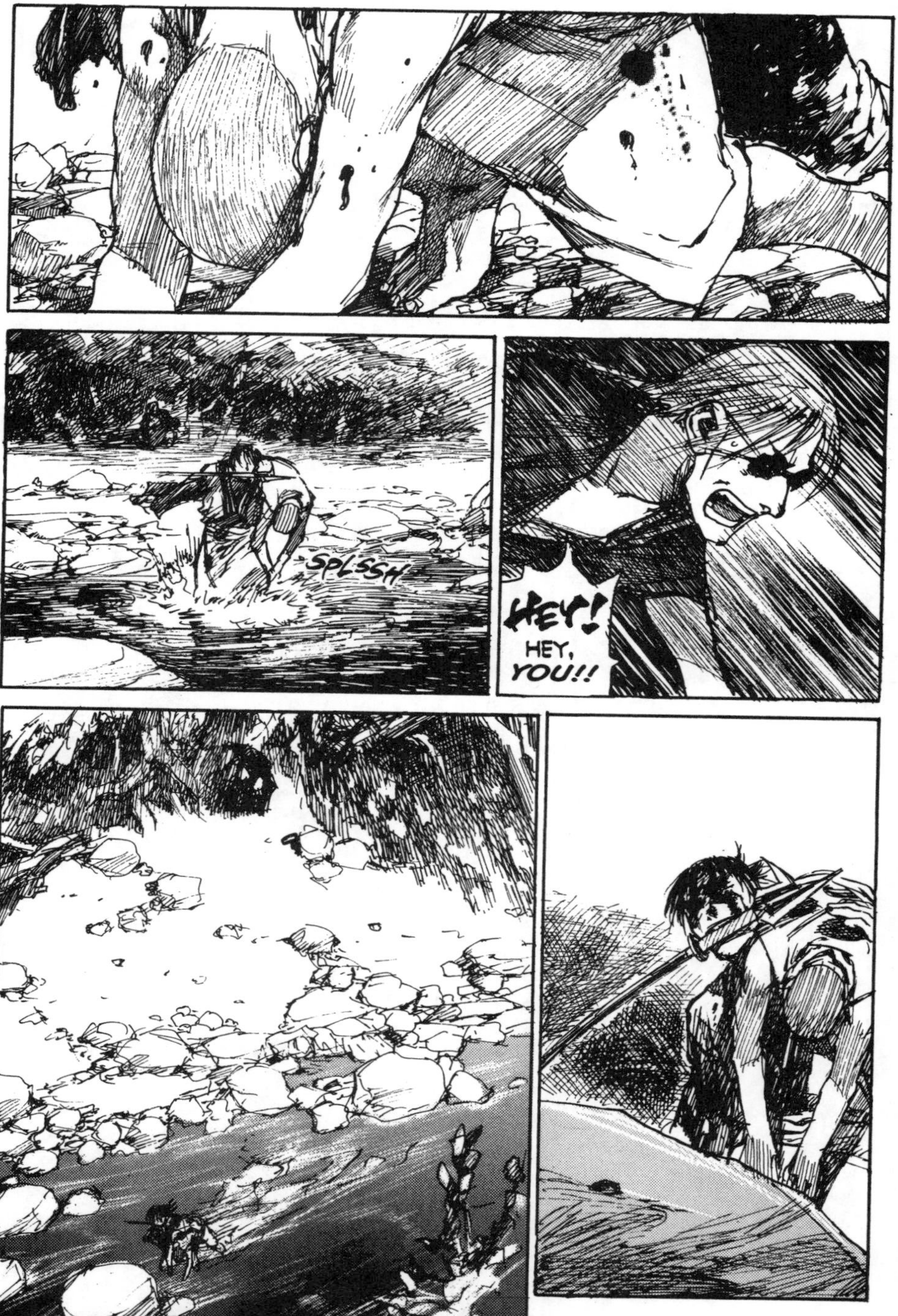
SPLSSH
HEY!
HEY, YOU!!

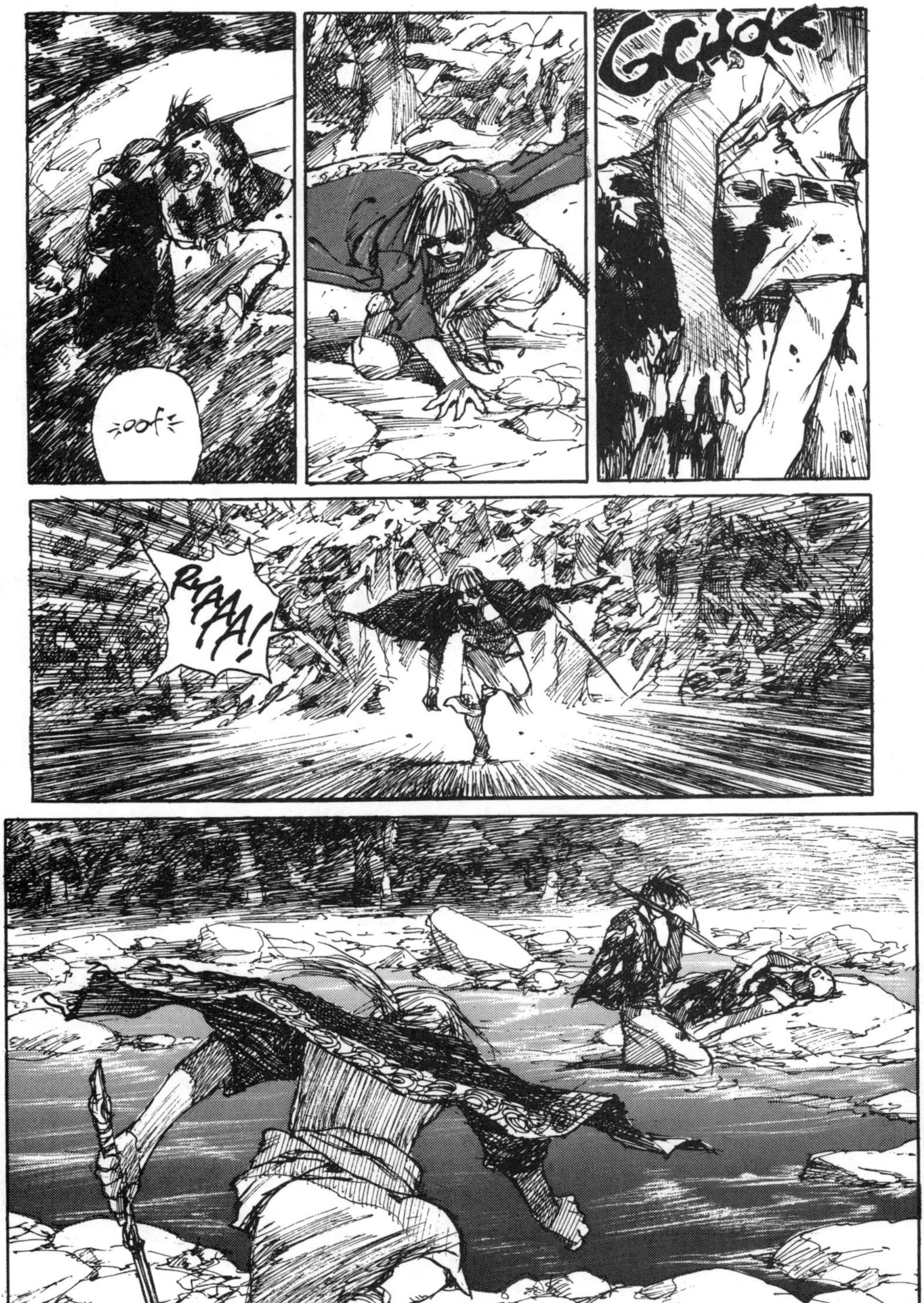

oof
GCHOK
RYAAAA!

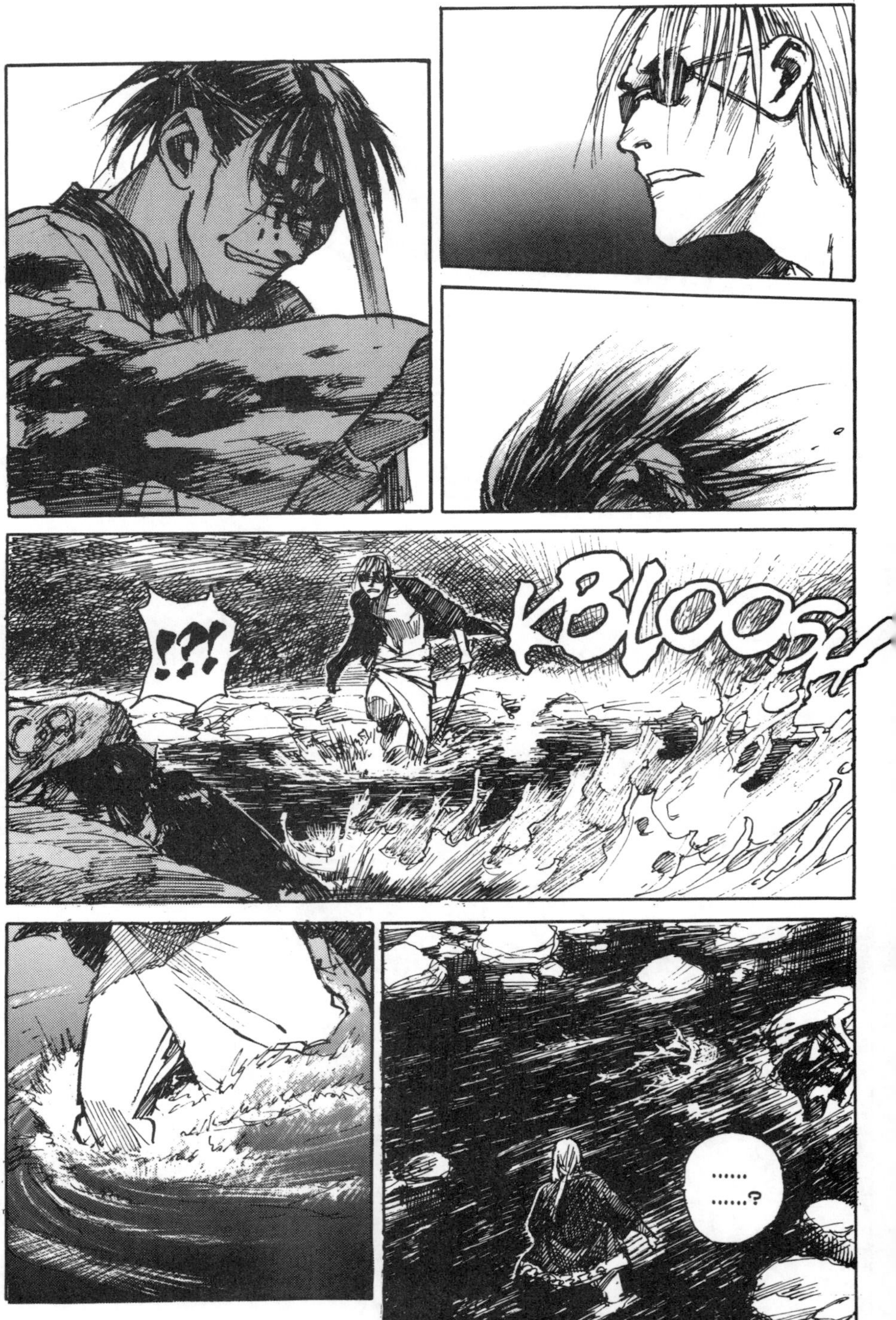

!?!
KBLOOSH
......
......?

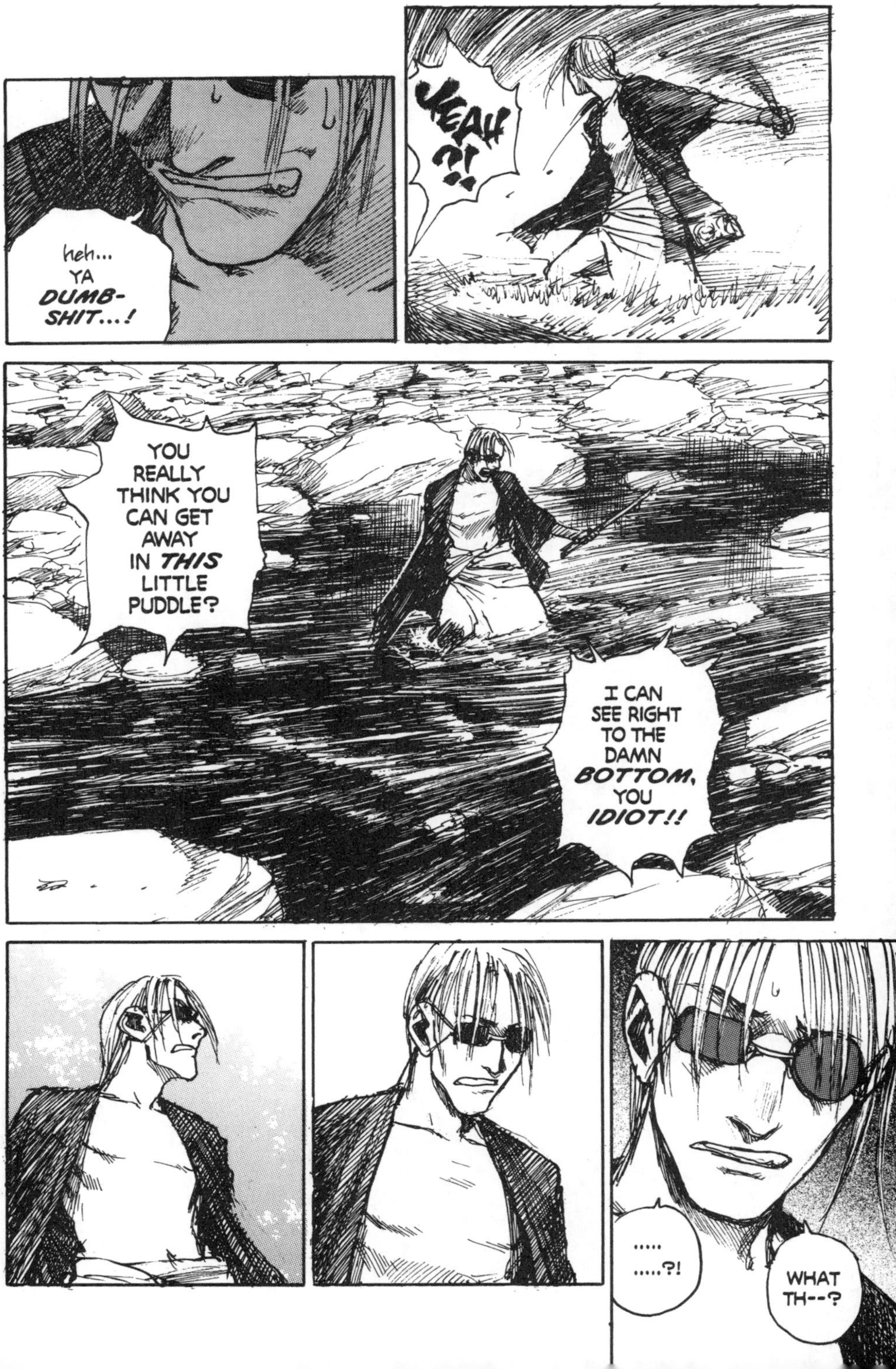
heh... YA DUMB-SHIT...!
JEAH ?!
YOU REALLY THINK YOU CAN GET AWAY IN THIS LITTLE PUDDLE?
I CAN SEE RIGHT TO THE DAMN BOTTOM, YOU IDIOT!!
....?!
WHAT TH--?

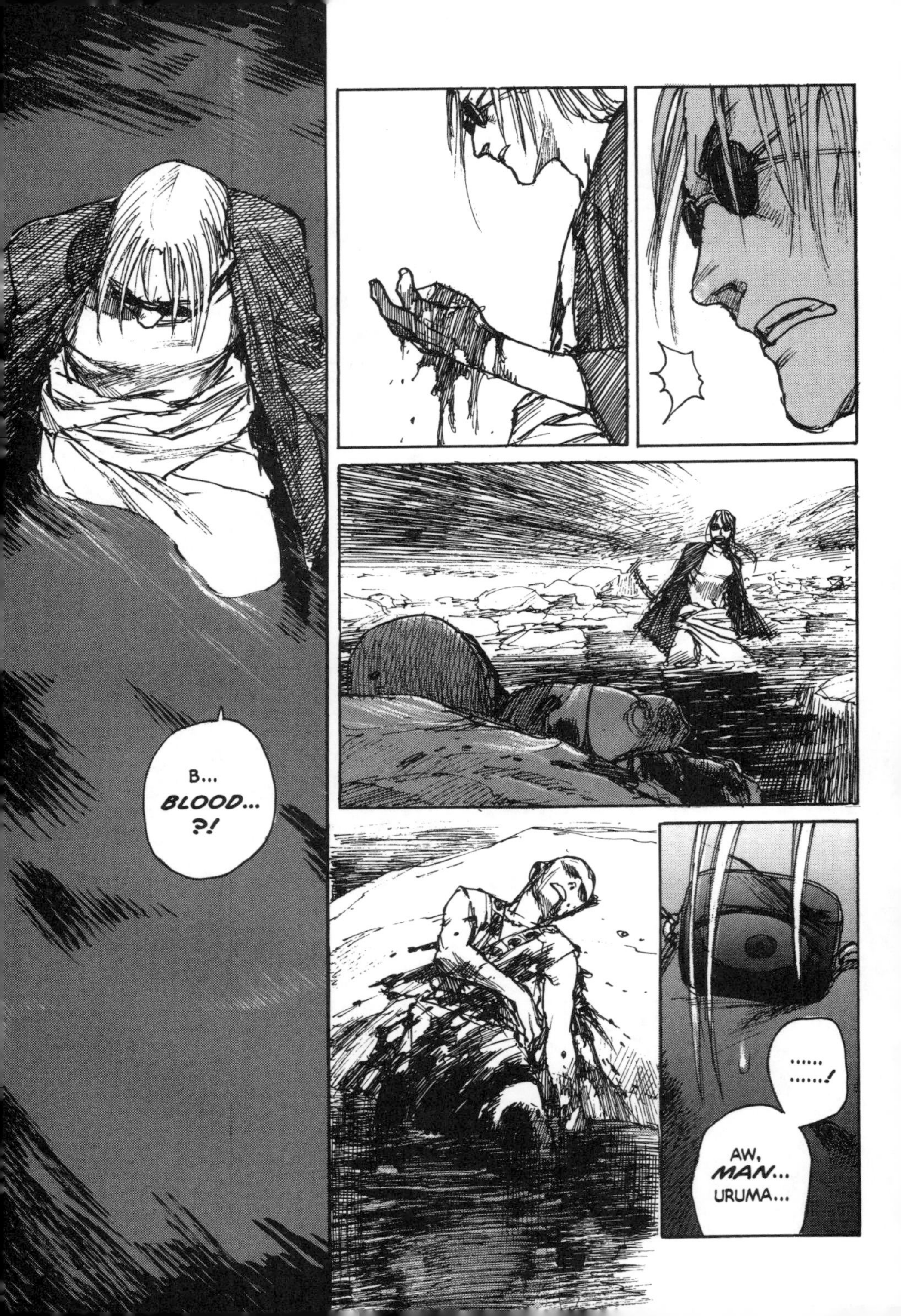
B... BLOOD... ?!
......
.......!
AW, MAN... URUMA...

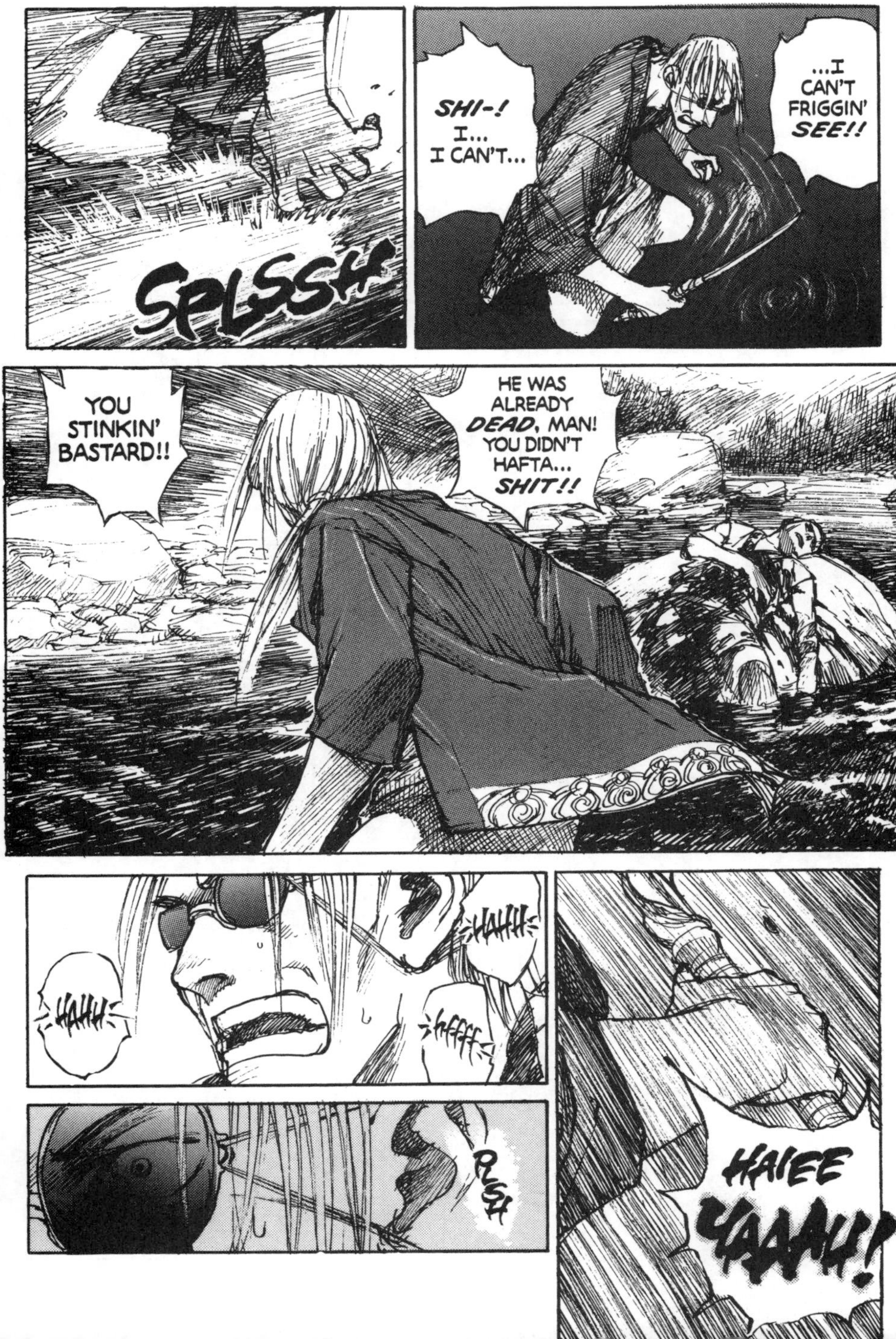
SPLSSH
SHI-! I... I CAN'T...
...I CAN'T FRIGGIN' SEE!!
YOU STINKIN' BASTARD!!
HE WAS ALREADY DEAD, MAN! YOU DIDN'T HAFTA... SHIT!!
HAHH
HAHH
hffff
PUSH
HAIEE YAAAH!

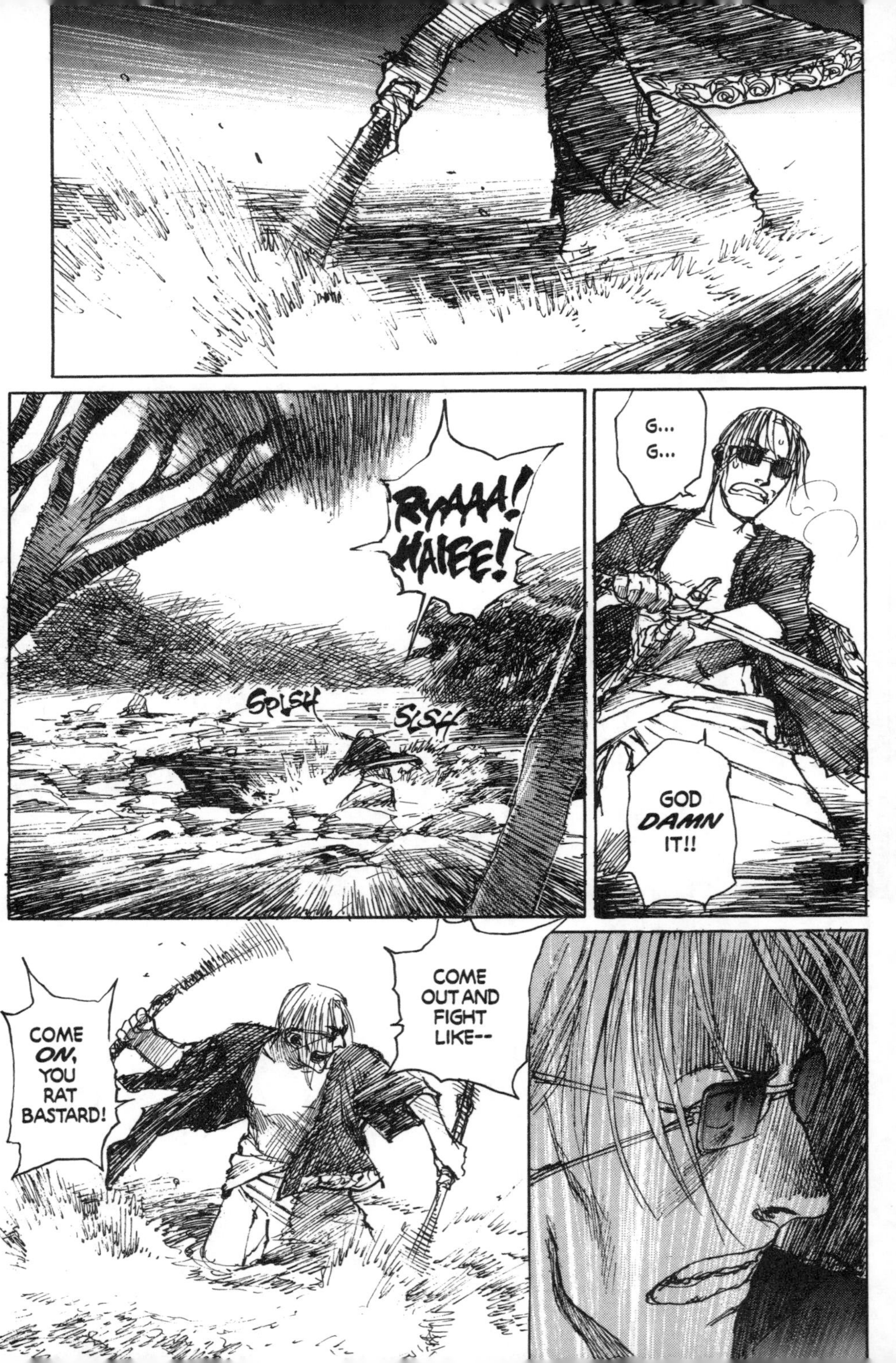
RYAAA! HAIEE!
SPLSH
SLSH
G... G...
GOD DAMN IT!!
COME ON, YOU RAT BASTARD!
COME OUT AND FIGHT LIKE--

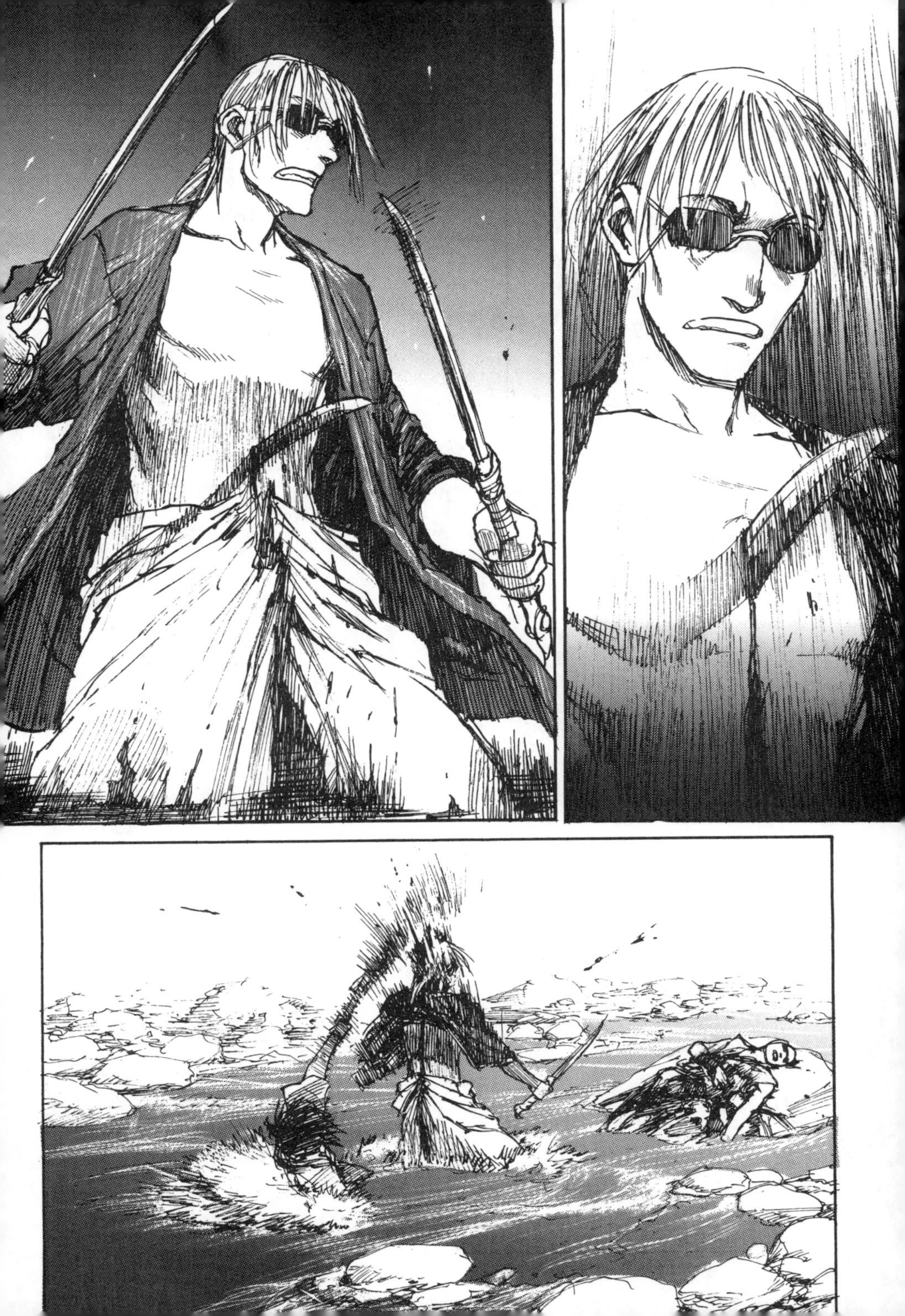

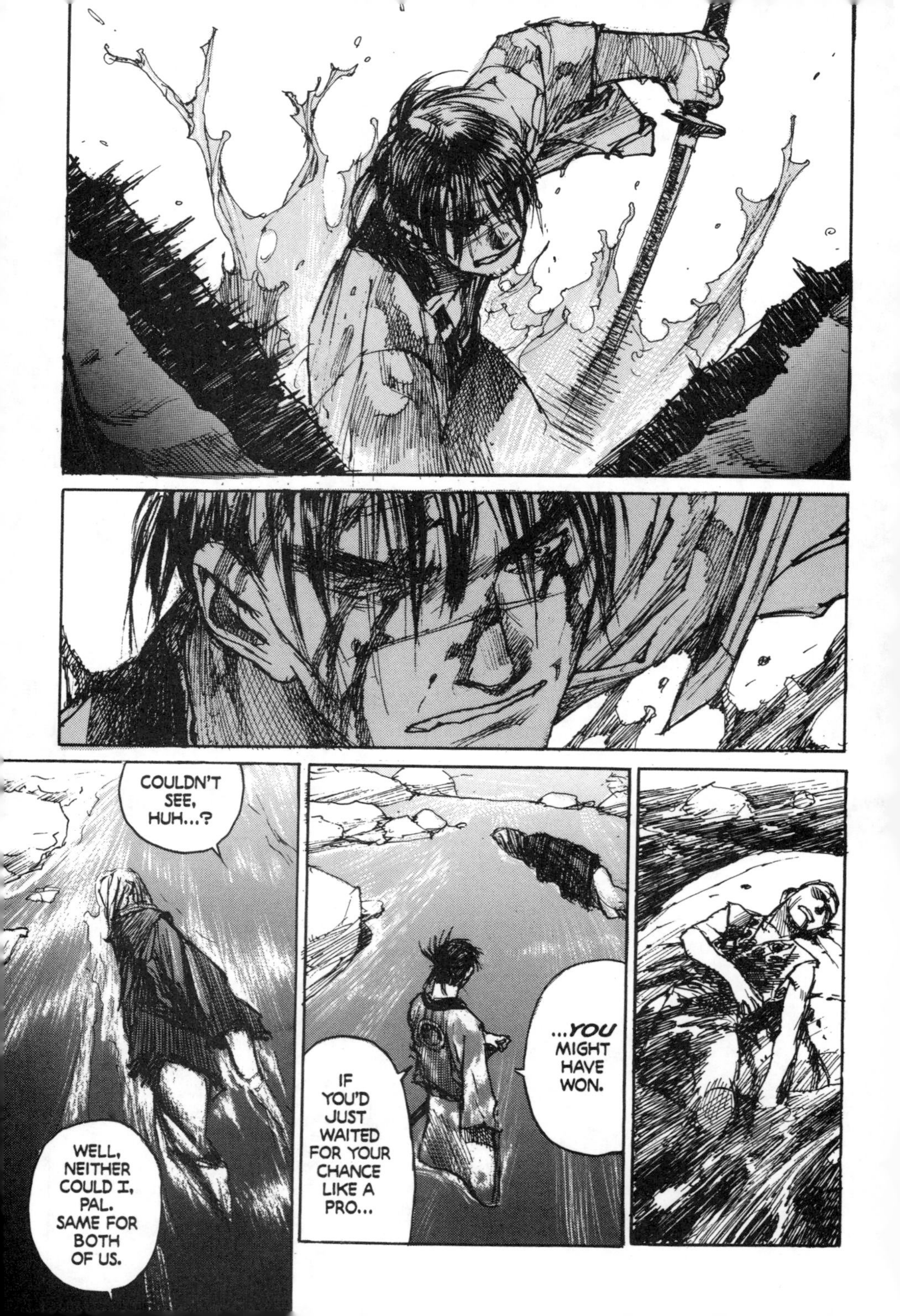
COULDN'T SEE, HUH...?
WELL, NEITHER COULD I, PAL. SAME FOR BOTH OF US.
IF YOU'D JUST WAITED FOR YOUR CHANCE LIKE A PRO...
...*YOU* MIGHT HAVE WON.

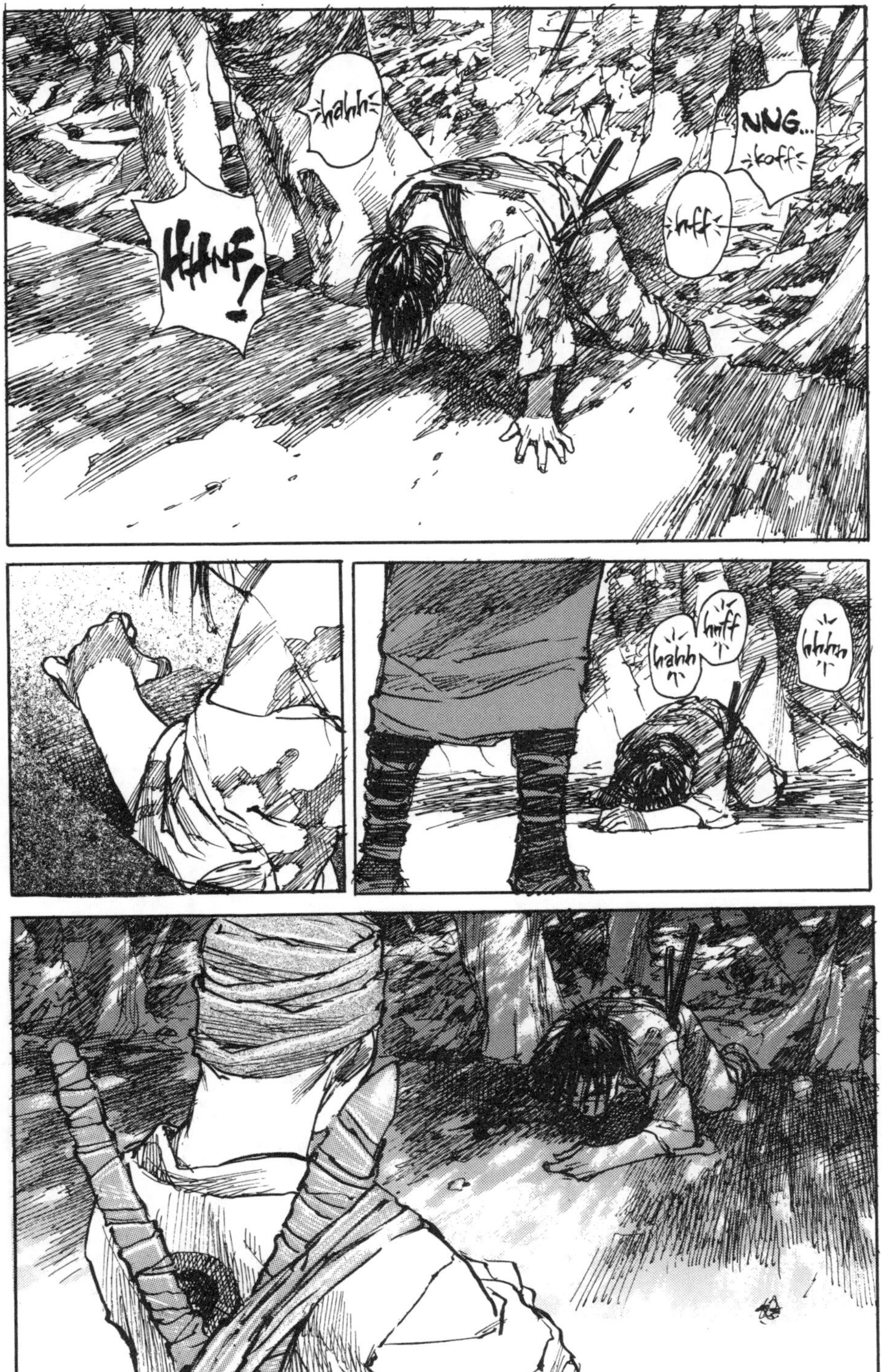
hahh
HHNF!
NNG... koff
hnff
hahh
hnff
hhhn

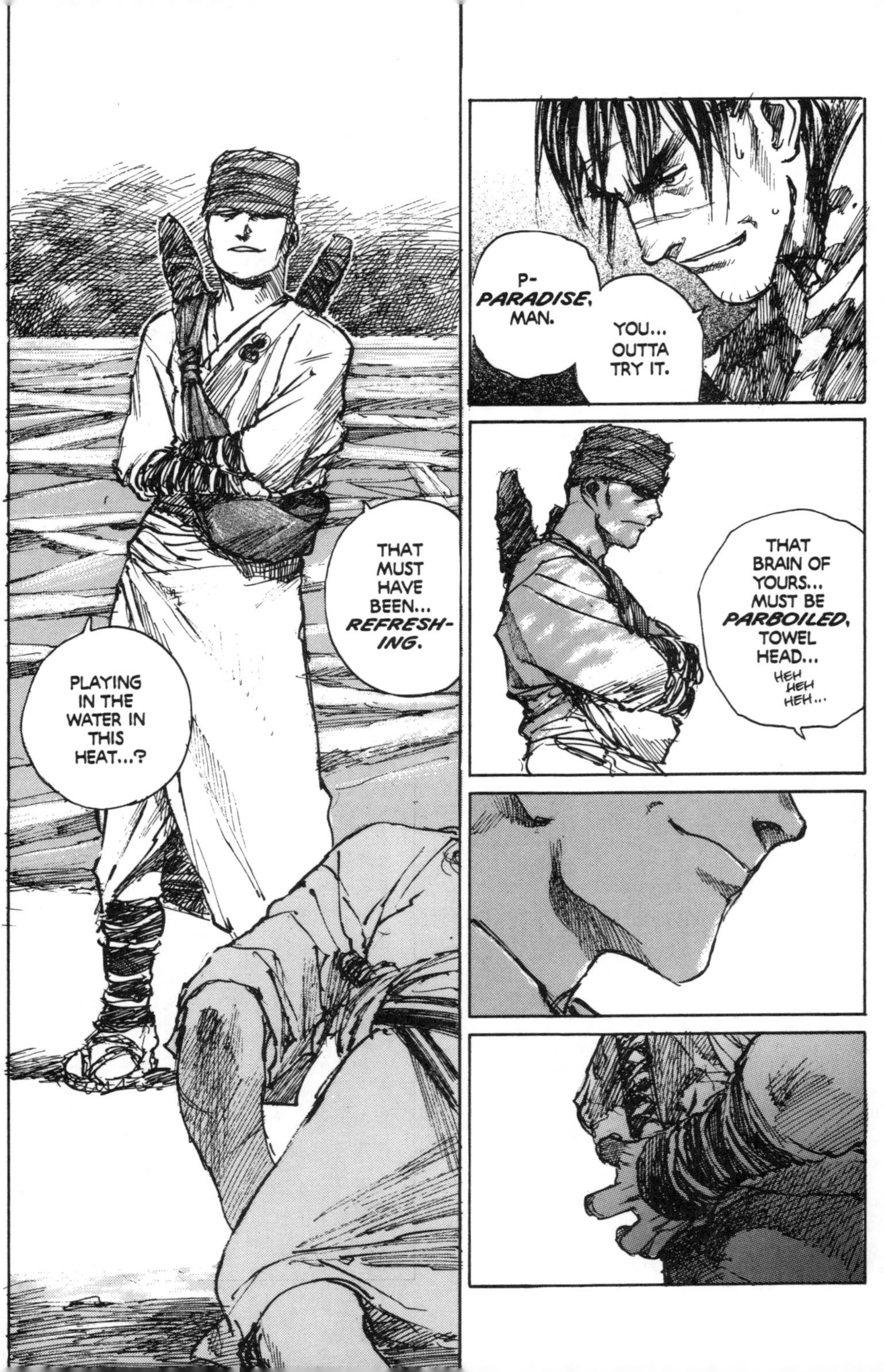
PLAYING IN THE WATER IN THIS HEAT...?
THAT MUST HAVE BEEN... REFRESHING.
P- PARADISE, MAN.
YOU... OUTTA TRY IT.
THAT BRAIN OF YOURS... MUST BE PARBOILED, TOWEL HEAD...
HEH HEH HEH...

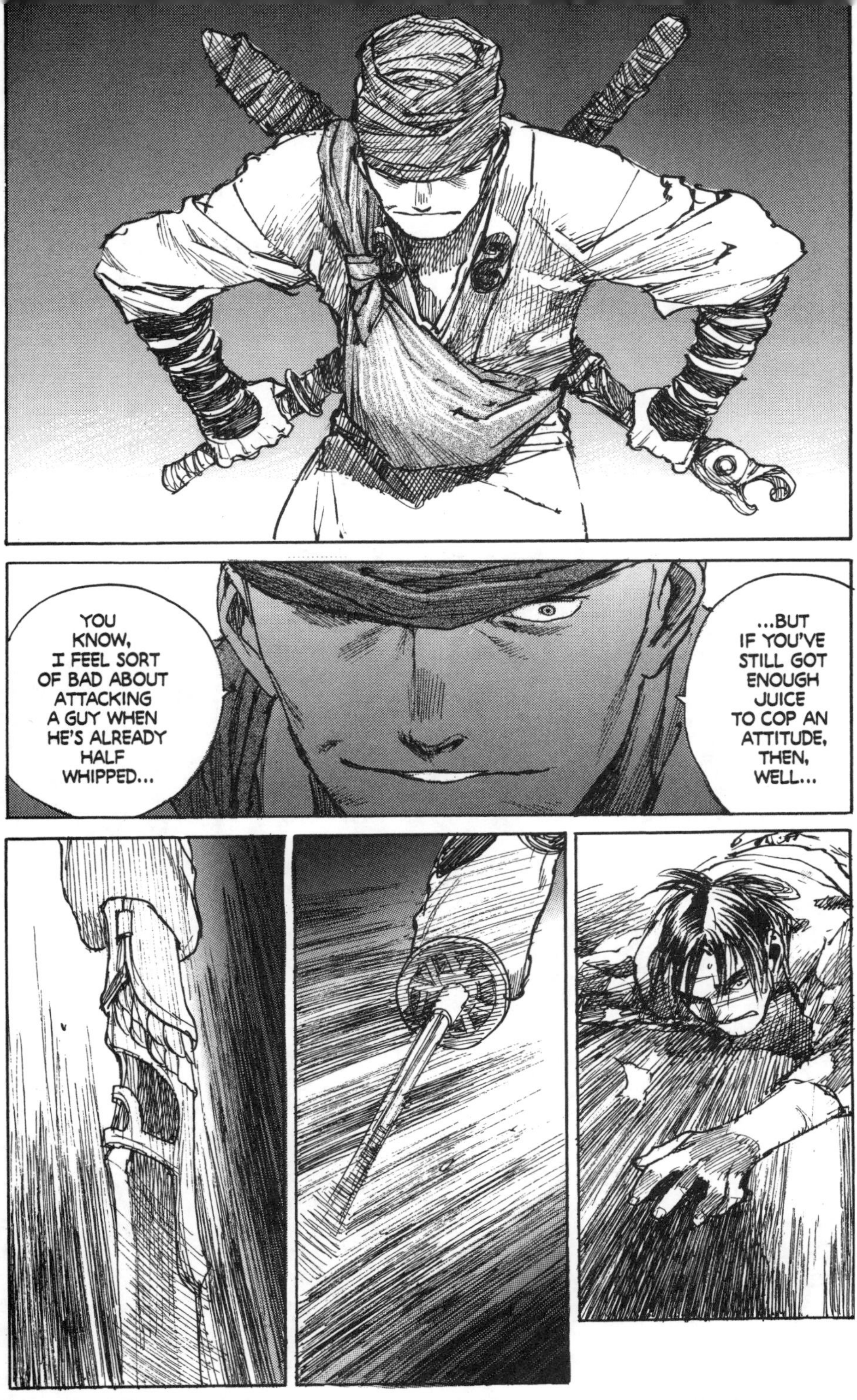
YOU KNOW, I FEEL SORT OF BAD ABOUT ATTACKING A GUY WHEN HE'S ALREADY HALF WHIPPED...
...BUT IF YOU'VE STILL GOT ENOUGH JUICE TO COP AN ATTITUDE, THEN, WELL...

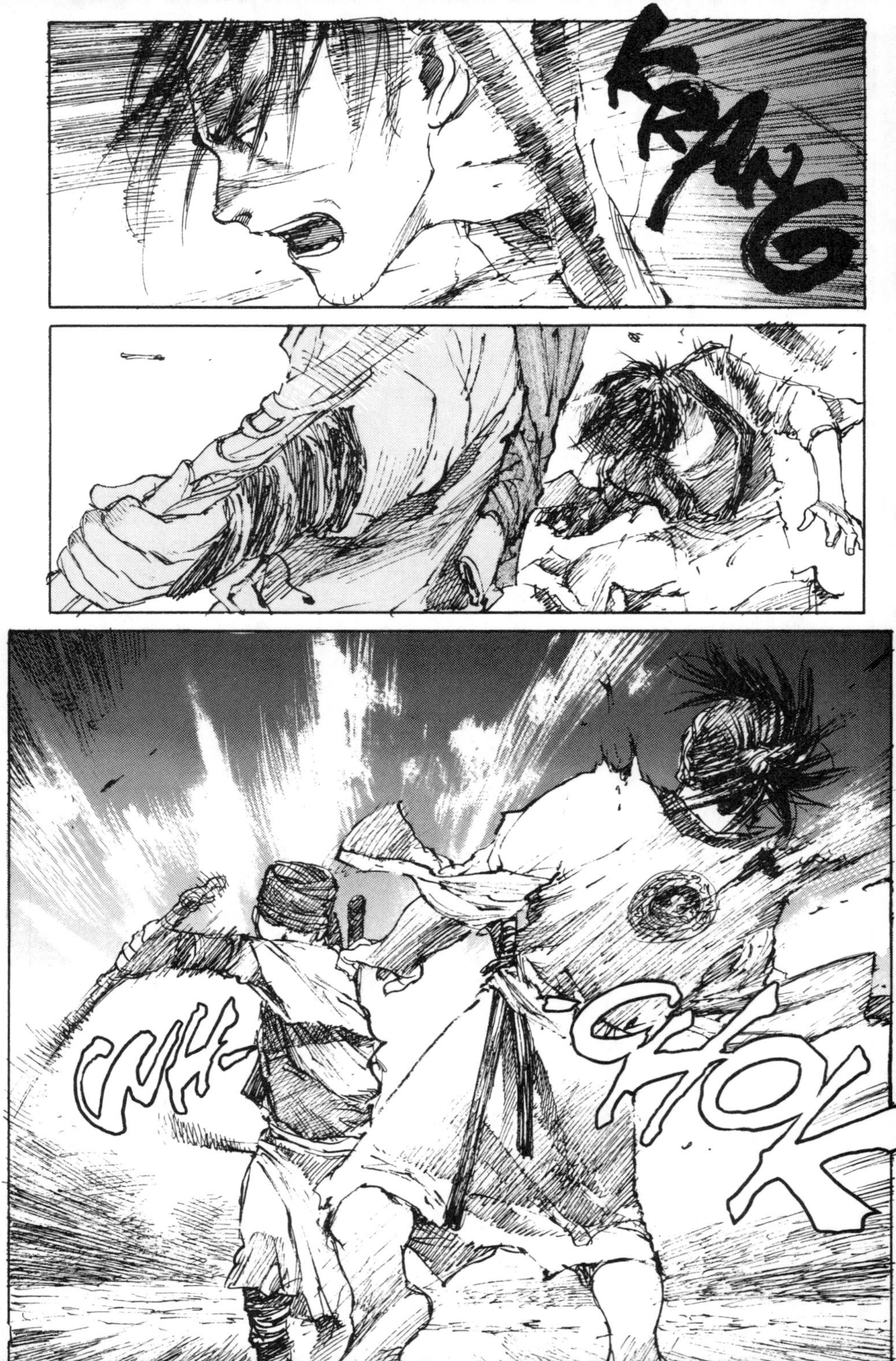
KRANG
GUH-
GHOK

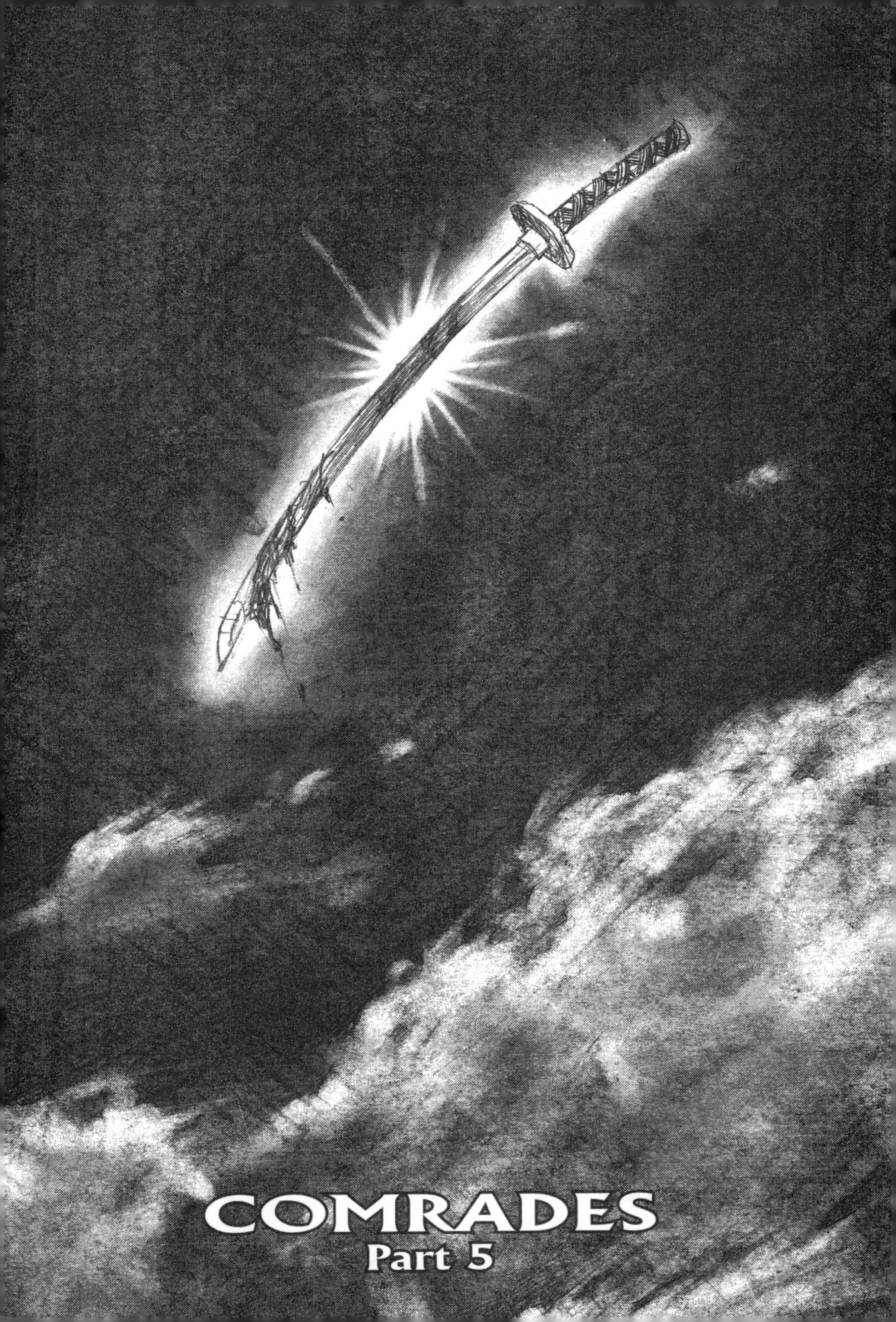

COMRADES
Part 5

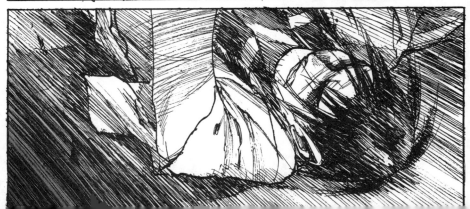

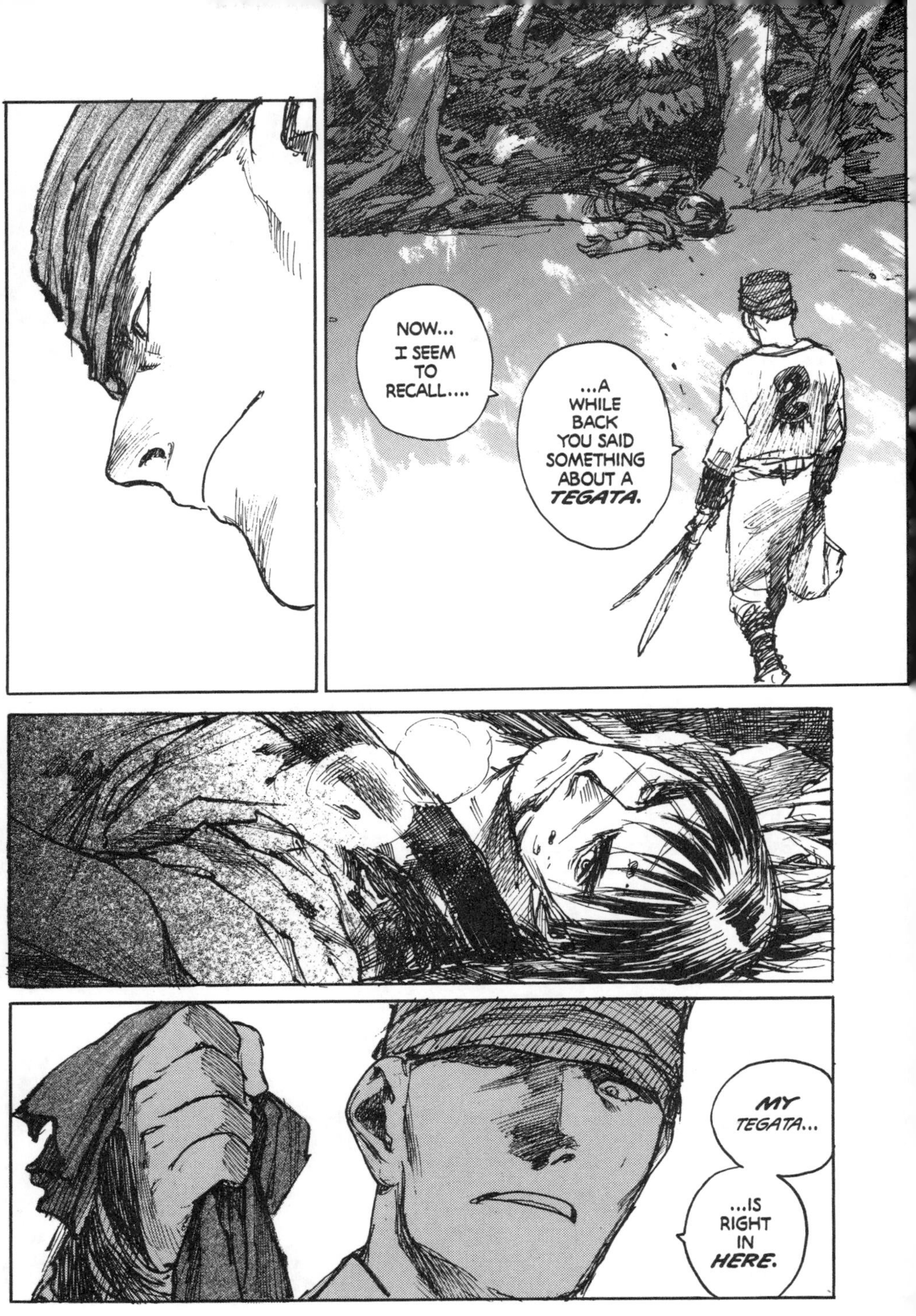
NOW... I SEEM TO RECALL....
...A WHILE BACK YOU SAID SOMETHING ABOUT A *TEGATA*.
MY TEGATA...
...IS RIGHT IN *HERE*.

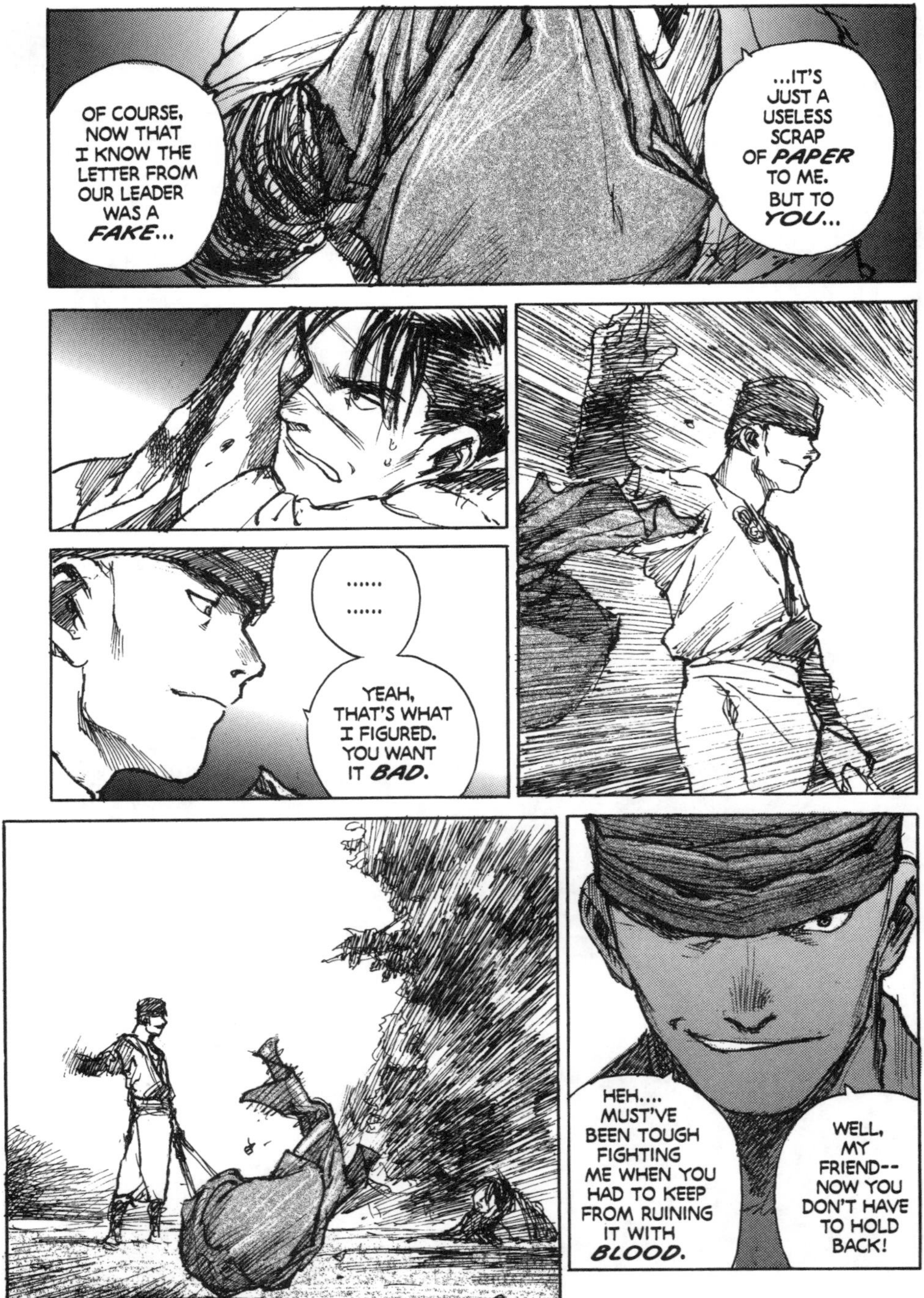
OF COURSE, NOW THAT I KNOW THE LETTER FROM OUR LEADER WAS A FAKE...
...IT'S JUST A USELESS SCRAP OF PAPER TO ME. BUT TO YOU...
....
YEAH, THAT'S WHAT I FIGURED. YOU WANT IT BAD.
HEH.... MUST'VE BEEN TOUGH FIGHTING ME WHEN YOU HAD TO KEEP FROM RUINING IT WITH BLOOD.
WELL, MY FRIEND-- NOW YOU DON'T HAVE TO HOLD BACK!

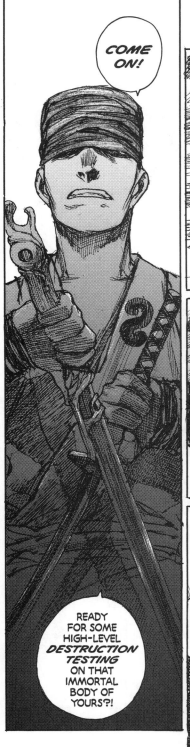

COME ON!

......
......

HEH.
HEH,
HEH!

HA HA
HA HA!

BWA
HAW
HAW!

READY
FOR SOME
HIGH-LEVEL
*DESTRUCTION
TESTING*
ON THAT
IMMORTAL
BODY OF
YOURS?!

YOU
*DUMB-
SHIT!*

WHAT A
LAUGH!
WELL,
THANKS,
ANYWAY!

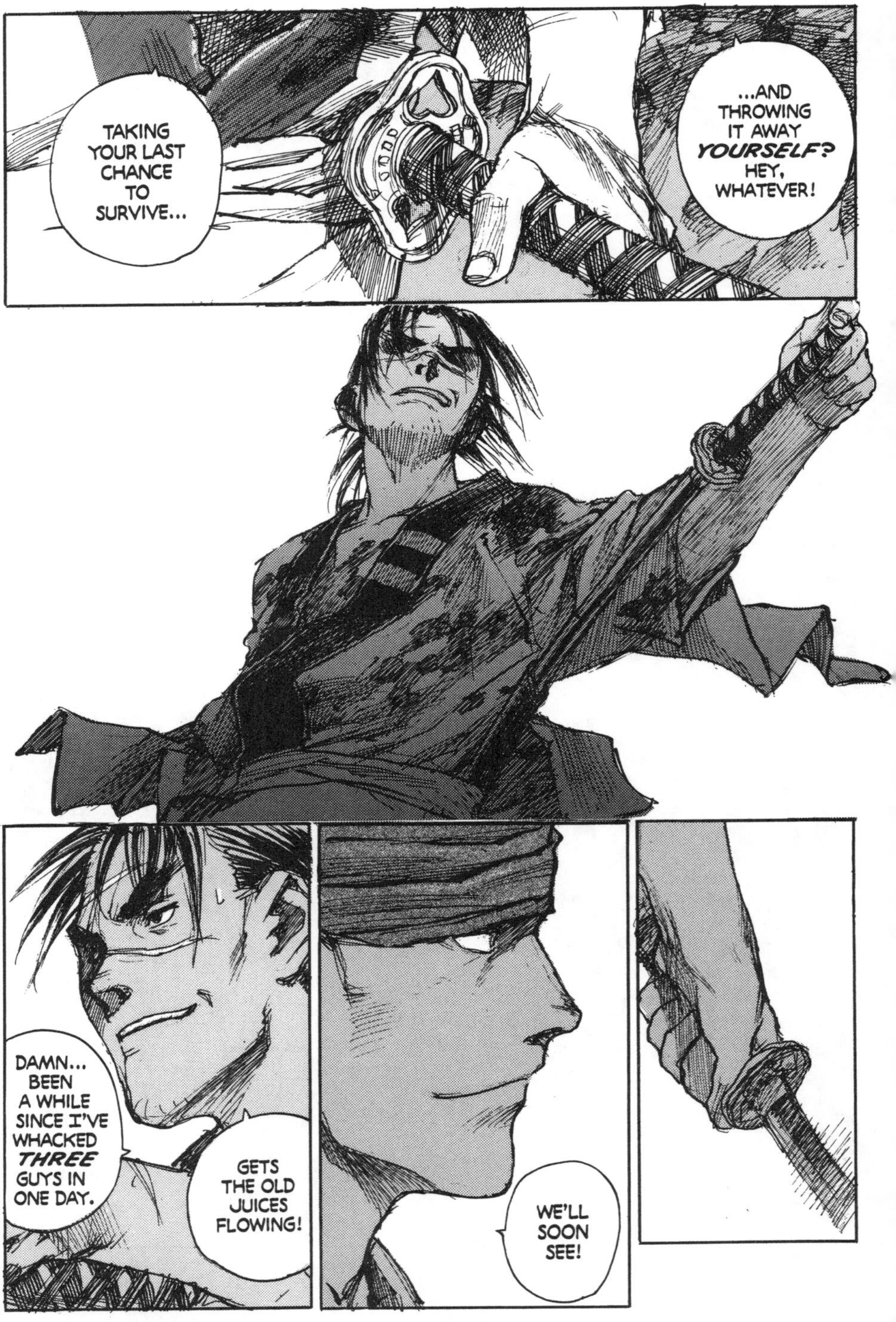

TAKING YOUR LAST CHANCE TO SURVIVE...
...AND THROWING IT AWAY *YOURSELF?* HEY, WHATEVER!
DAMN... BEEN A WHILE SINCE I'VE WHACKED *THREE* GUYS IN ONE DAY.
GETS THE OLD JUICES FLOWING!
WE'LL SOON SEE!

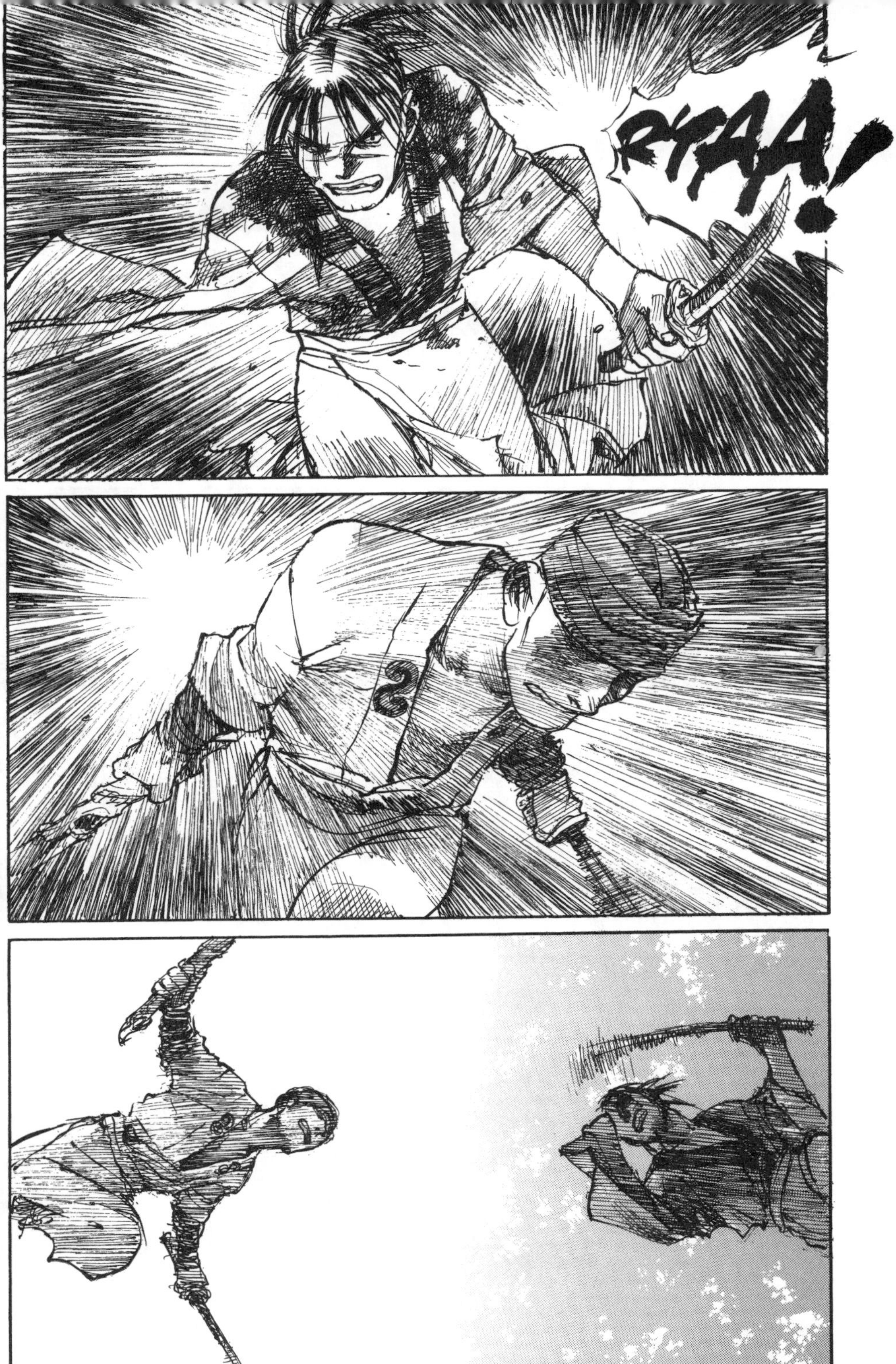
RYAA!

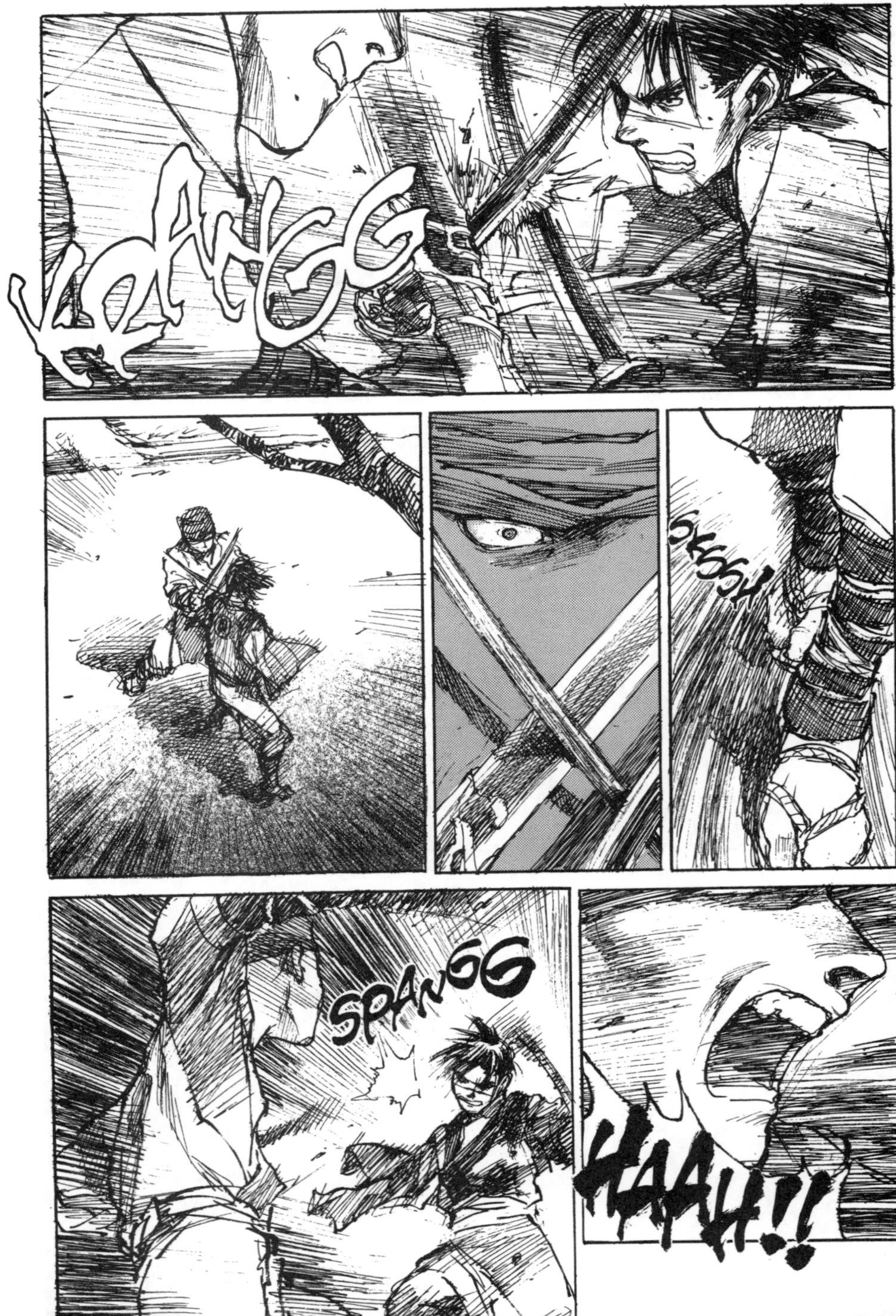
SKSSH
SPANGG
HAAH!!

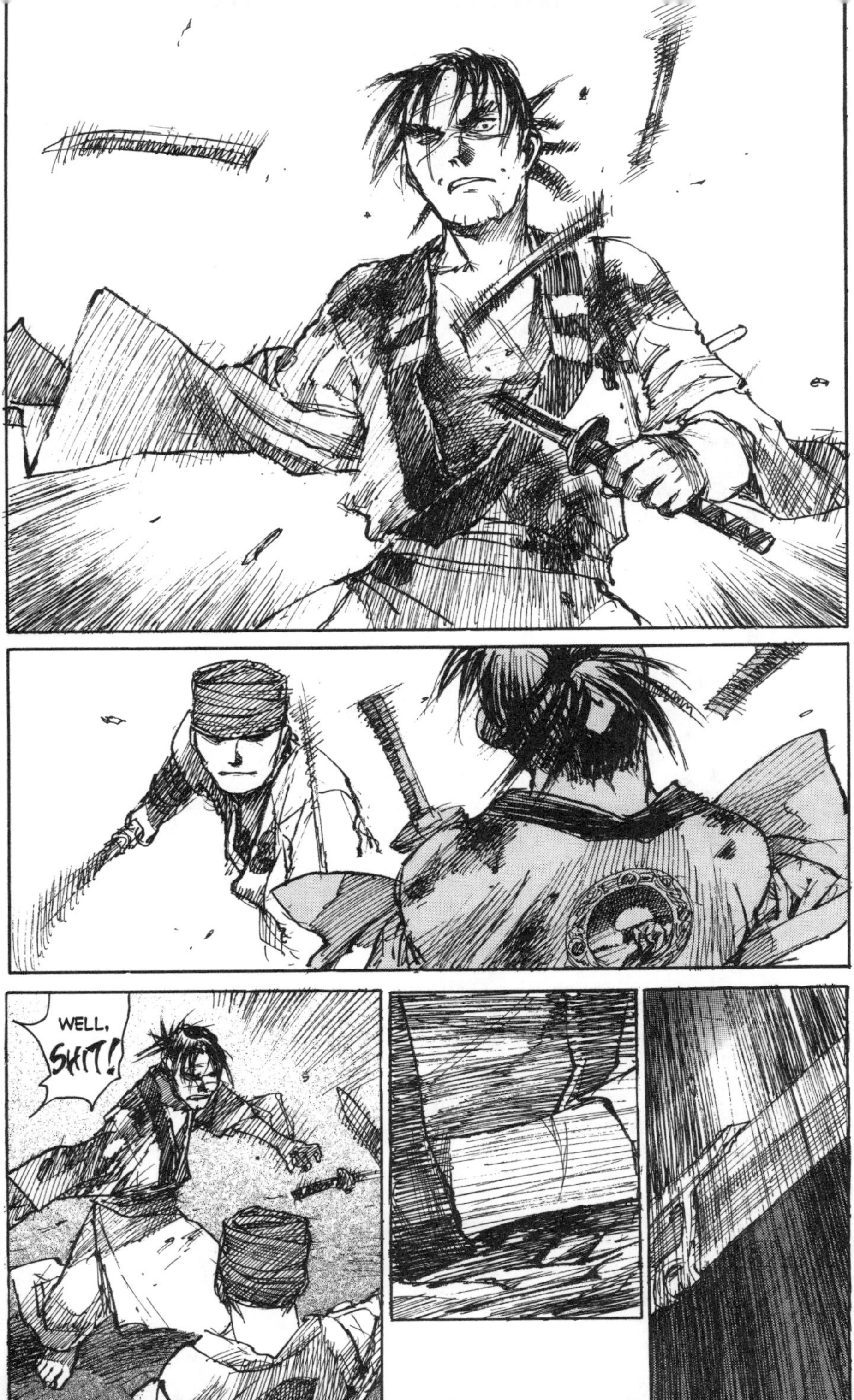
WELL, SHIT!

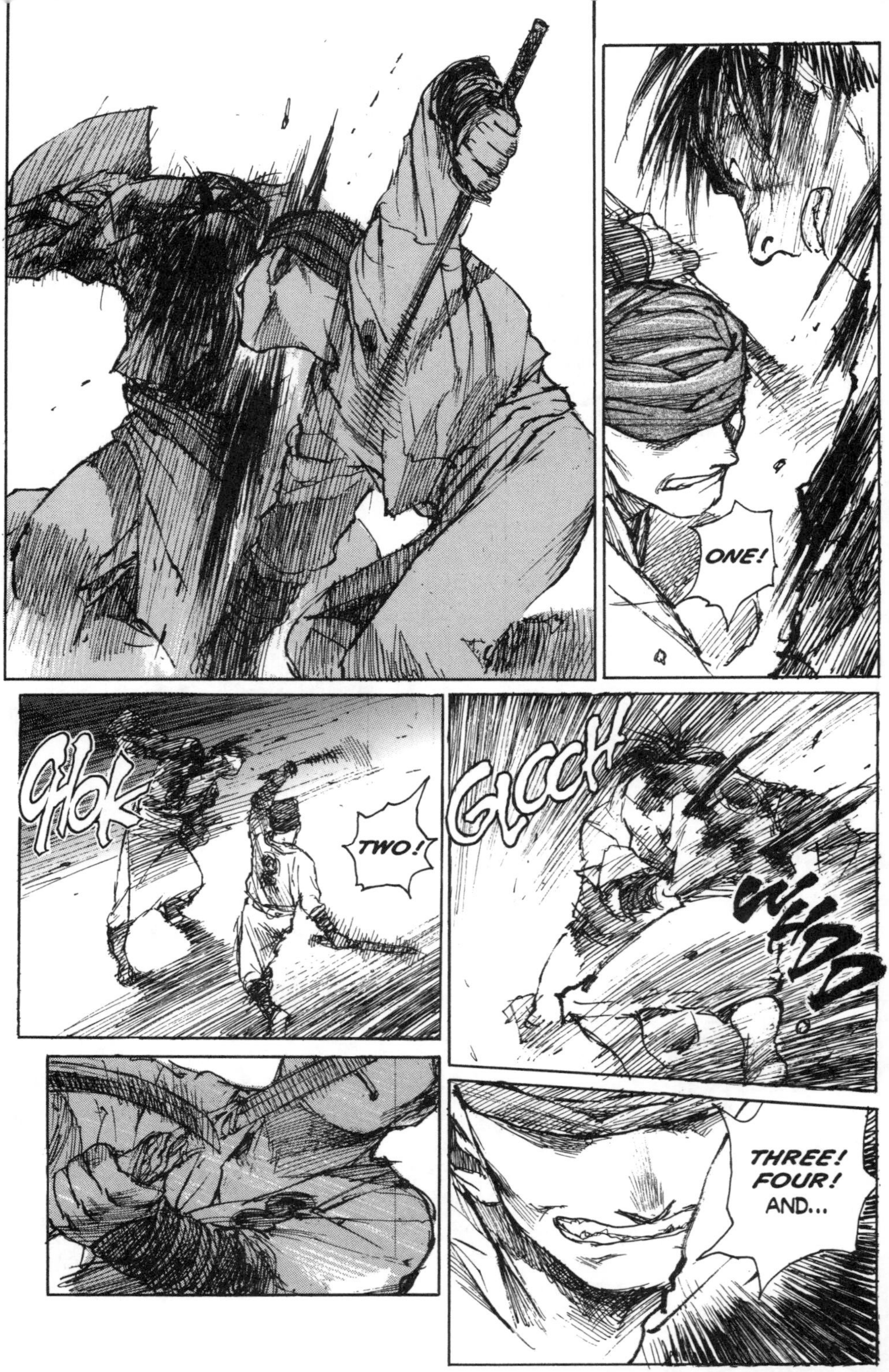
ONE!
GLOK
TWO!
GLCCH
WHOO!
THREE! FOUR! AND...

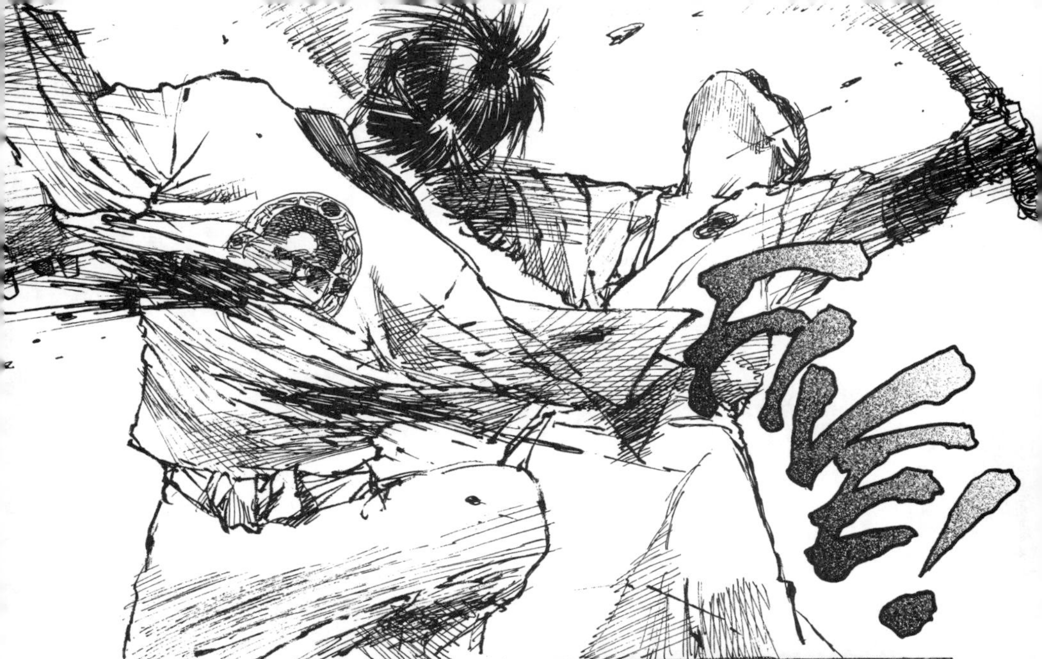

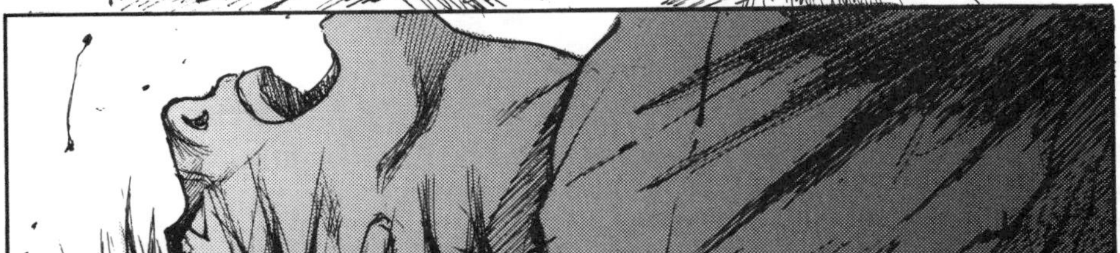

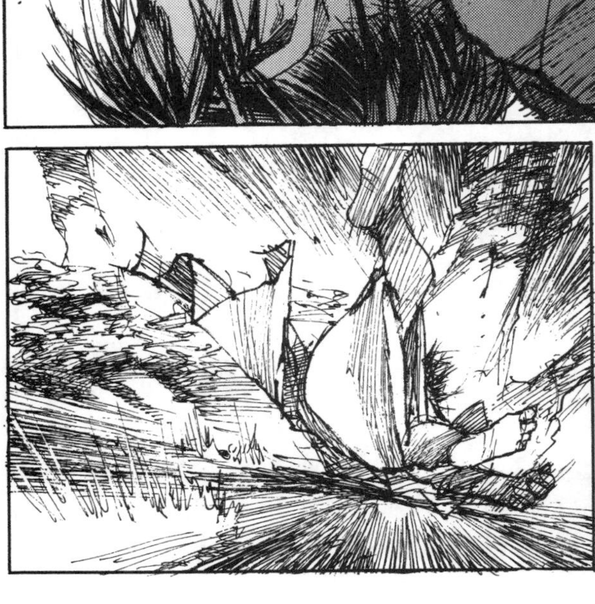

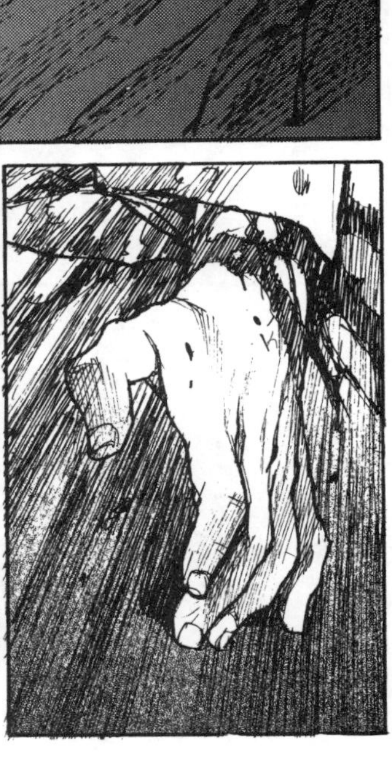

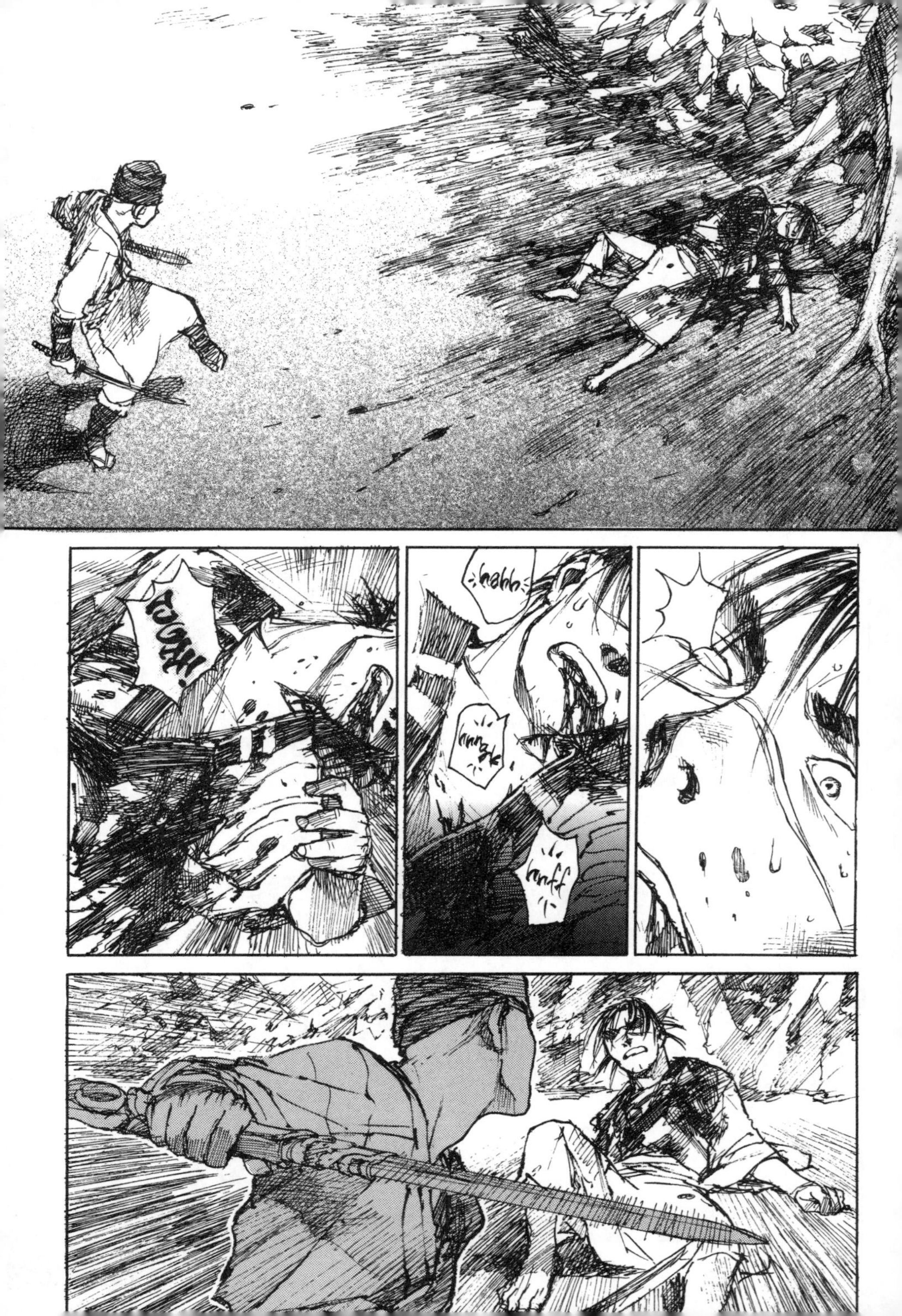
hahh
hnngk
hnff

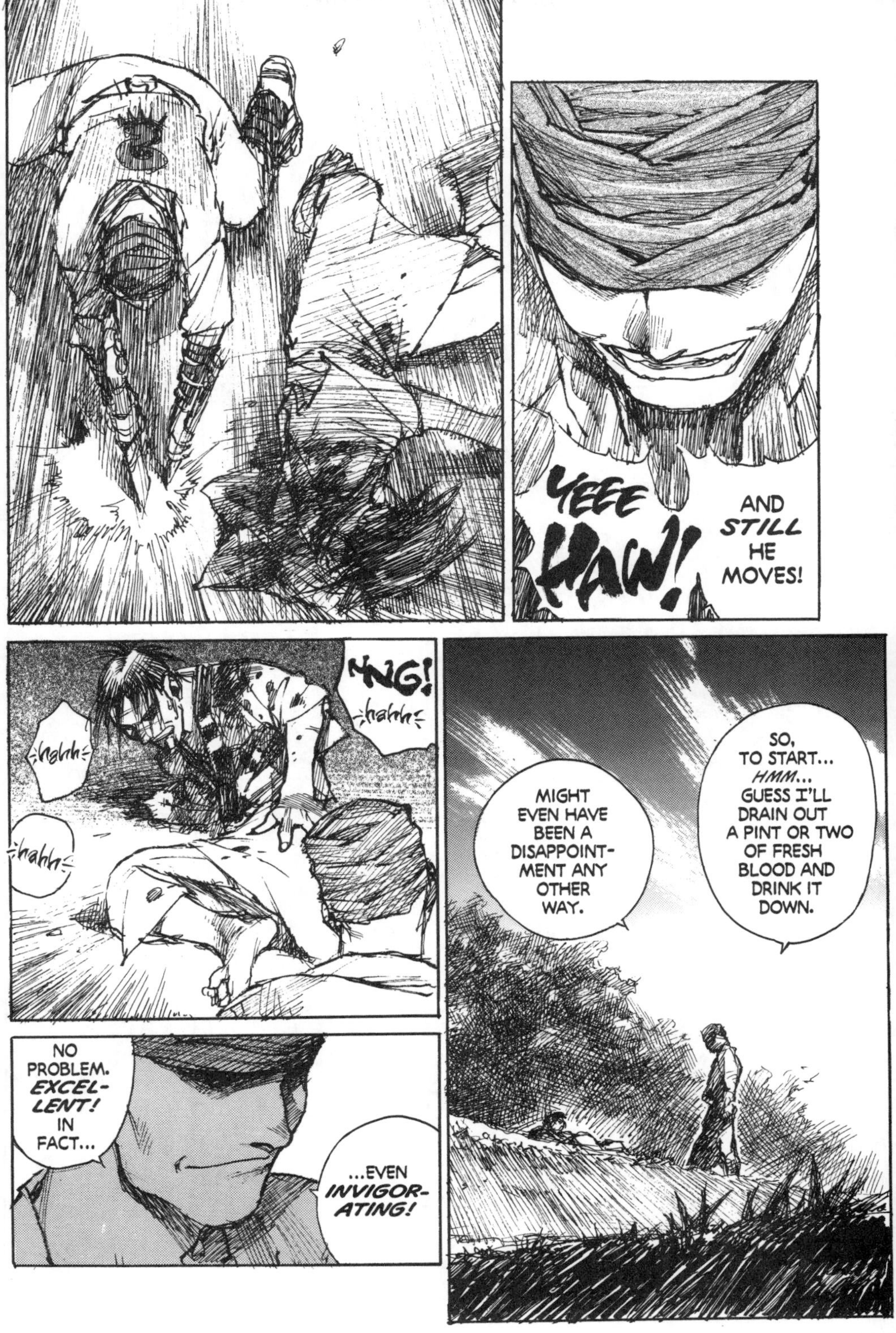
YEEE HAW!
AND STILL HE MOVES!
HNG!
hahh
hahh
hahh
NO PROBLEM. EXCEL-LENT! IN FACT...
...EVEN INVIGOR-ATING!
MIGHT EVEN HAVE BEEN A DISAPPOINT-MENT ANY OTHER WAY.
SO, TO START... HMM... GUESS I'LL DRAIN OUT A PINT OR TWO OF FRESH BLOOD AND DRINK IT DOWN.

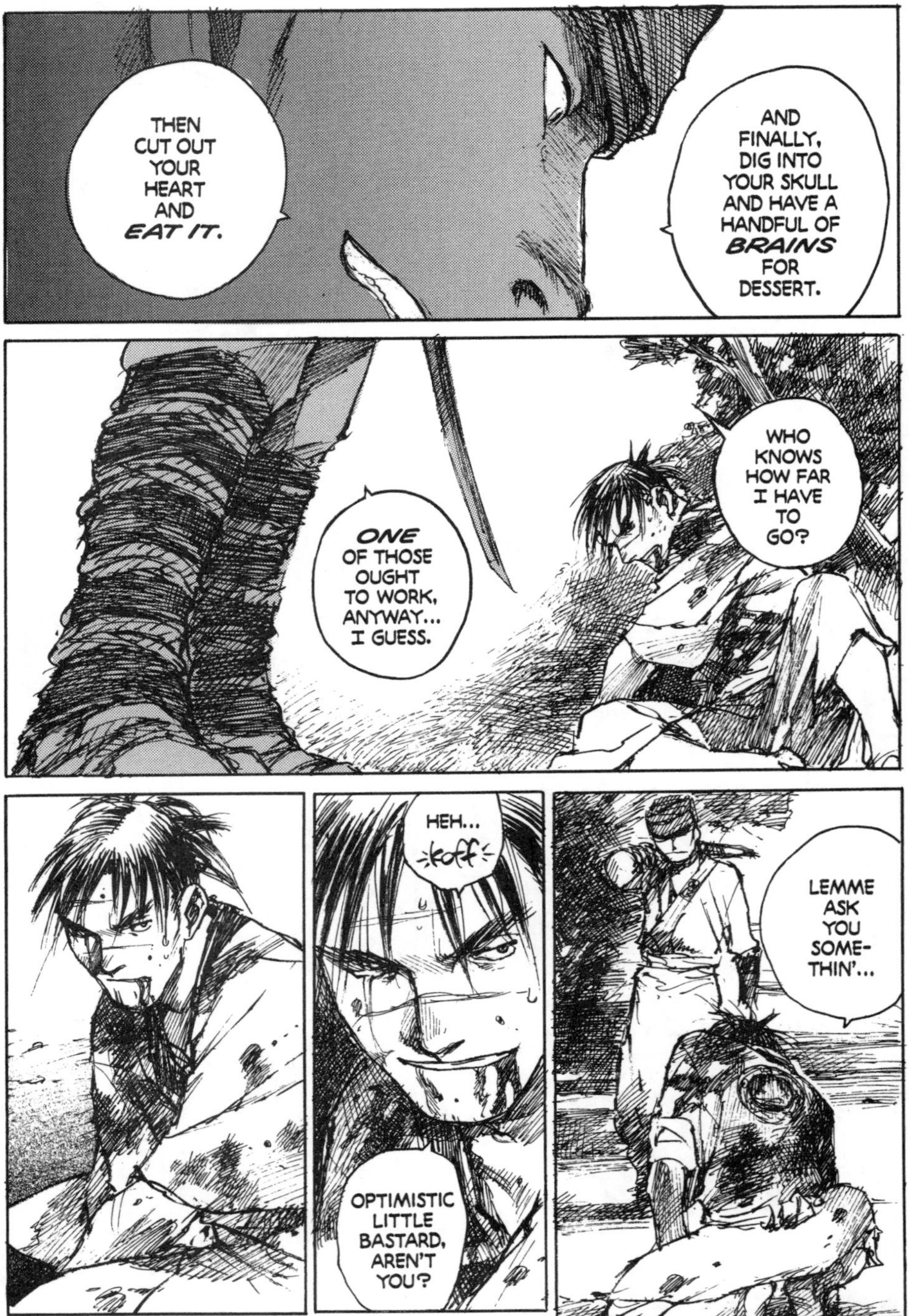
THEN CUT OUT YOUR HEART AND EAT IT.
AND FINALLY, DIG INTO YOUR SKULL AND HAVE A HANDFUL OF BRAINS FOR DESSERT.
ONE OF THOSE OUGHT TO WORK, ANYWAY... I GUESS.
WHO KNOWS HOW FAR I HAVE TO GO?
HEH...
koff
OPTIMISTIC LITTLE BASTARD, AREN'T YOU?
LEMME ASK YOU SOME-THIN'...

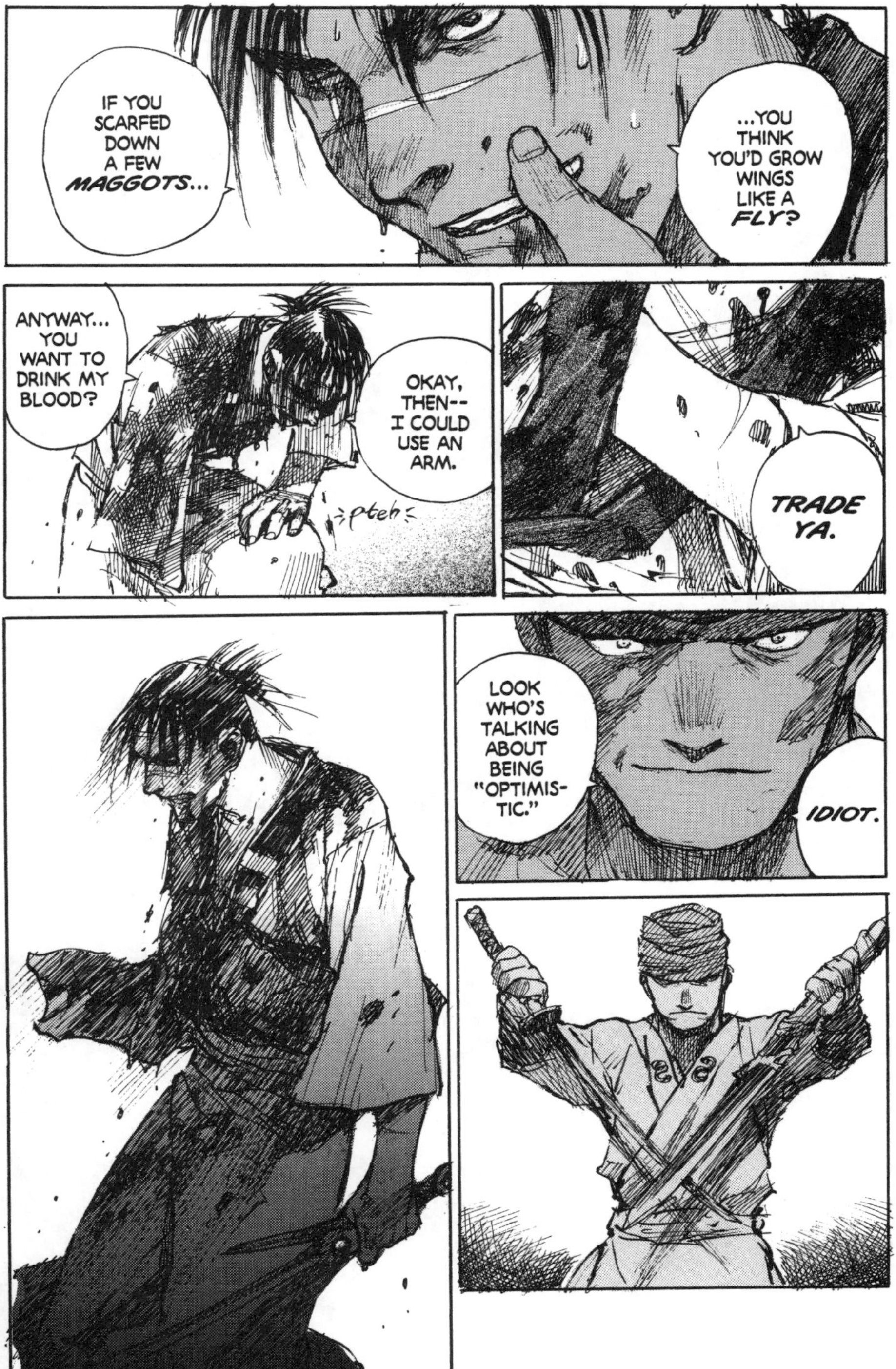
IF YOU SCARFED DOWN A FEW MAGGOTS...
...YOU THINK YOU'D GROW WINGS LIKE A FLY?
ANYWAY... YOU WANT TO DRINK MY BLOOD?
OKAY, THEN-- I COULD USE AN ARM.
pteh
TRADE YA.
LOOK WHO'S TALKING ABOUT BEING "OPTIMISTIC."
IDIOT.

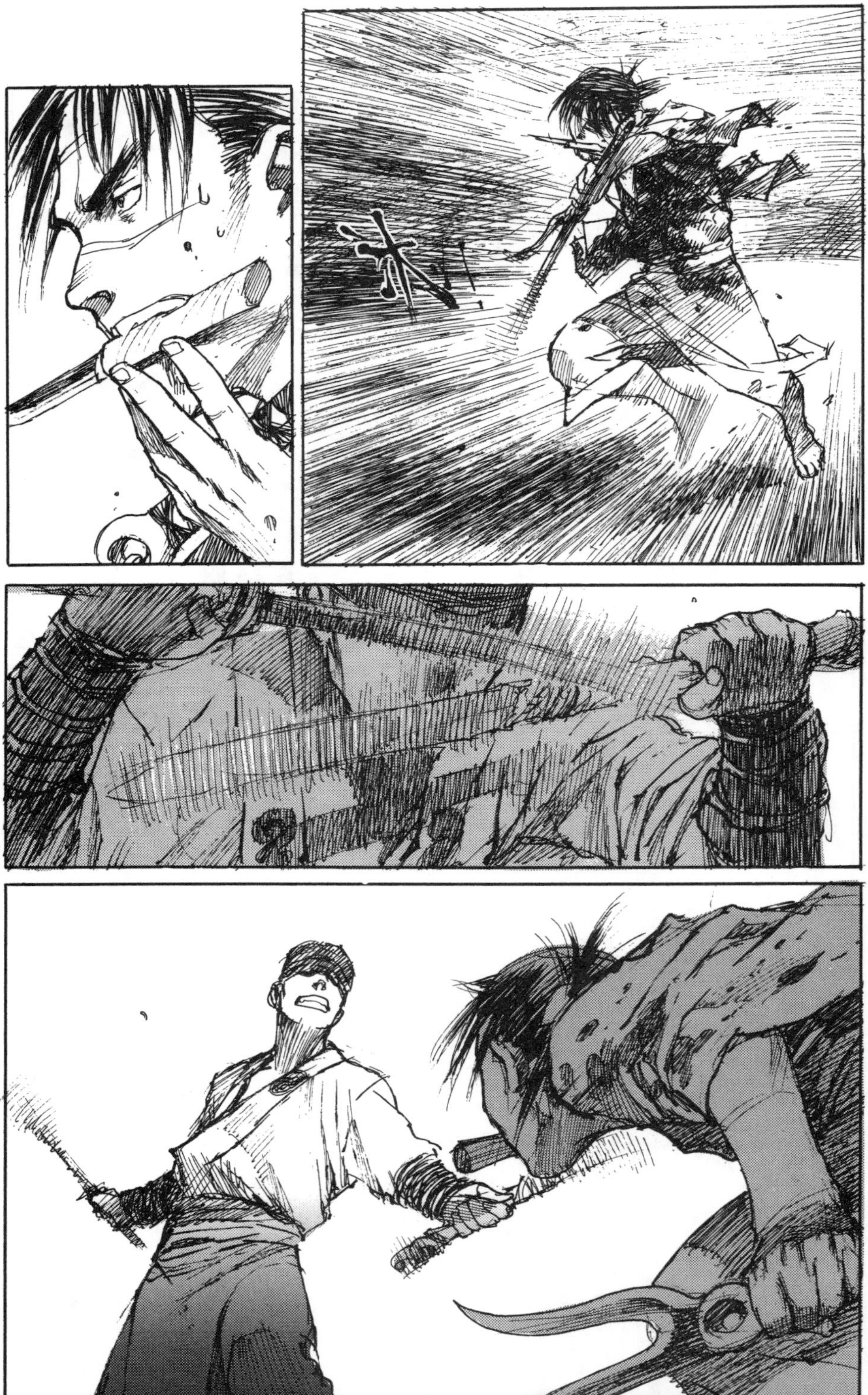

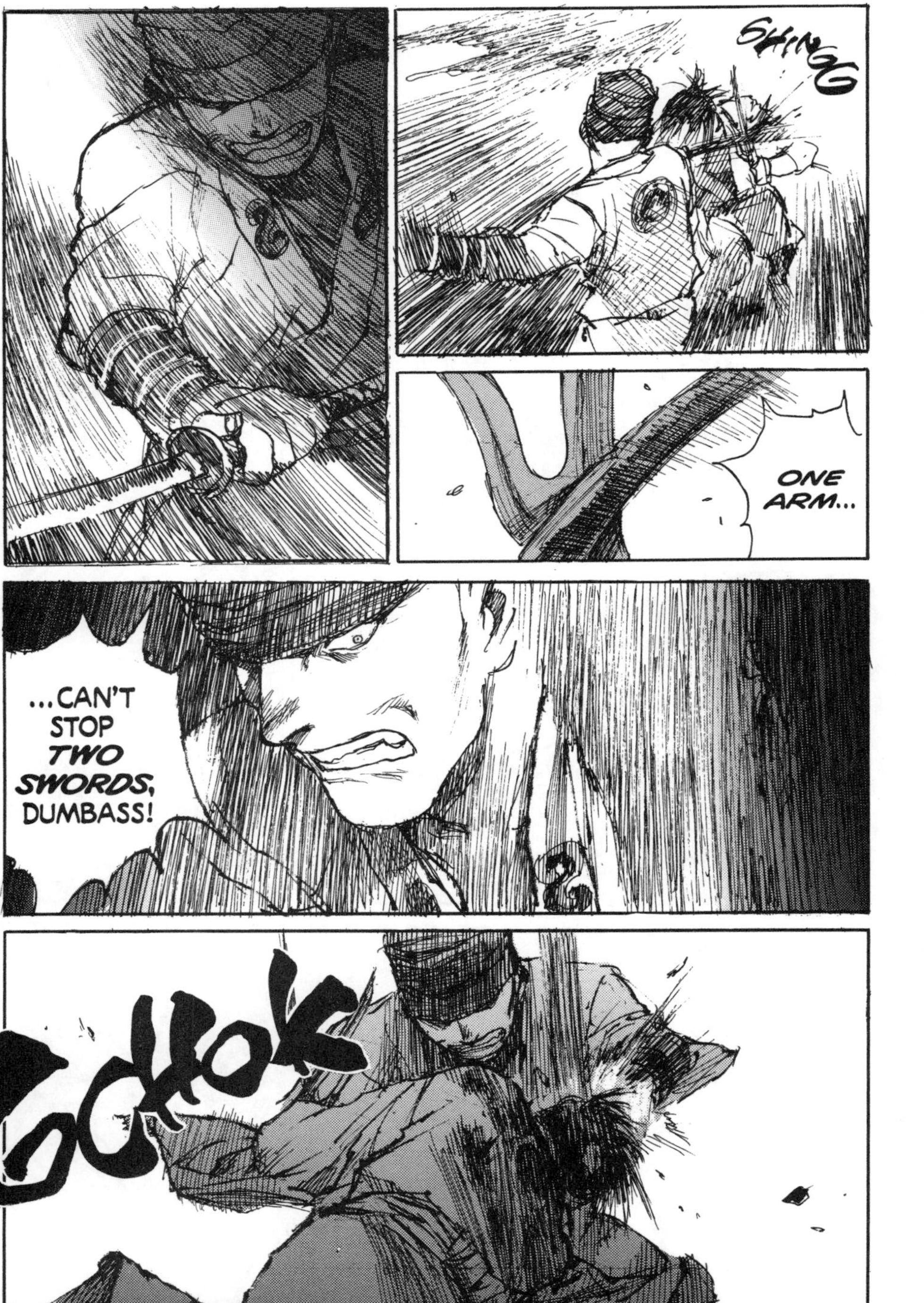
SHINGG
ONE ARM...
...CAN'T STOP TWO SWORDS, DUMBASS!
GCHOK

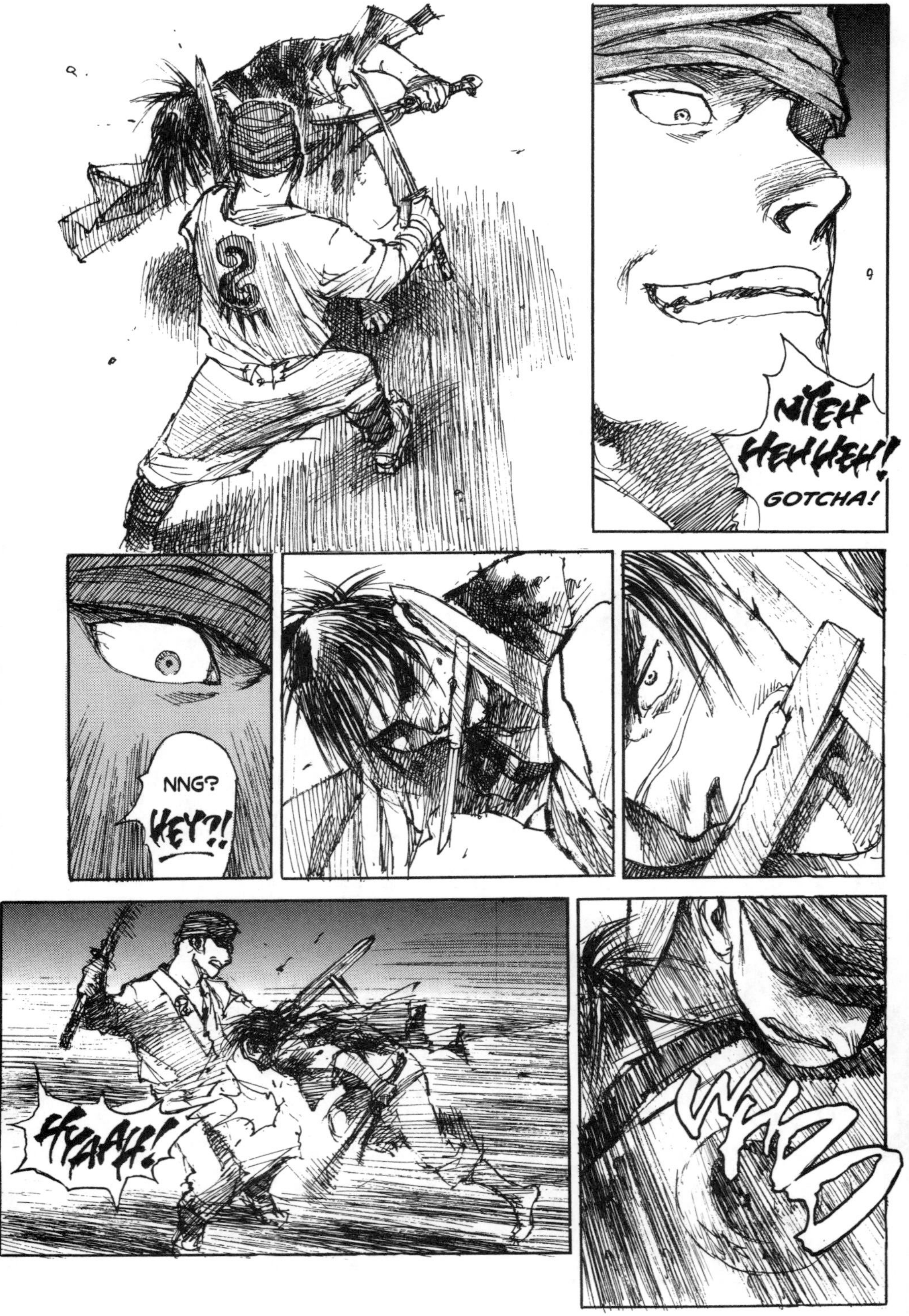
NYEH HEH HEH!♥
GOTCHA!
NNG?
HEY?!
HYAAH!
UWAAO

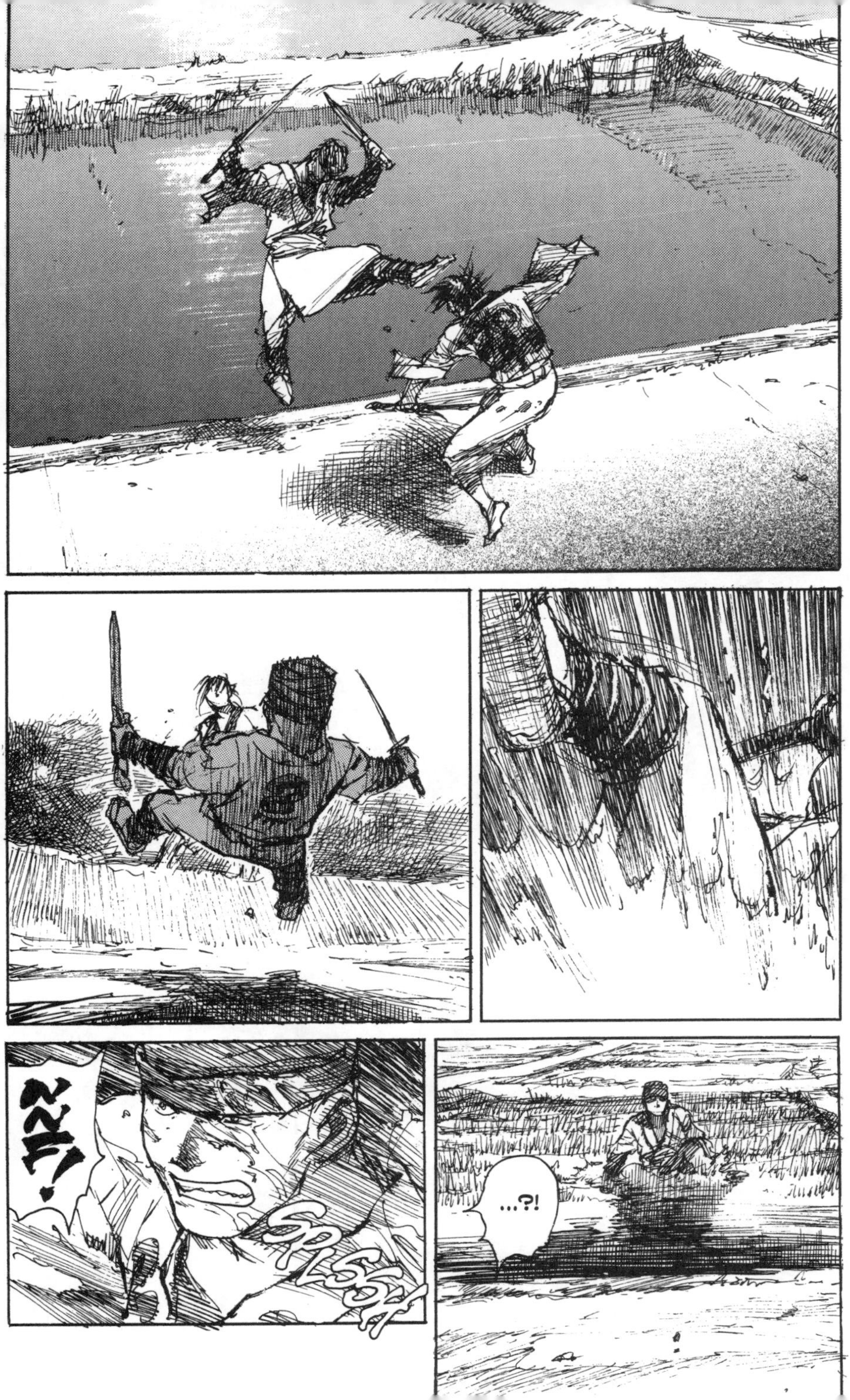
NNH!
SPLSSH
...?!

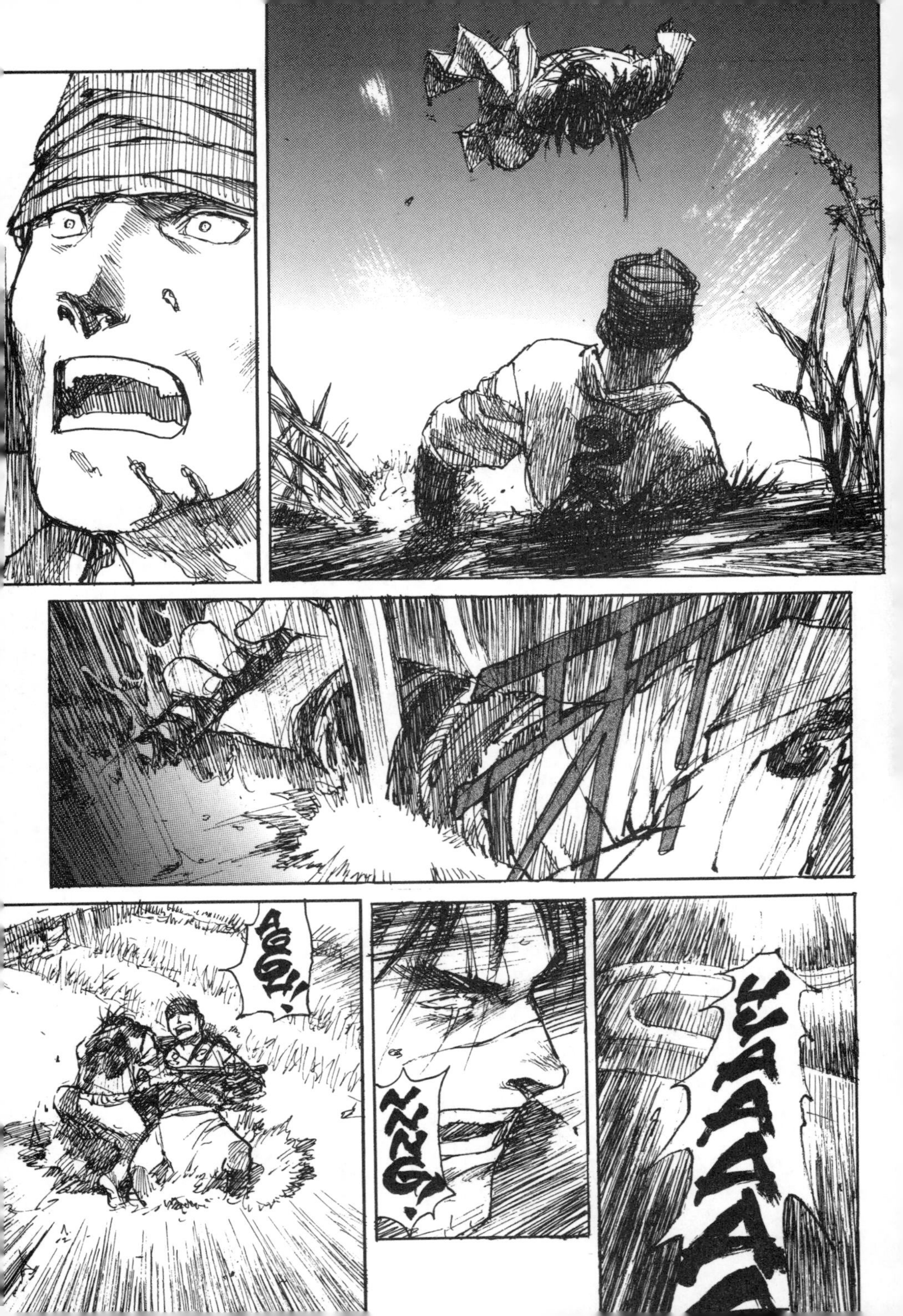
AGGH!
NNNG!
HAAAAAA

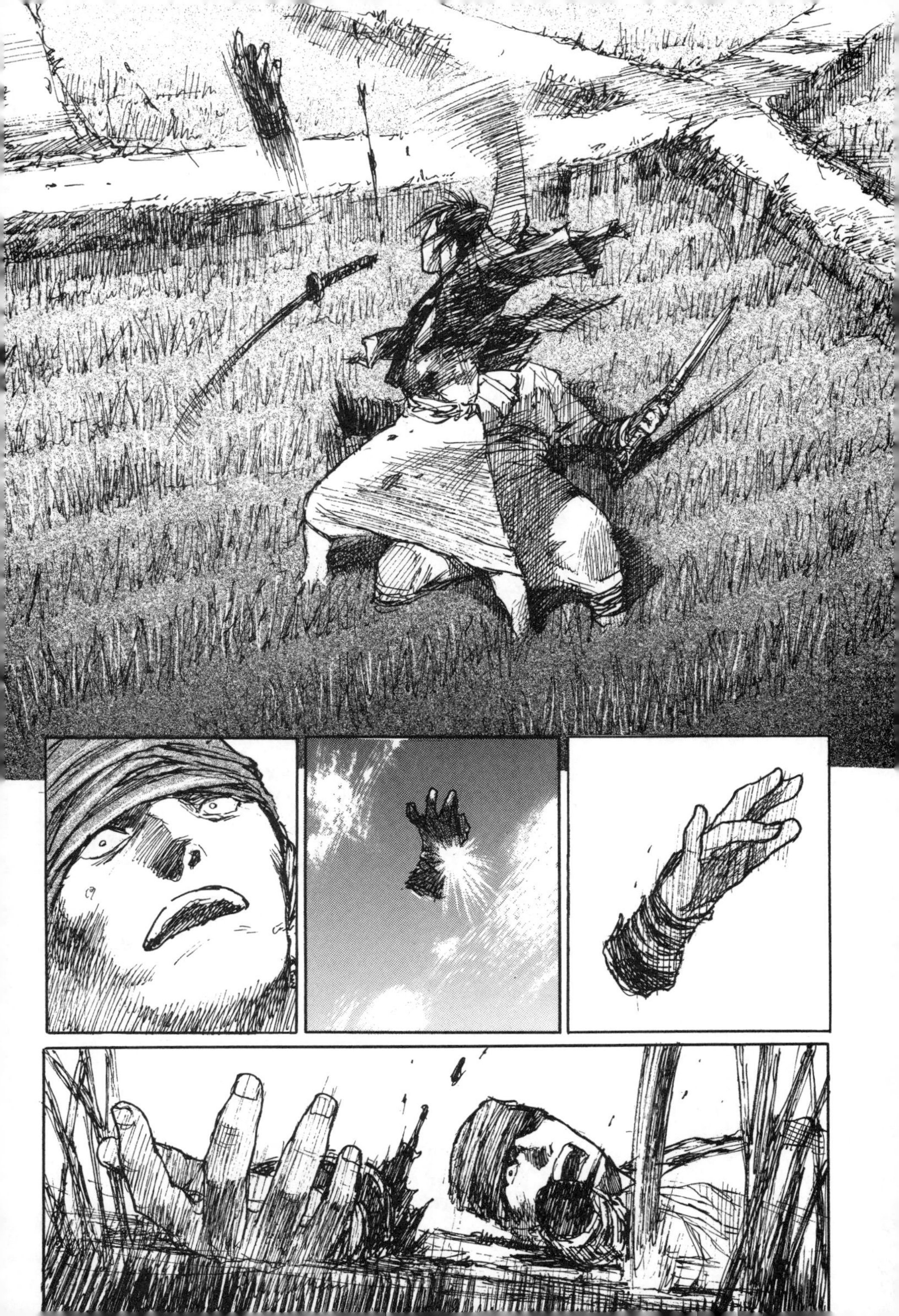

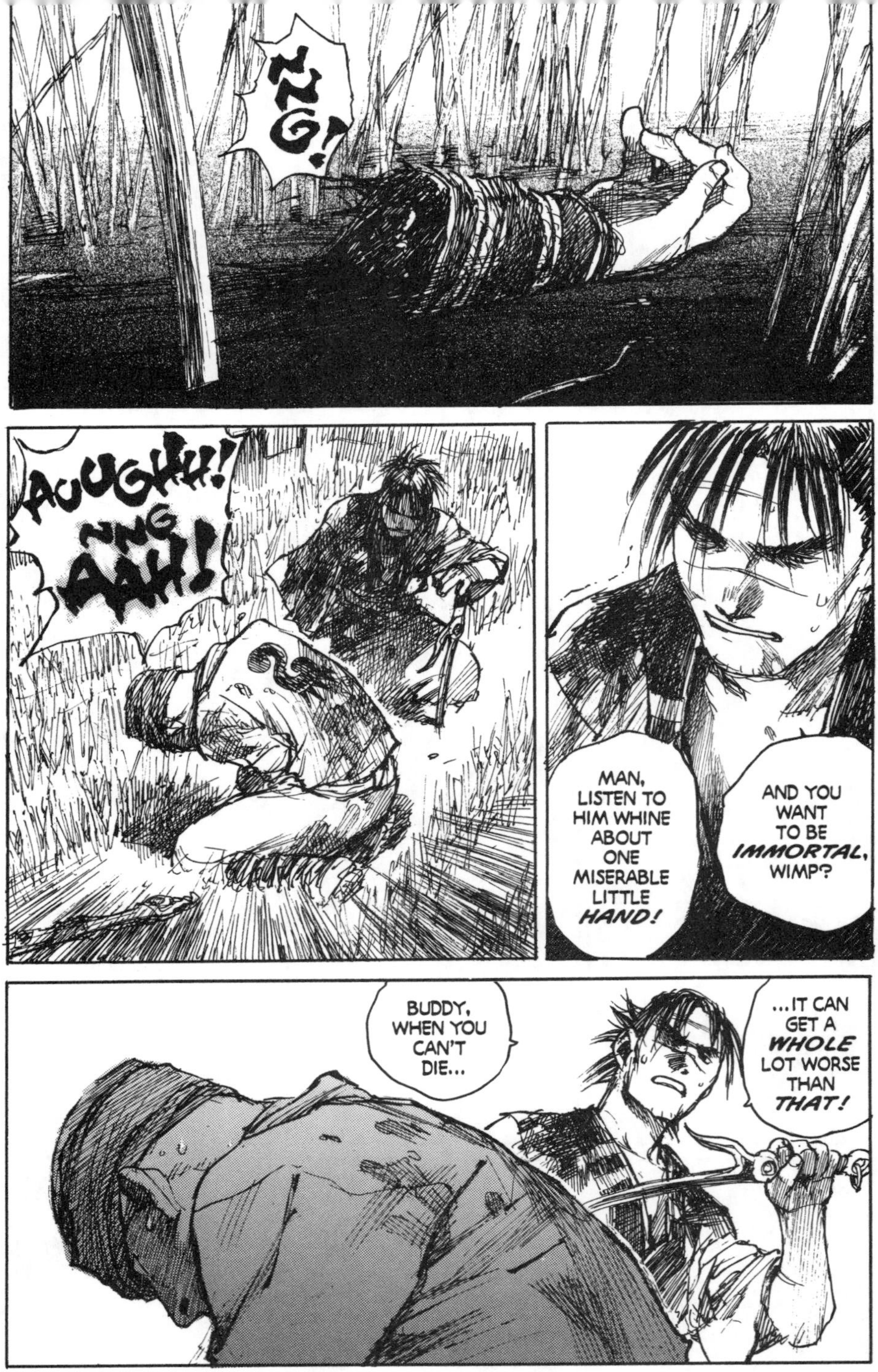
NNG!
AUUGHH! NNG AAH!
MAN, LISTEN TO HIM WHINE ABOUT ONE MISERABLE LITTLE *HAND!*
AND YOU WANT TO BE *IMMORTAL*, WIMP?
BUDDY, WHEN YOU CAN'T DIE...
...IT CAN GET A *WHOLE* LOT WORSE THAN *THAT!*

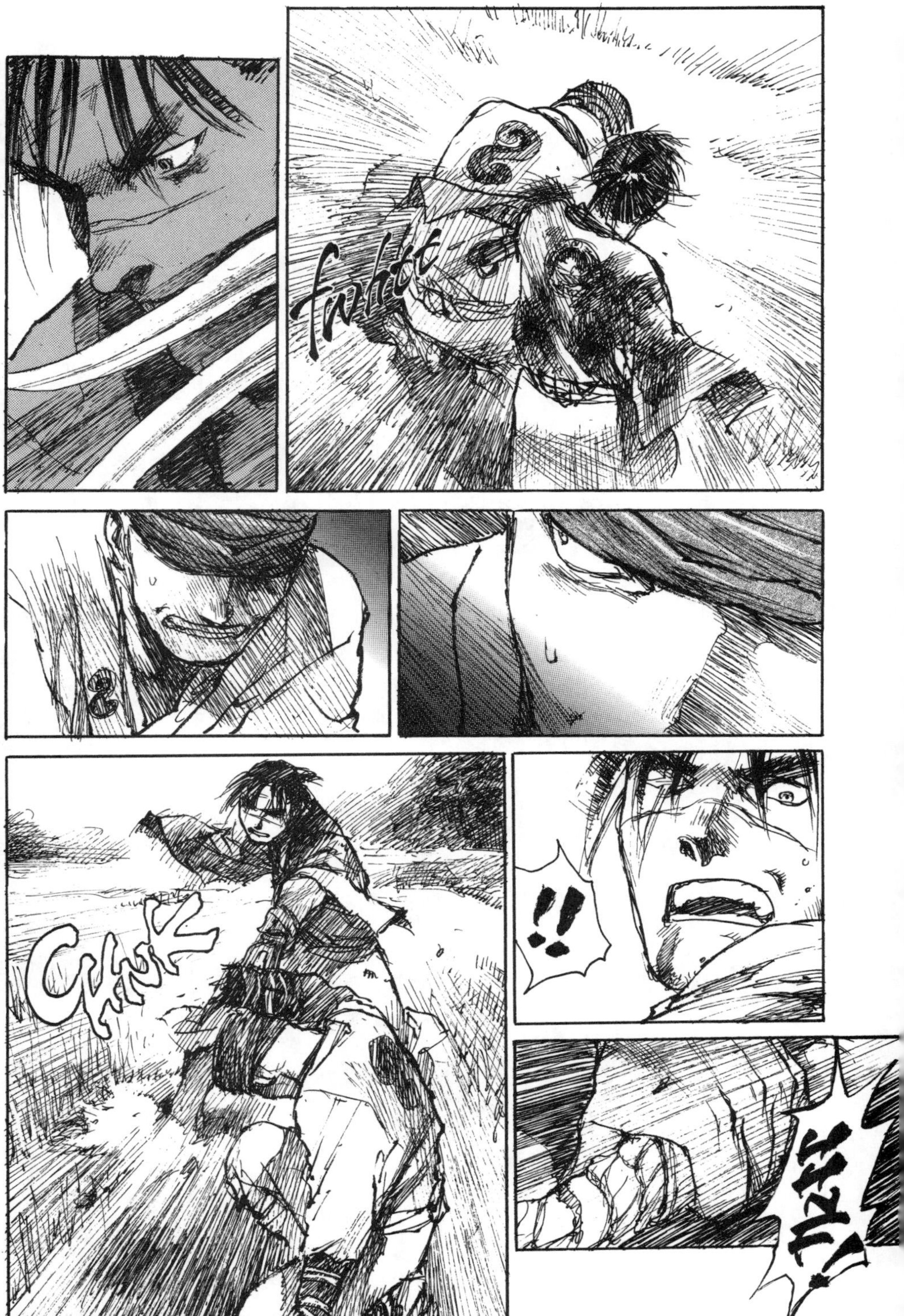
fwhtt
!!

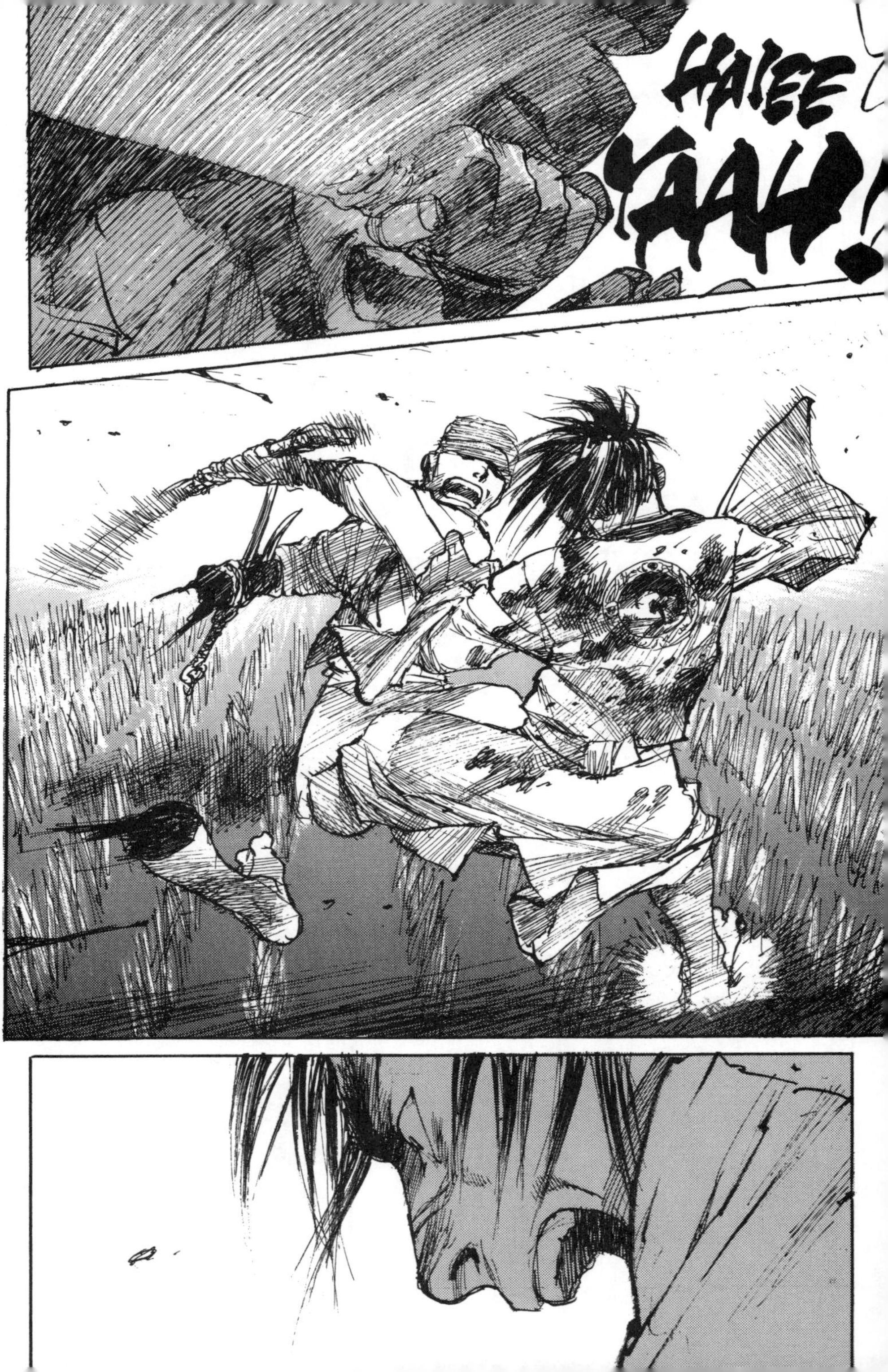
HAIEE YAAH!!

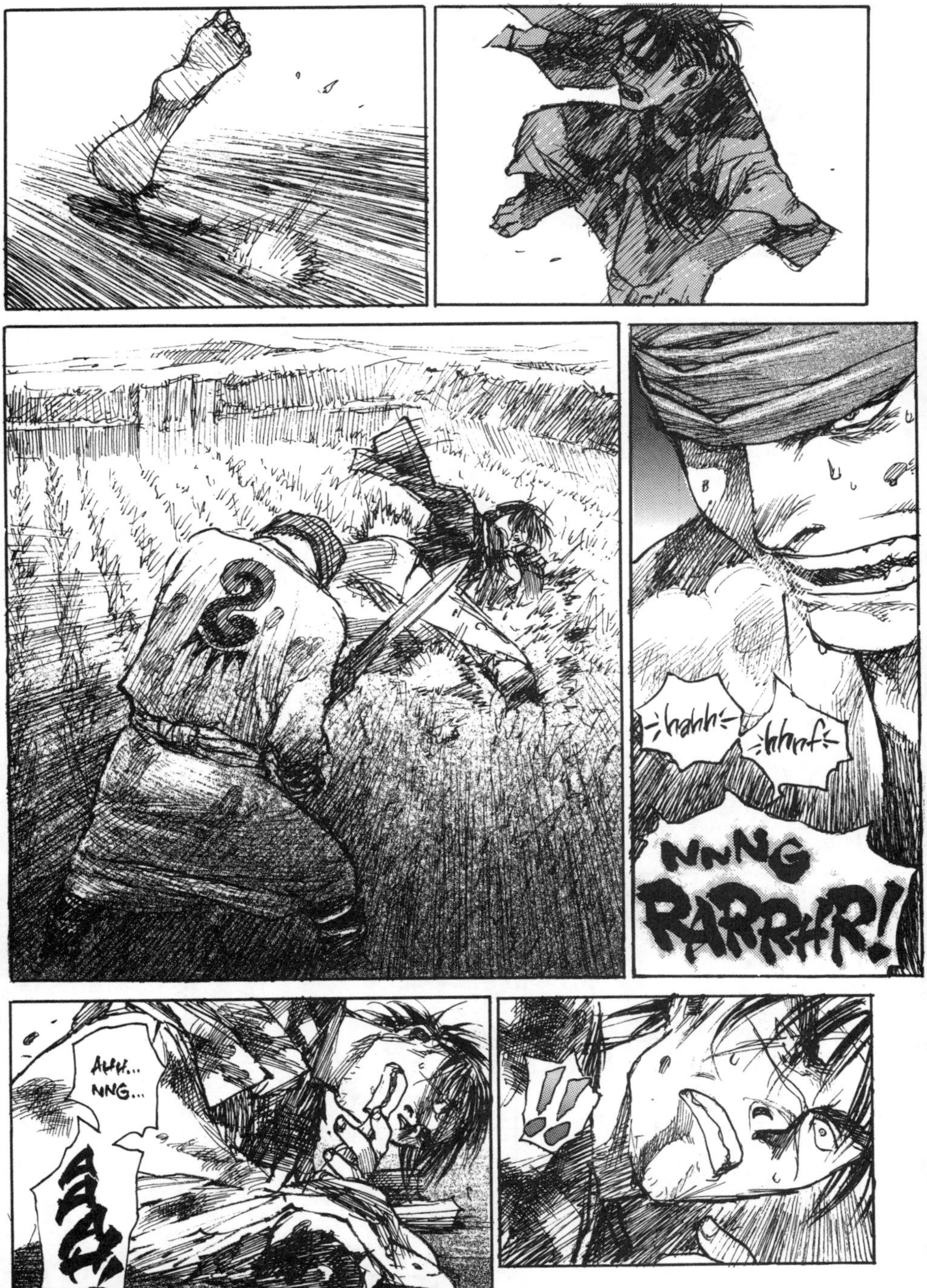
hahh
hhnf
NNNG RARRHR!
AHH... NNG...
AAGH!

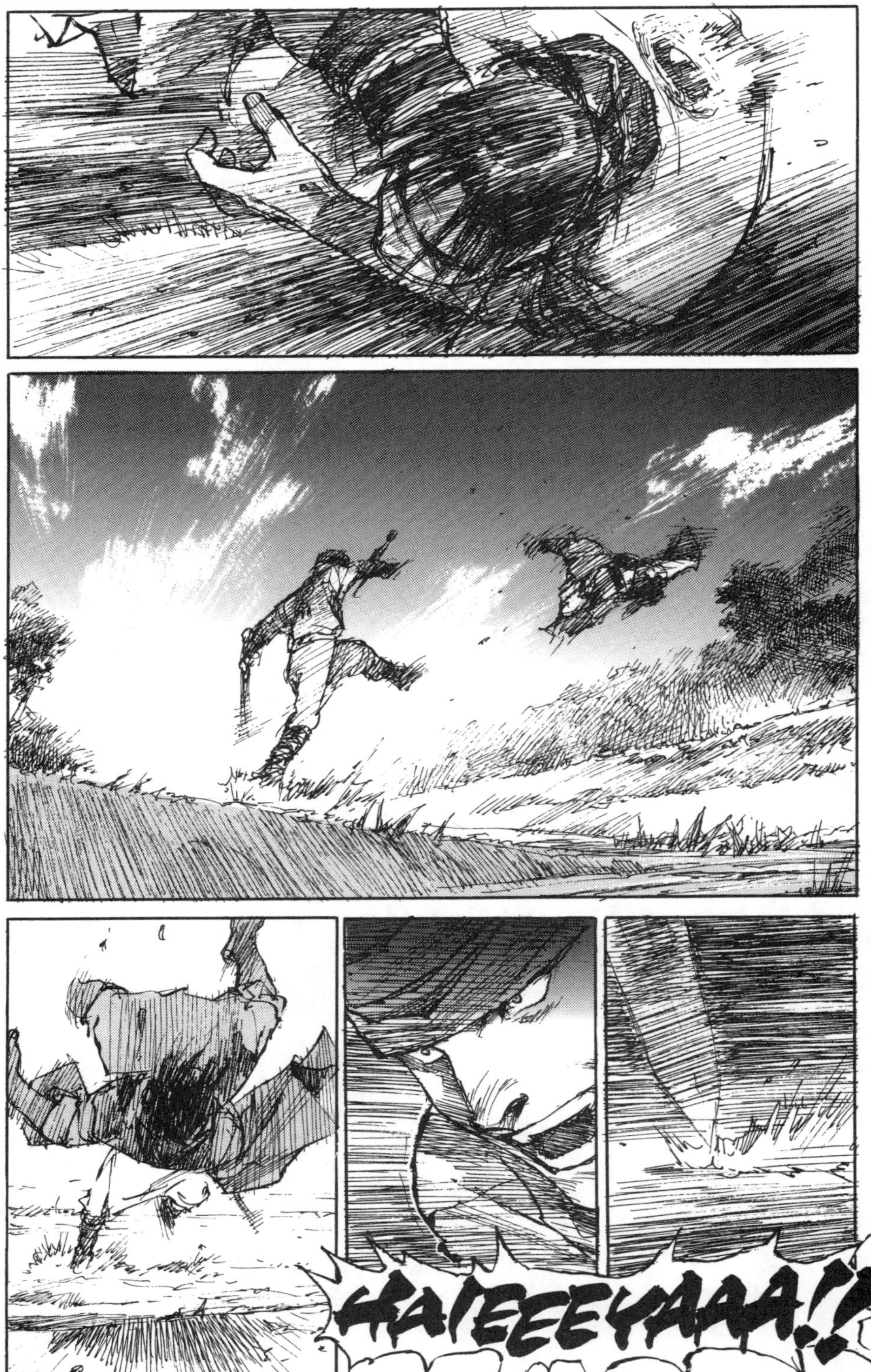
HAIEEEYAAA!?

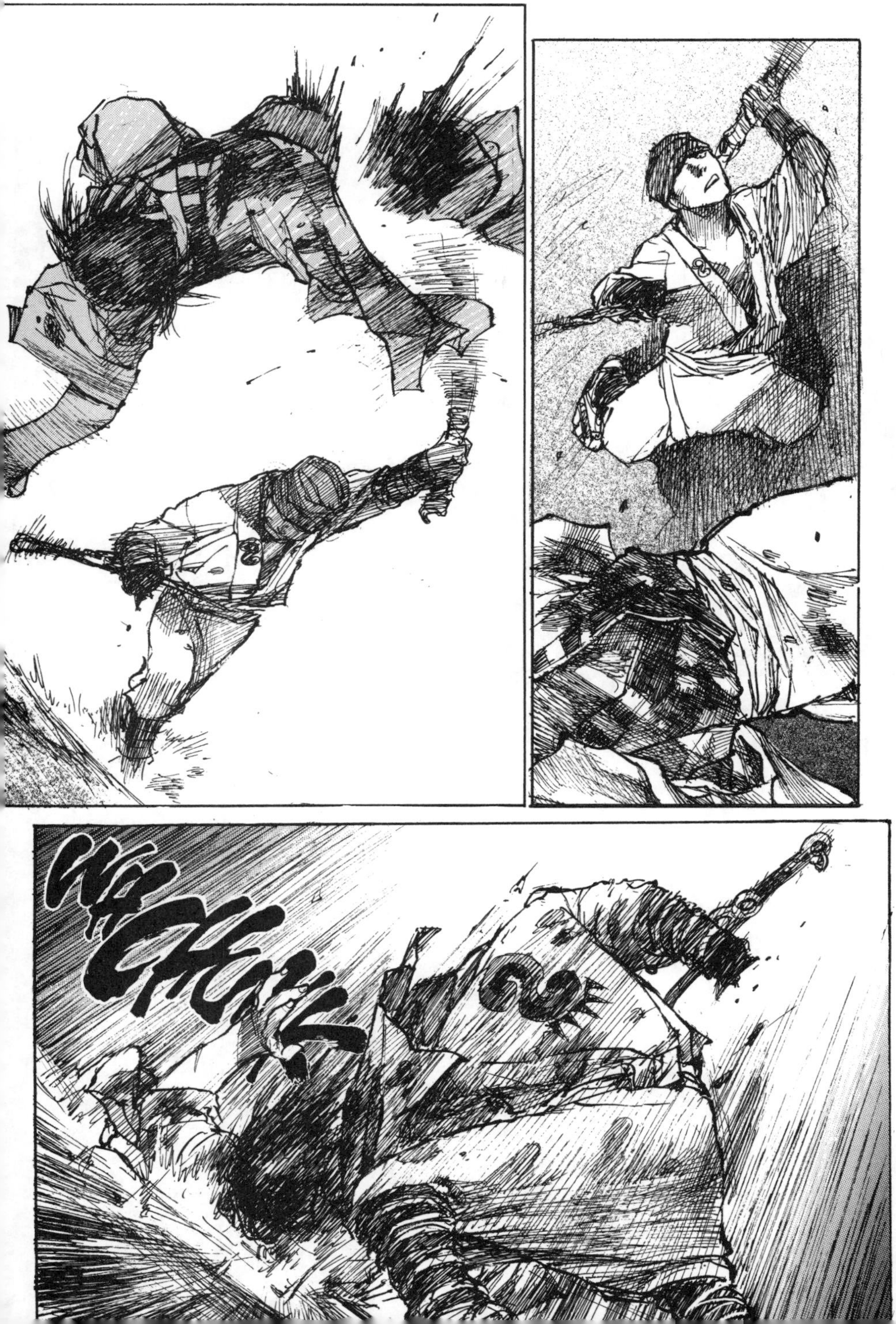
WACHUNK

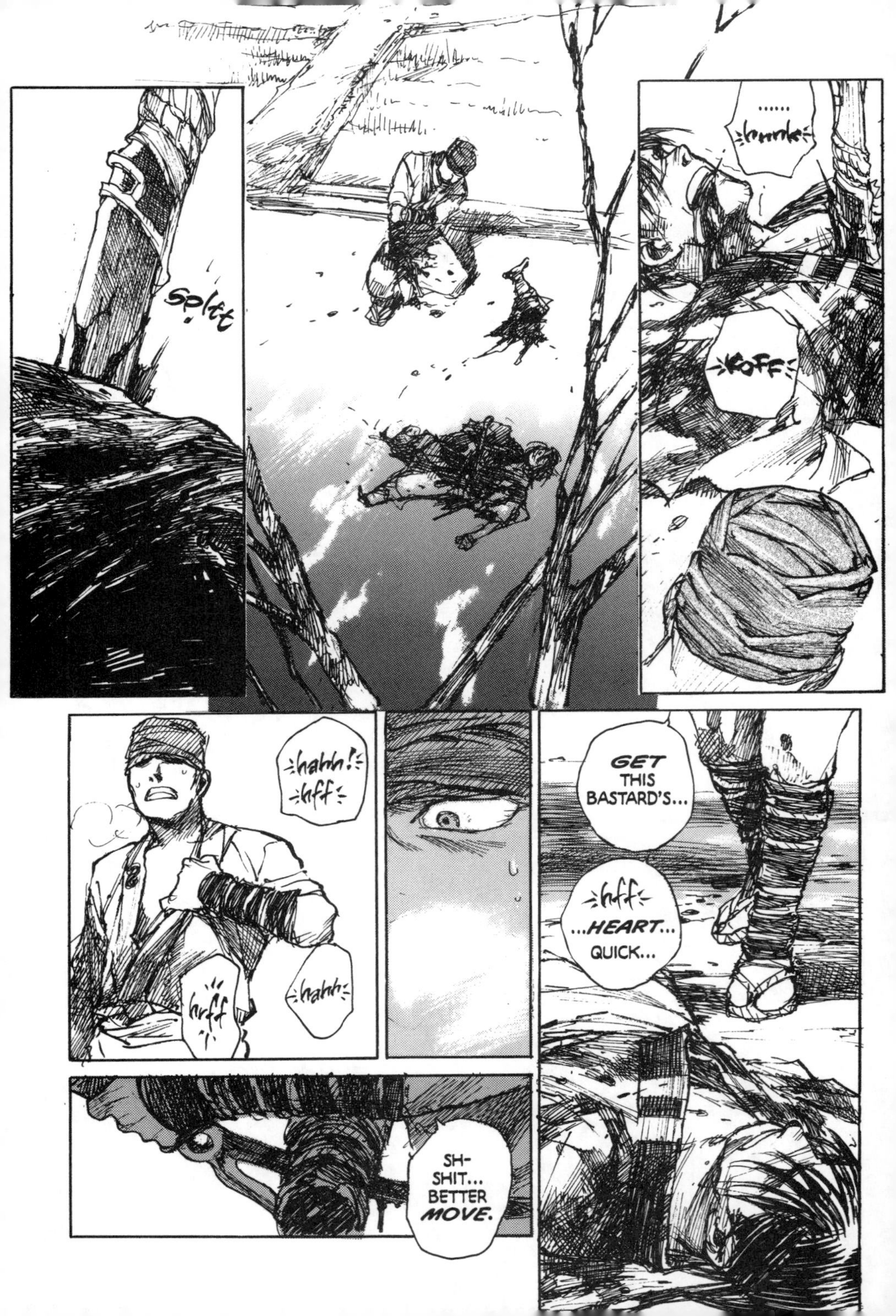
splitt
......
hnnnk
koff
hahh!
hff
hrff
hahh
GET THIS BASTARD'S...
hff
...HEART...
QUICK...
SH-SHIT... BETTER MOVE.

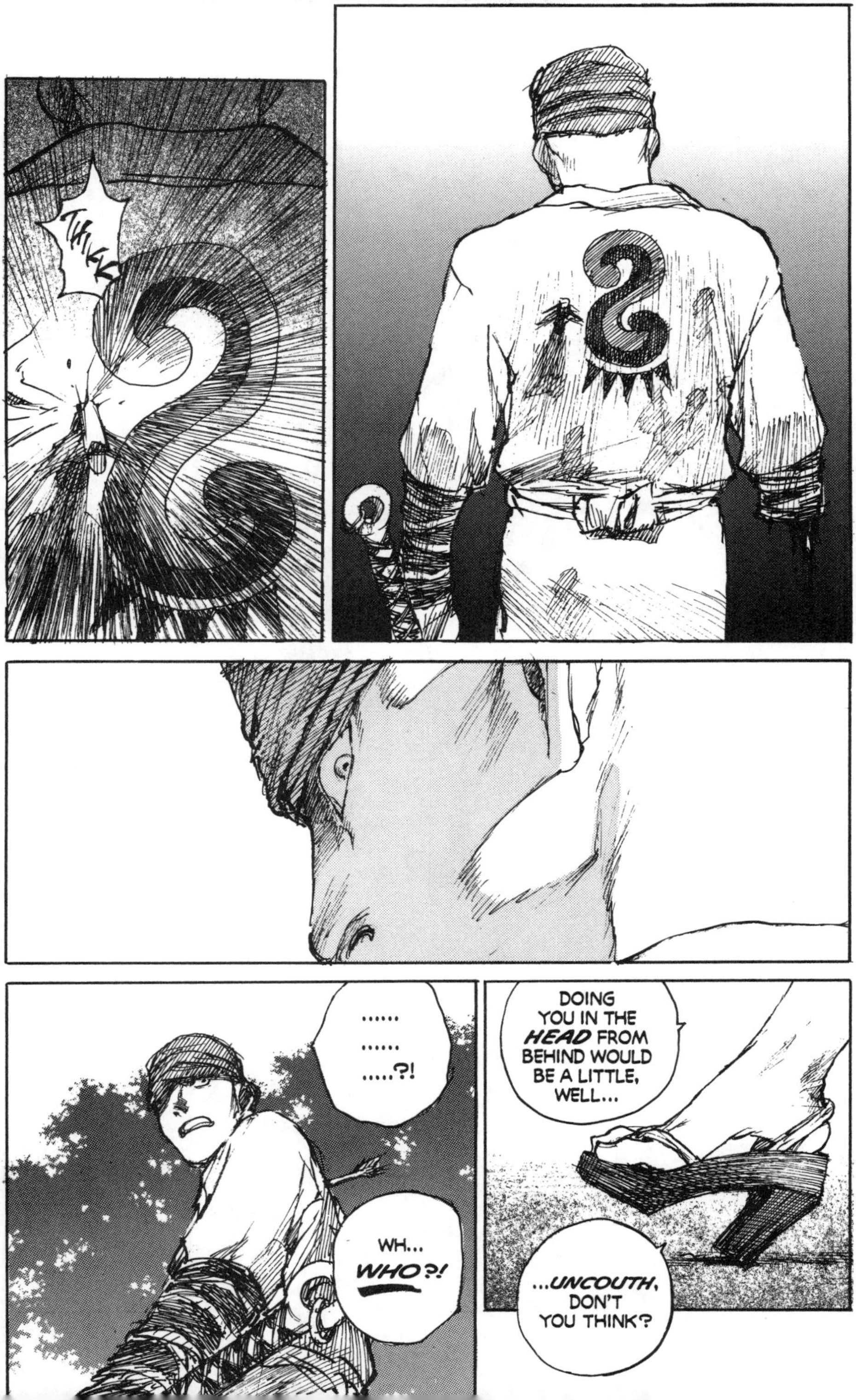
THUKK
......
......
.....?!
WH...
WHO?!
DOING YOU IN THE HEAD FROM BEHIND WOULD BE A LITTLE, WELL...
...UNCOUTH, DON'T YOU THINK?

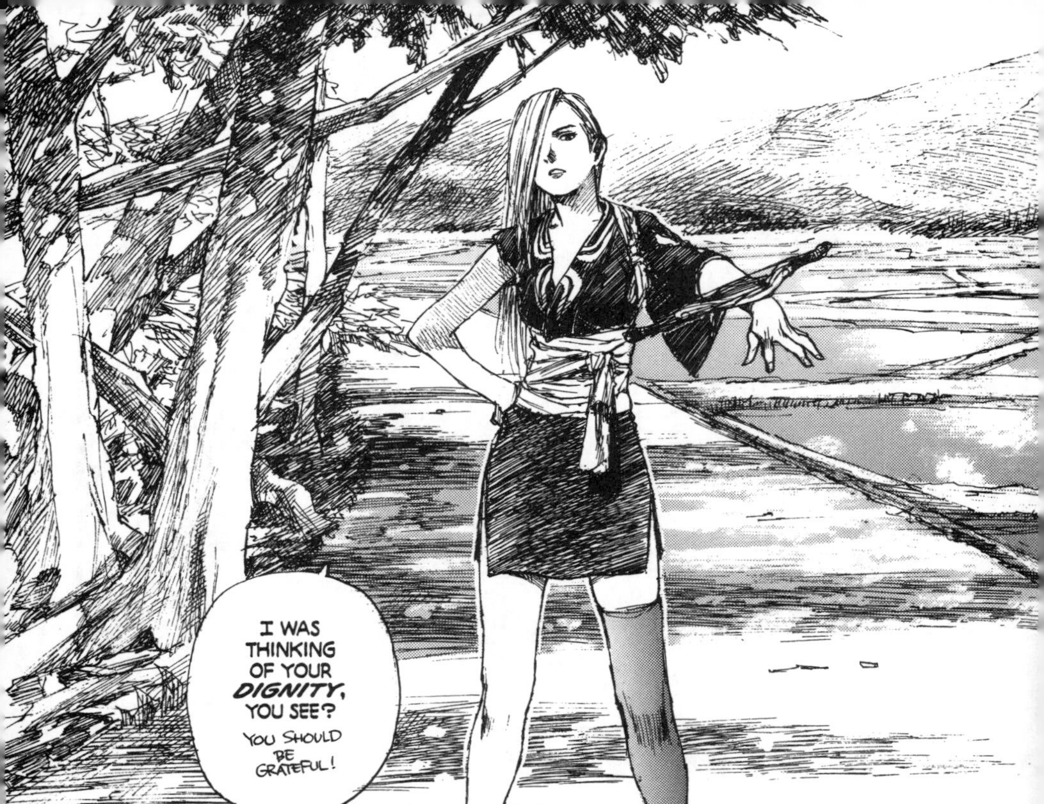
I WAS THINKING OF YOUR *DIGNITY*, YOU SEE?
YOU SHOULD BE GRATEFUL!

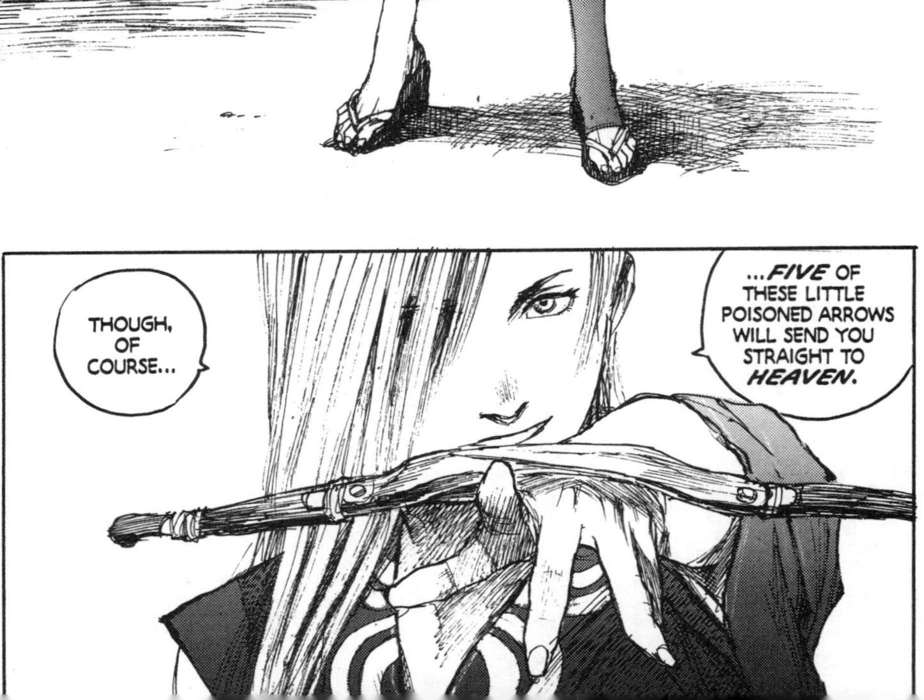
THOUGH, OF COURSE...
...*FIVE* OF THESE LITTLE POISONED ARROWS WILL SEND YOU STRAIGHT TO *HEAVEN*.

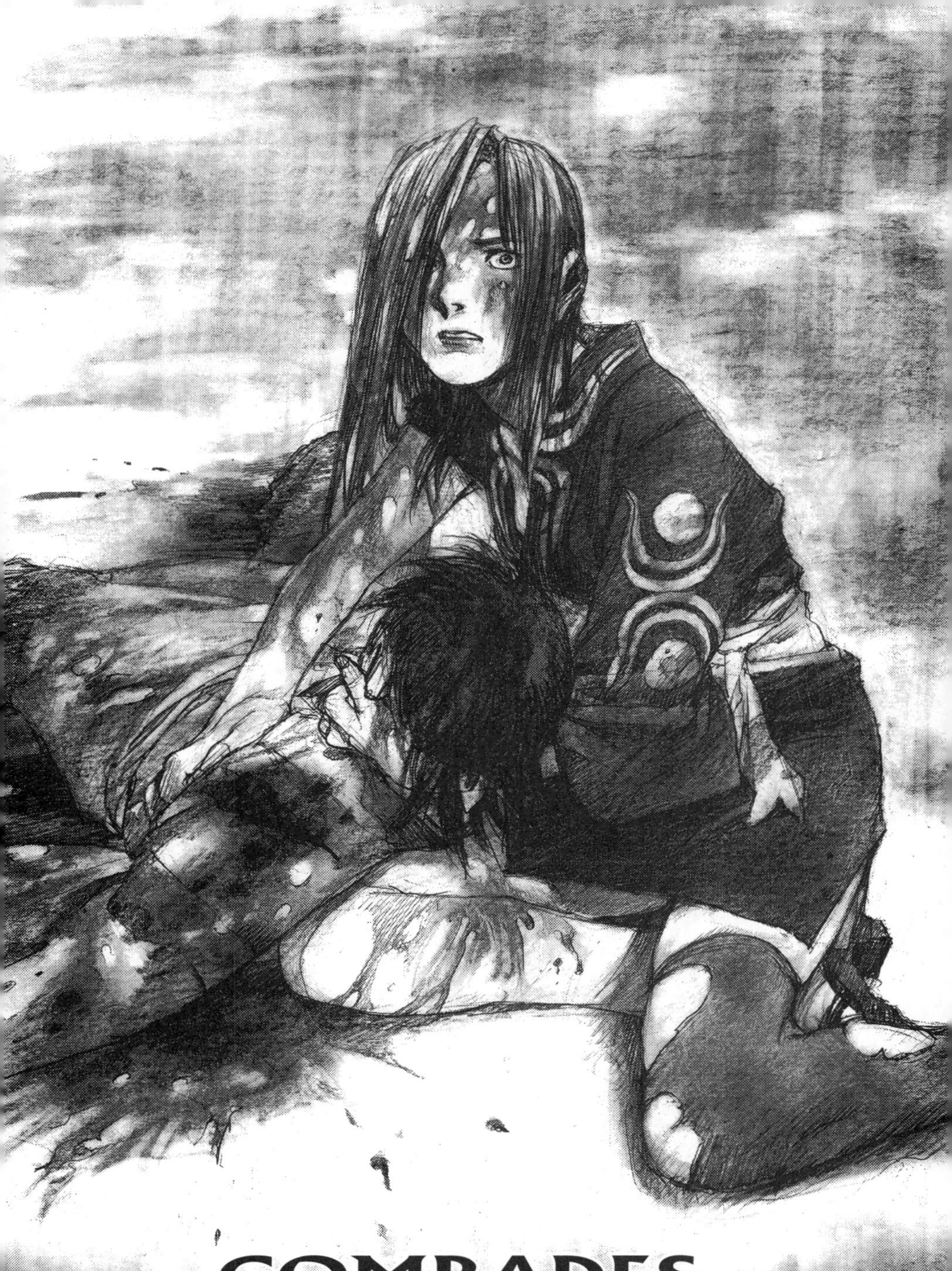

COMRADES
Part 6

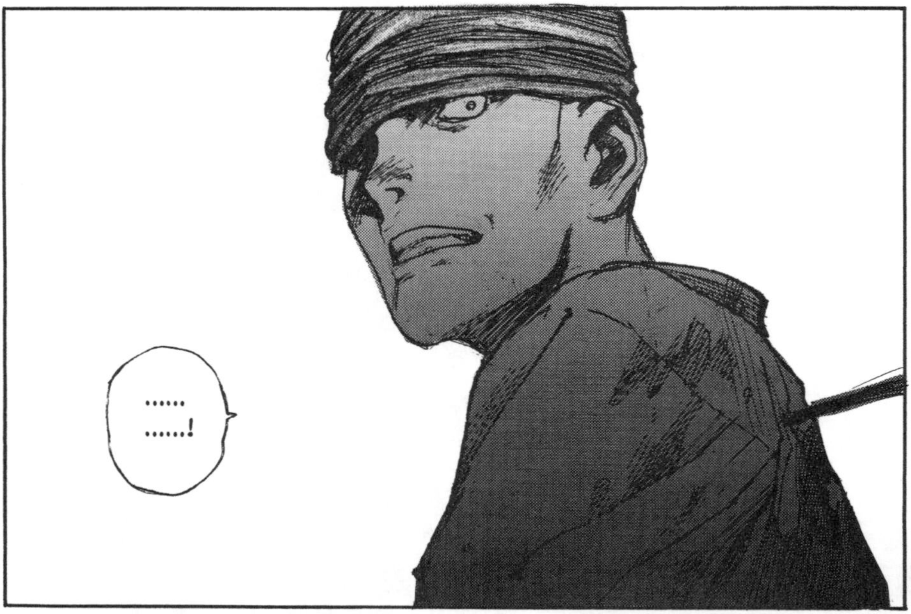
......
......!

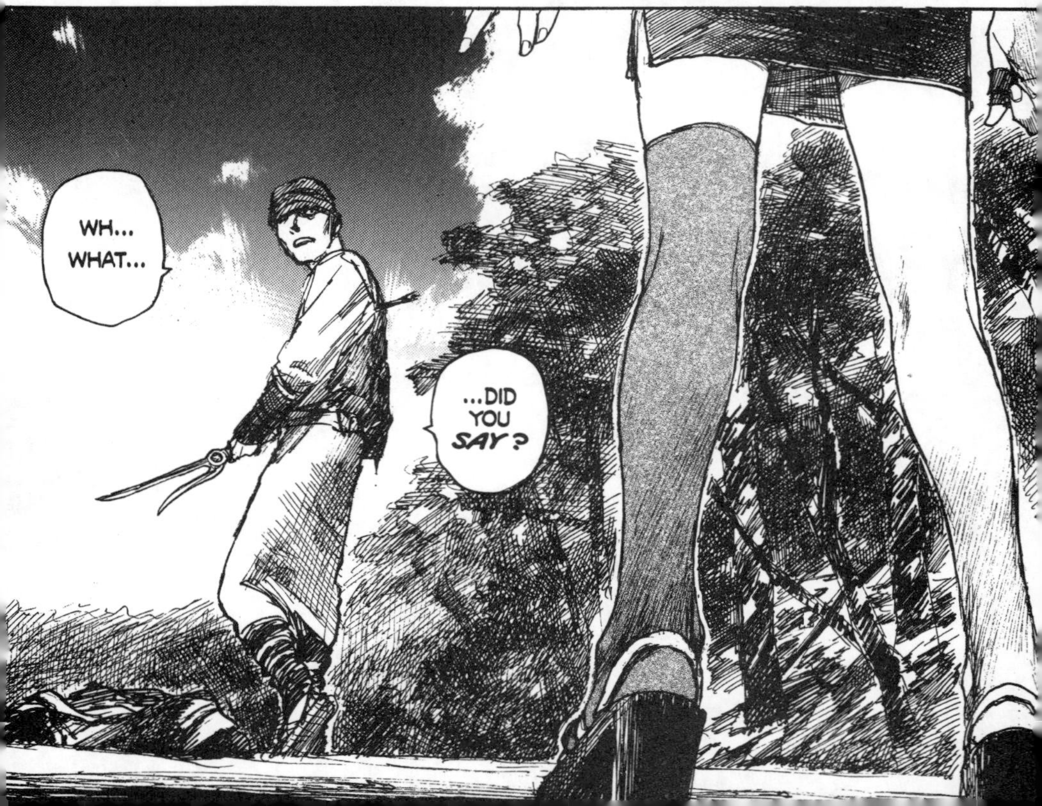
WH... WHAT...
...DID YOU SAY?

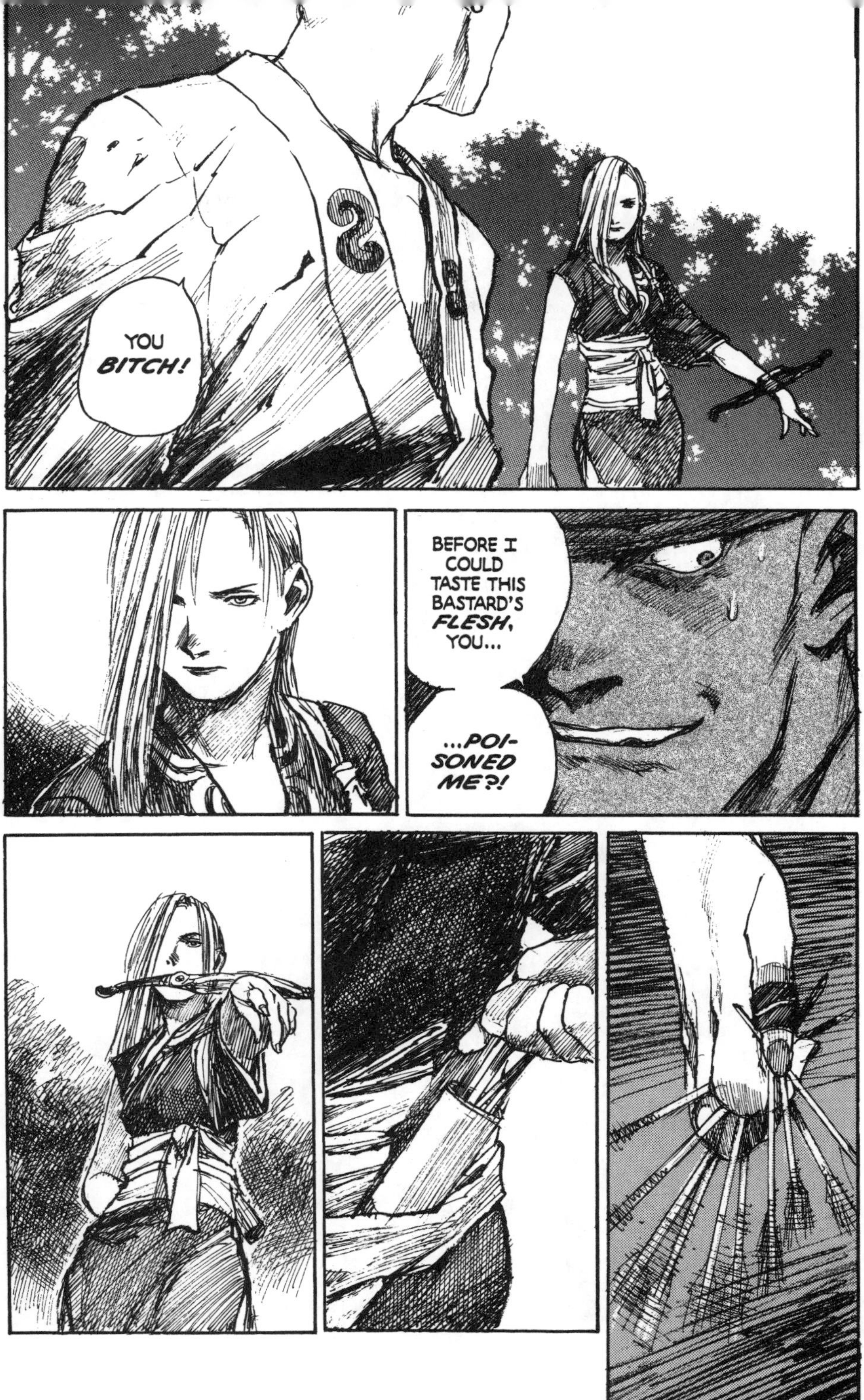
YOU BITCH!
BEFORE I COULD TASTE THIS BASTARD'S FLESH, YOU...
...POI-SONED ME?!

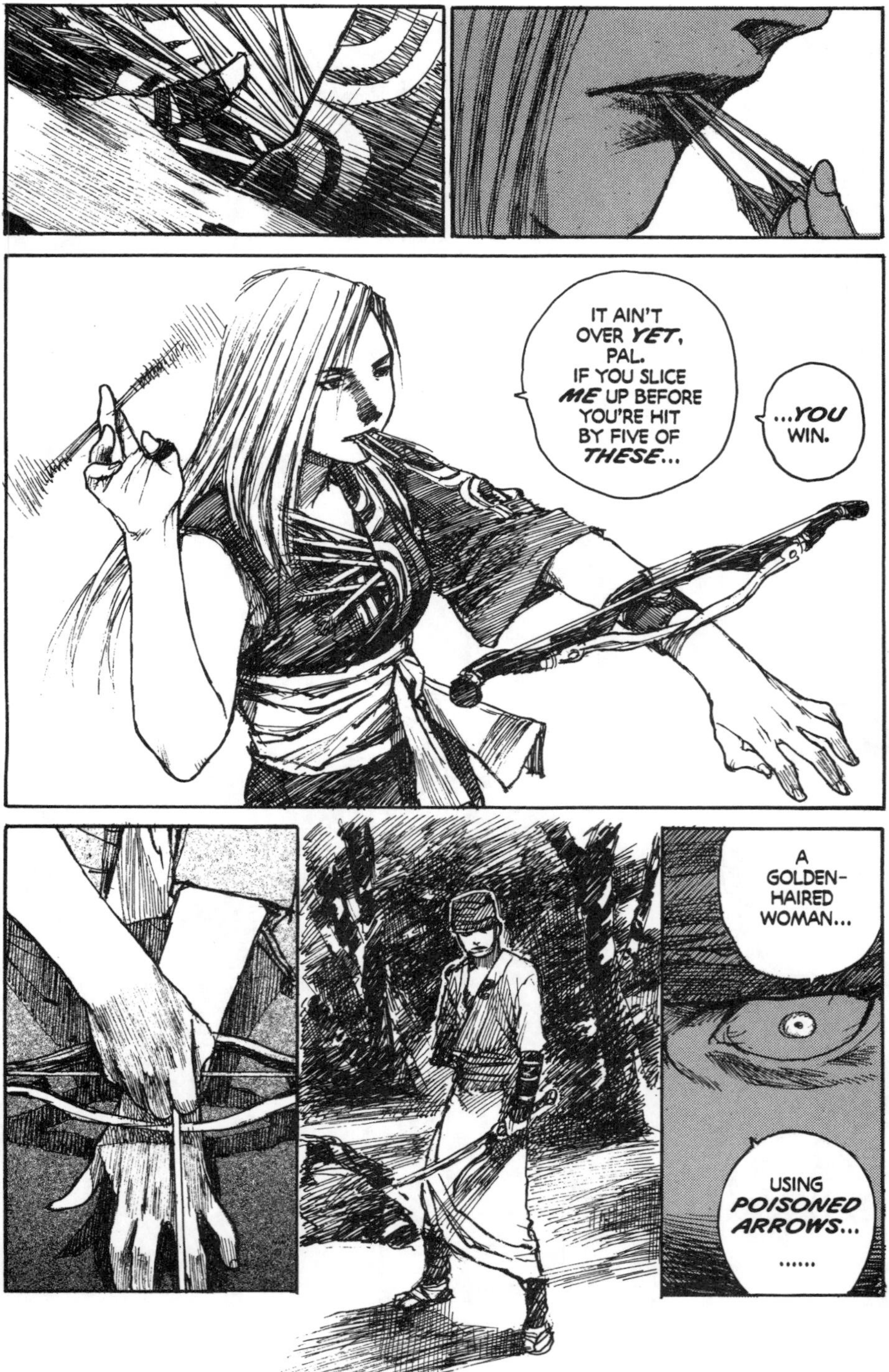
IT AIN'T OVER *YET*, PAL. IF YOU SLICE *ME* UP BEFORE YOU'RE HIT BY FIVE OF *THESE*...
...*YOU* WIN.
A GOLDEN-HAIRED WOMAN...
USING *POISONED ARROWS*...
......

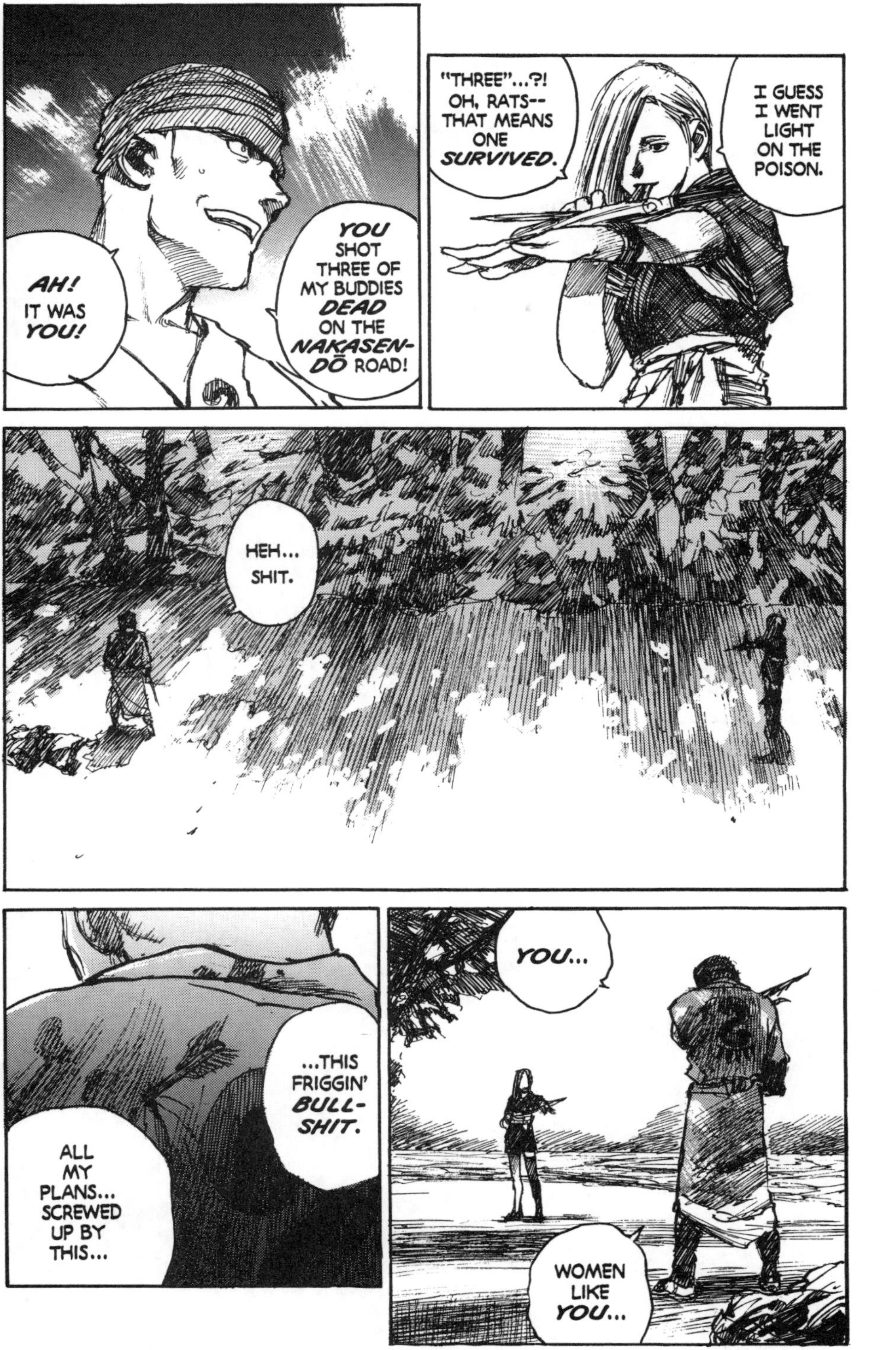
AH! IT WAS YOU!
YOU SHOT THREE OF MY BUDDIES DEAD ON THE NAKASEN-DŌ ROAD!
"THREE"...?! OH, RATS-- THAT MEANS ONE SURVIVED.
I GUESS I WENT LIGHT ON THE POISON.
HEH... SHIT.
ALL MY PLANS... SCREWED UP BY THIS...
...THIS FRIGGIN' BULL-SHIT.
YOU...
WOMEN LIKE YOU...

THERE'S ONLY *ONE THING* YOU'RE GOOD FOR--

--TO BE *BUTCHERED* LIKE A PIG!!

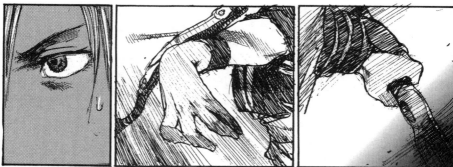

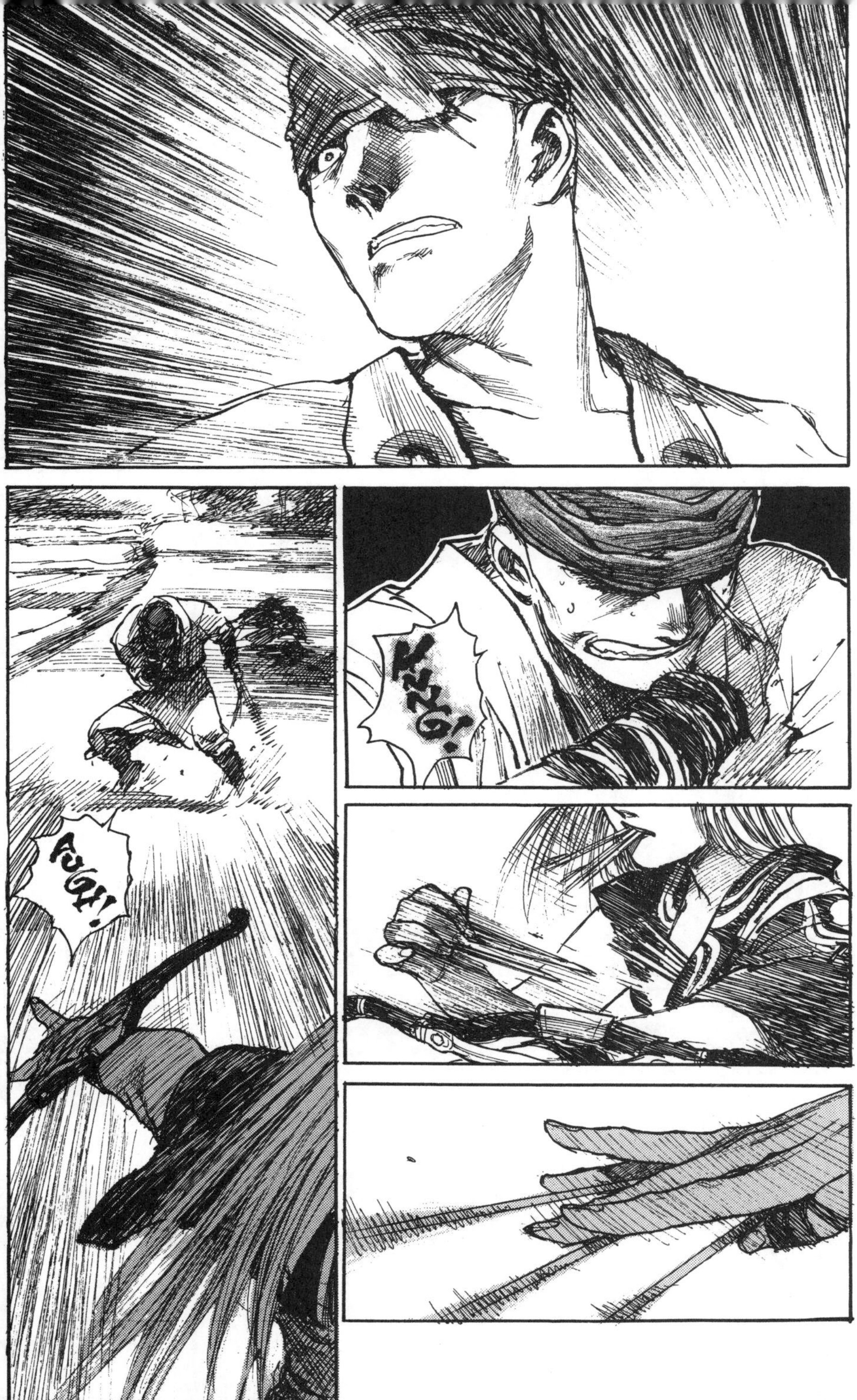
AUGH!
KNNG!

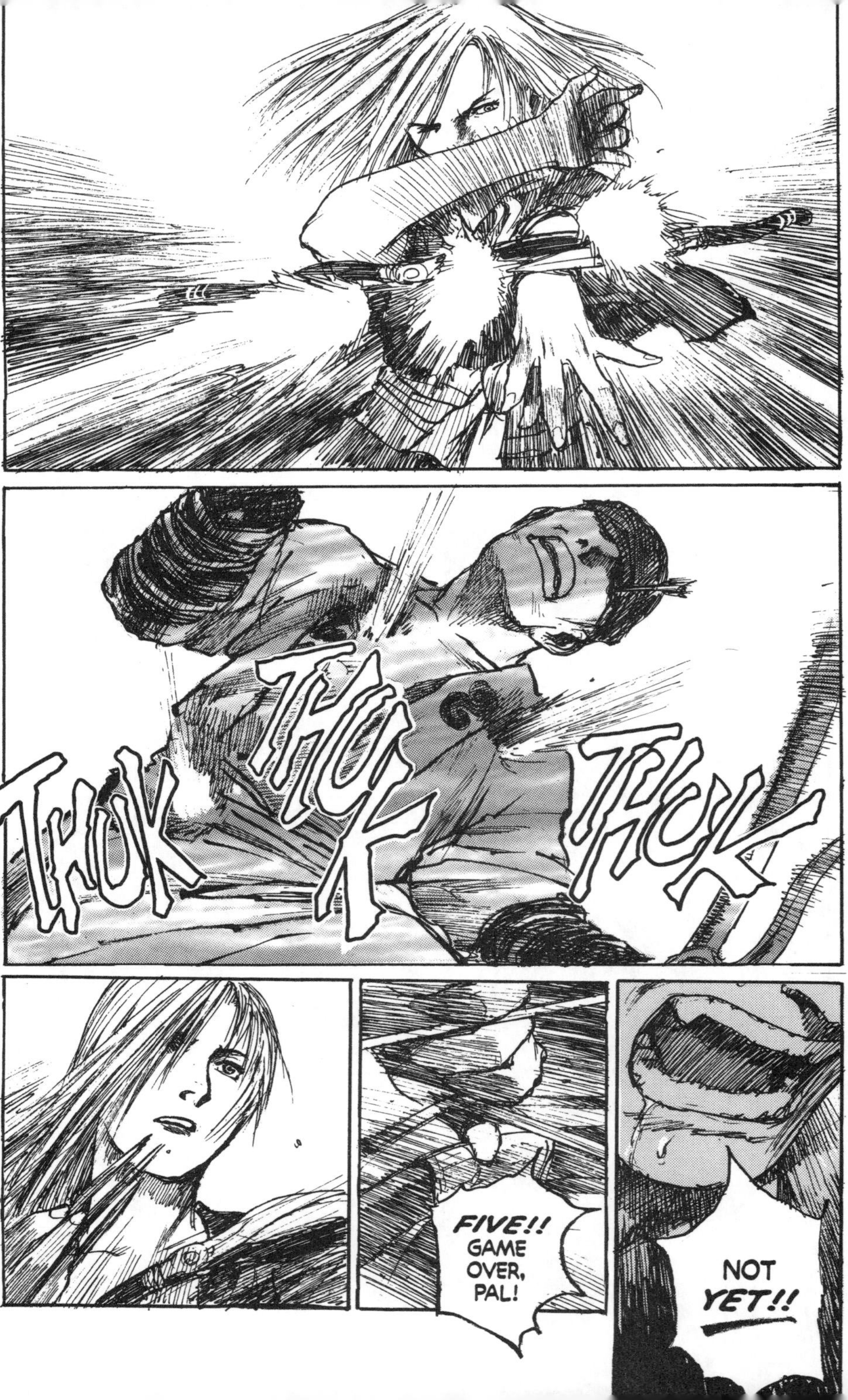
THUK
THUK
THUK
FIVE!! GAME OVER, PAL!
NOT YET!!

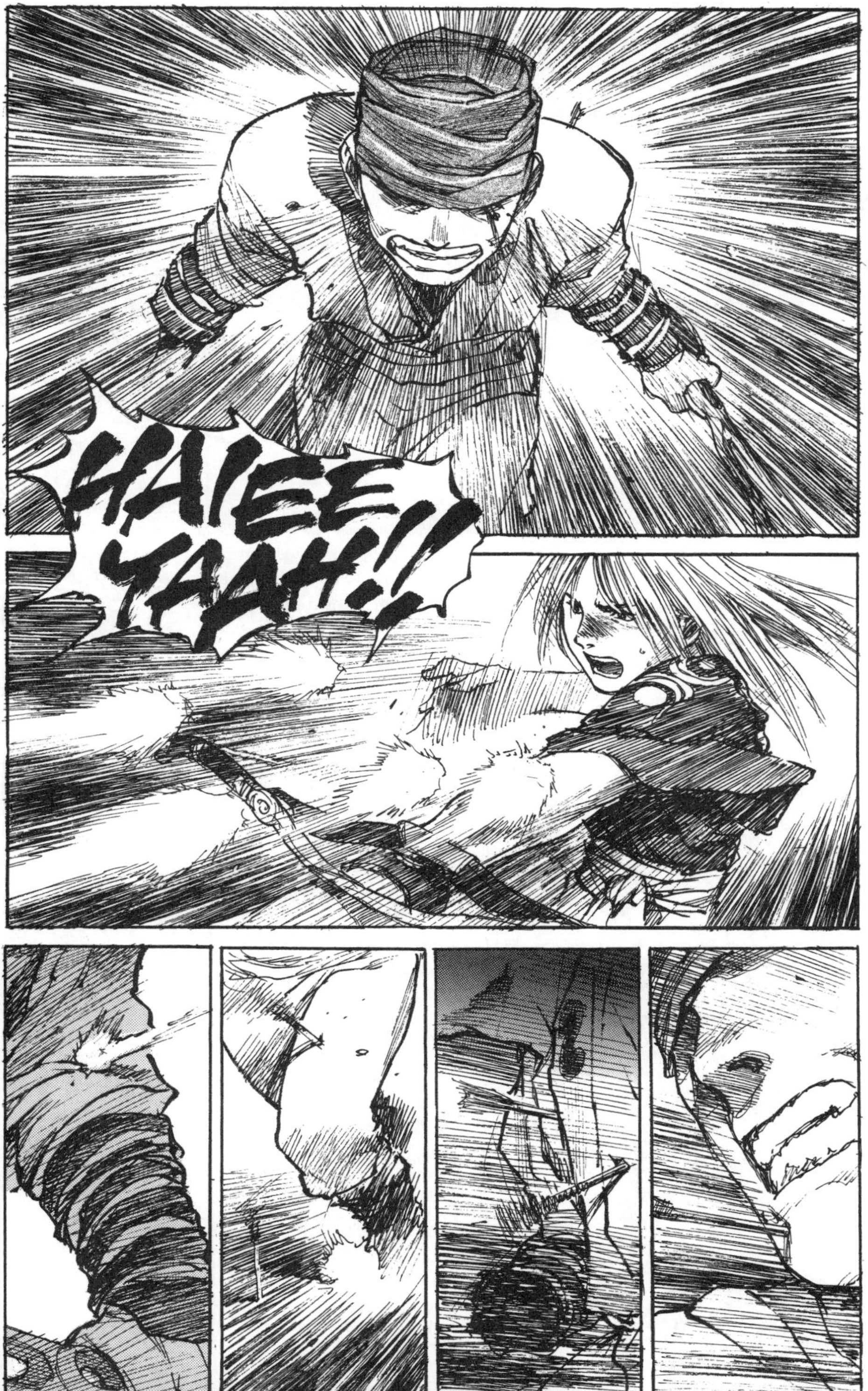
HAIEE YAAH!!

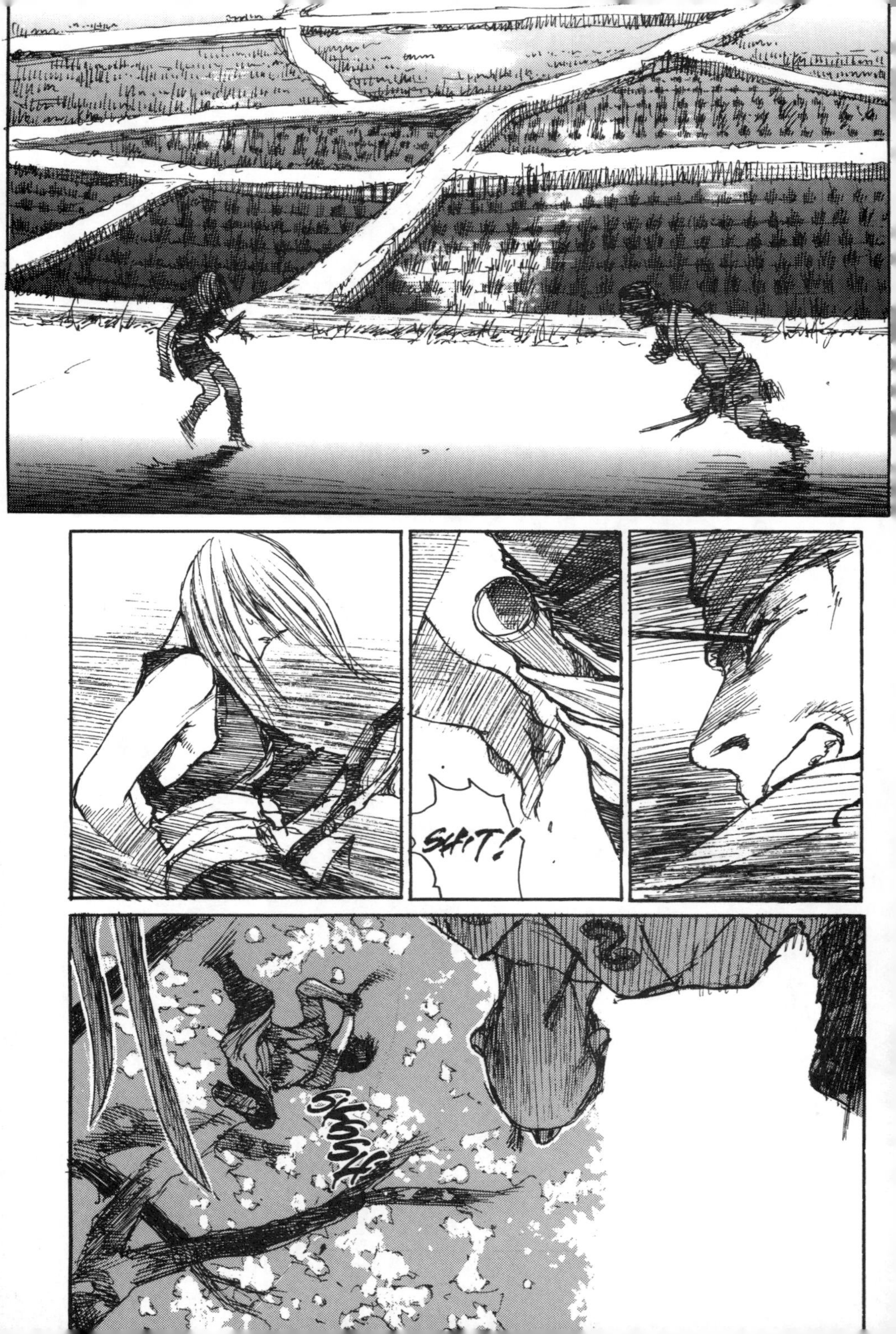
SHIT!
SKOSH

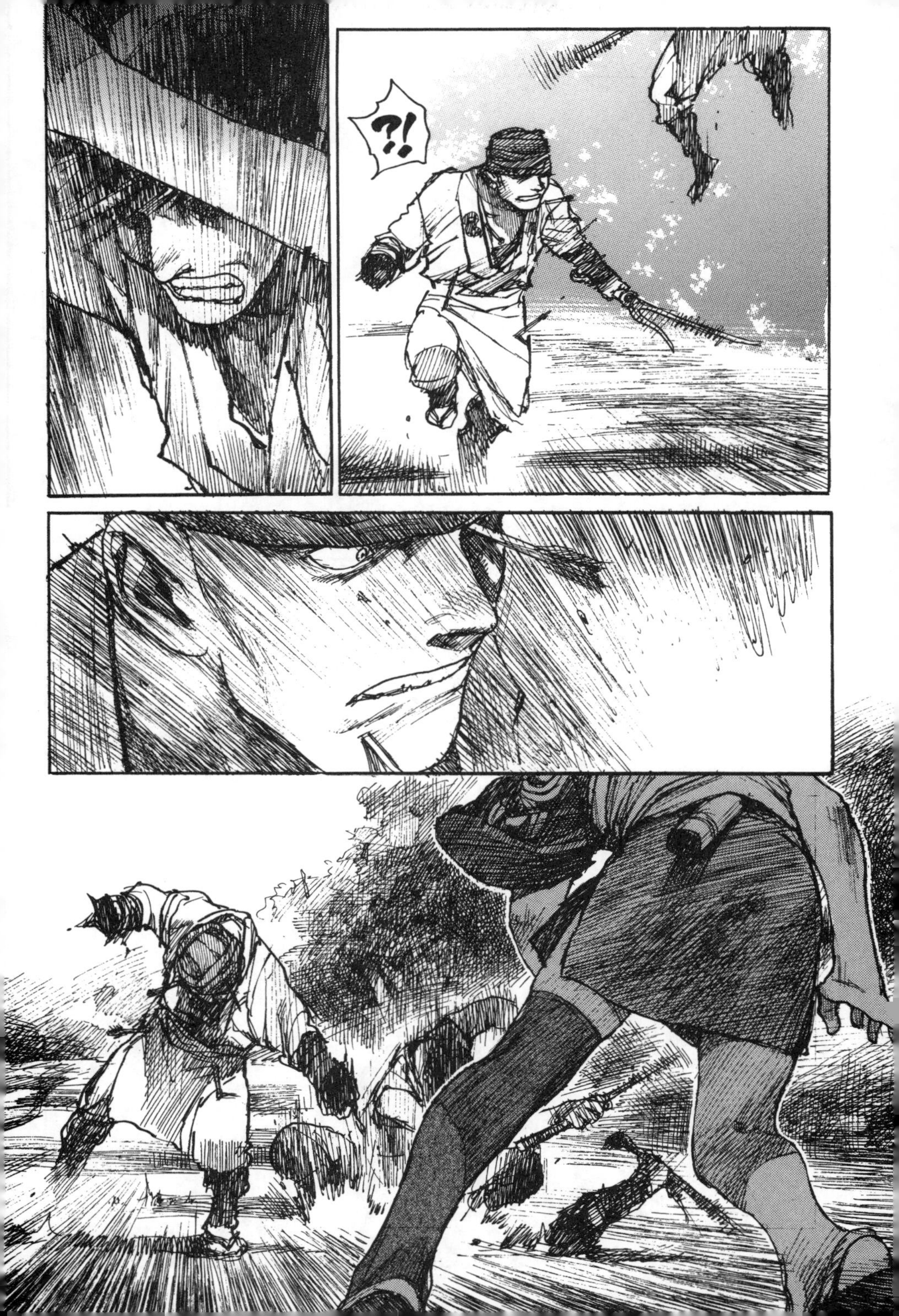
?!

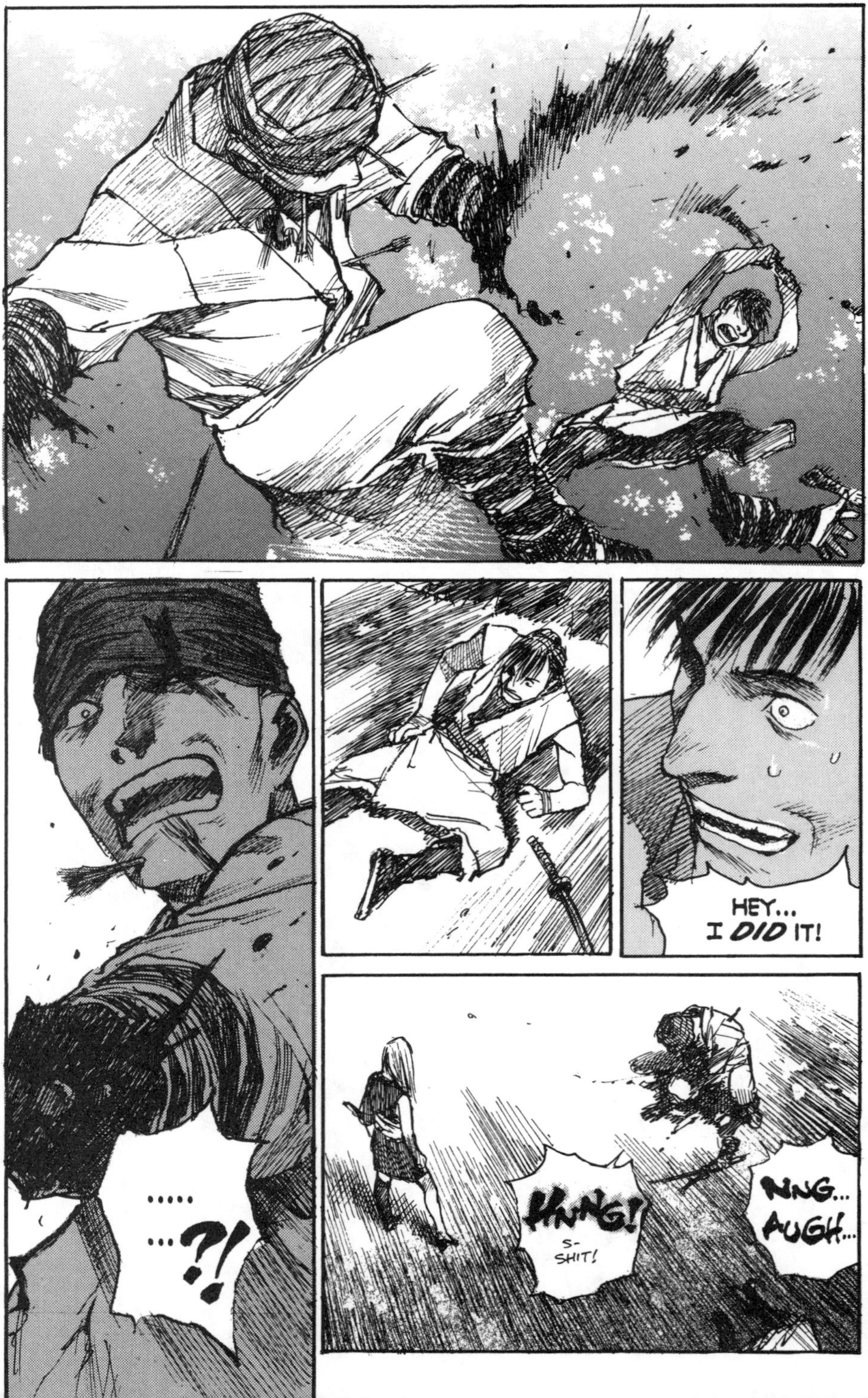
.....
...?!
HEY...
I DID IT!
HNNG!
S-
SHIT!
NNG...
AUGH...

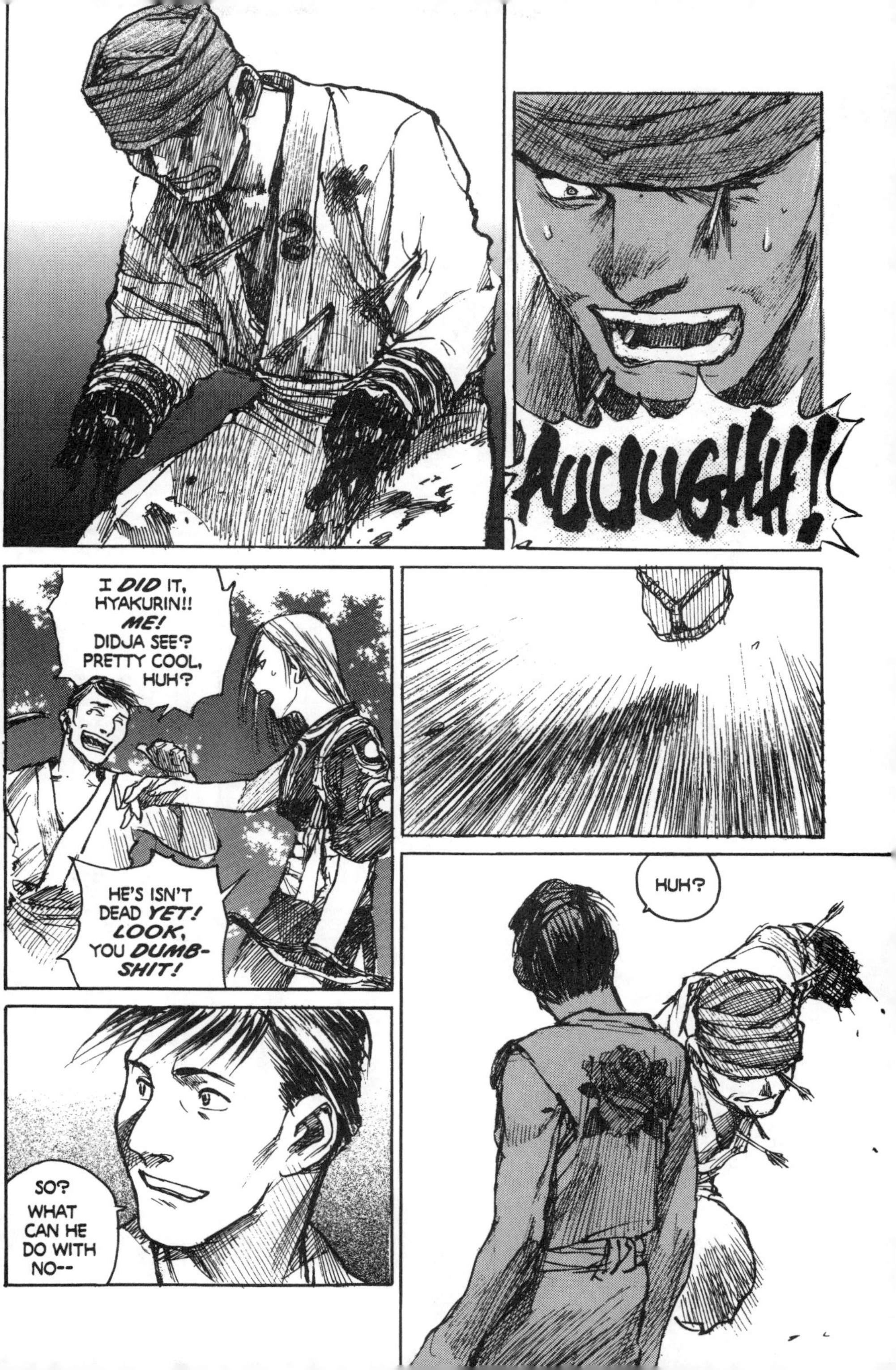
AUUUGHH!
I DID IT, HYAKURIN!! ME! DIDJA SEE? PRETTY COOL, HUH?
HE'S ISN'T DEAD YET! LOOK, YOU DUMB-SHIT!
HUH?
SO? WHAT CAN HE DO WITH NO--

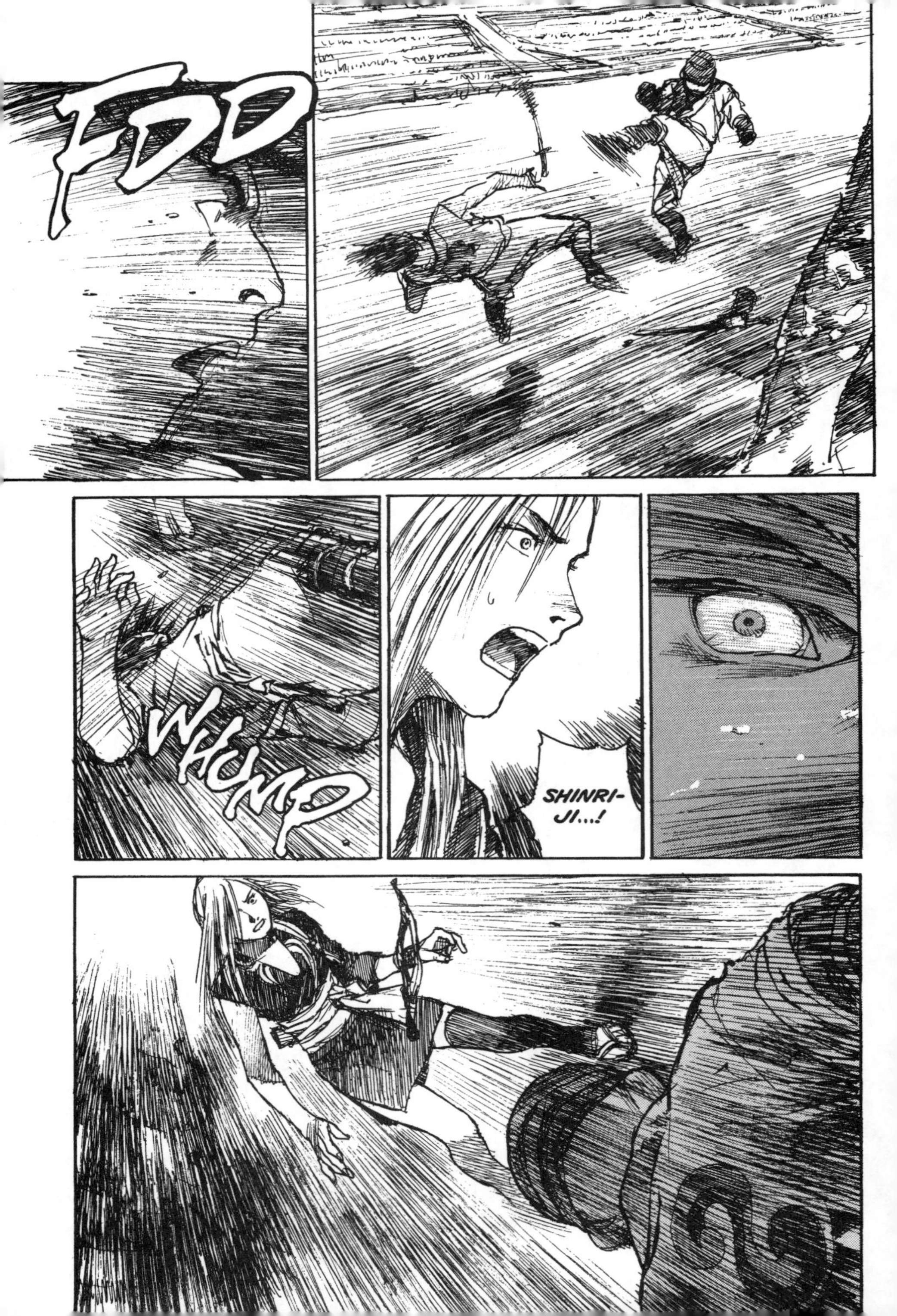
FDD
WHUMP
SHINRI-JI...!

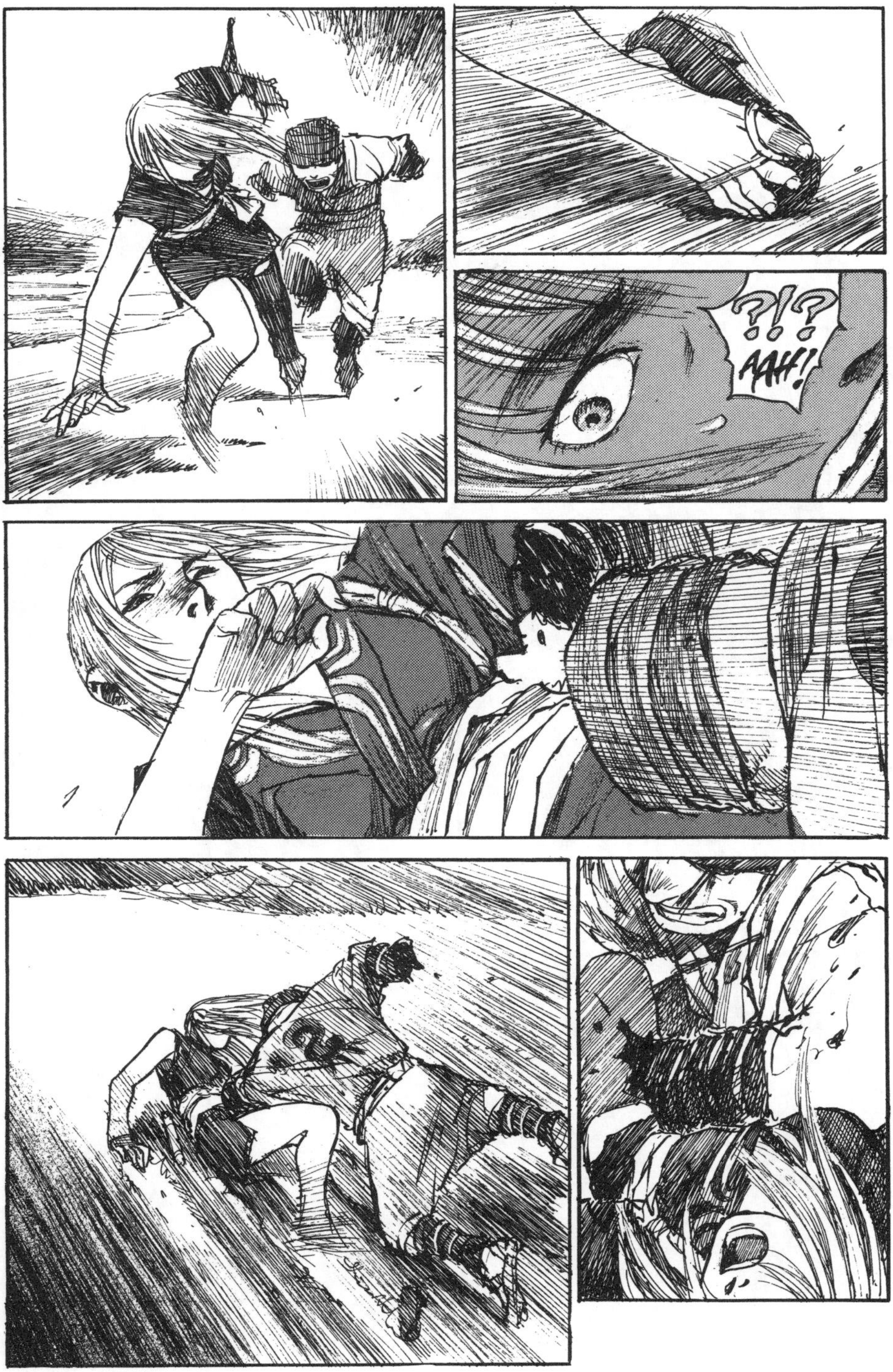
?!?
AAH!

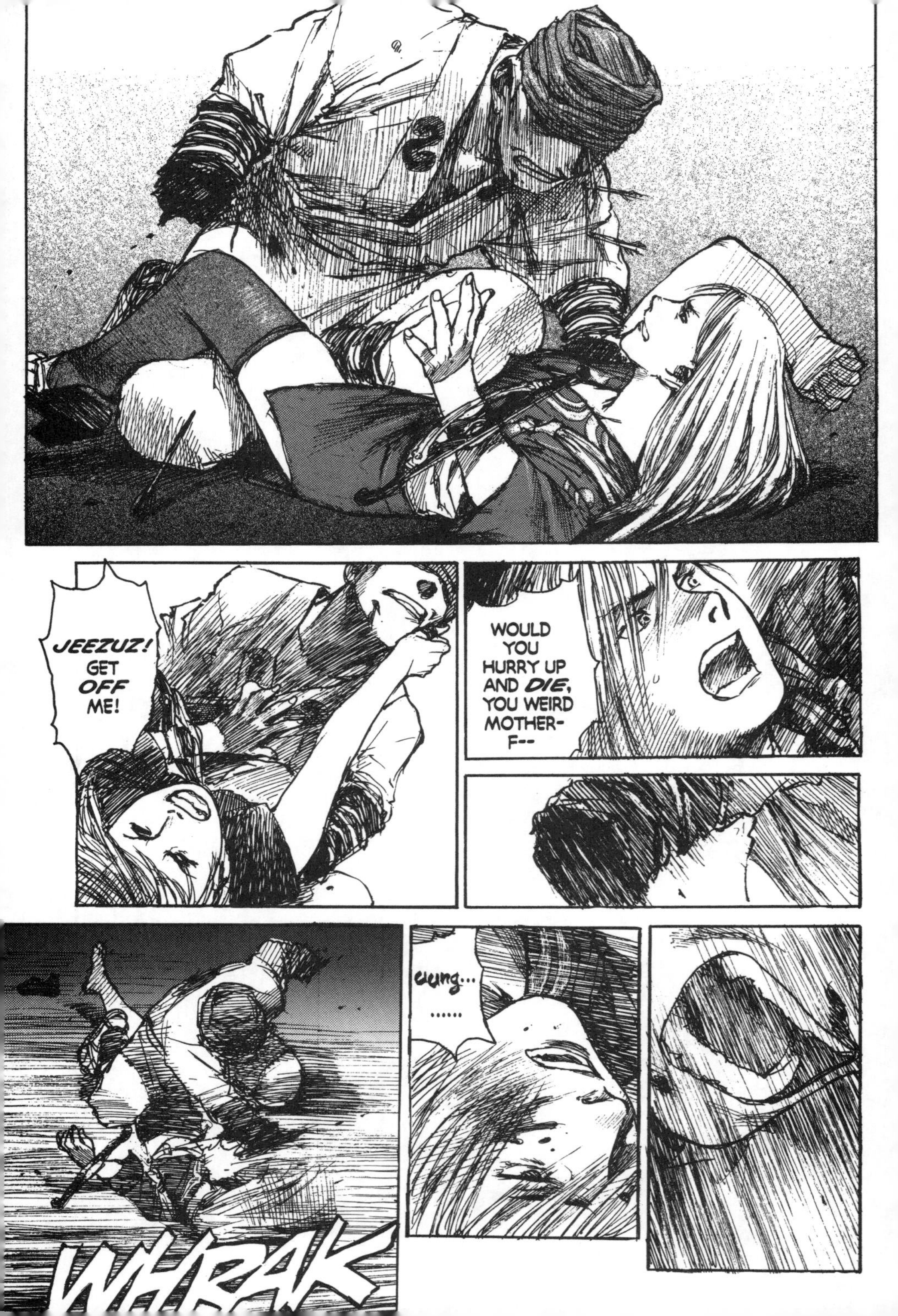
JEEZUZ! GET OFF ME!
WOULD YOU HURRY UP AND DIE, YOU WEIRD MOTHER-F--
WHRAK
uung...
......

?!?
AAH?!

AAUGGH!!

KRNCH

SKRNCH

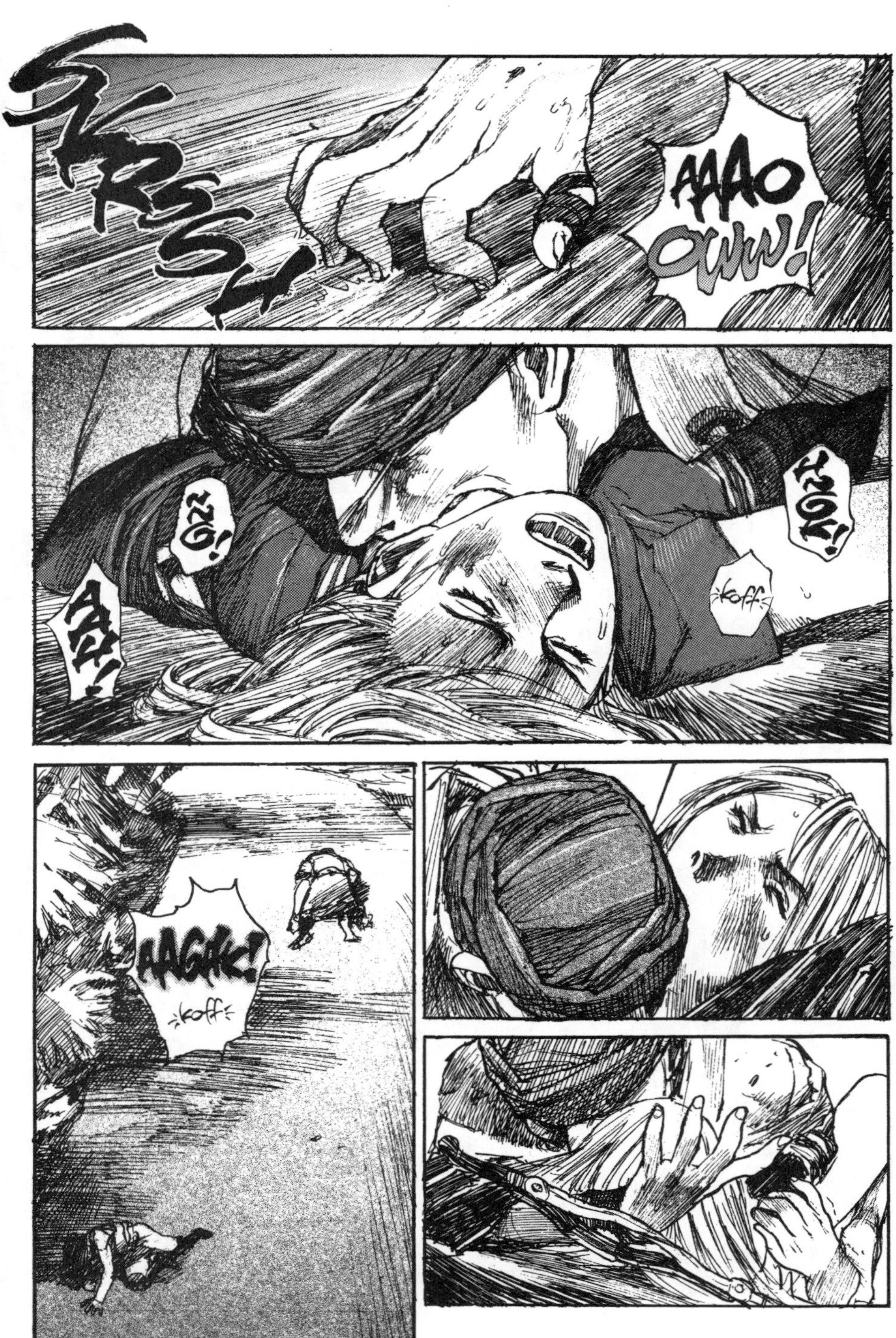
SKRSSH
AAAO OWW!
NG!
AAH!
KNGK!
koff
AAGAK!
koff

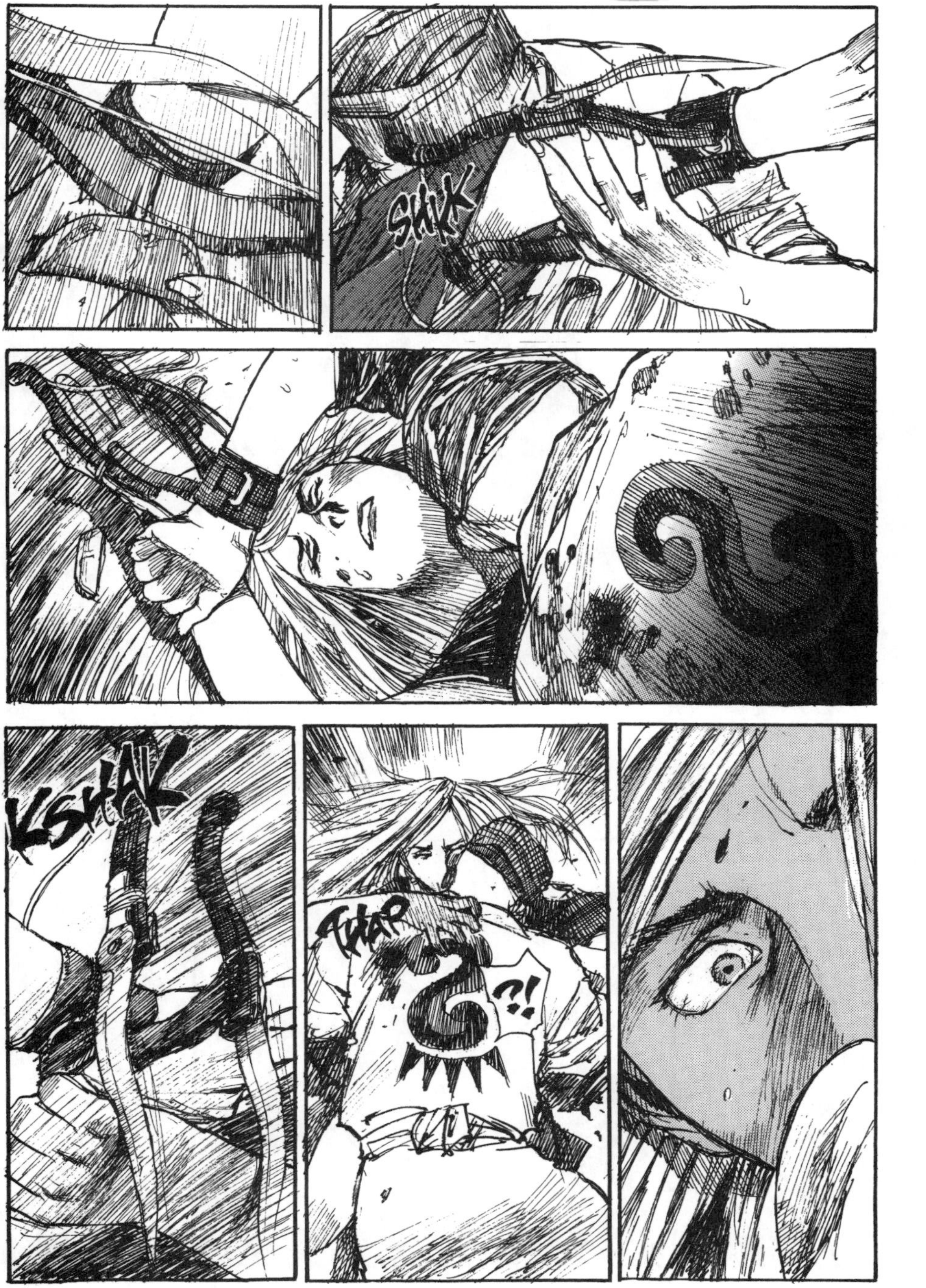
SHVK
KSHAK
FWAP
?!

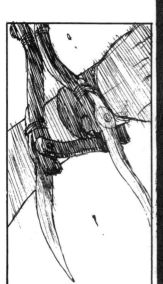

......!

≥hehh≥ ≥hnff≥

HRGG...

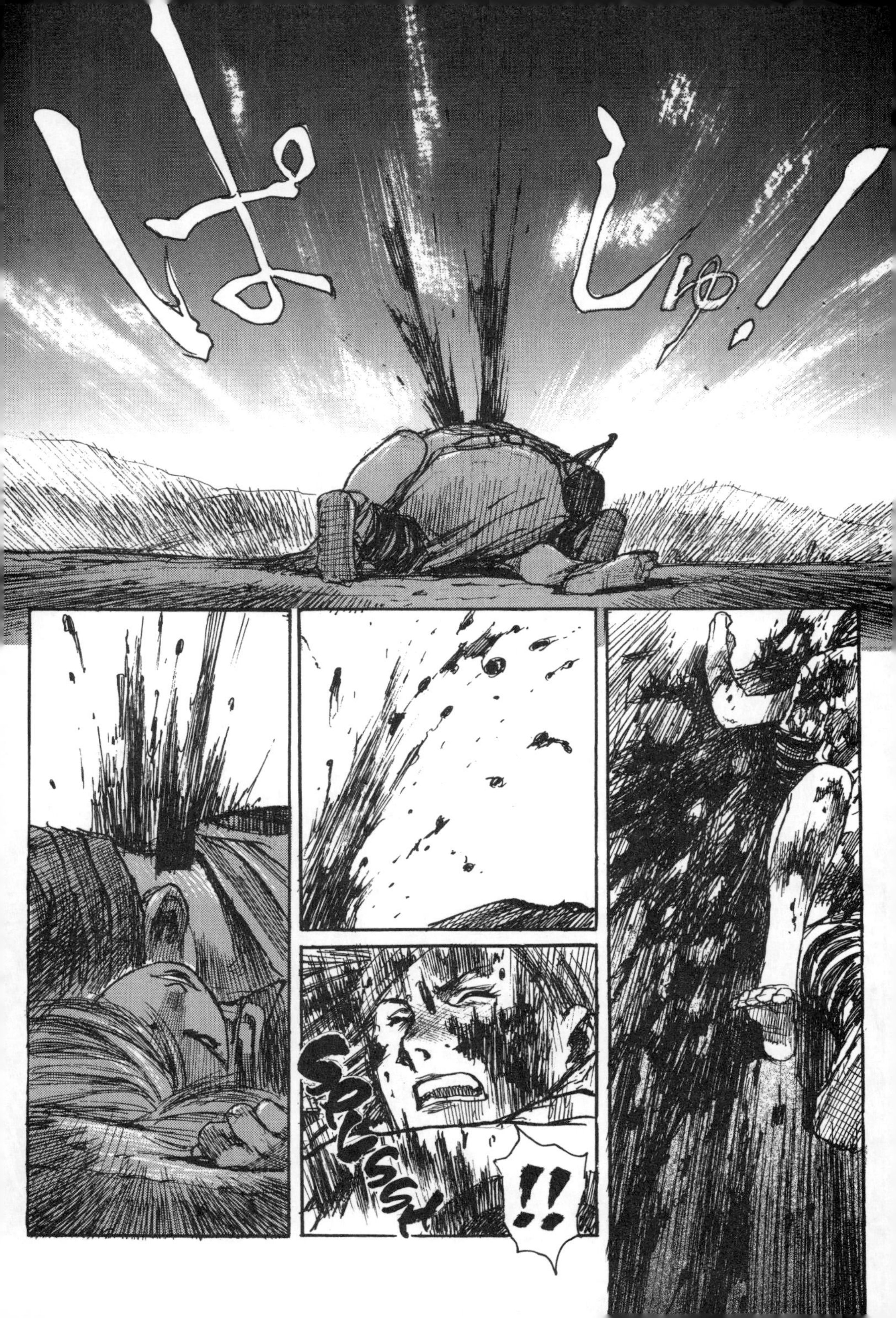
ぱしゅ!
SPLSSSH
!!

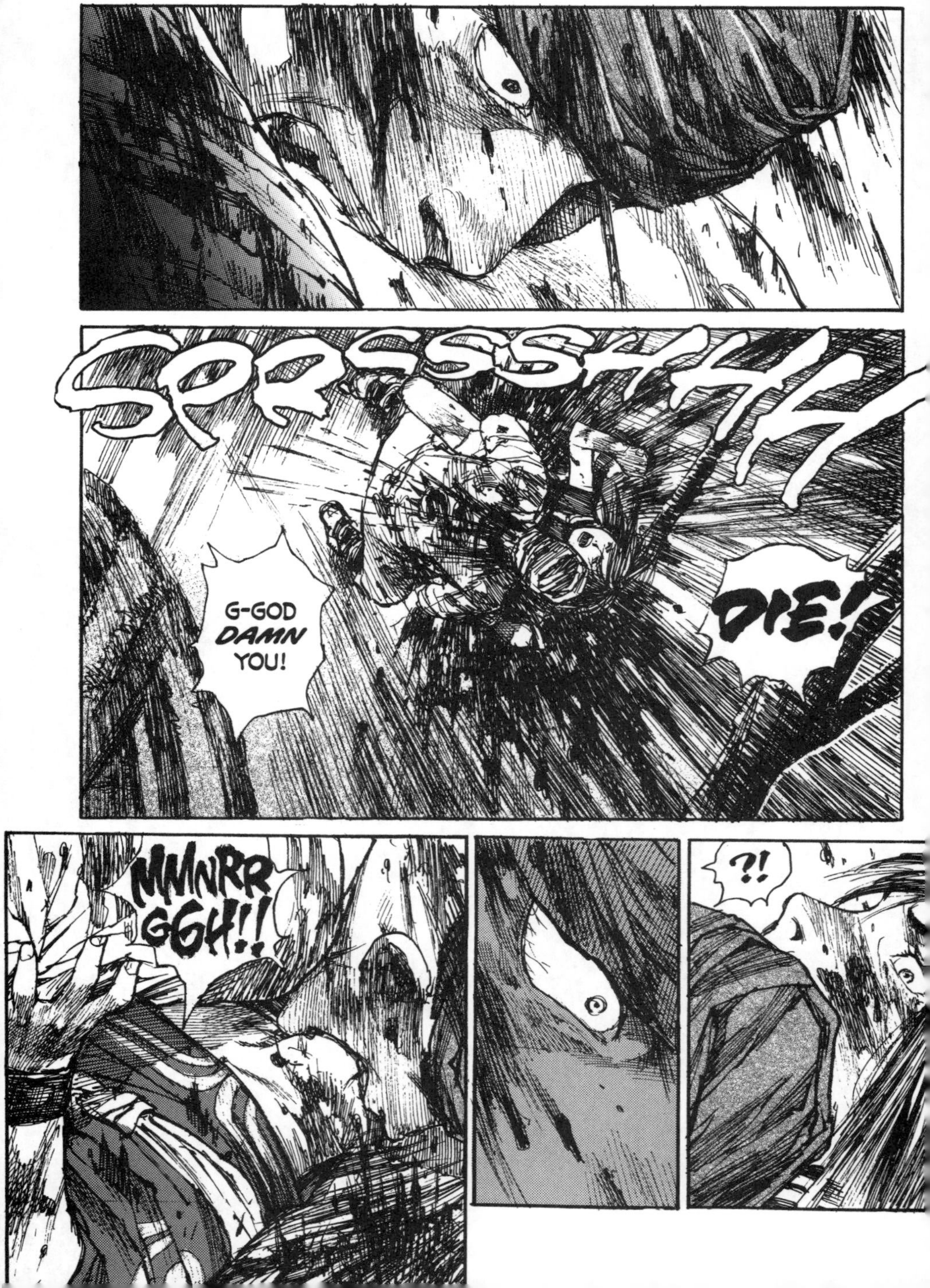
SPRSSHHH
G-GOD DAMN YOU!
DIE!!
MMNRR GGH!!
?!

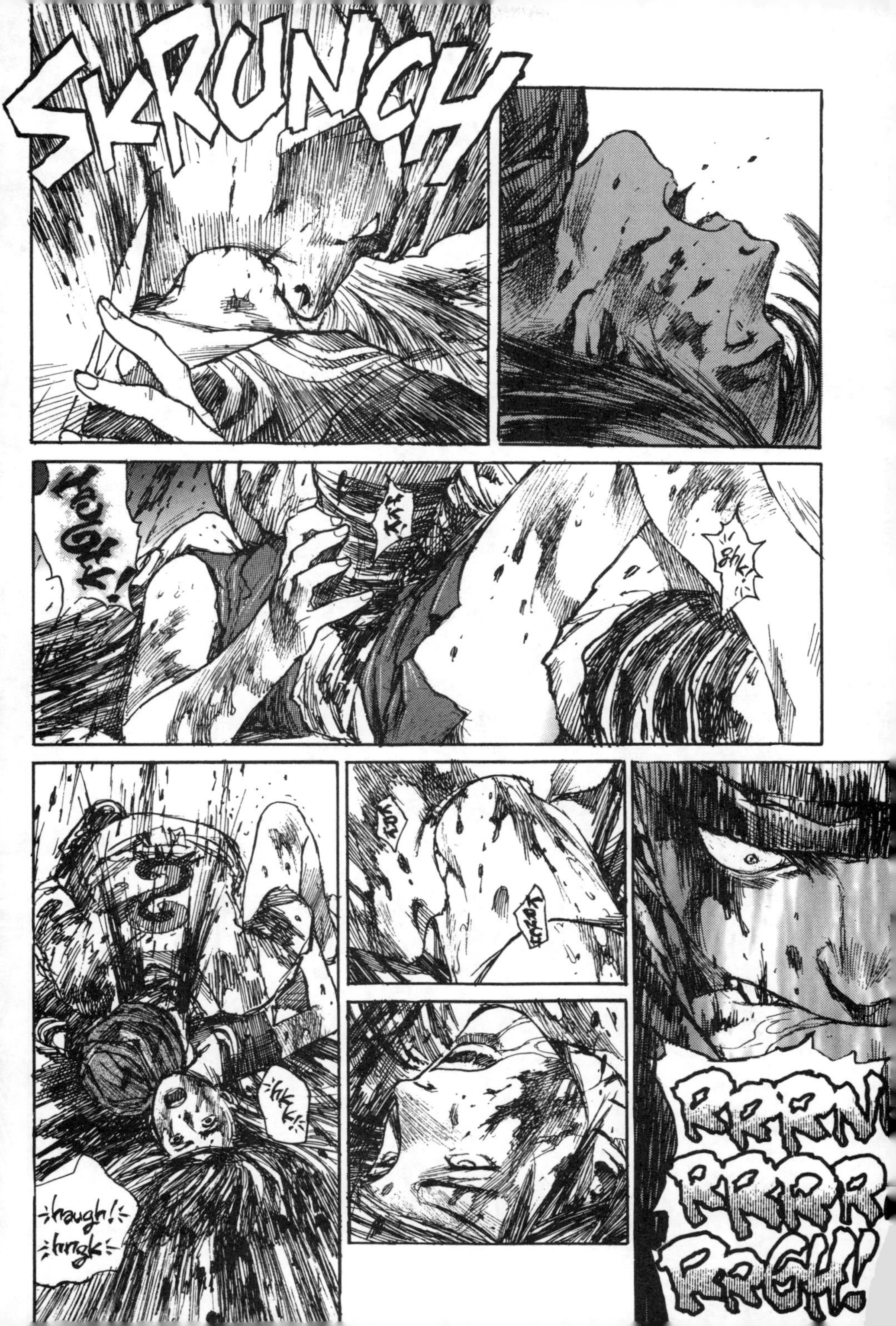
SKRUNCH
ghk!
hkk
haugh!
hngk
RRRR
RRRR
RRGH!

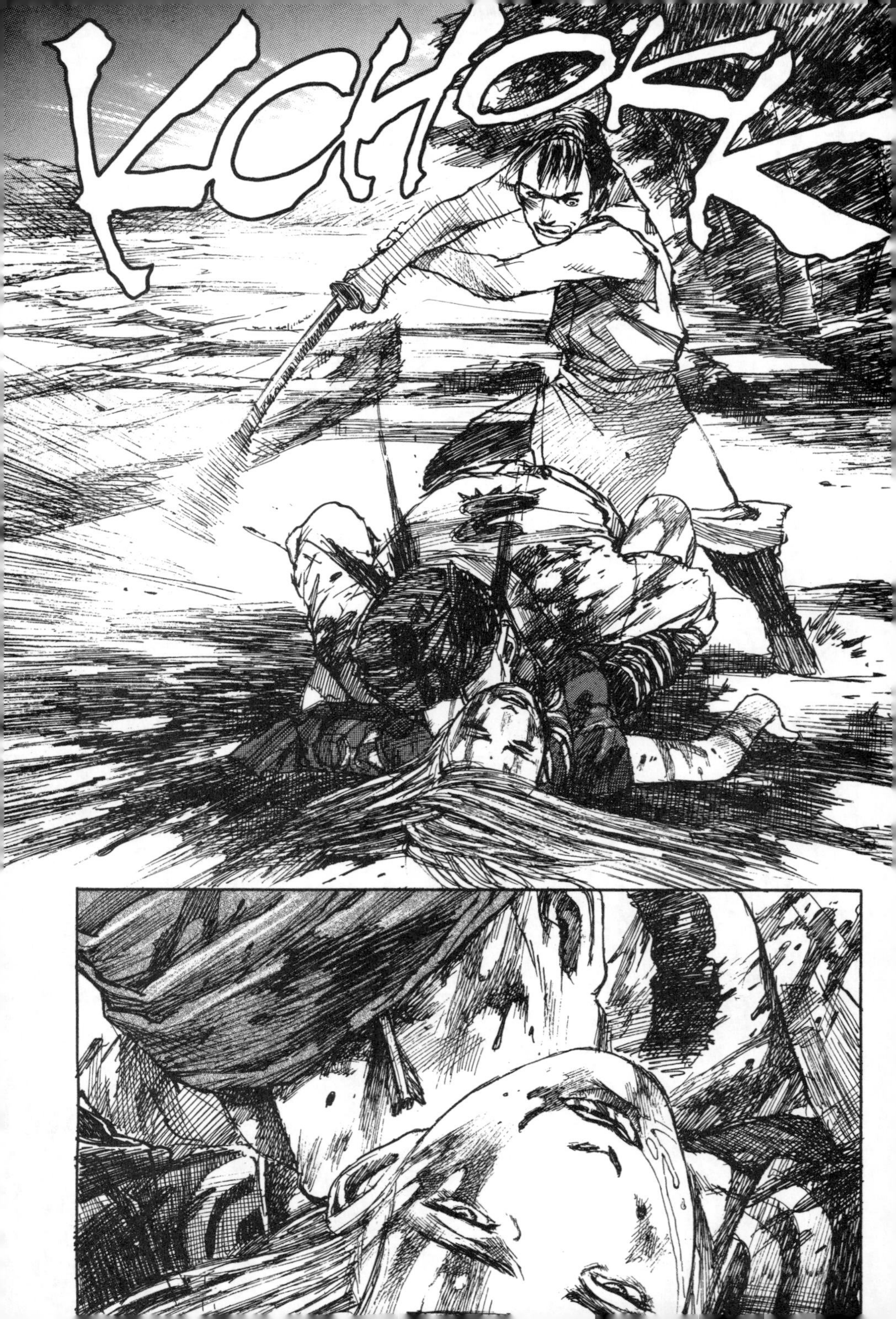
KCHOK

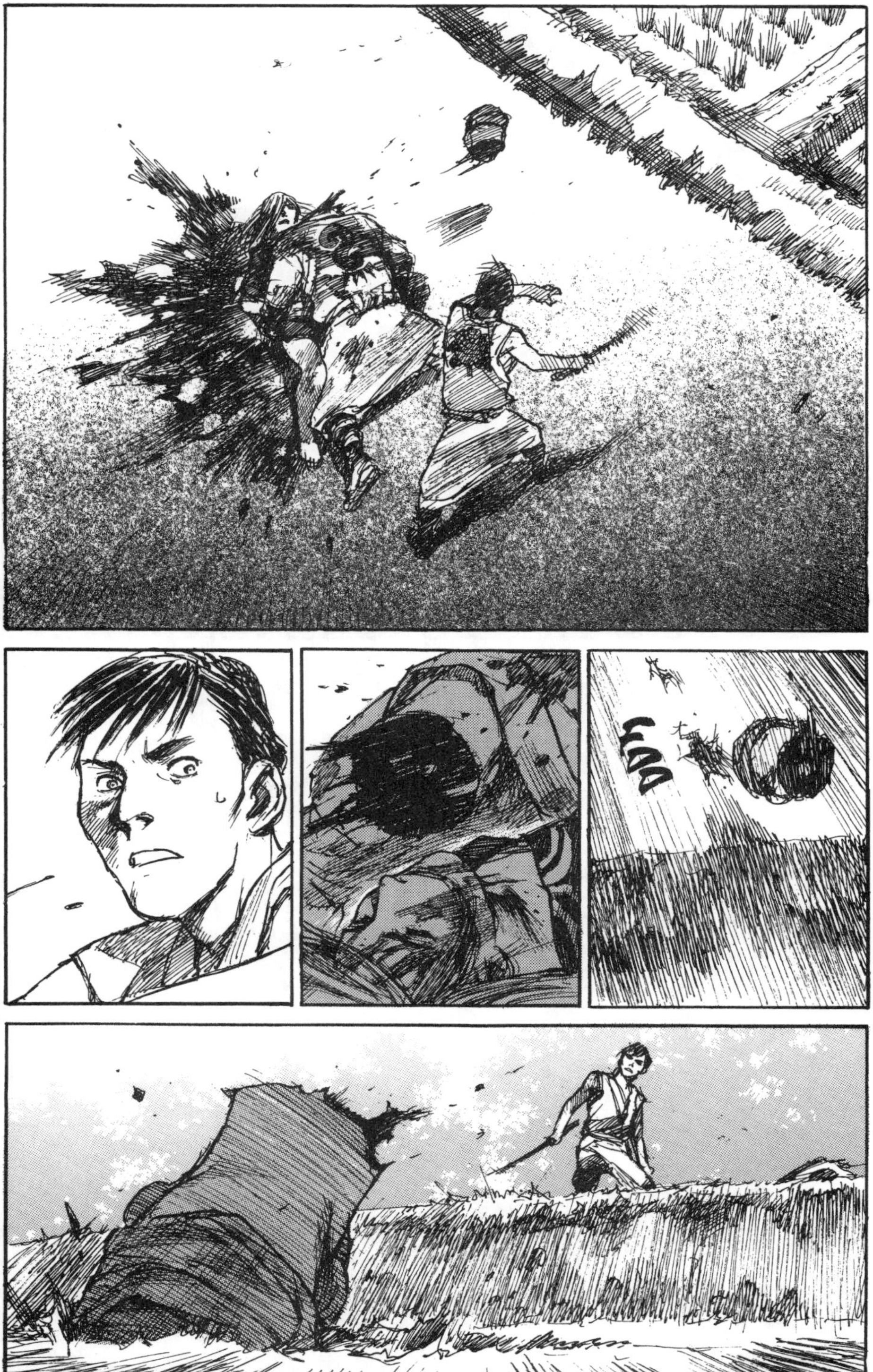

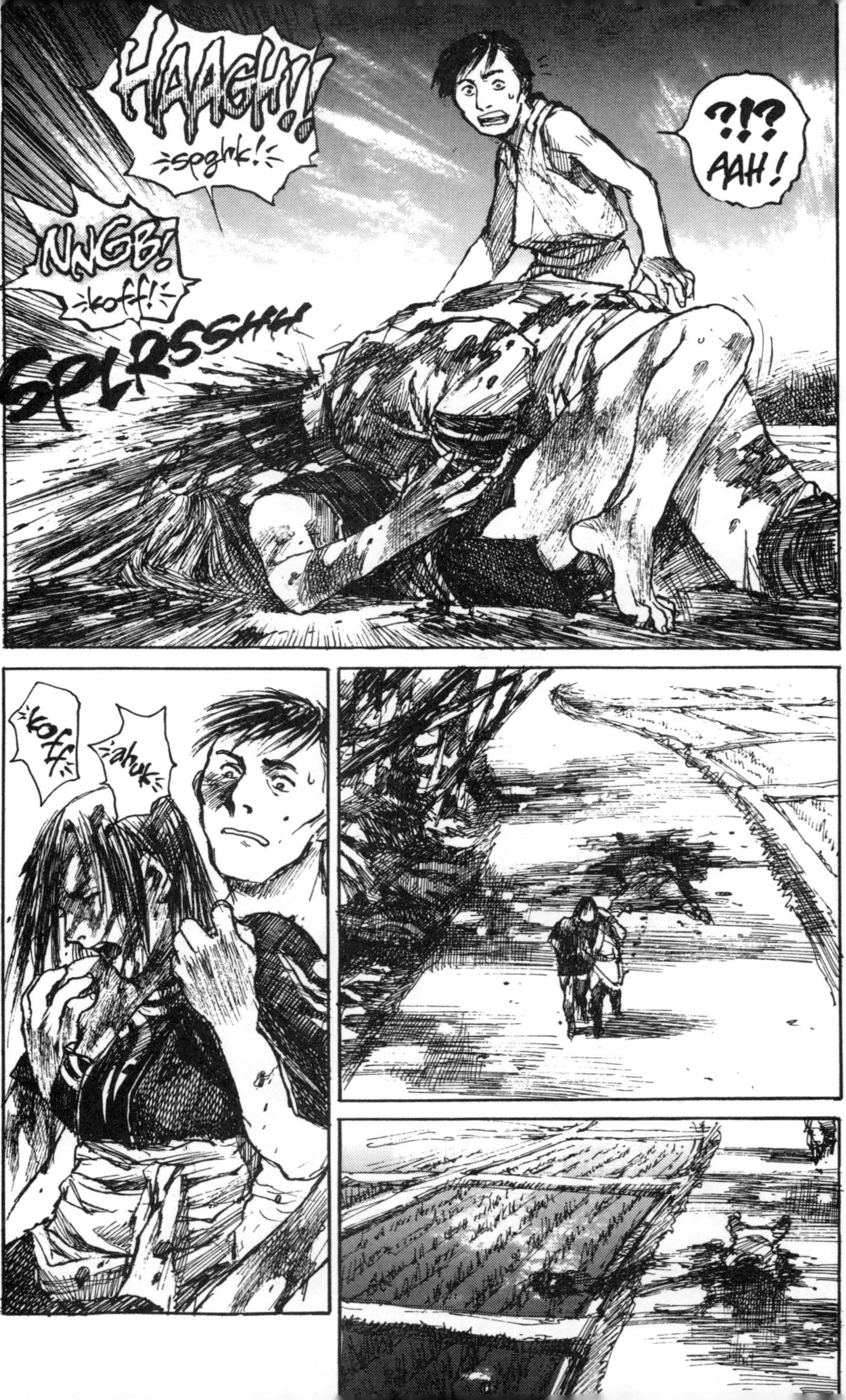
HAAGH!!
spghk!
?!?
AAH!
NNGB!
koff!
SPLRSSHH
koff
ahuk

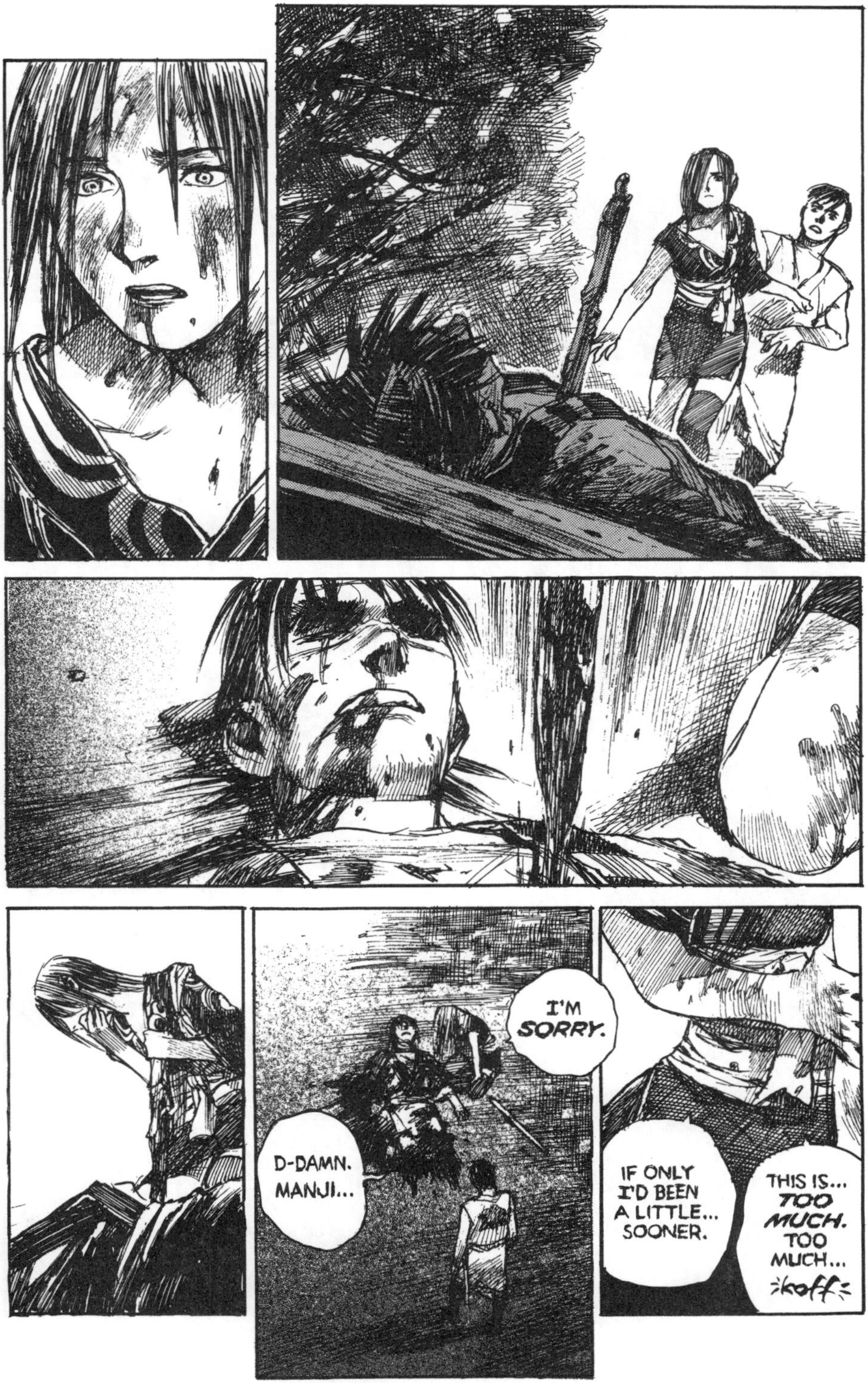
I'M SORRY.
D-DAMN. MANJI...
IF ONLY I'D BEEN A LITTLE... SOONER.
THIS IS... TOO MUCH. TOO MUCH...
koff

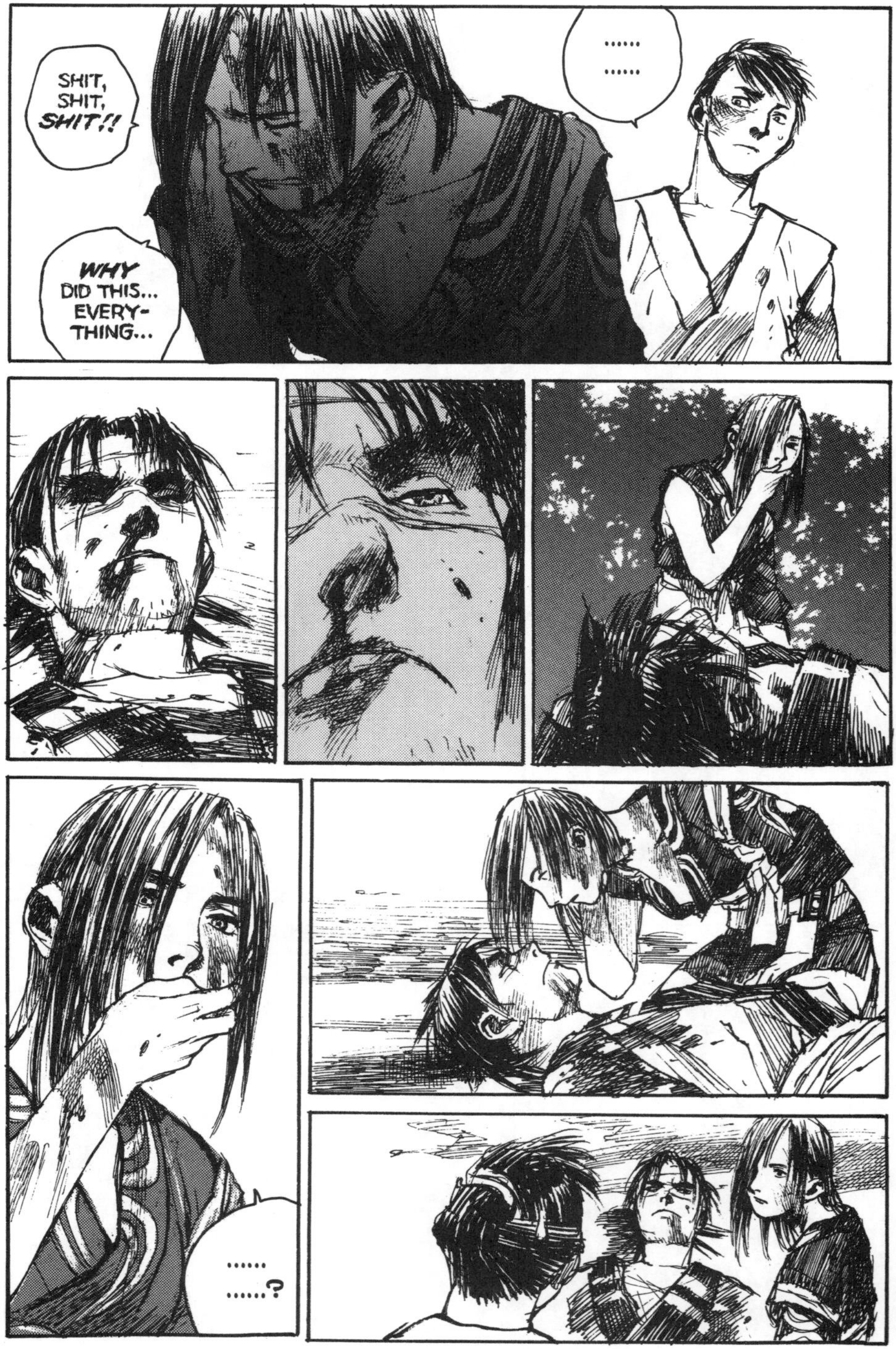
SHIT, SHIT, SHIT!!
WHY DID THIS... EVERYTHING...
......
......
......
......?

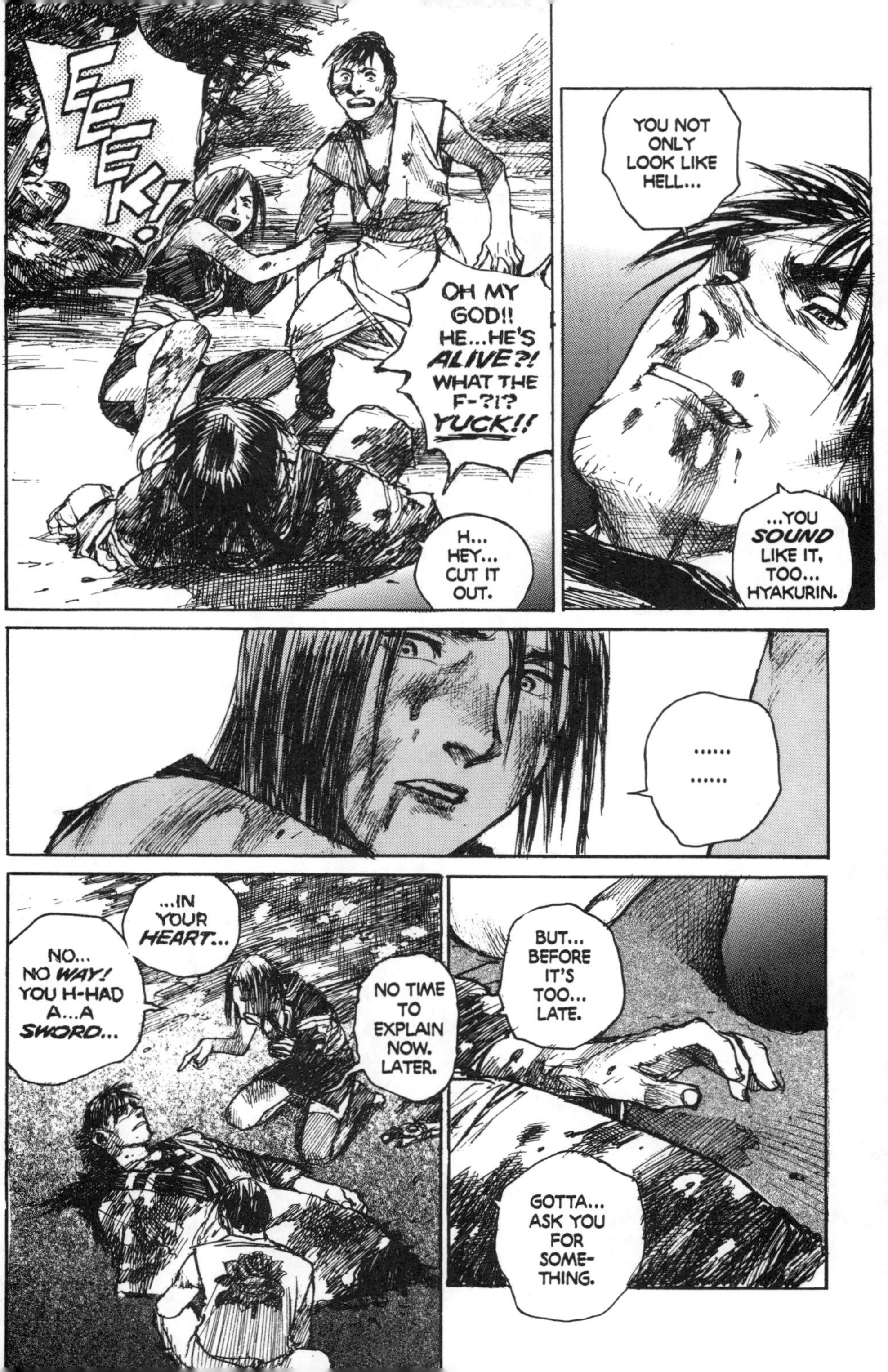
EEEEK!
OH MY GOD!! HE...HE'S ALIVE?! WHAT THE F-?!? YUCK!!
H... HEY... CUT IT OUT.
YOU NOT ONLY LOOK LIKE HELL...
...YOU SOUND LIKE IT, TOO... HYAKURIN.
......
......
NO... NO WAY! YOU H-HAD A...A SWORD...
...IN YOUR HEART...
NO TIME TO EXPLAIN NOW. LATER.
BUT... BEFORE IT'S TOO... LATE.
GOTTA... ASK YOU FOR SOMETHING.

SOME-WHERE... IN THOSE *TREES*... RICE *PADDIES*... ⸮koff⸮

MY *ARMS* AND *LEGS* OUGHTA BE... *LYING* OUT THERE. *BRING* 'EM...

NO... WAIT A SEC.

BEFORE THAT... GET THE *TEGATA*... ⸮hnggk⸮

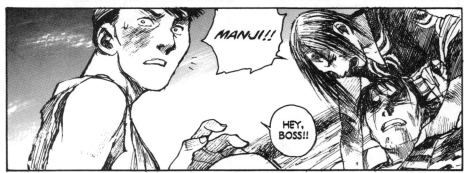

MANJI!!

HEY, BOSS!!

WELL, WELL... JUST *LOOK* AT THIS MESS!

ON THE SHŌGUN'S HIGHWAY, TOO.

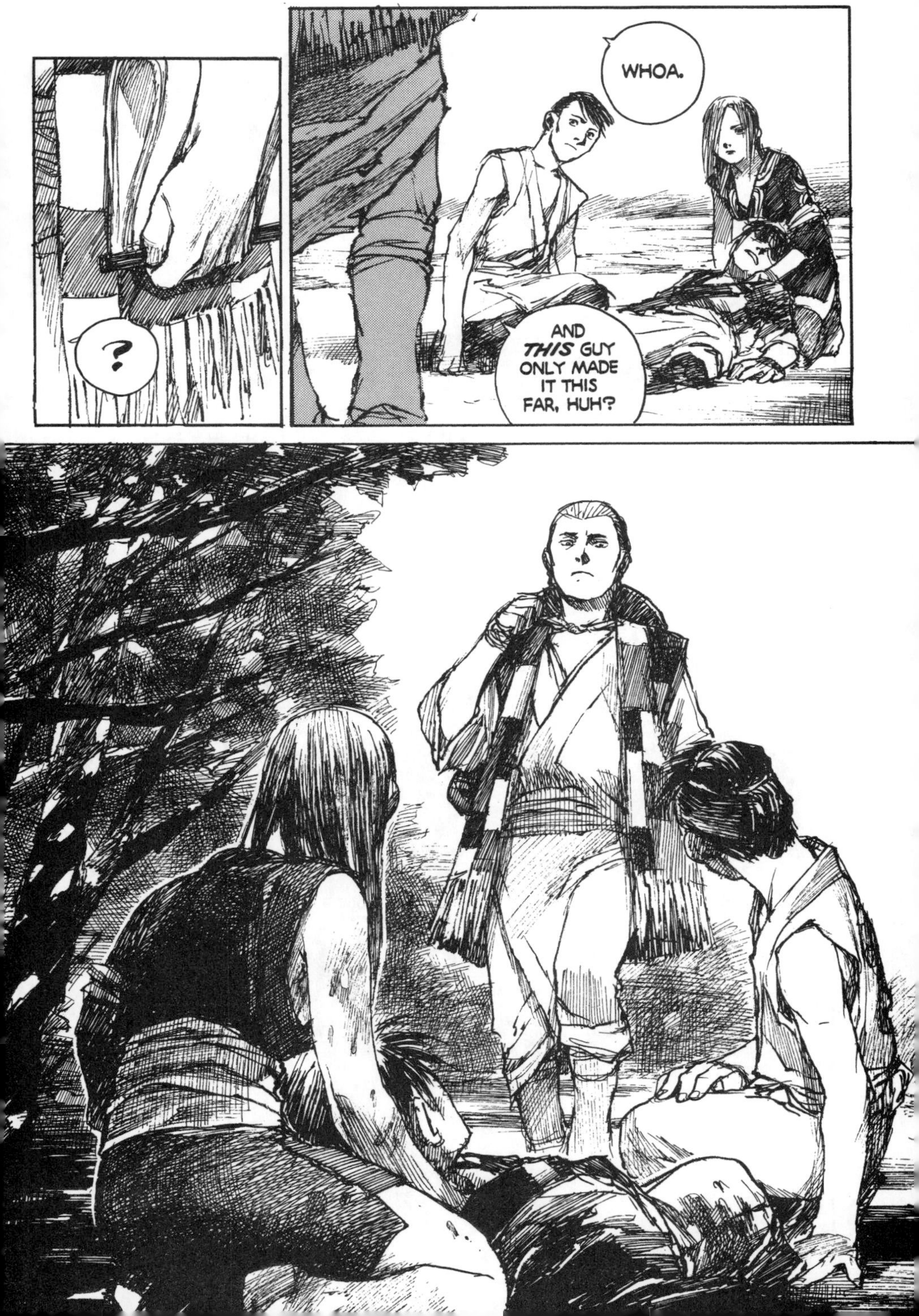
?
WHOA.
AND *THIS* GUY ONLY MADE IT THIS FAR, HUH?

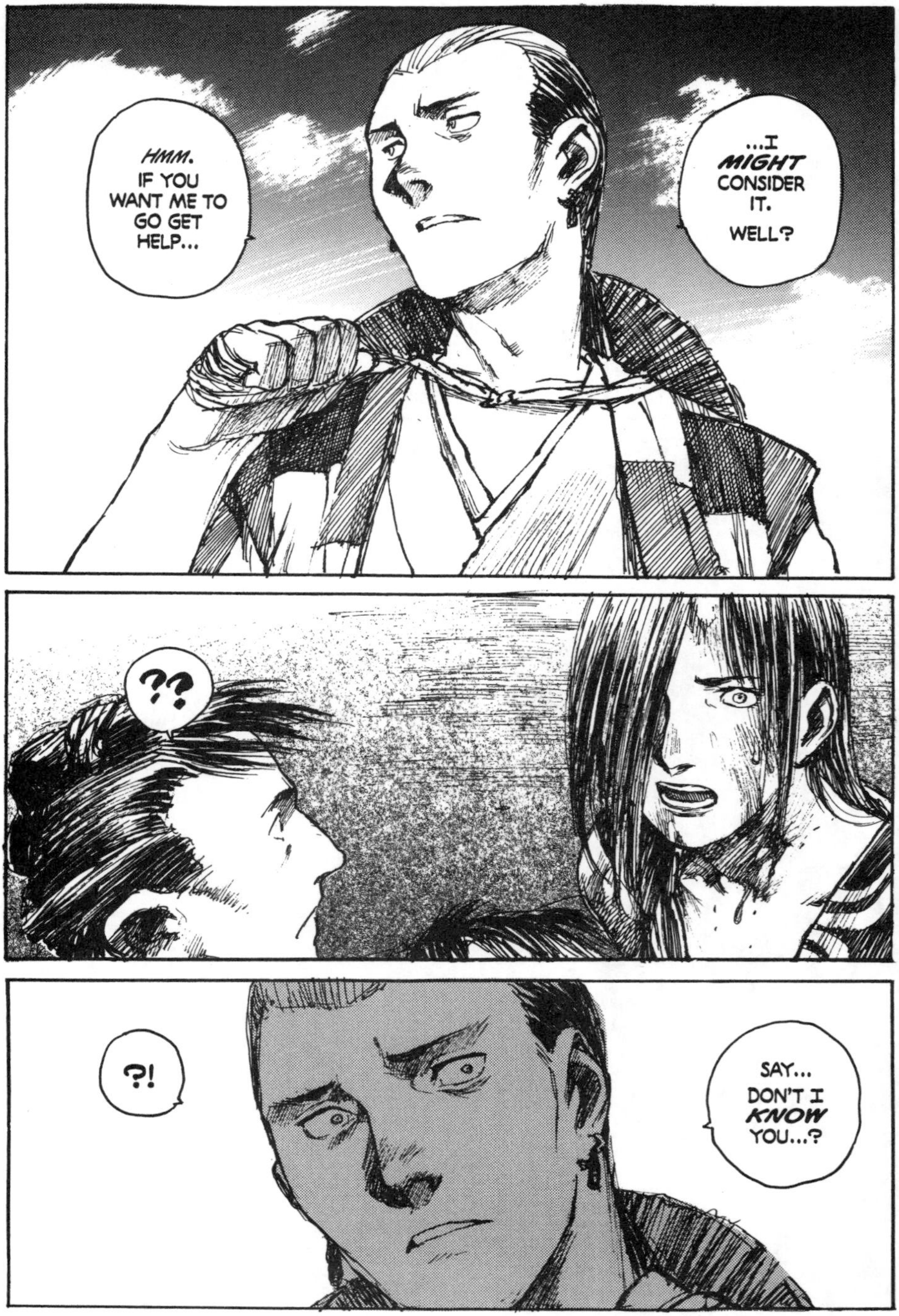
HMM. IF YOU WANT ME TO GO GET HELP...
...I MIGHT CONSIDER IT.
WELL?
??
?!
SAY... DON'T I KNOW YOU...?

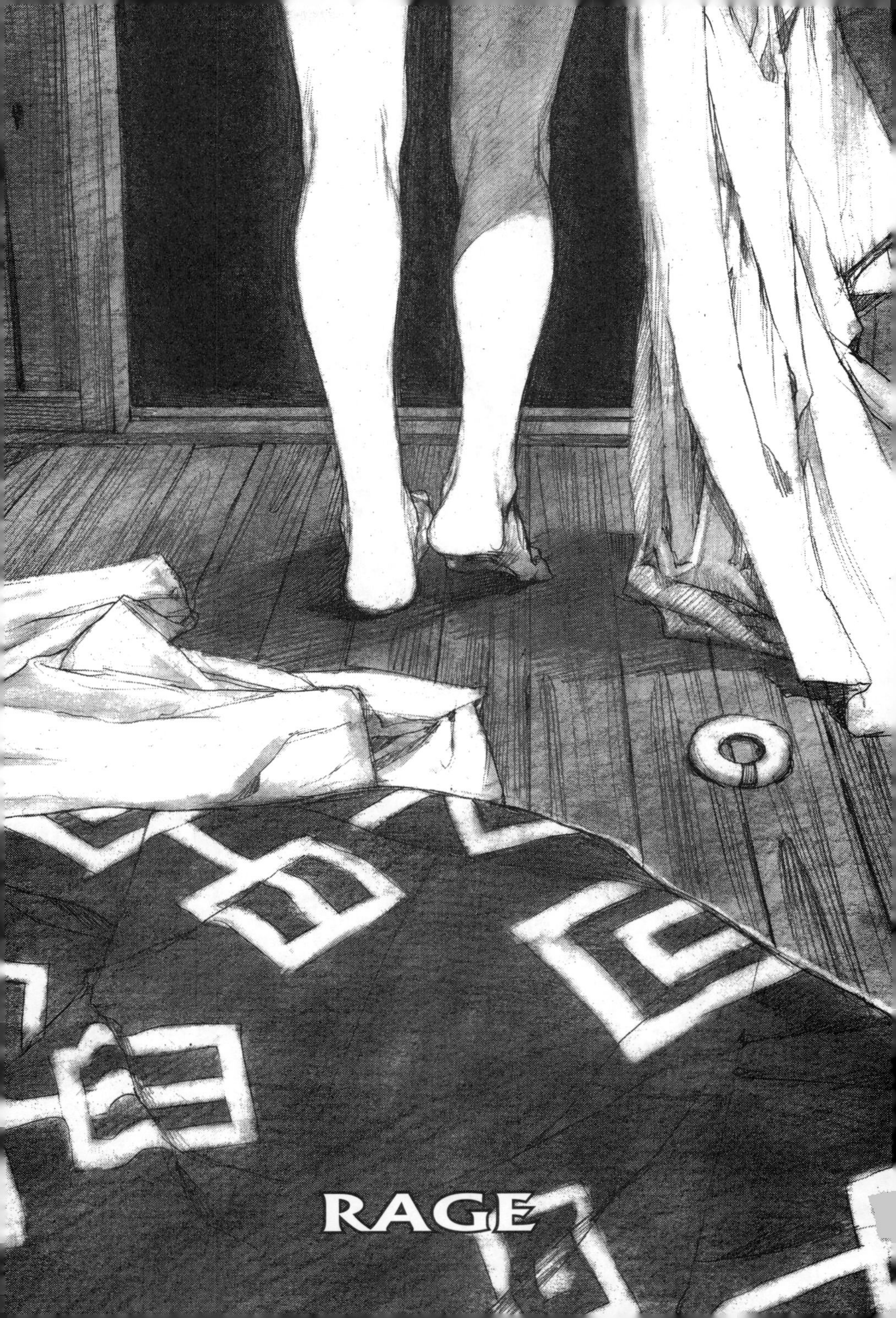
RAGE

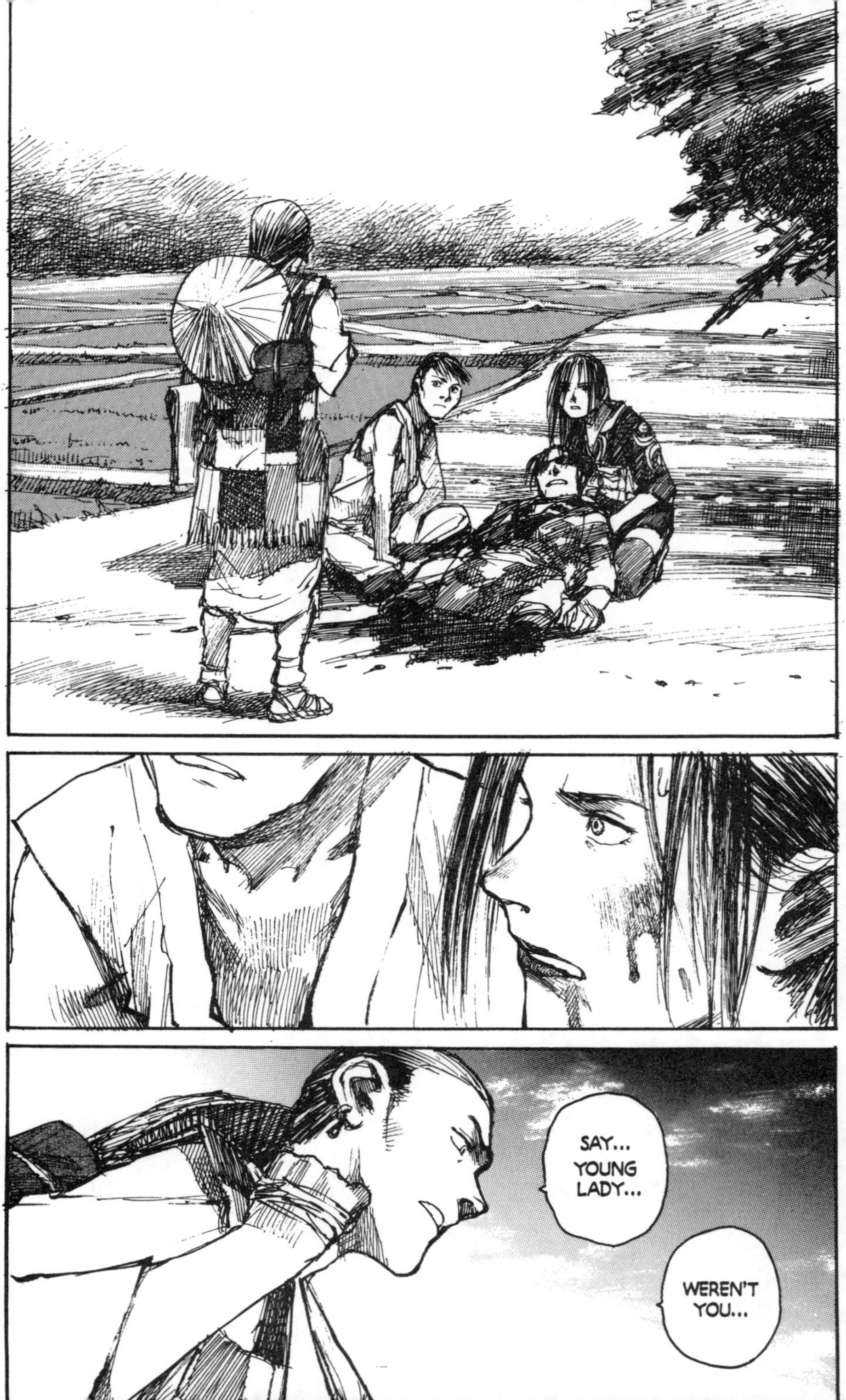
SAY... YOUNG LADY...
WEREN'T YOU...

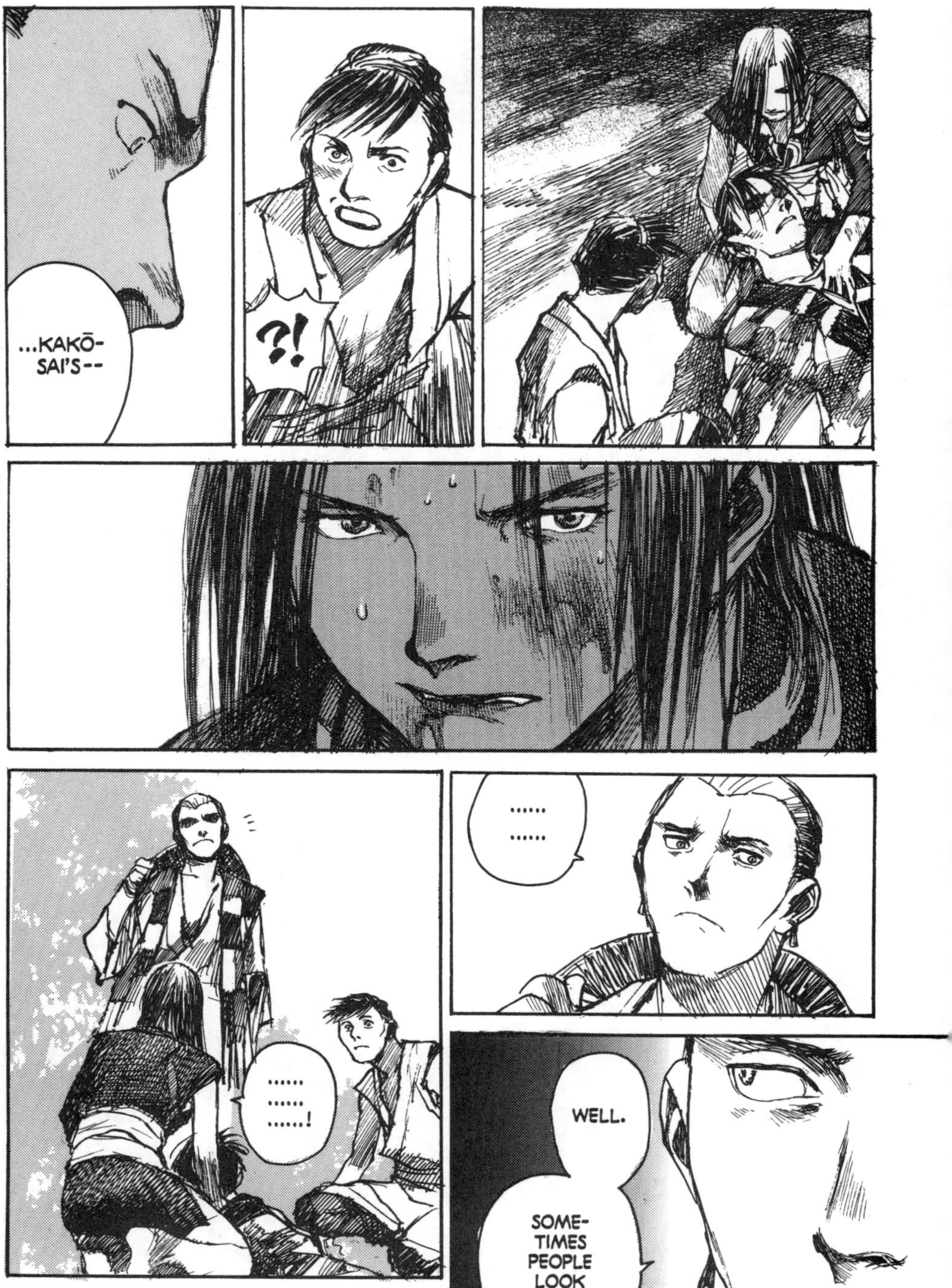
...KAKŌ-SAI'S--
?!
....!
....
WELL.
SOME-TIMES PEOPLE LOOK ALIKE.

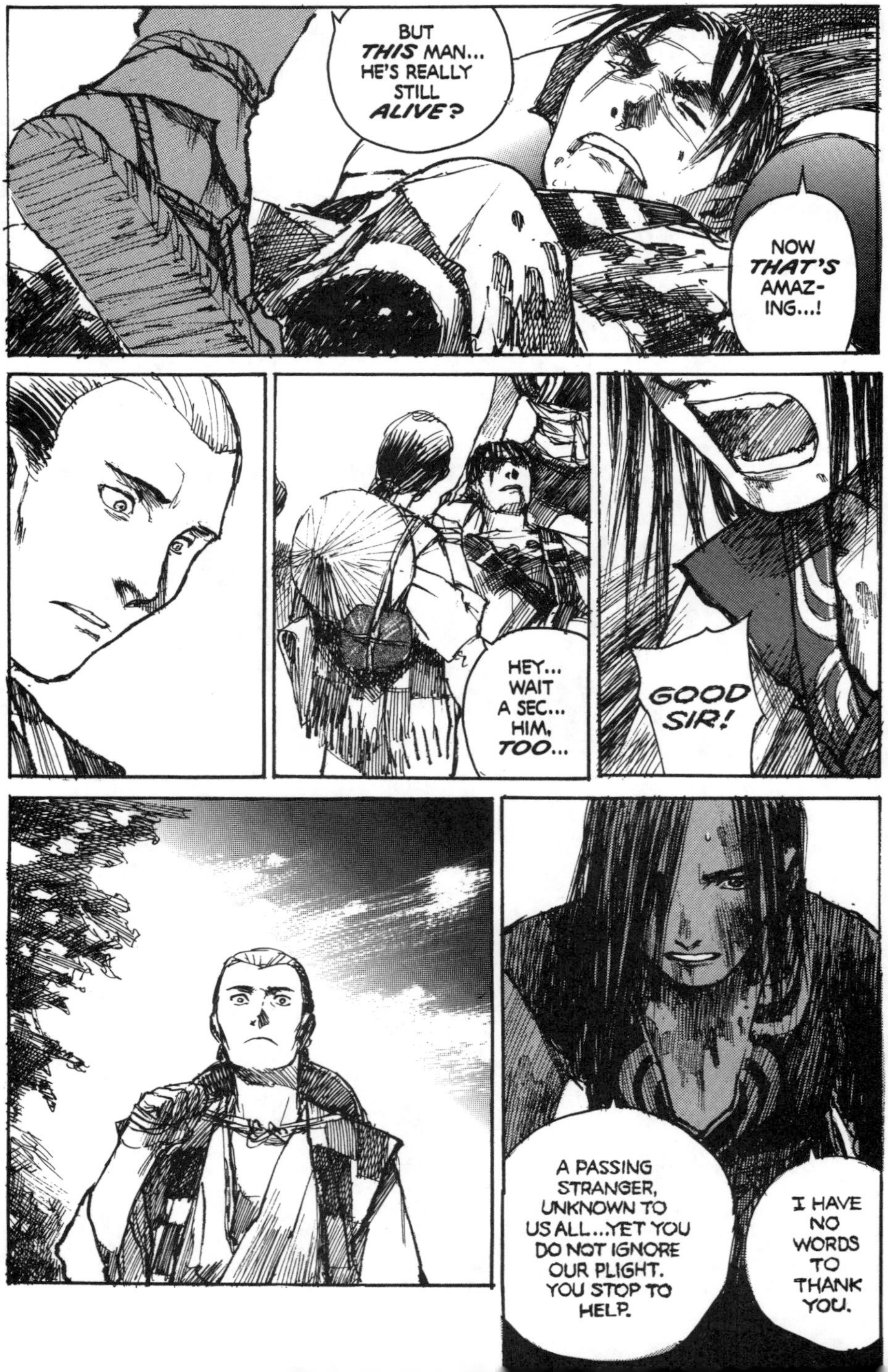
BUT THIS MAN... HE'S REALLY STILL ALIVE?
NOW THAT'S AMAZ-ING...!
HEY... WAIT A SEC... HIM, TOO...
GOOD SIR!
A PASSING STRANGER, UNKNOWN TO US ALL...YET YOU DO NOT IGNORE OUR PLIGHT. YOU STOP TO HELP.
I HAVE NO WORDS TO THANK YOU.

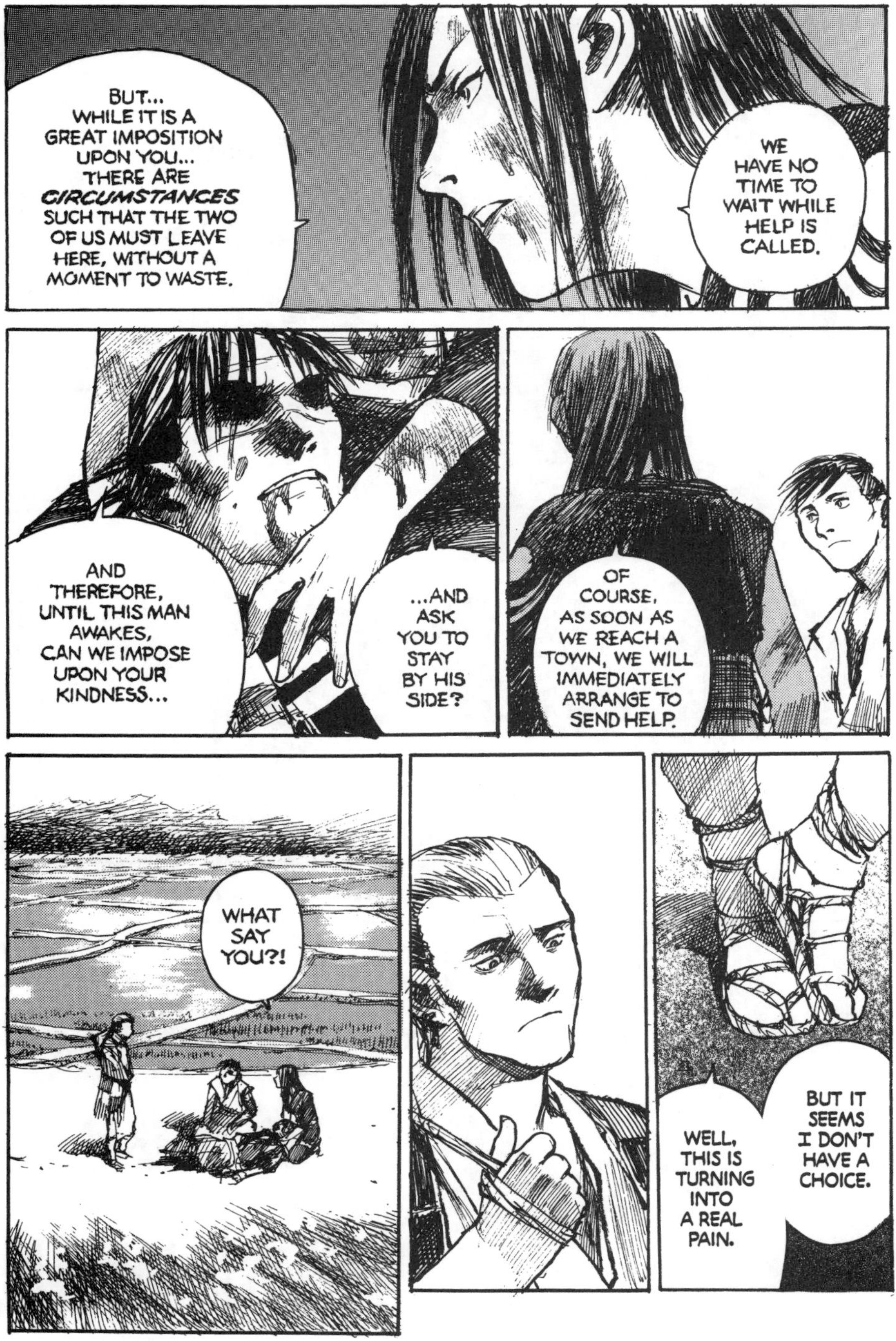
BUT... WHILE IT IS A GREAT IMPOSITION UPON YOU... THERE ARE *CIRCUMSTANCES* SUCH THAT THE TWO OF US MUST LEAVE HERE, WITHOUT A MOMENT TO WASTE.
WE HAVE NO TIME TO WAIT WHILE HELP IS CALLED.
AND THEREFORE, UNTIL THIS MAN AWAKES, CAN WE IMPOSE UPON YOUR KINDNESS...
...AND ASK YOU TO STAY BY HIS SIDE?
OF COURSE, AS SOON AS WE REACH A TOWN, WE WILL IMMEDIATELY ARRANGE TO SEND HELP.
WHAT SAY YOU?!
WELL, THIS IS TURNING INTO A REAL PAIN.
BUT IT SEEMS I DON'T HAVE A CHOICE.

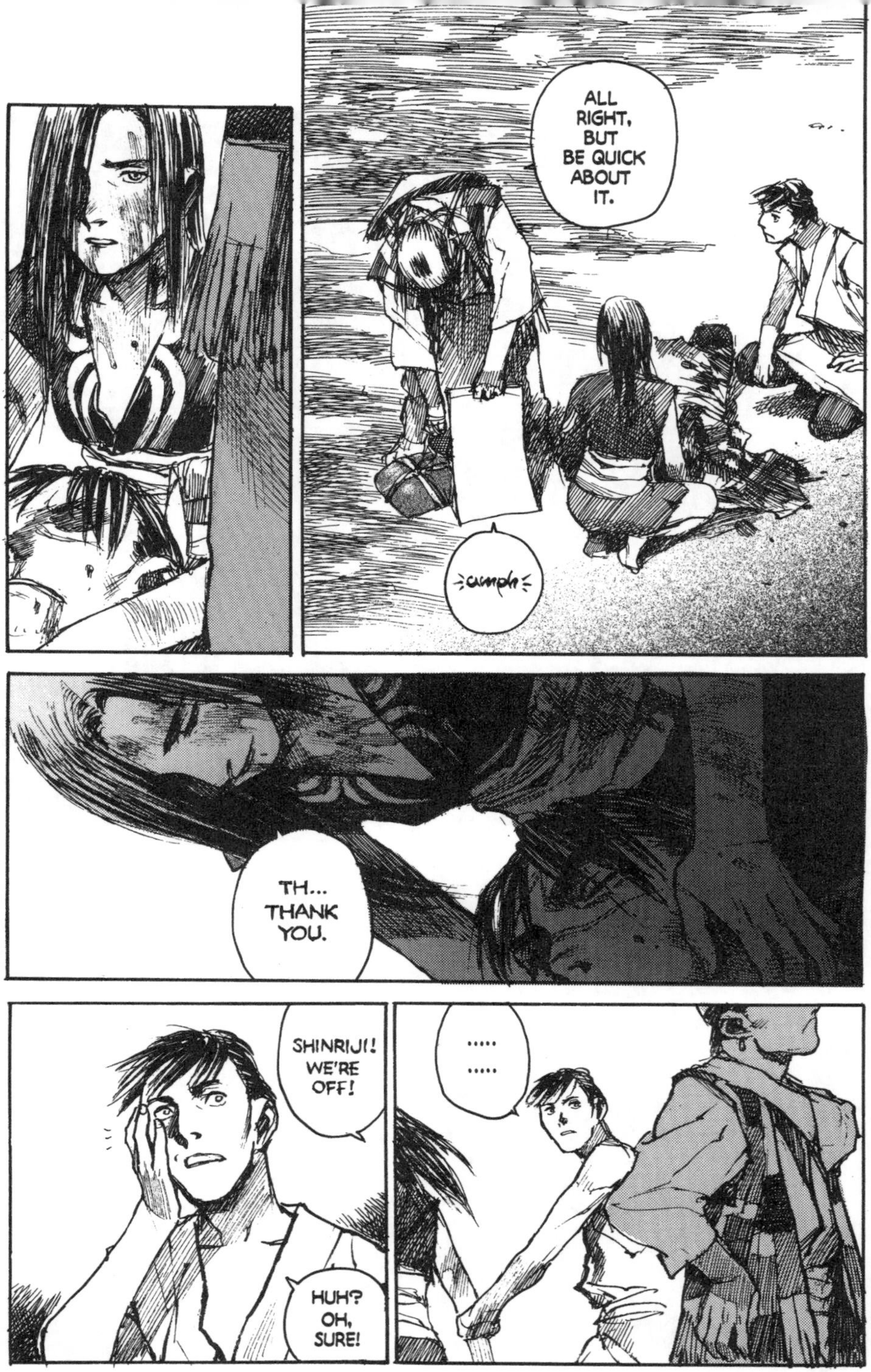
ALL RIGHT, BUT BE QUICK ABOUT IT.
umph
TH... THANK YOU.
SHINRIJI! WE'RE OFF!
HUH? OH, SURE!
.....
.....

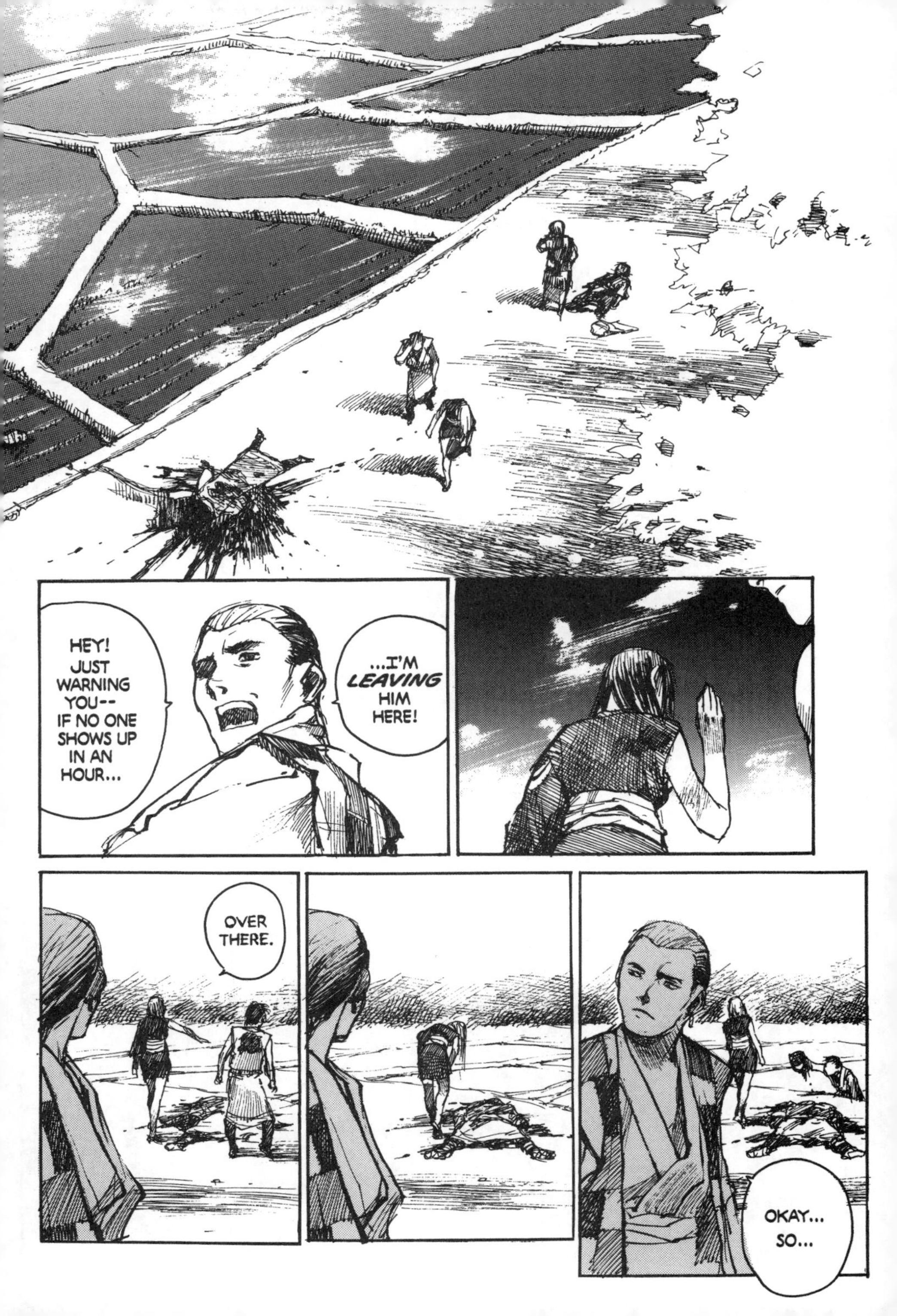
HEY! JUST WARNING YOU-- IF NO ONE SHOWS UP IN AN HOUR...
...I'M *LEAVING* HIM HERE!
OVER THERE.
OKAY... SO...

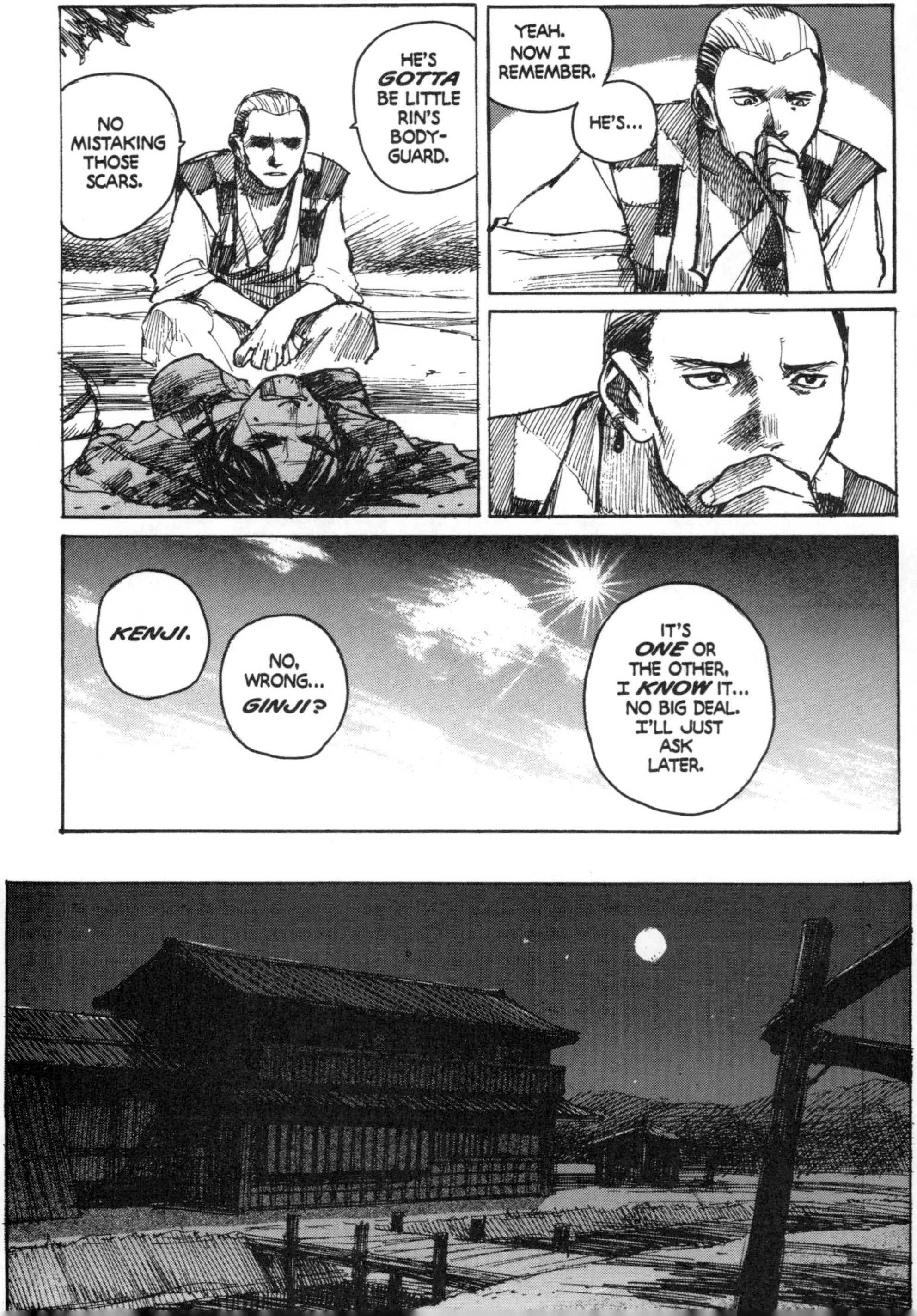
NO MISTAKING THOSE SCARS.
HE'S *GOTTA* BE LITTLE RIN'S BODY-GUARD.
YEAH. NOW I REMEMBER.
HE'S...
KENJI.
NO, WRONG... *GINJI?*
IT'S *ONE* OR THE OTHER, I *KNOW* IT... NO BIG DEAL. I'LL JUST ASK LATER.

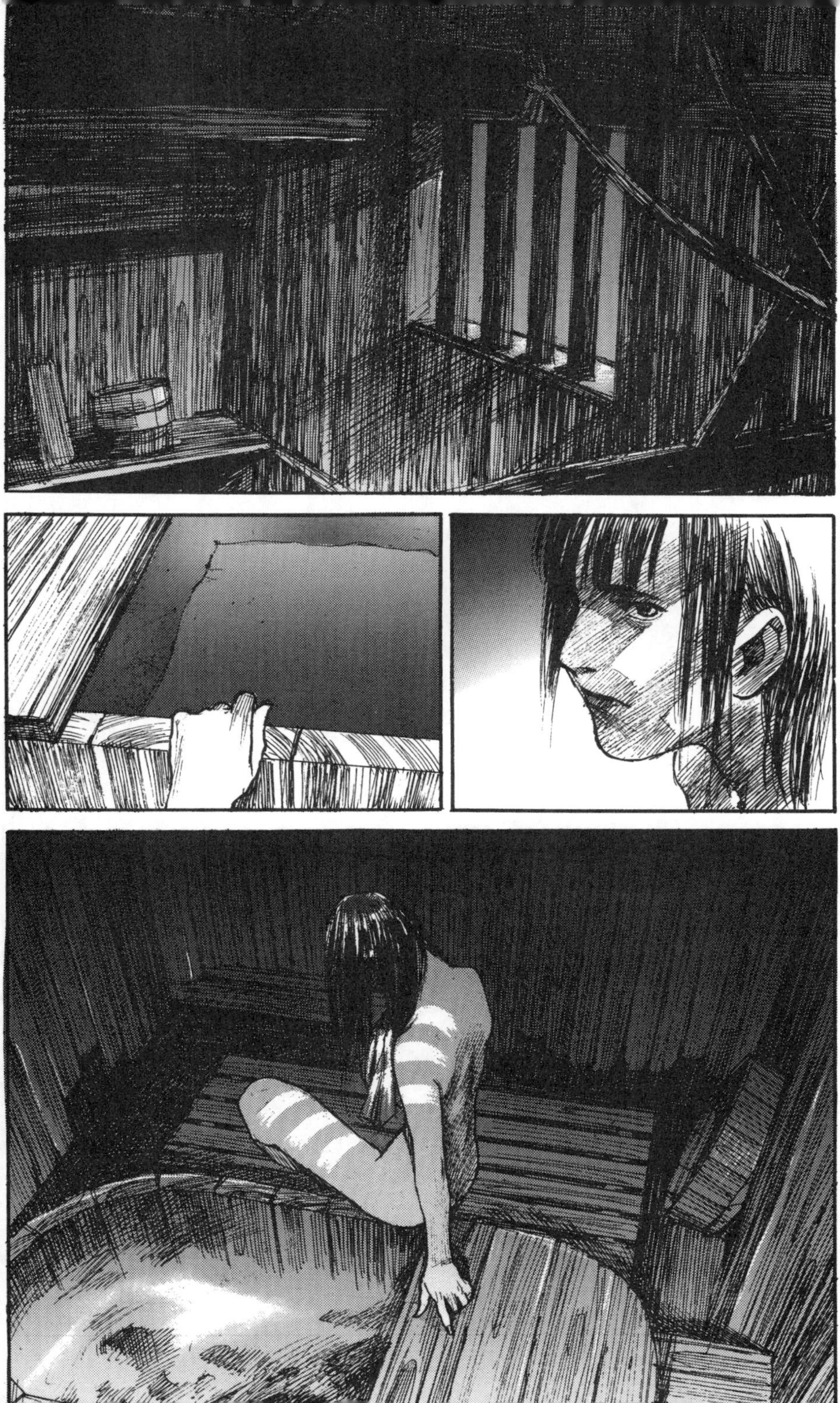

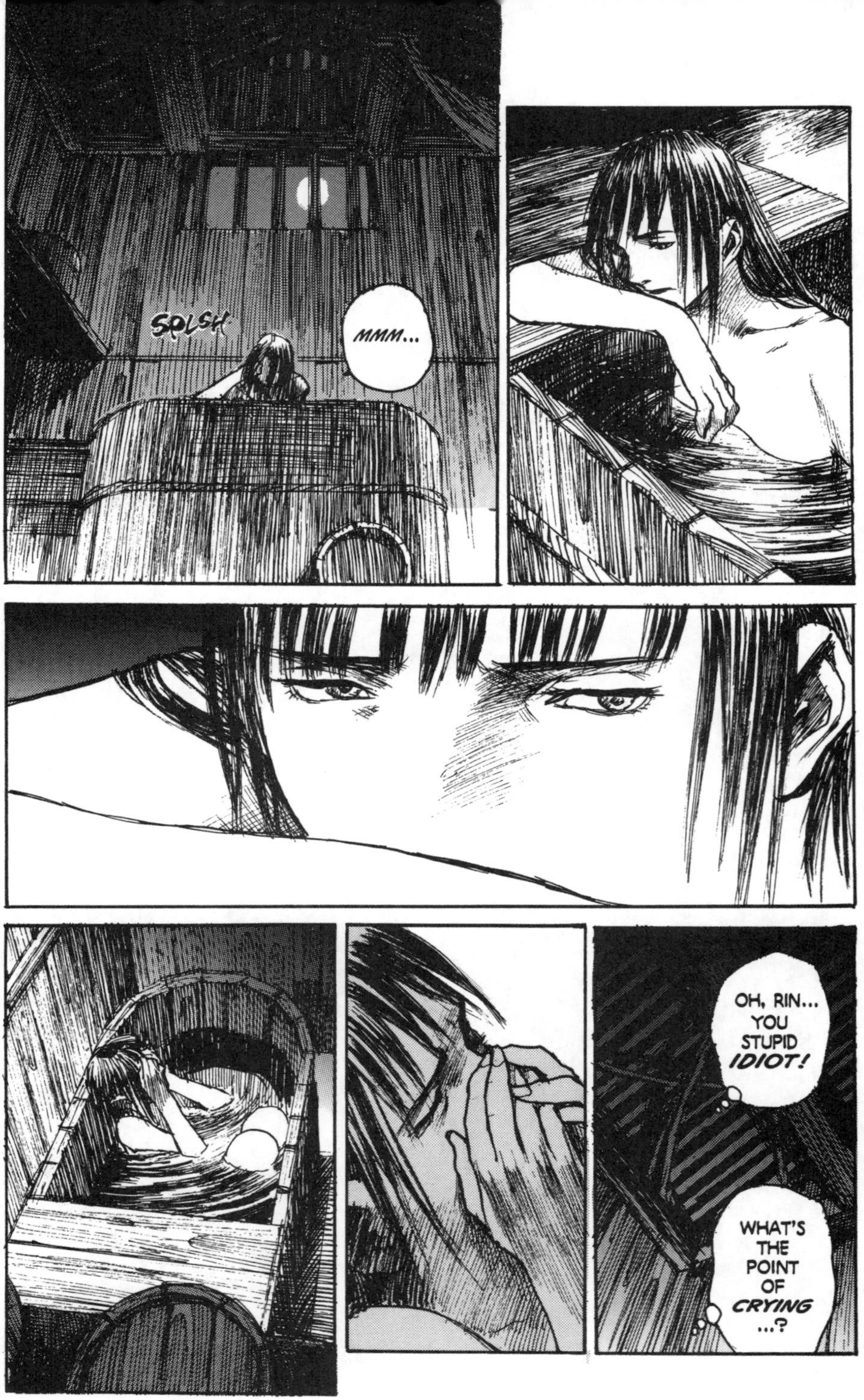
SPLSH
MMM...
OH, RIN... YOU STUPID IDIOT!
WHAT'S THE POINT OF CRYING ...?

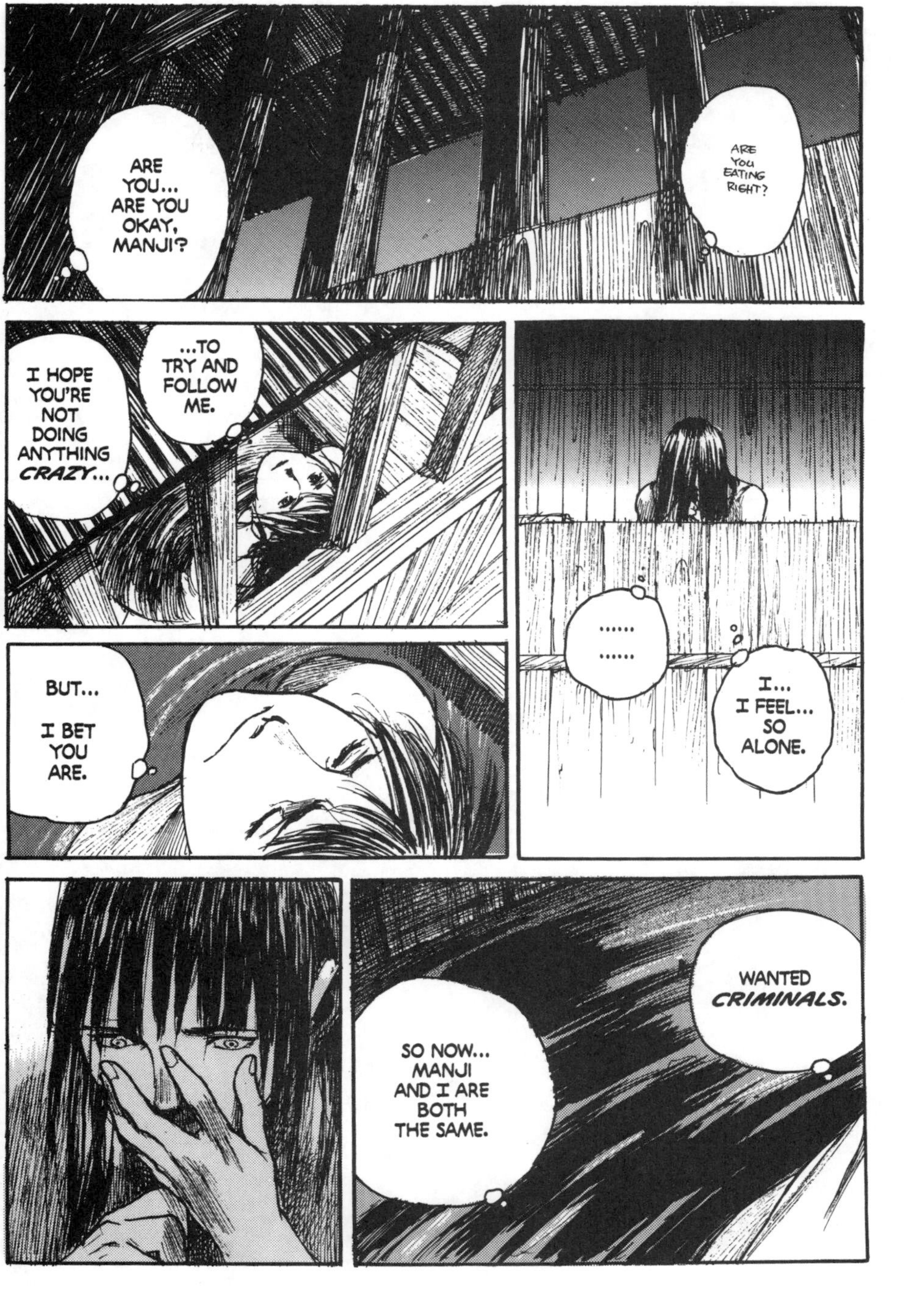
ARE YOU... ARE YOU OKAY, MANJI?
ARE YOU EATING RIGHT?
I HOPE YOU'RE NOT DOING ANYTHING *CRAZY*...
...TO TRY AND FOLLOW ME.
BUT... I BET YOU ARE.
......
......
I... I FEEL... SO ALONE.
SO NOW... MANJI AND I ARE BOTH THE SAME.
WANTED *CRIMINALS.*

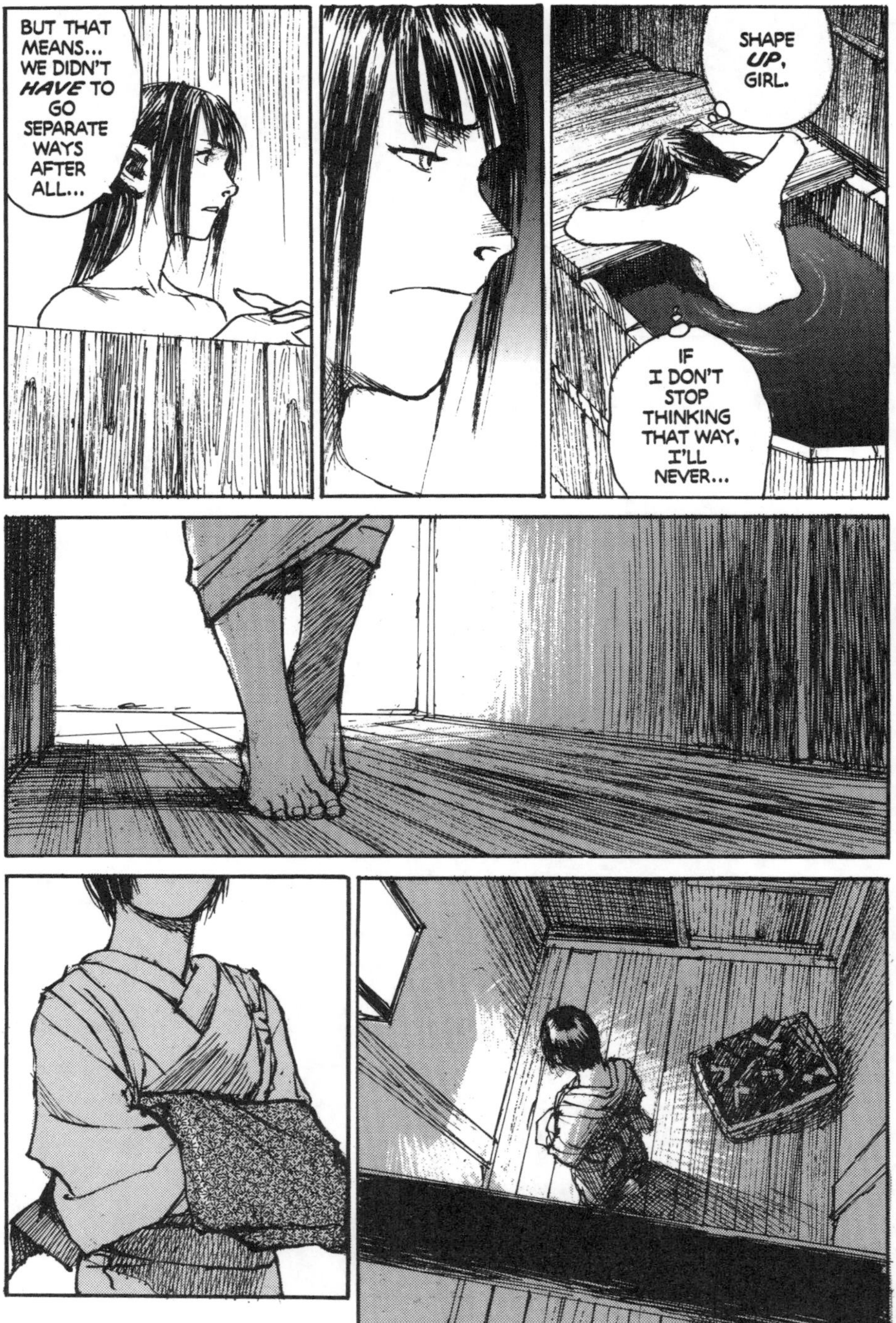
BUT THAT MEANS... WE DIDN'T *HAVE* TO GO SEPARATE WAYS AFTER ALL...
SHAPE *UP*, GIRL.
IF I DON'T STOP THINKING THAT WAY, I'LL NEVER...

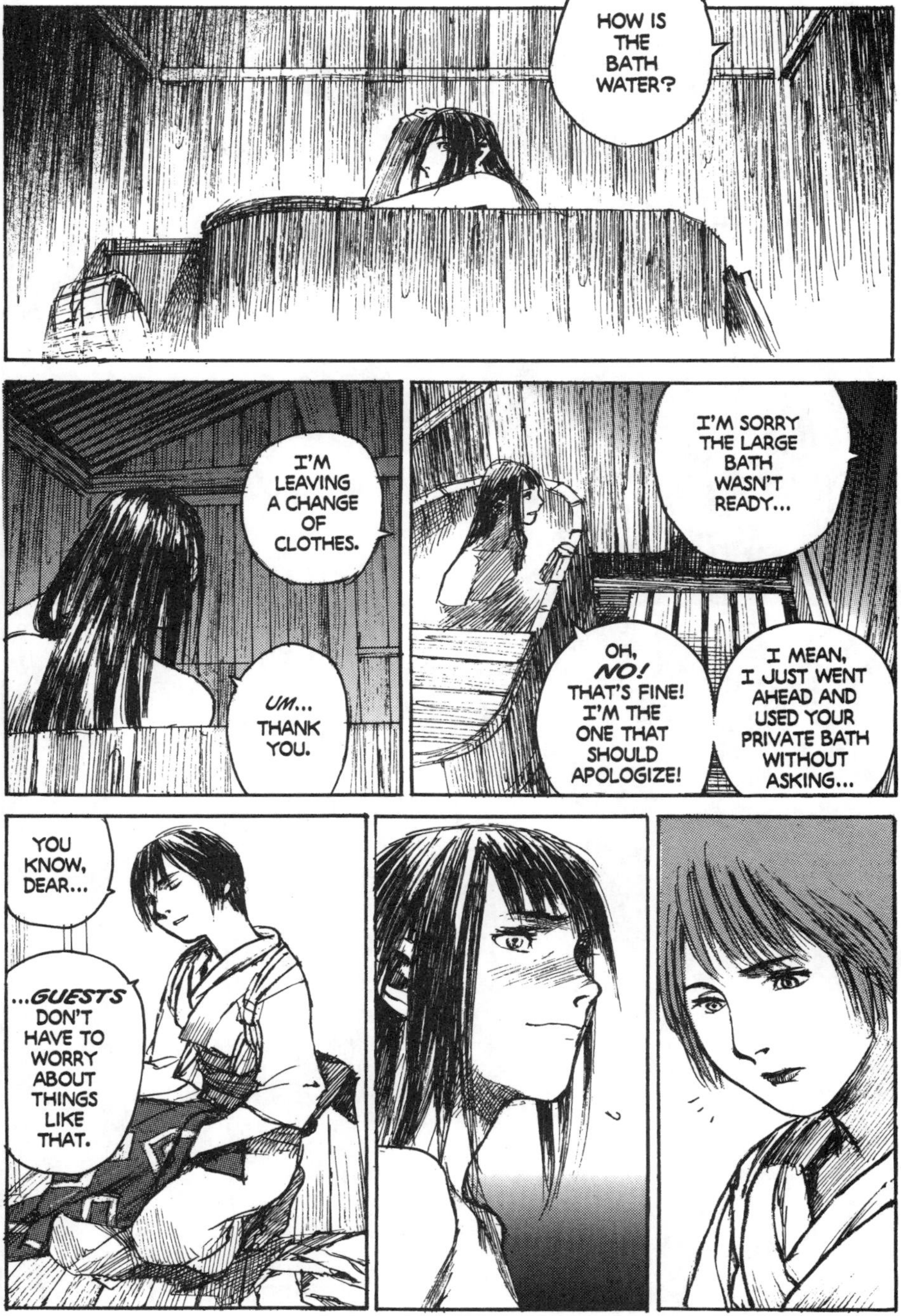
HOW IS THE BATH WATER?
I'M LEAVING A CHANGE OF CLOTHES.
UM... THANK YOU.
I'M SORRY THE LARGE BATH WASN'T READY...
OH, NO! THAT'S FINE! I'M THE ONE THAT SHOULD APOLOGIZE!
I MEAN, I JUST WENT AHEAD AND USED YOUR PRIVATE BATH WITHOUT ASKING...
YOU KNOW, DEAR...
...GUESTS DON'T HAVE TO WORRY ABOUT THINGS LIKE THAT.

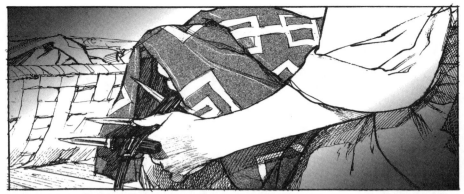

Y...
YES?

UM...

ABOUT...
YOU
KNOW...
WHAT I
SAID THIS
AFTER-
NOON...?

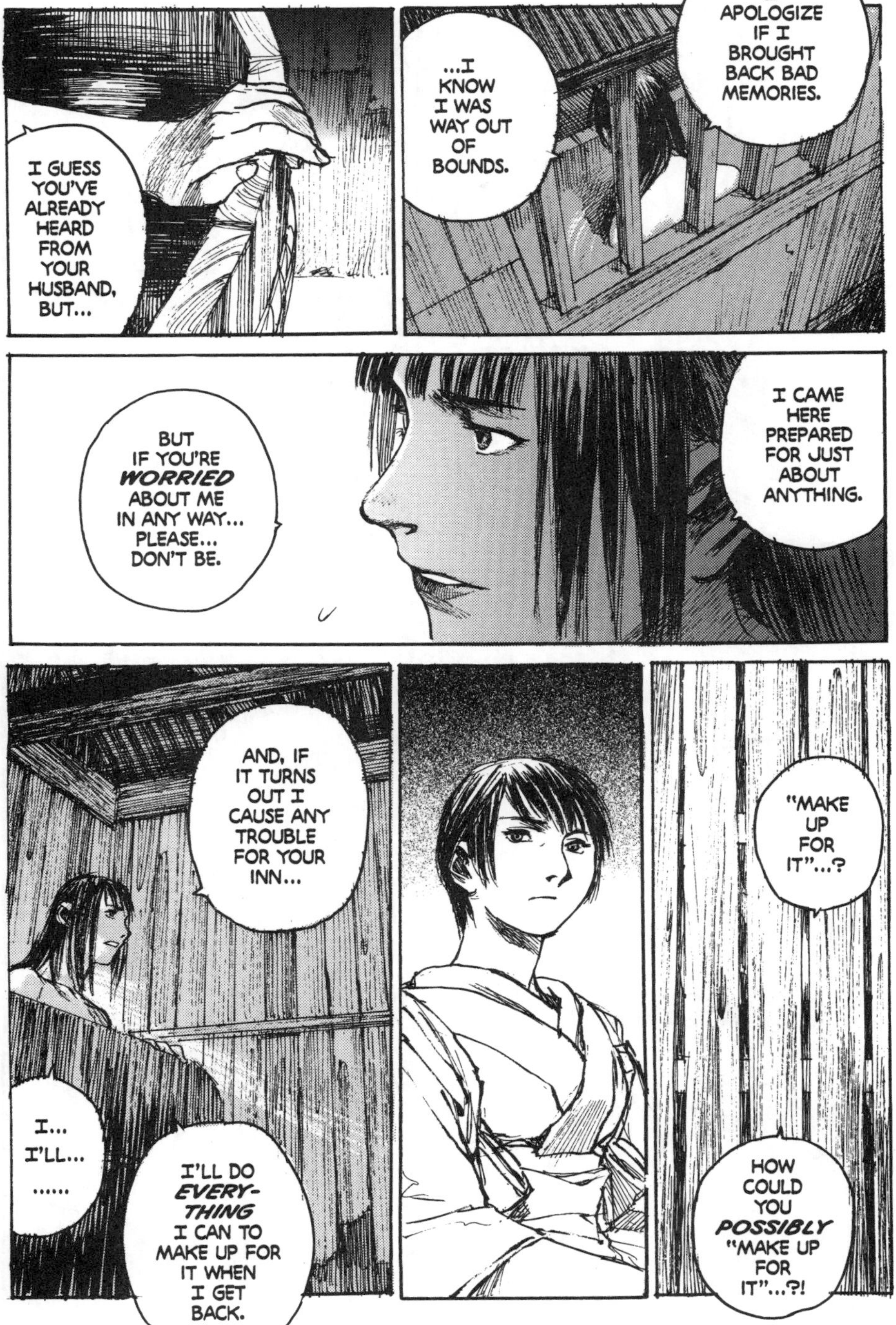
I GUESS YOU'VE ALREADY HEARD FROM YOUR HUSBAND, BUT...
...I KNOW I WAS WAY OUT OF BOUNDS.
I APOLOGIZE IF I BROUGHT BACK BAD MEMORIES.
BUT IF YOU'RE *WORRIED* ABOUT ME IN ANY WAY... PLEASE... DON'T BE.
I CAME HERE PREPARED FOR JUST ABOUT ANYTHING.
AND, IF IT TURNS OUT I CAUSE ANY TROUBLE FOR YOUR INN...
I... I'LL... ......
I'LL DO *EVERYTHING* I CAN TO MAKE UP FOR IT WHEN I GET BACK.
"MAKE UP FOR IT"...?
HOW COULD YOU *POSSIBLY* "MAKE UP FOR IT"...?!

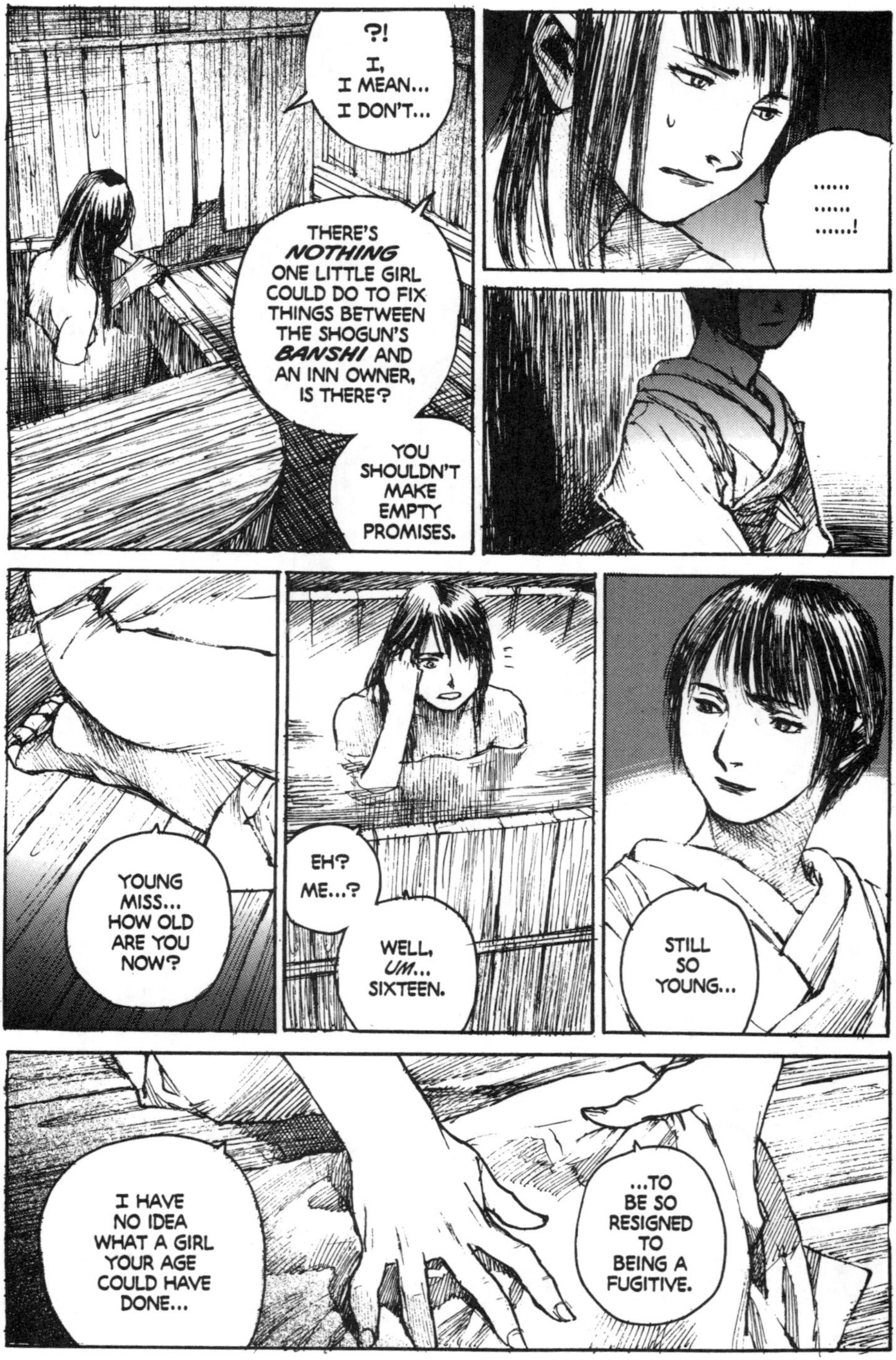
?!
I, I MEAN... I DON'T...
THERE'S *NOTHING* ONE LITTLE GIRL COULD DO TO FIX THINGS BETWEEN THE SHOGUN'S *BANSHI* AND AN INN OWNER, IS THERE?
YOU SHOULDN'T MAKE EMPTY PROMISES.
....!
YOUNG MISS... HOW OLD ARE YOU NOW?
EH? ME...?
WELL, *UM*... SIXTEEN.
STILL SO YOUNG...
I HAVE NO IDEA WHAT A GIRL YOUR AGE COULD HAVE DONE...
...TO BE SO RESIGNED TO BEING A FUGITIVE.

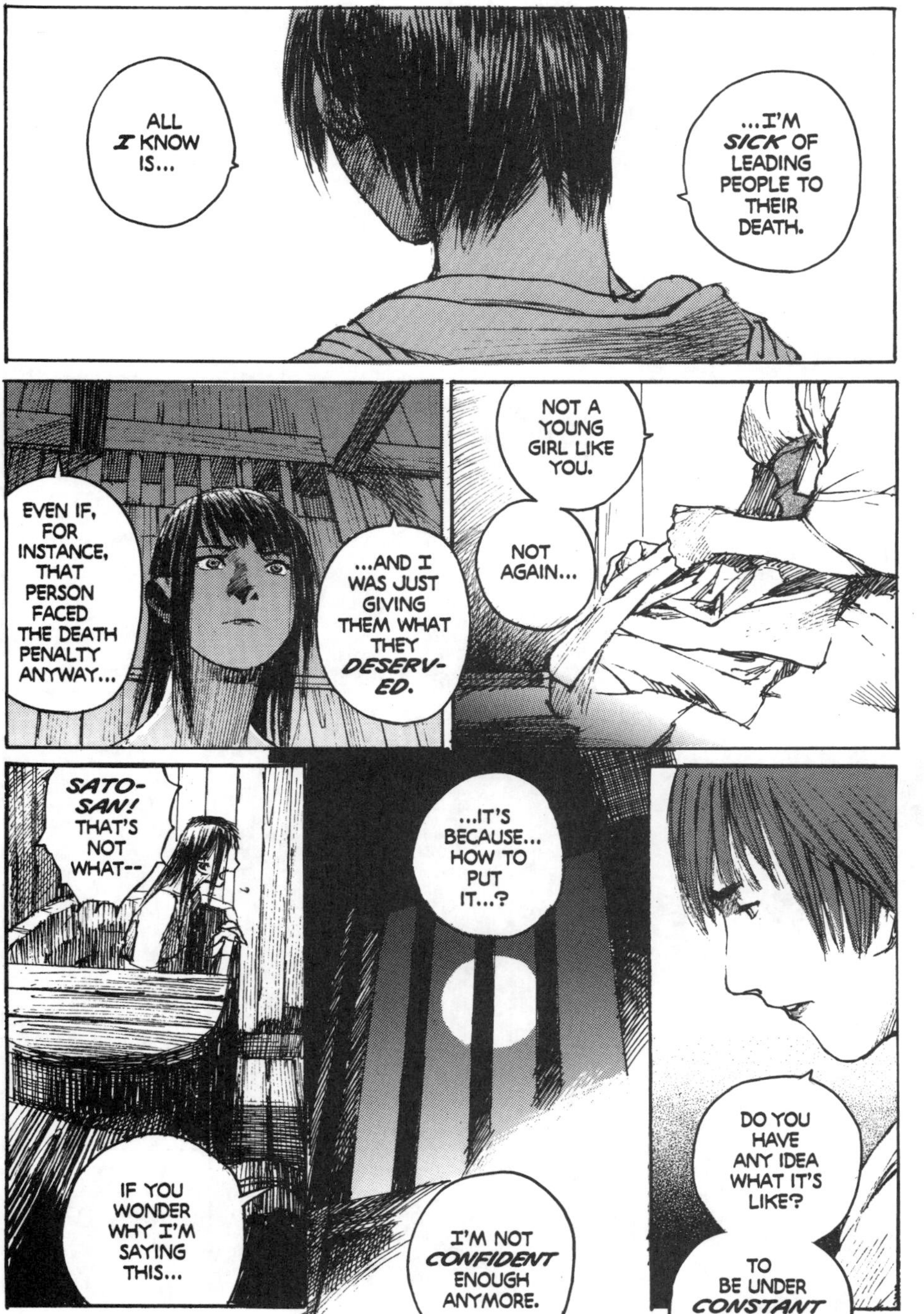
ALL I KNOW IS...
...I'M SICK OF LEADING PEOPLE TO THEIR DEATH.
EVEN IF, FOR INSTANCE, THAT PERSON FACED THE DEATH PENALTY ANYWAY...
...AND I WAS JUST GIVING THEM WHAT THEY DESERV-ED.
NOT A YOUNG GIRL LIKE YOU.
NOT AGAIN...
SATO-SAN! THAT'S NOT WHAT--
IF YOU WONDER WHY I'M SAYING THIS...
...IT'S BECAUSE... HOW TO PUT IT...?
I'M NOT CONFIDENT ENOUGH ANYMORE.
DO YOU HAVE ANY IDEA WHAT IT'S LIKE?
TO BE UNDER CONSTANT SURVEIL-LANCE?

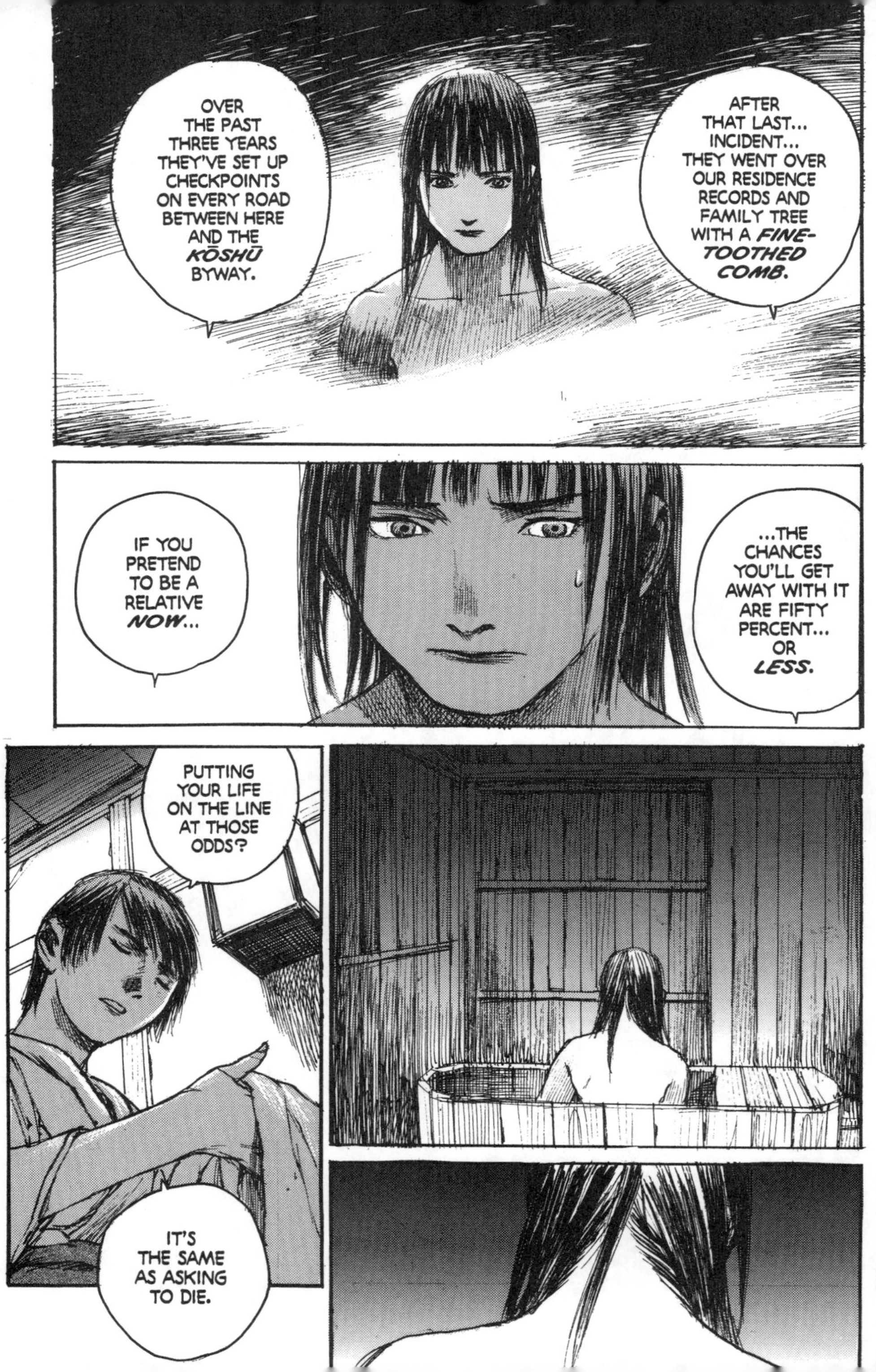
OVER THE PAST THREE YEARS THEY'VE SET UP CHECKPOINTS ON EVERY ROAD BETWEEN HERE AND THE KŌSHŪ BYWAY.
AFTER THAT LAST... INCIDENT... THEY WENT OVER OUR RESIDENCE RECORDS AND FAMILY TREE WITH A FINE-TOOTHED COMB.
IF YOU PRETEND TO BE A RELATIVE NOW...
...THE CHANCES YOU'LL GET AWAY WITH IT ARE FIFTY PERCENT... OR LESS.
PUTTING YOUR LIFE ON THE LINE AT THOSE ODDS?
IT'S THE SAME AS ASKING TO DIE.

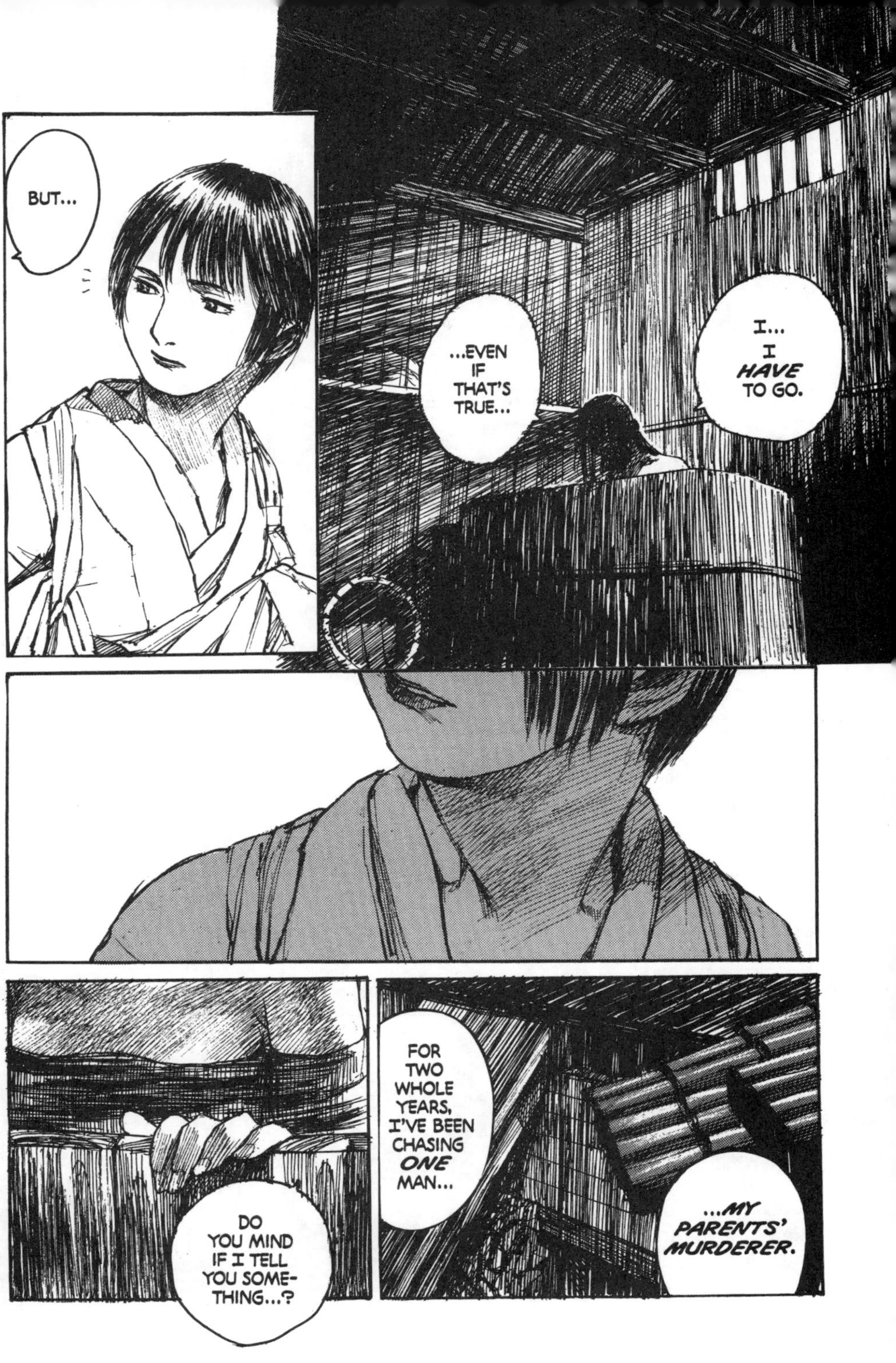
BUT...
...EVEN IF THAT'S TRUE...
I... I *HAVE* TO GO.
DO YOU MIND IF I TELL YOU SOME-THING...?
FOR TWO WHOLE YEARS, I'VE BEEN CHASING *ONE* MAN...
...MY PARENTS' MURDERER.

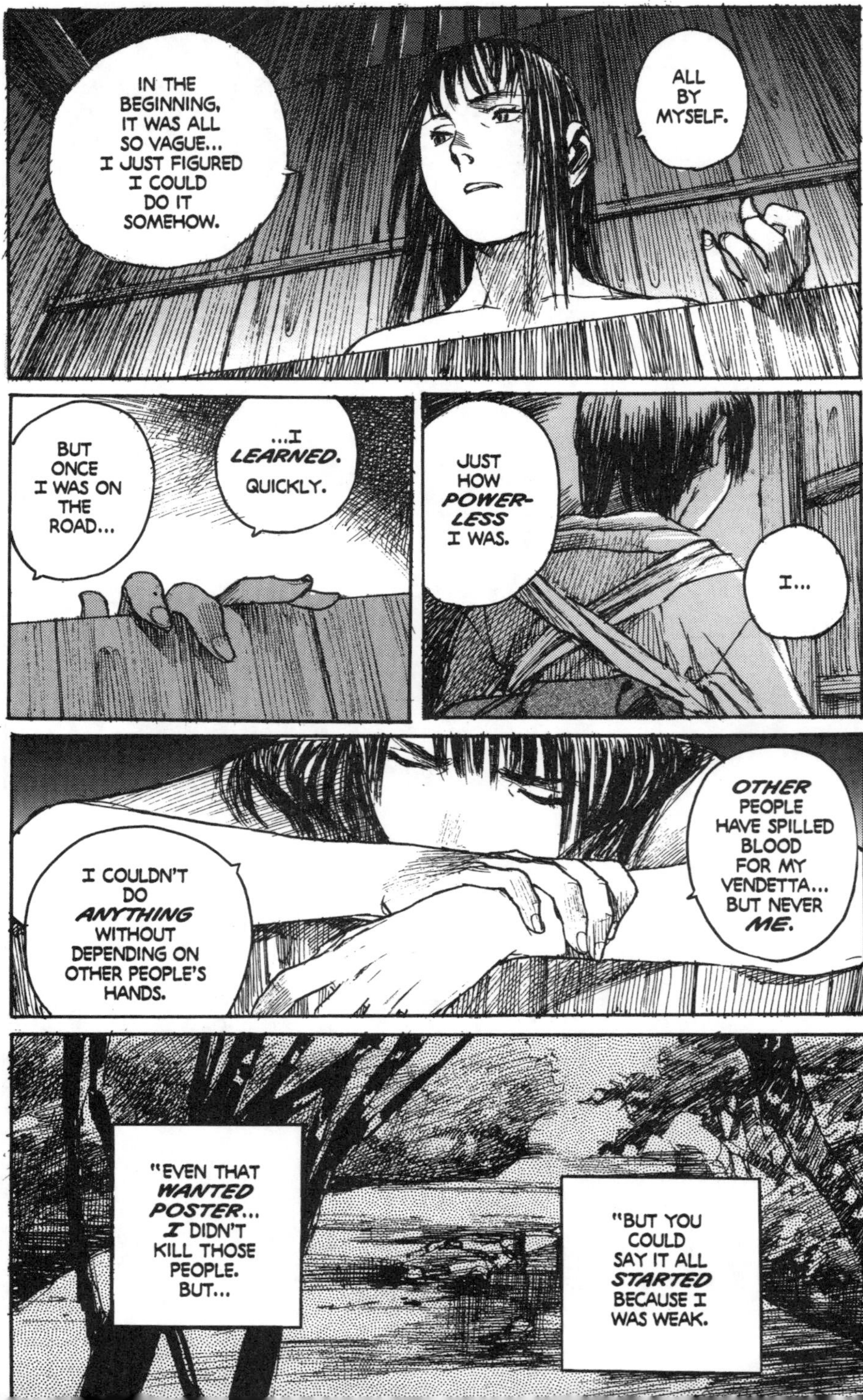
IN THE BEGINNING, IT WAS ALL SO VAGUE... I JUST FIGURED I COULD DO IT SOMEHOW.
ALL BY MYSELF.
BUT ONCE I WAS ON THE ROAD...
...I *LEARNED*. QUICKLY.
JUST HOW *POWERLESS* I WAS.
I...
I COULDN'T DO *ANYTHING* WITHOUT DEPENDING ON OTHER PEOPLE'S HANDS.
OTHER PEOPLE HAVE SPILLED BLOOD FOR MY VENDETTA... BUT NEVER *ME*.
"EVEN THAT *WANTED POSTER*... *I* DIDN'T KILL THOSE PEOPLE. BUT...
"BUT YOU COULD SAY IT ALL *STARTED* BECAUSE I WAS WEAK.

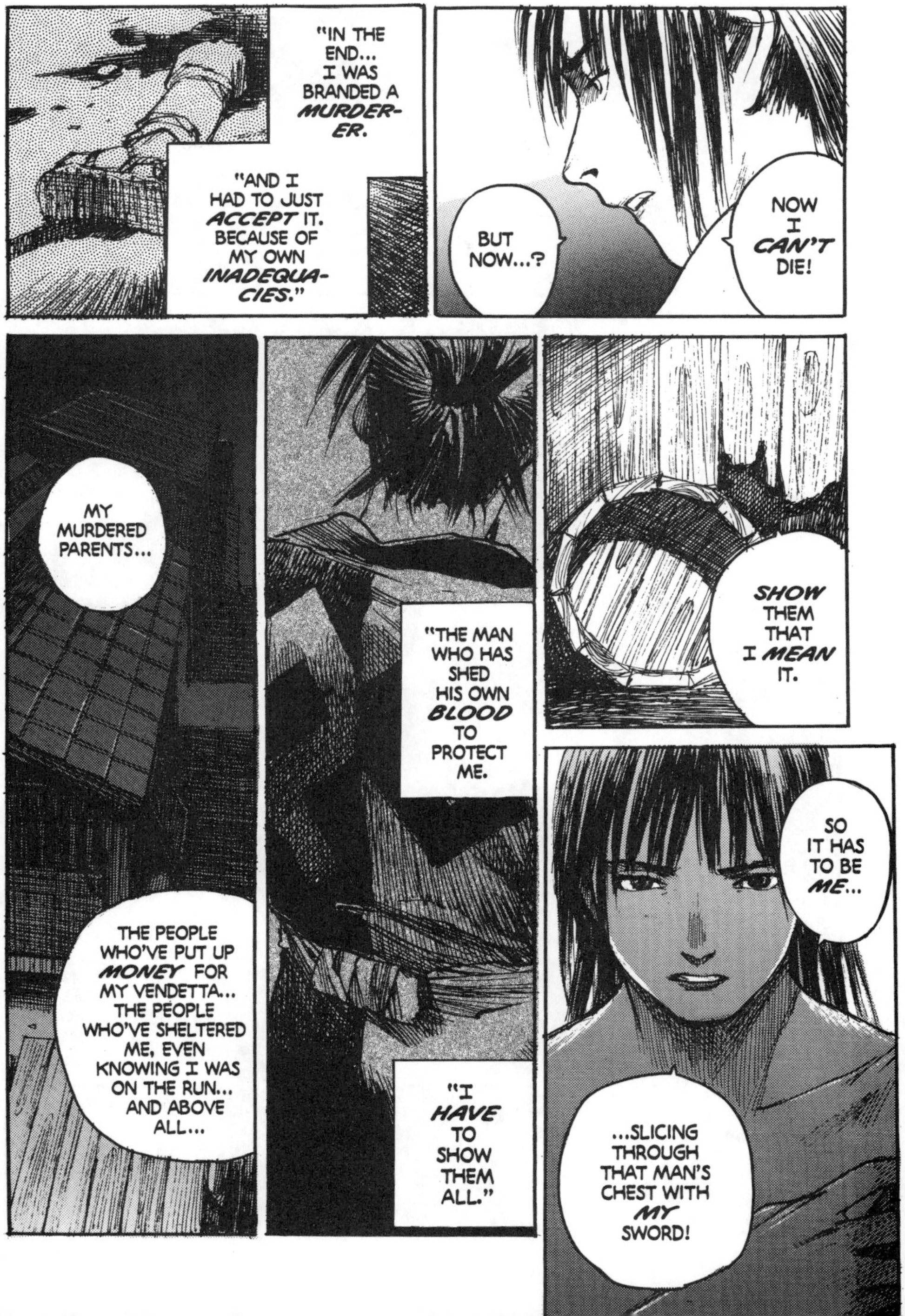
"IN THE END... I WAS BRANDED A MURDERER.
"AND I HAD TO JUST ACCEPT IT. BECAUSE OF MY OWN INADEQUACIES."
BUT NOW...?
NOW I CAN'T DIE!
MY MURDERED PARENTS...
THE PEOPLE WHO'VE PUT UP MONEY FOR MY VENDETTA... THE PEOPLE WHO'VE SHELTERED ME, EVEN KNOWING I WAS ON THE RUN... AND ABOVE ALL...
"THE MAN WHO HAS SHED HIS OWN BLOOD TO PROTECT ME.
"I HAVE TO SHOW THEM ALL."
SHOW THEM THAT I MEAN IT.
SO IT HAS TO BE ME...
...SLICING THROUGH THAT MAN'S CHEST WITH MY SWORD!

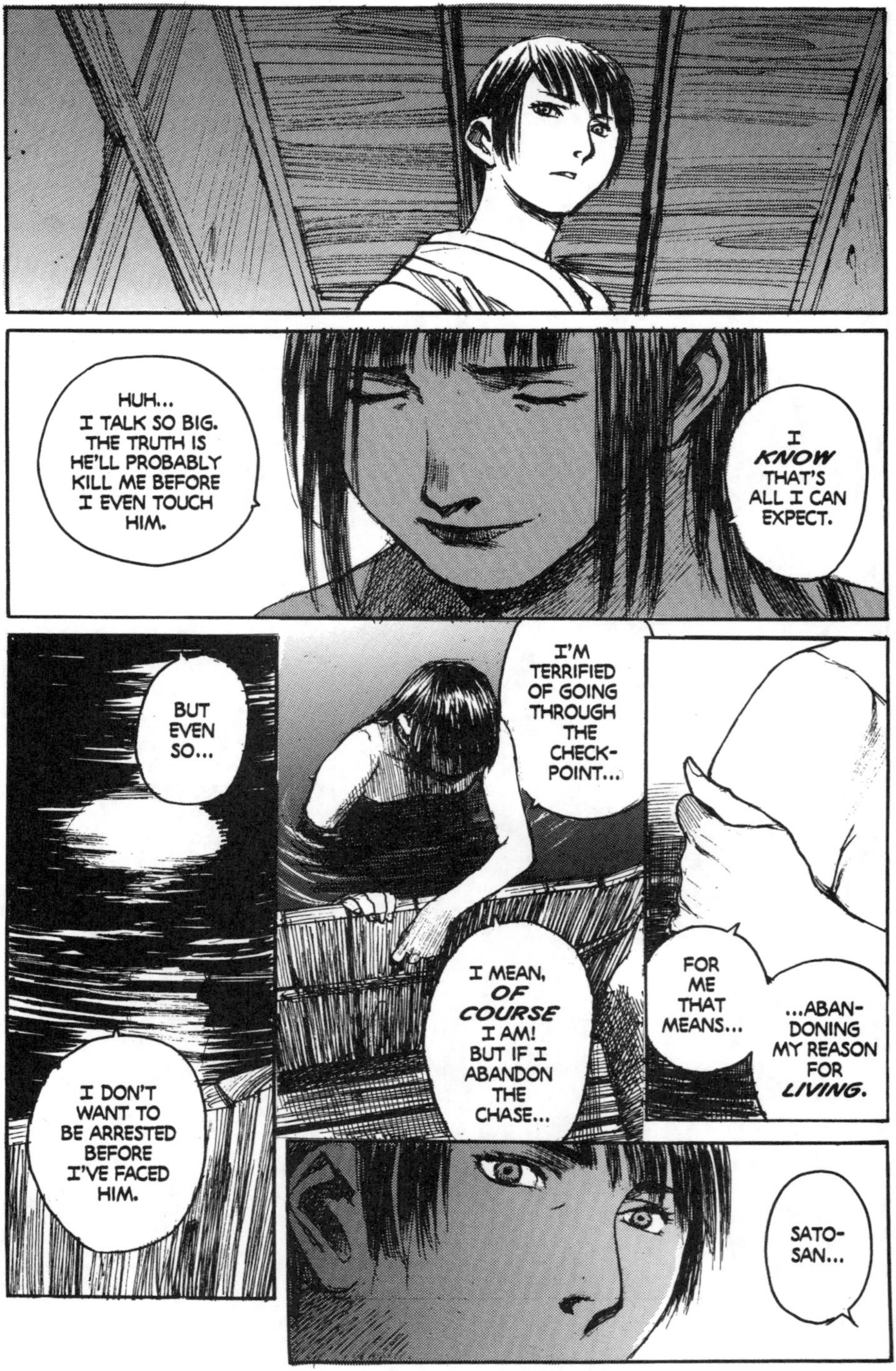
HUH... I TALK SO BIG. THE TRUTH IS HE'LL PROBABLY KILL ME BEFORE I EVEN TOUCH HIM.
I *KNOW* THAT'S ALL I CAN EXPECT.
BUT EVEN SO...
I DON'T WANT TO BE ARRESTED BEFORE I'VE FACED HIM.
I'M TERRIFIED OF GOING THROUGH THE CHECK-POINT...
I MEAN, *OF COURSE* I AM! BUT IF I ABANDON THE CHASE...
FOR ME THAT MEANS...
...ABAN-DONING MY REASON FOR *LIVING*.
SATO-SAN...

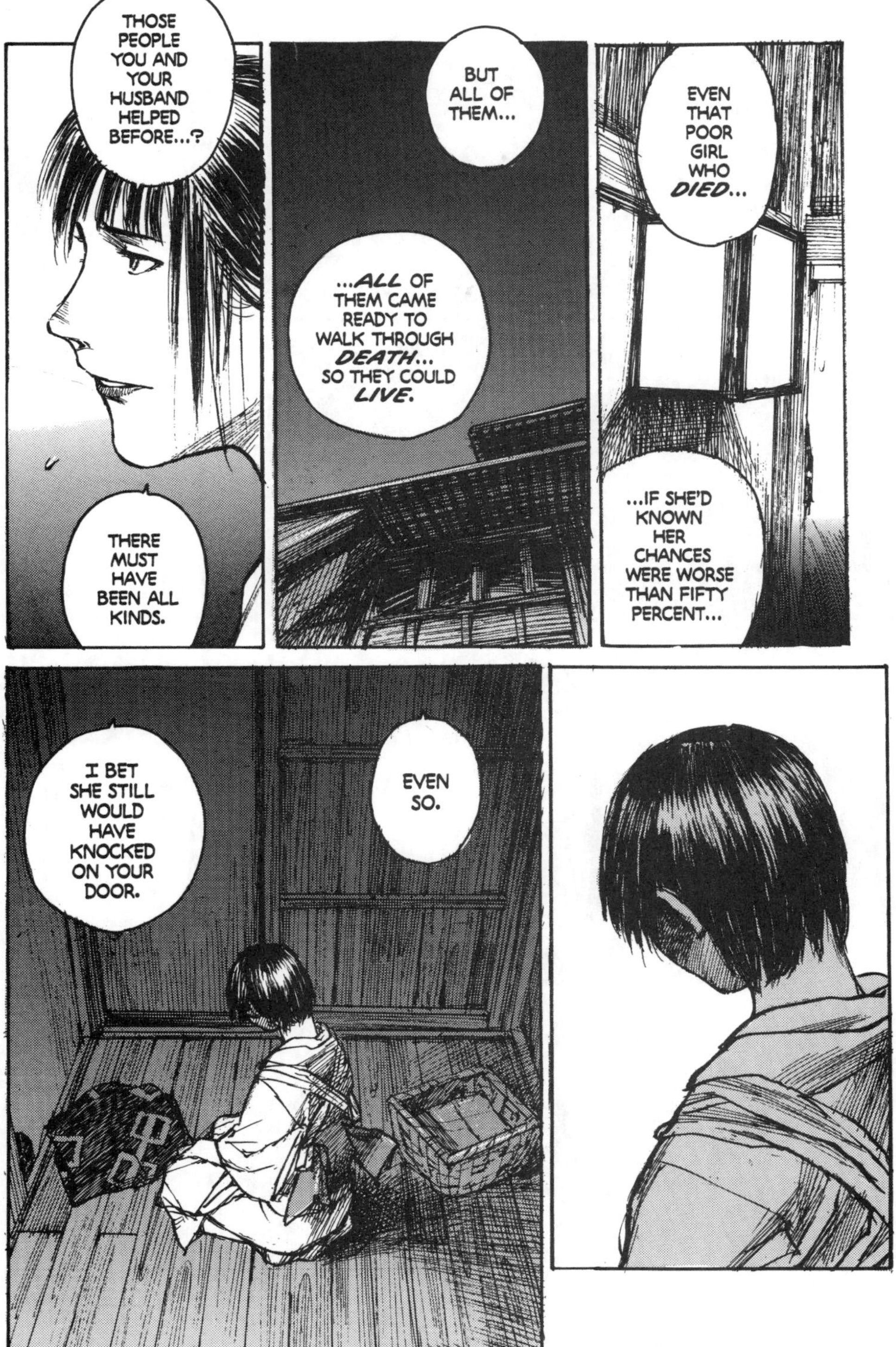
THOSE PEOPLE YOU AND YOUR HUSBAND HELPED BEFORE...?
THERE MUST HAVE BEEN ALL KINDS.
BUT ALL OF THEM...
...ALL OF THEM CAME READY TO WALK THROUGH DEATH... SO THEY COULD LIVE.
EVEN THAT POOR GIRL WHO DIED...
...IF SHE'D KNOWN HER CHANCES WERE WORSE THAN FIFTY PERCENT...
I BET SHE STILL WOULD HAVE KNOCKED ON YOUR DOOR.
EVEN SO.

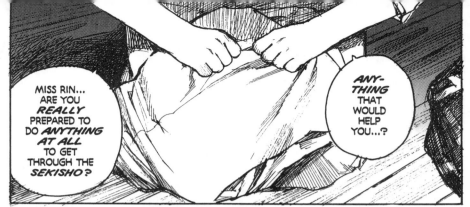

MISS RIN...
ARE YOU
REALLY
PREPARED
TO DO *ANYTHING*
AT ALL
TO GET
THROUGH THE
SEKISHO?

*ANY-
THING*
THAT
WOULD
HELP
YOU...?

?!

WELL...?
PLEASE
ANSWER.

......
I SEE.

THEN...
DON'T
FORGET
YOUR
ANSWER.

Y-
YES!

OF
COURSE!

......
......?

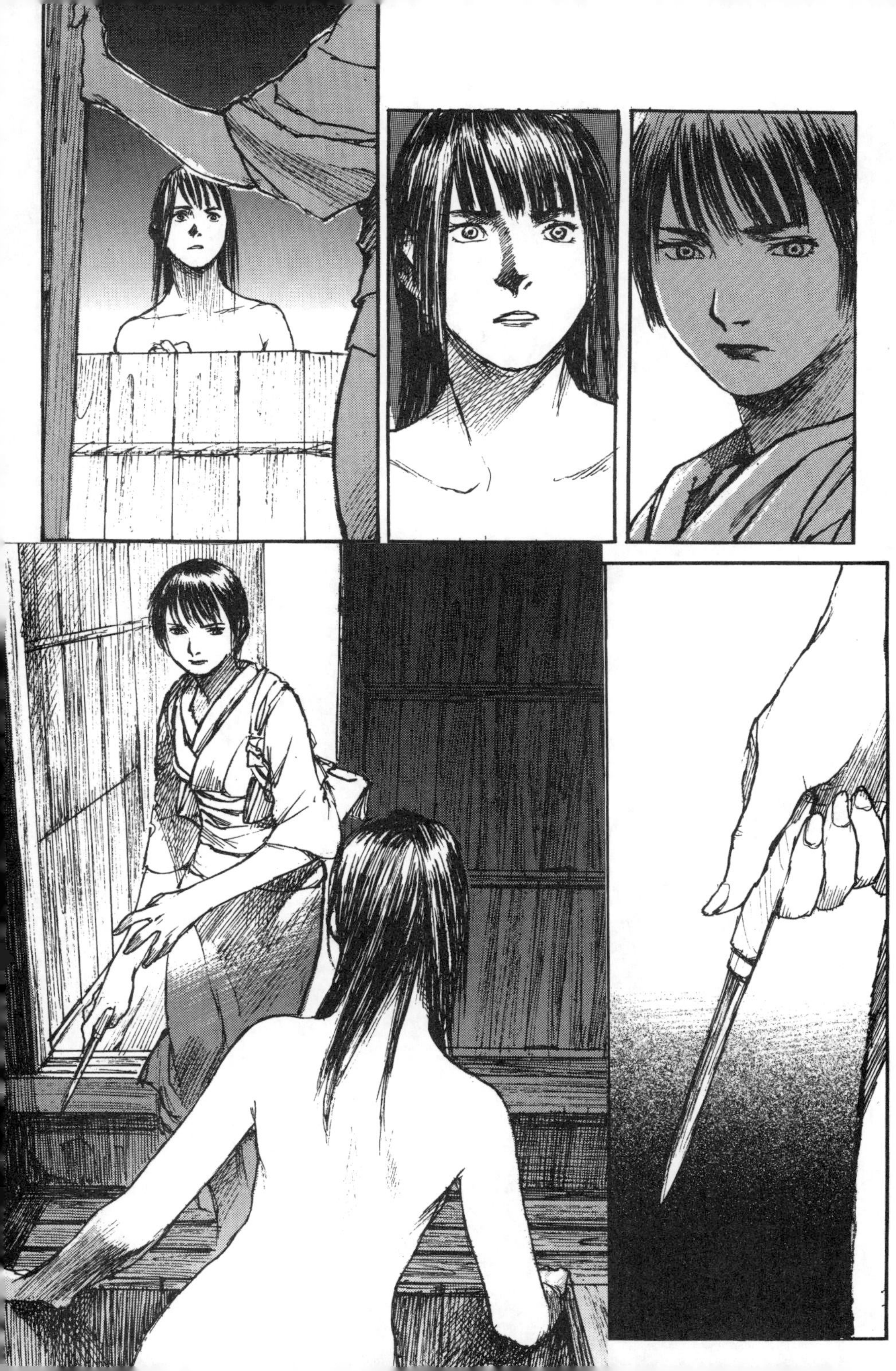

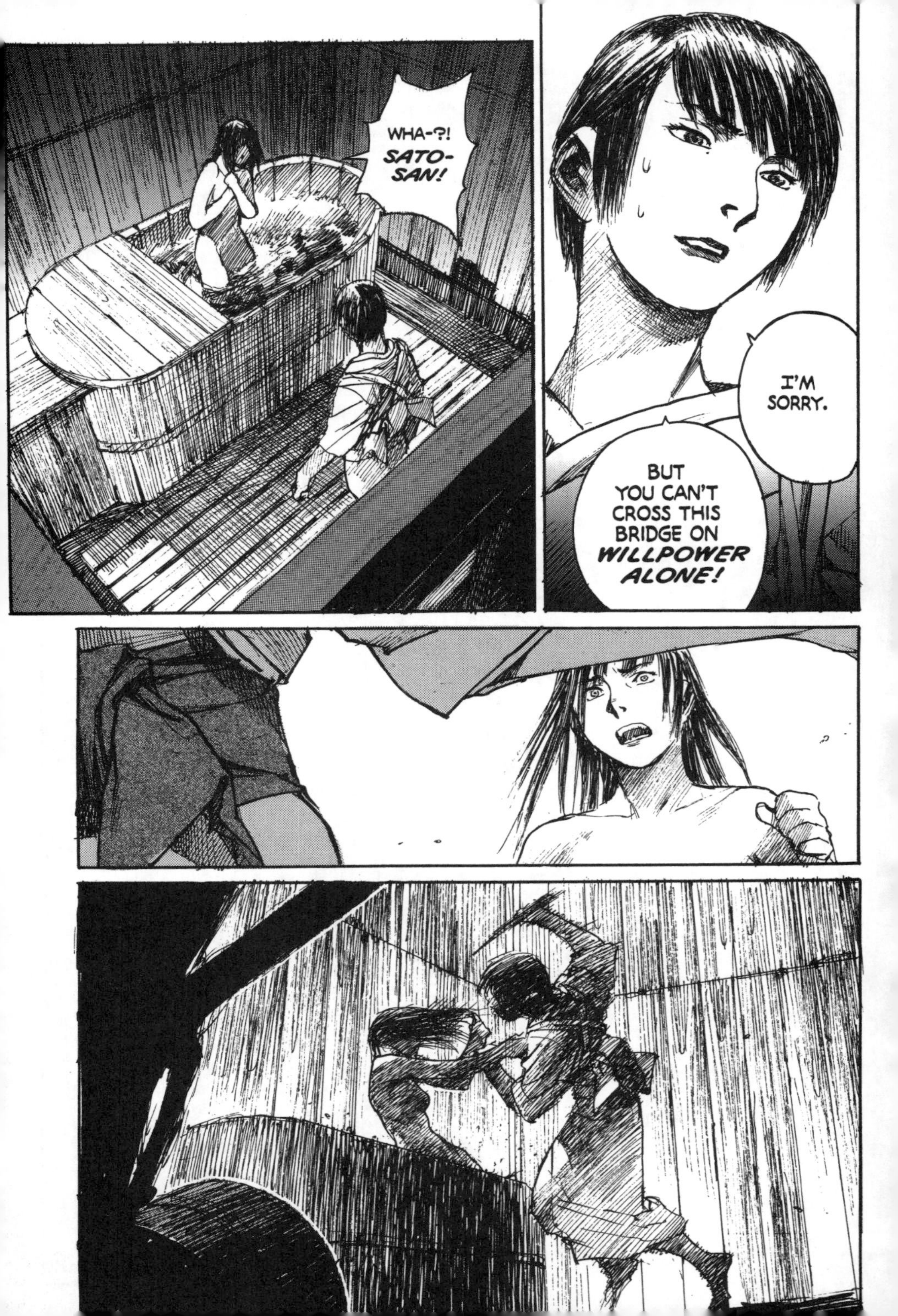
WHA-?! SATO-SAN!
I'M SORRY.
BUT YOU CAN'T CROSS THIS BRIDGE ON WILLPOWER ALONE!

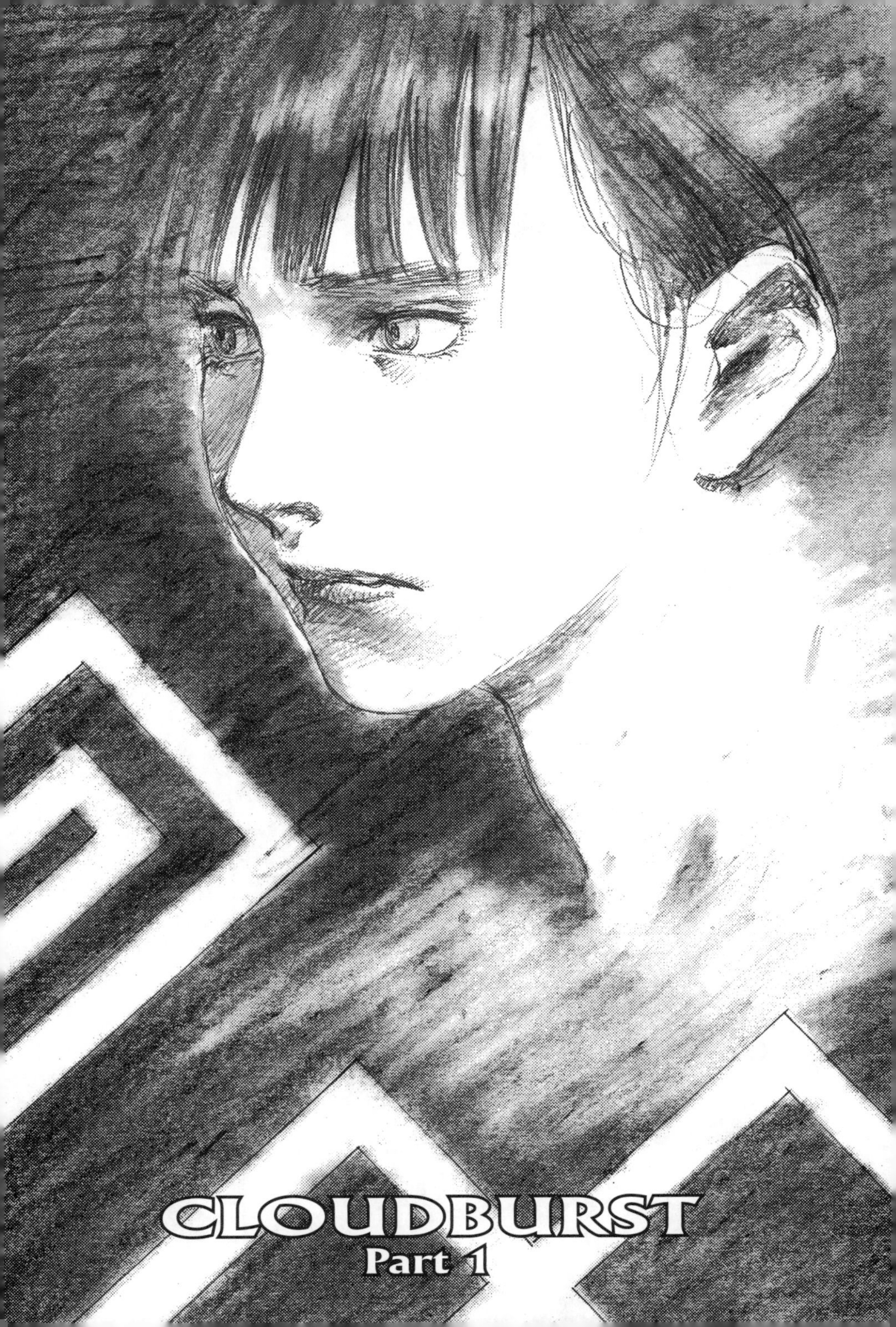
CLOUDBURST
Part 1

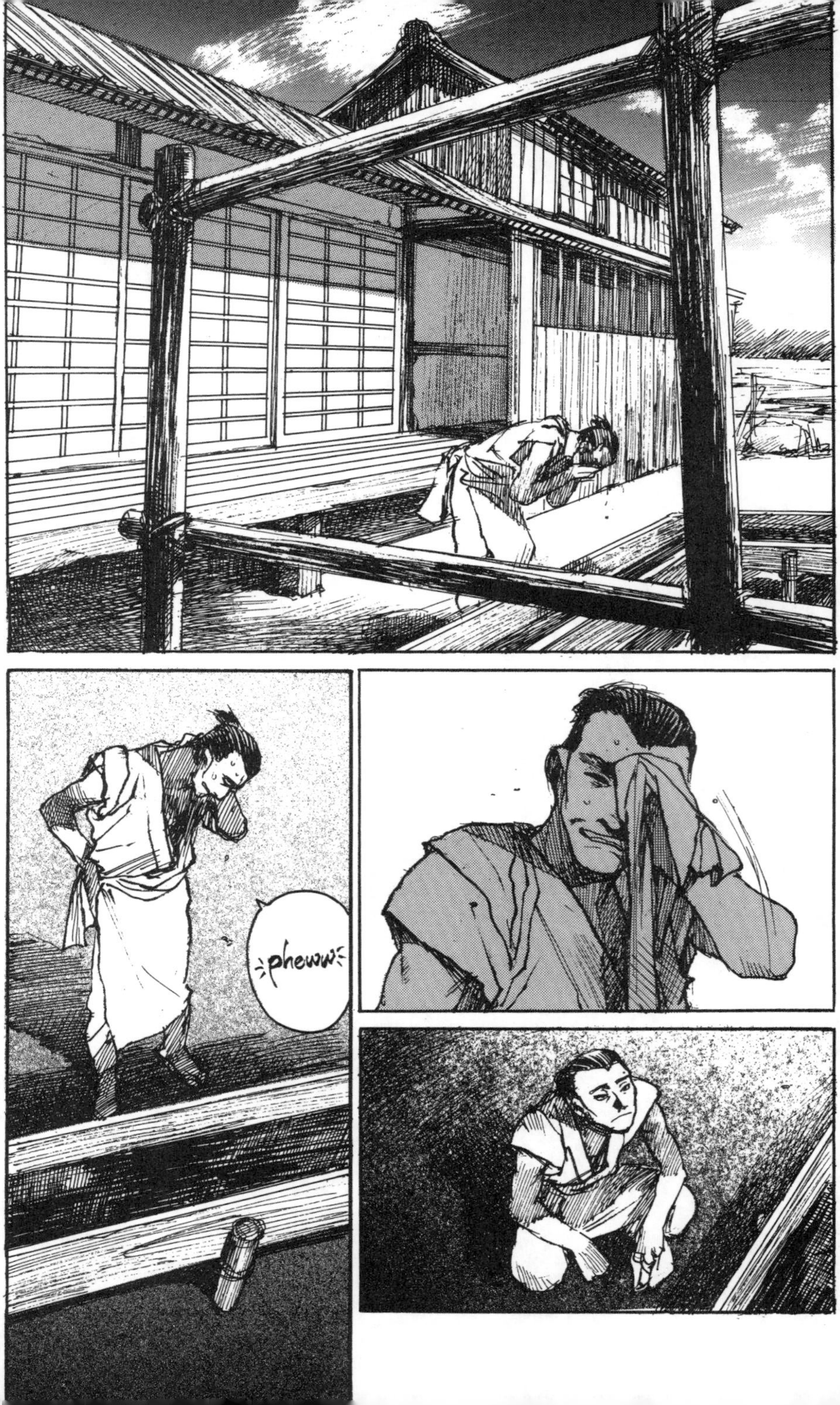
phewww

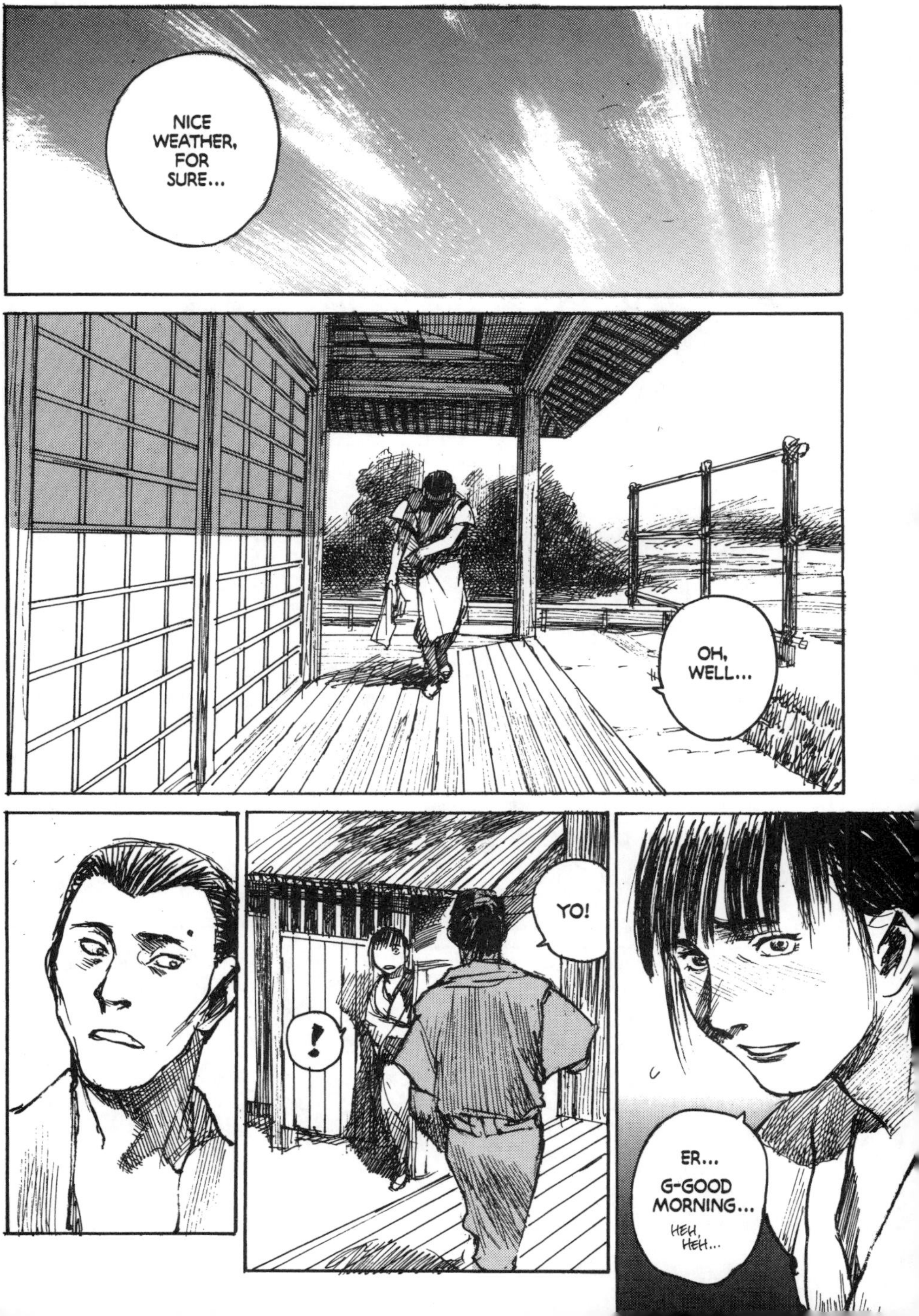
NICE WEATHER, FOR SURE...
OH, WELL...
YO!
!
ER... G-GOOD MORNING...
HEH, HEH...

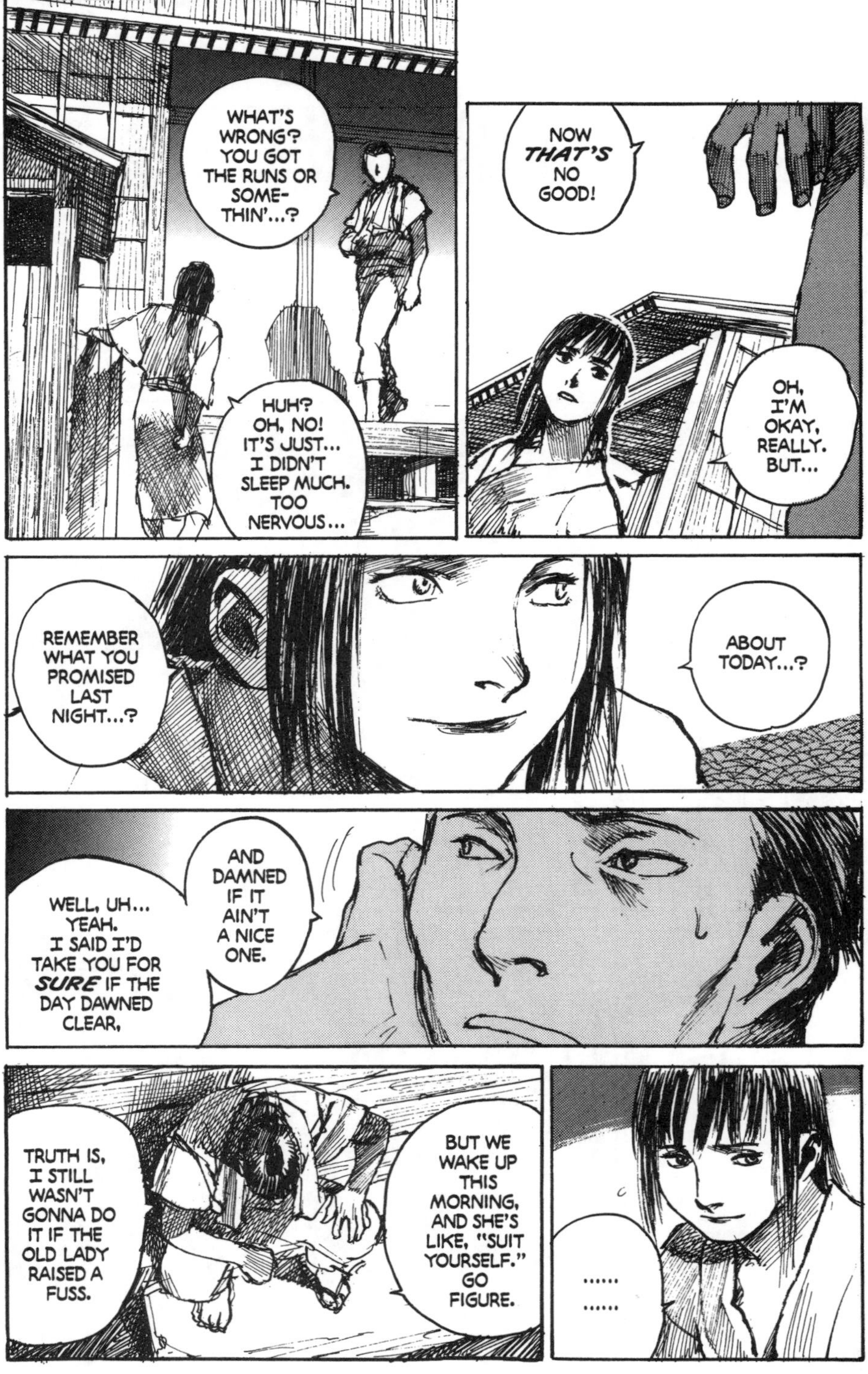
WHAT'S WRONG? YOU GOT THE RUNS OR SOME-THIN'...?
HUH? OH, NO! IT'S JUST... I DIDN'T SLEEP MUCH. TOO NERVOUS...
NOW *THAT'S* NO GOOD!
OH, I'M OKAY, REALLY. BUT...
REMEMBER WHAT YOU PROMISED LAST NIGHT...?
ABOUT TODAY...?
WELL, UH... YEAH. I SAID I'D TAKE YOU FOR *SURE* IF THE DAY DAWNED CLEAR,
AND DAMNED IF IT AIN'T A NICE ONE.
TRUTH IS, I STILL WASN'T GONNA DO IT IF THE OLD LADY RAISED A FUSS.
BUT WE WAKE UP THIS MORNING, AND SHE'S LIKE, "SUIT YOURSELF." GO FIGURE.
....

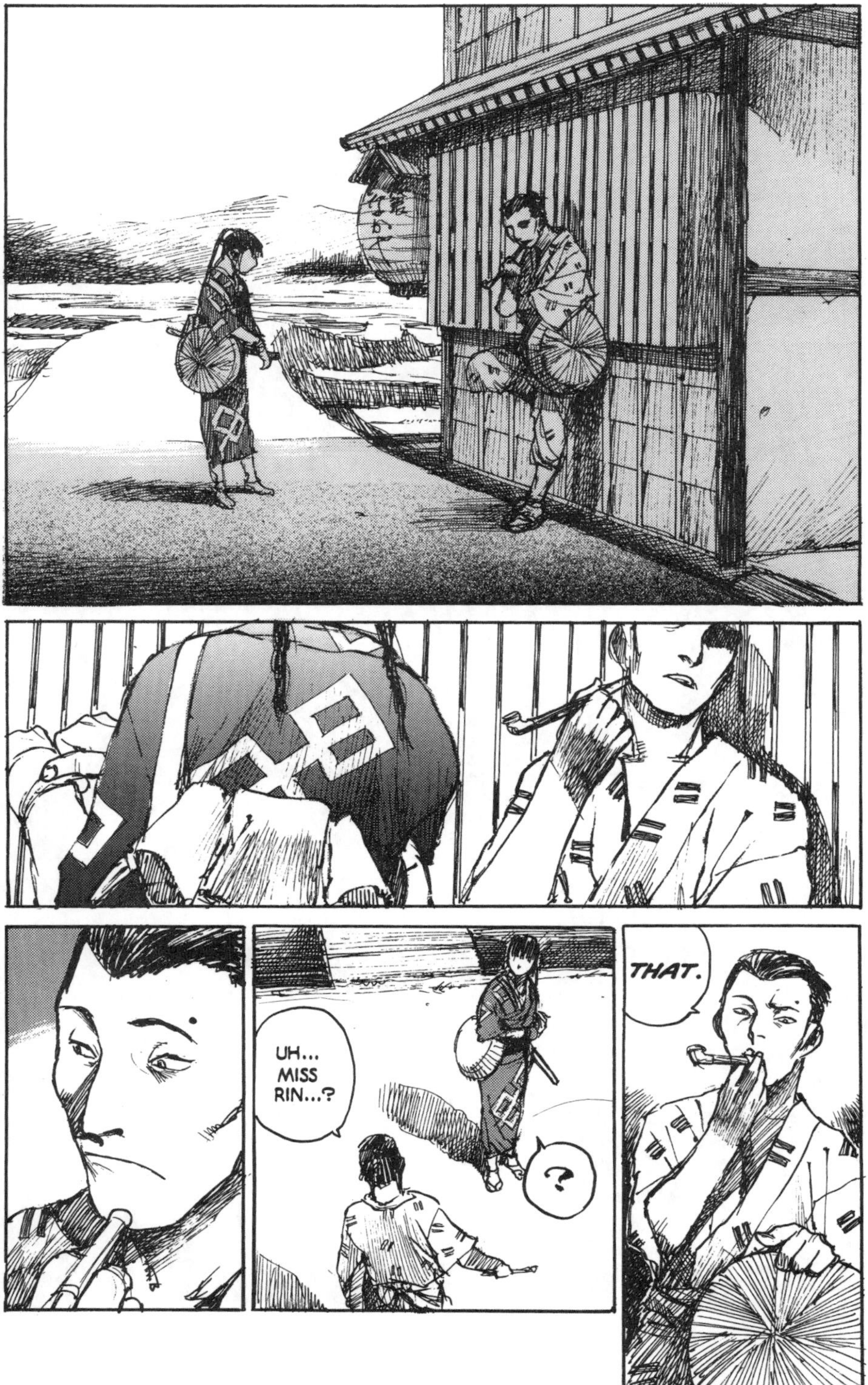
UH... MISS RIN...?
?
THAT.

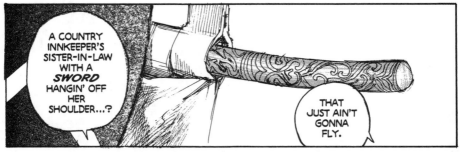

A COUNTRY INNKEEPER'S SISTER-IN-LAW WITH A **SWORD** HANGIN' OFF HER SHOULDER...?

THAT JUST AIN'T GONNA FLY.

...?! AH!

OF... OF **COURSE!** BUT...

WHY NOT PARK IT HERE?

ONCE YOU KNOW WHERE YOU'LL BE, WE'LL SEND IT TO YOU. HECK, IT'S AIN'T LIKE YOU'RE OFF TO KAGA TO CHOP UP SOME POOR SLOB...RIGHT?

UM... HA, HA... RIGHT.

OKAY, THEN. I'LL LEAVE IT HERE.

THANKS.

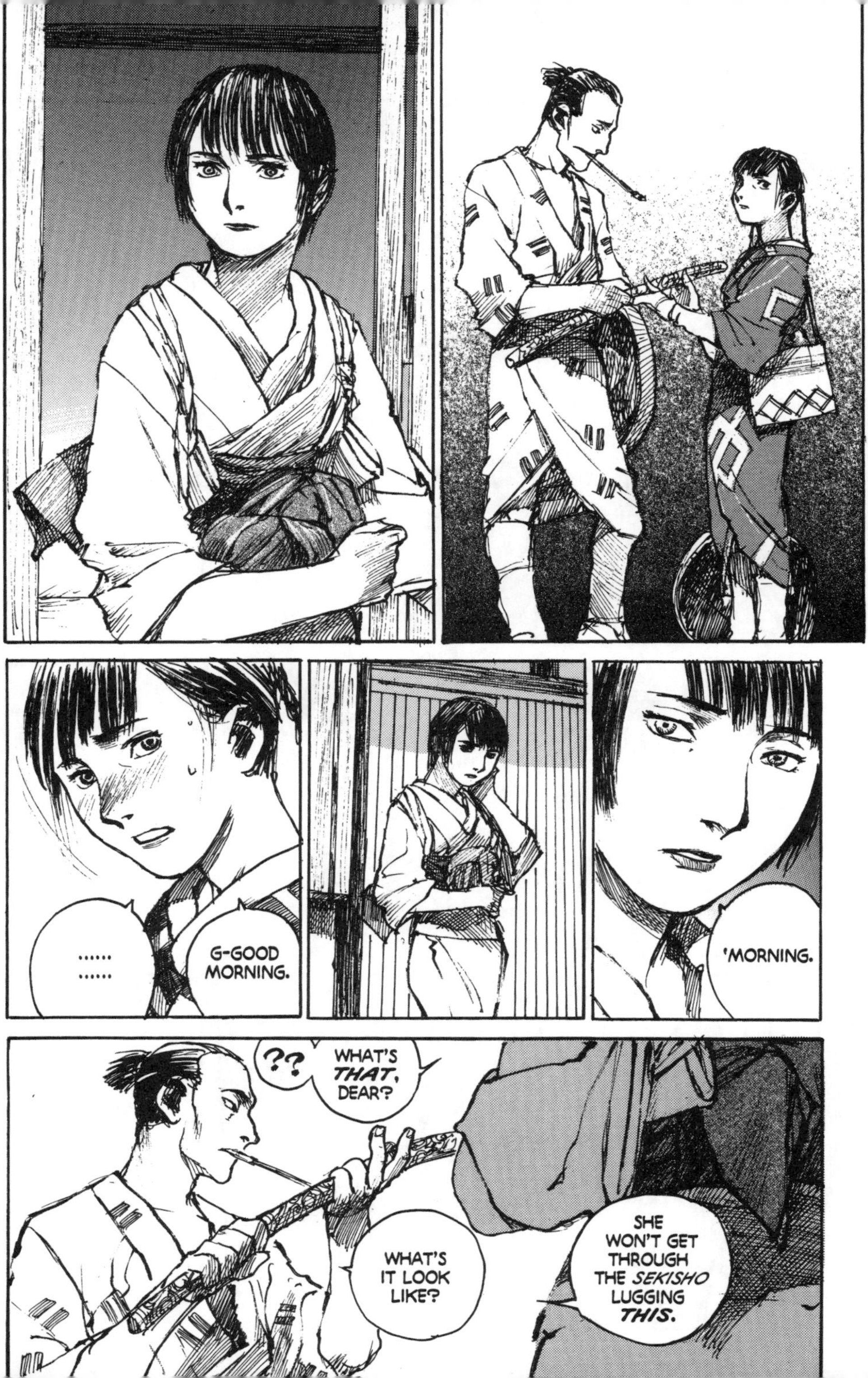

......
......
G-GOOD MORNING.
'MORNING.
??
WHAT'S *THAT*, DEAR?
WHAT'S IT LOOK LIKE?
SHE WON'T GET THROUGH THE *SEKISHO* LUGGING *THIS*.

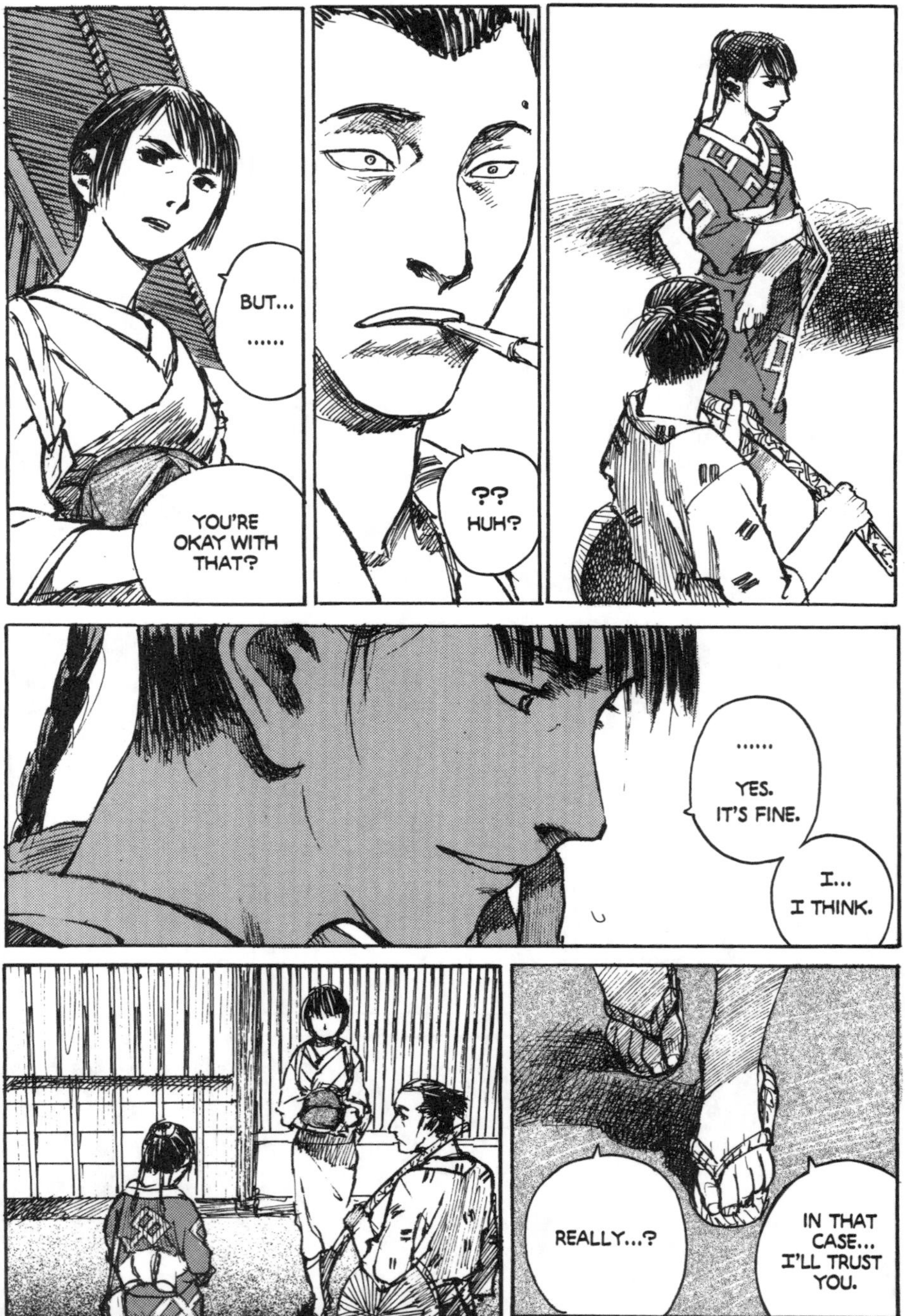
BUT...
......
YOU'RE OKAY WITH THAT?
?? HUH?
......
YES. IT'S FINE.
I... I THINK.
REALLY...?
IN THAT CASE... I'LL TRUST YOU.

HERE. TAKE THIS.

SINCE YOU DIDN'T HAVE TIME FOR BREAKFAST...

AH...EH?! *OH!* TH-THANK YOU! THANK YOU *SO MUCH!*

EAT THEM *AFTER* YOU'RE THROUGH THE *SEKISHO,* ALL RIGHT?

?? *UM...* SURE. I WILL!

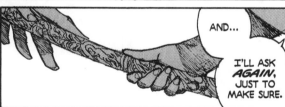

I'LL TAKE *THAT,* SŌHACHI.

OKAY, OKAY.

AND...

I'LL ASK *AGAIN,* JUST TO MAKE SURE.

YOU CAN'T USE THE BACK WAY. AND AFTER LAST TIME, WE HAD TO GIVE THEM COPIES OF OUR FAMILY TREES. IT WON'T BE EASY TO PASS HER OFF AS A RELATIVE.

YOU'RE *SURE* YOU CAN DO IT?

LOOK, SATO... FAMILY TREES...

...THEY DON'T GOT NO *FACES* ON 'EM, RIGHT?

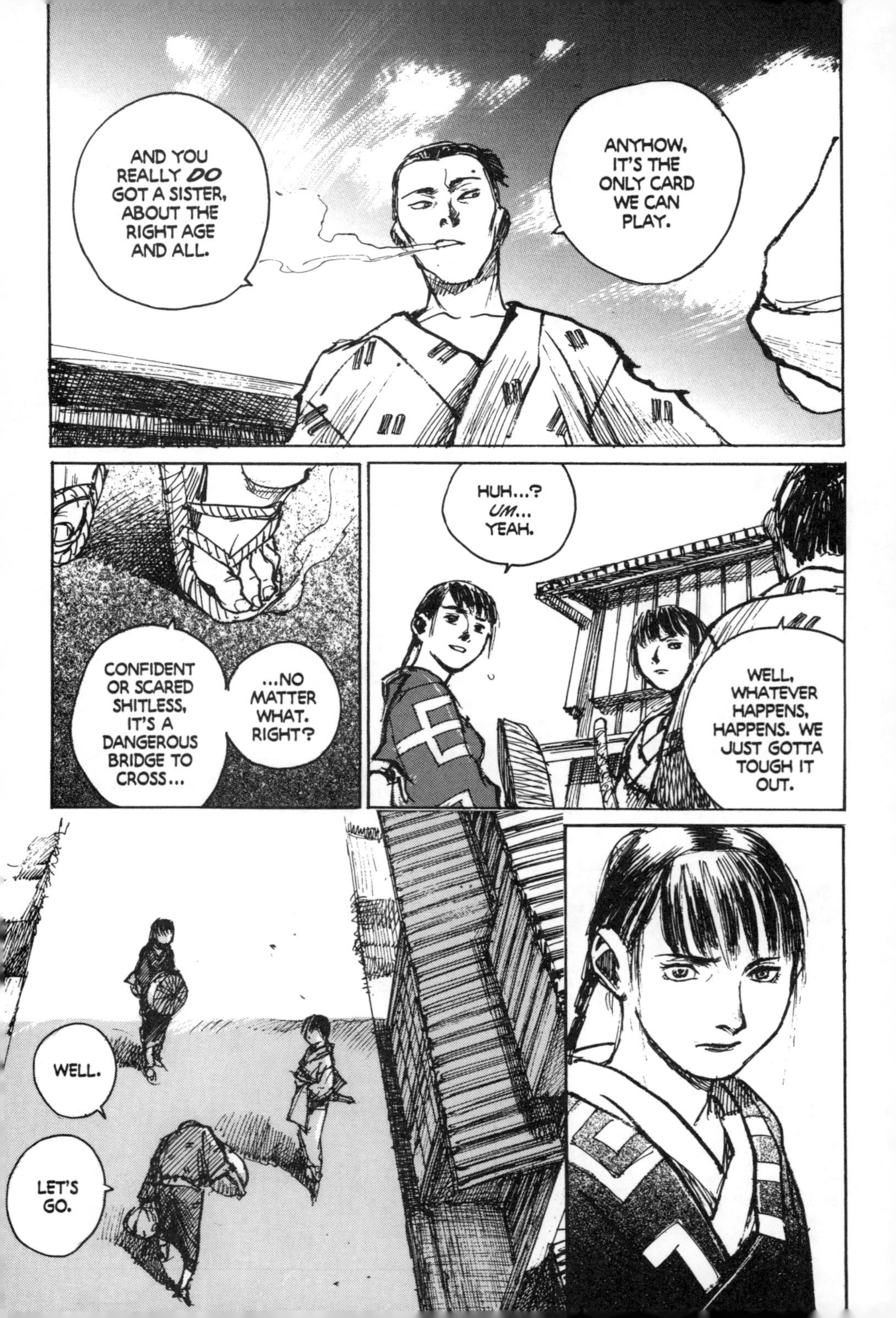
AND YOU REALLY *DO* GOT A SISTER, ABOUT THE RIGHT AGE AND ALL.
ANYHOW, IT'S THE ONLY CARD WE CAN PLAY.
CONFIDENT OR SCARED SHITLESS, IT'S A DANGEROUS BRIDGE TO CROSS...
...NO MATTER WHAT. RIGHT?
HUH...? *UM*... YEAH.
WELL, WHATEVER HAPPENS, HAPPENS. WE JUST GOTTA TOUGH IT OUT.
WELL.
LET'S GO.

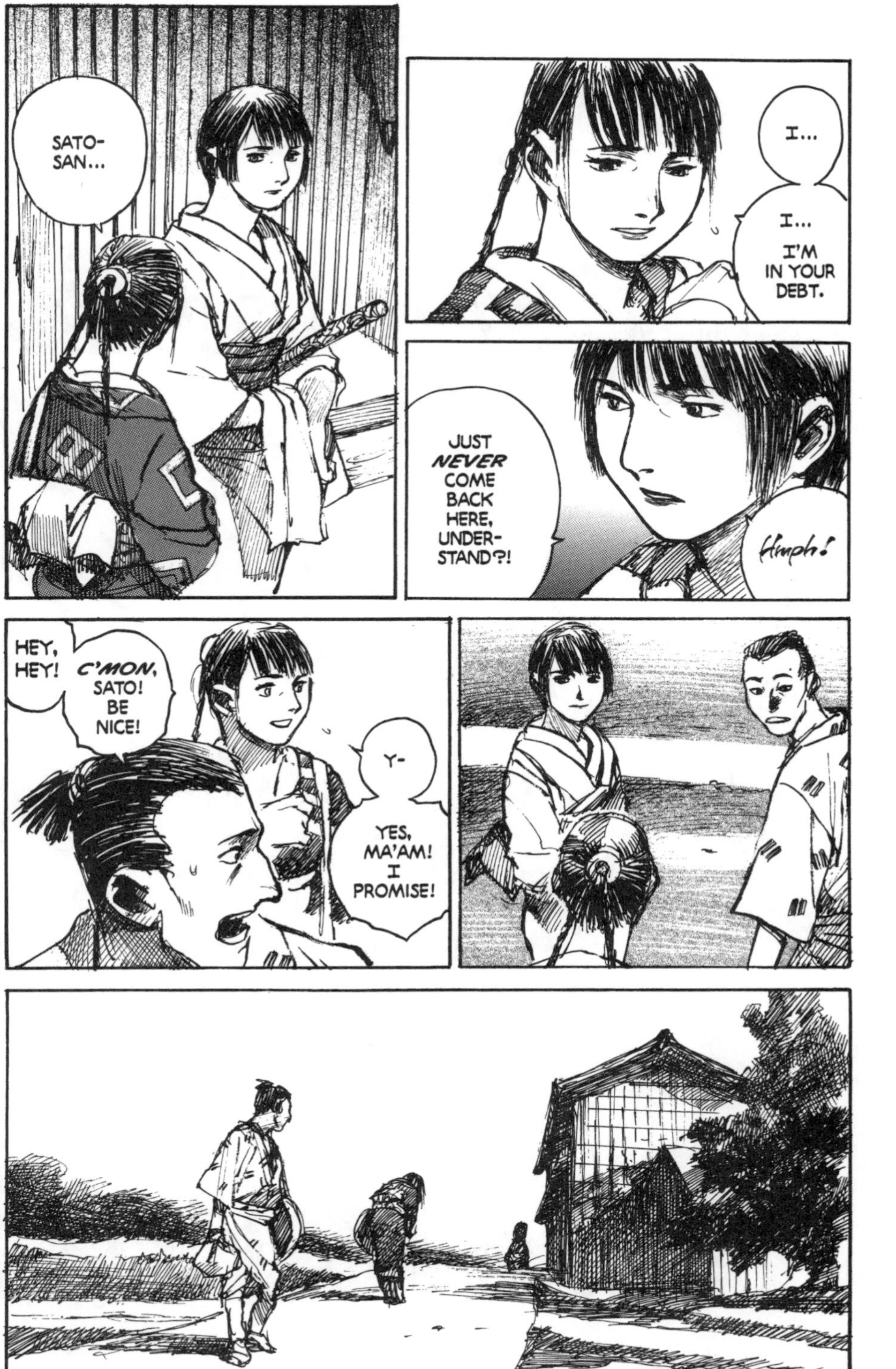
SATO-SAN...
I...
I... I'M IN YOUR DEBT.
JUST *NEVER* COME BACK HERE, UNDERSTAND?!
Hmph!
HEY, HEY!
C'MON, SATO! BE NICE!
Y-
YES, MA'AM! I PROMISE!

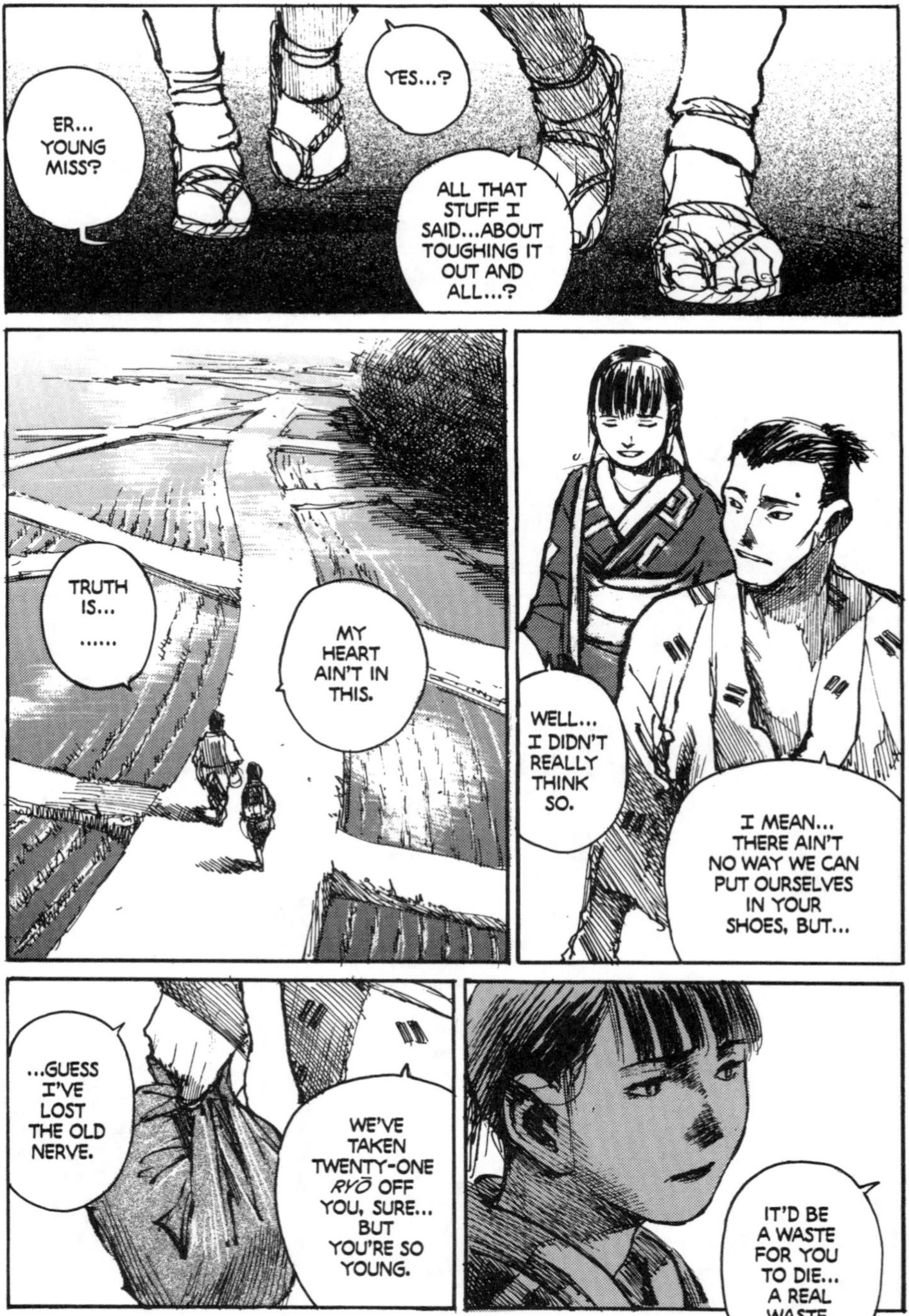
ER... YOUNG MISS?
YES...?
ALL THAT STUFF I SAID...ABOUT TOUGHING IT OUT AND ALL...?
TRUTH IS... ......
MY HEART AIN'T IN THIS.
WELL... I DIDN'T REALLY THINK SO.
I MEAN... THERE AIN'T NO WAY WE CAN PUT OURSELVES IN YOUR SHOES, BUT...
...GUESS I'VE LOST THE OLD NERVE.
WE'VE TAKEN TWENTY-ONE *RYŌ* OFF YOU, SURE... BUT YOU'RE SO YOUNG.
IT'D BE A WASTE FOR YOU TO DIE... A REAL WASTE.

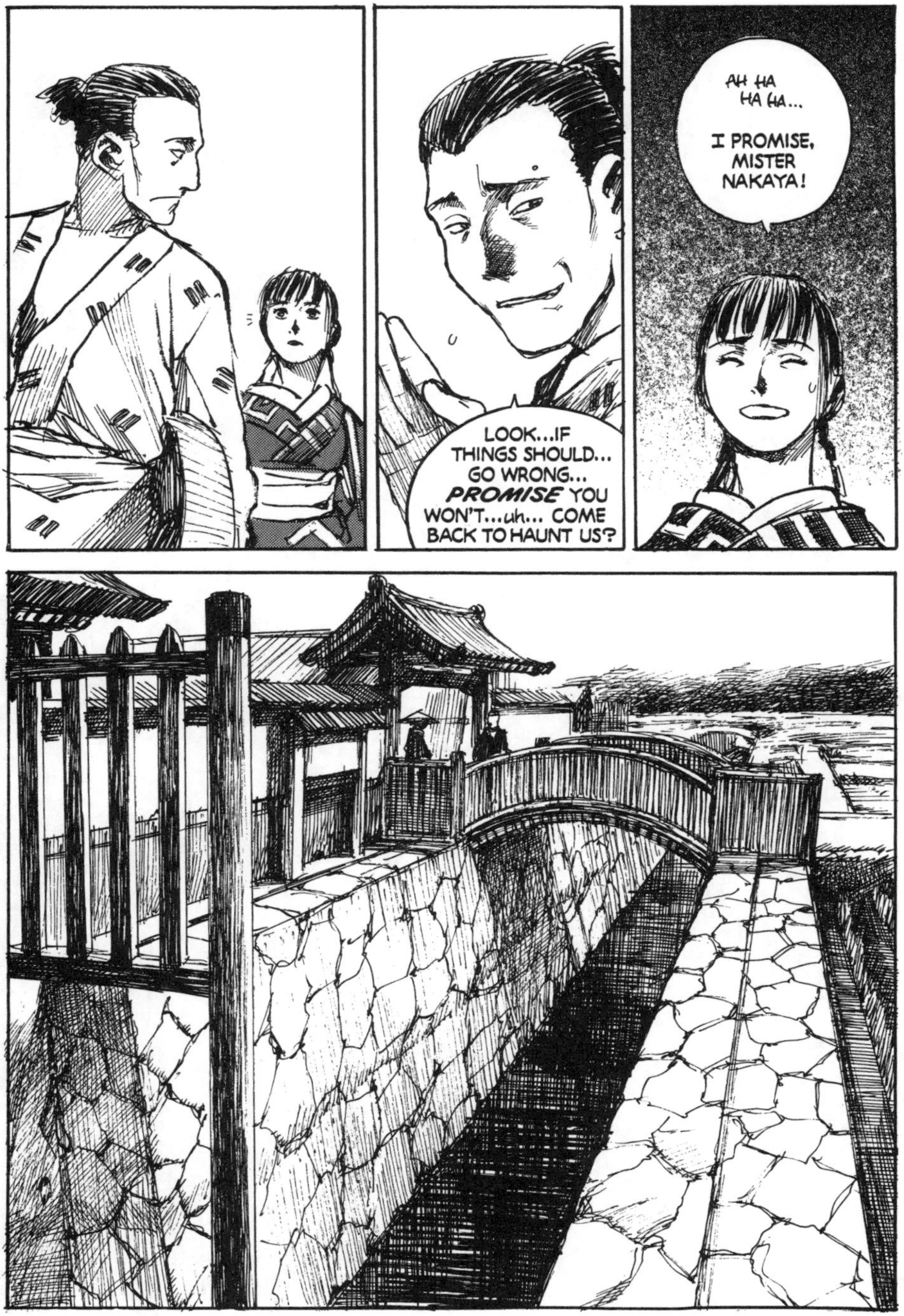
LOOK...IF THINGS SHOULD... GO WRONG... PROMISE YOU WON'T...uh... COME BACK TO HAUNT US?
AH HA HA HA...
I PROMISE, MISTER NAKAYA!

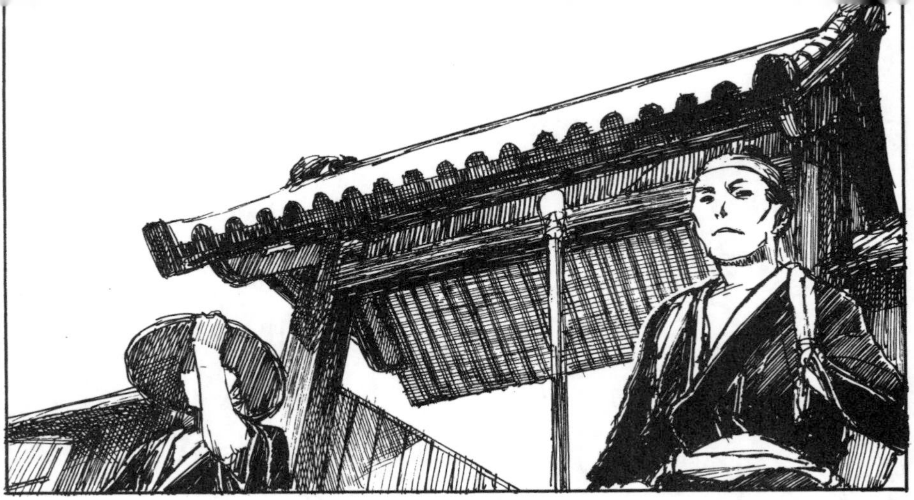
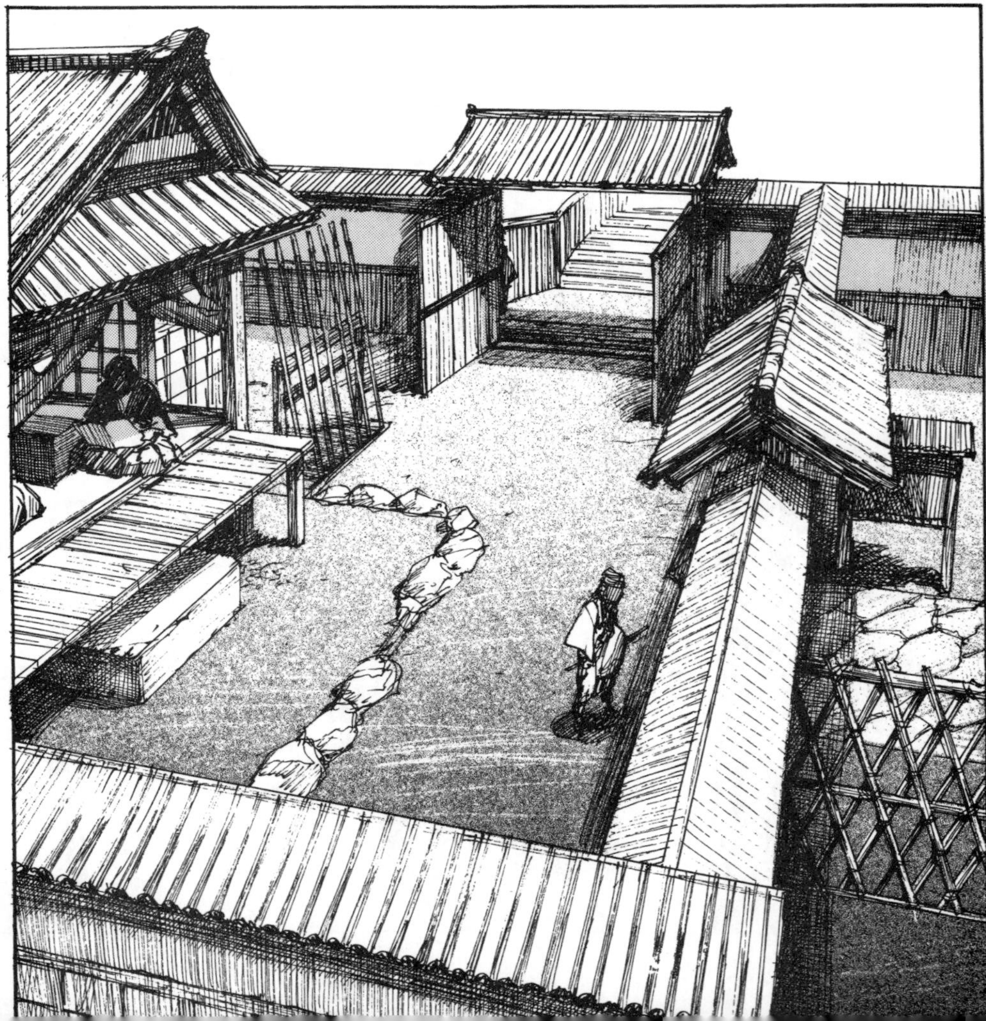

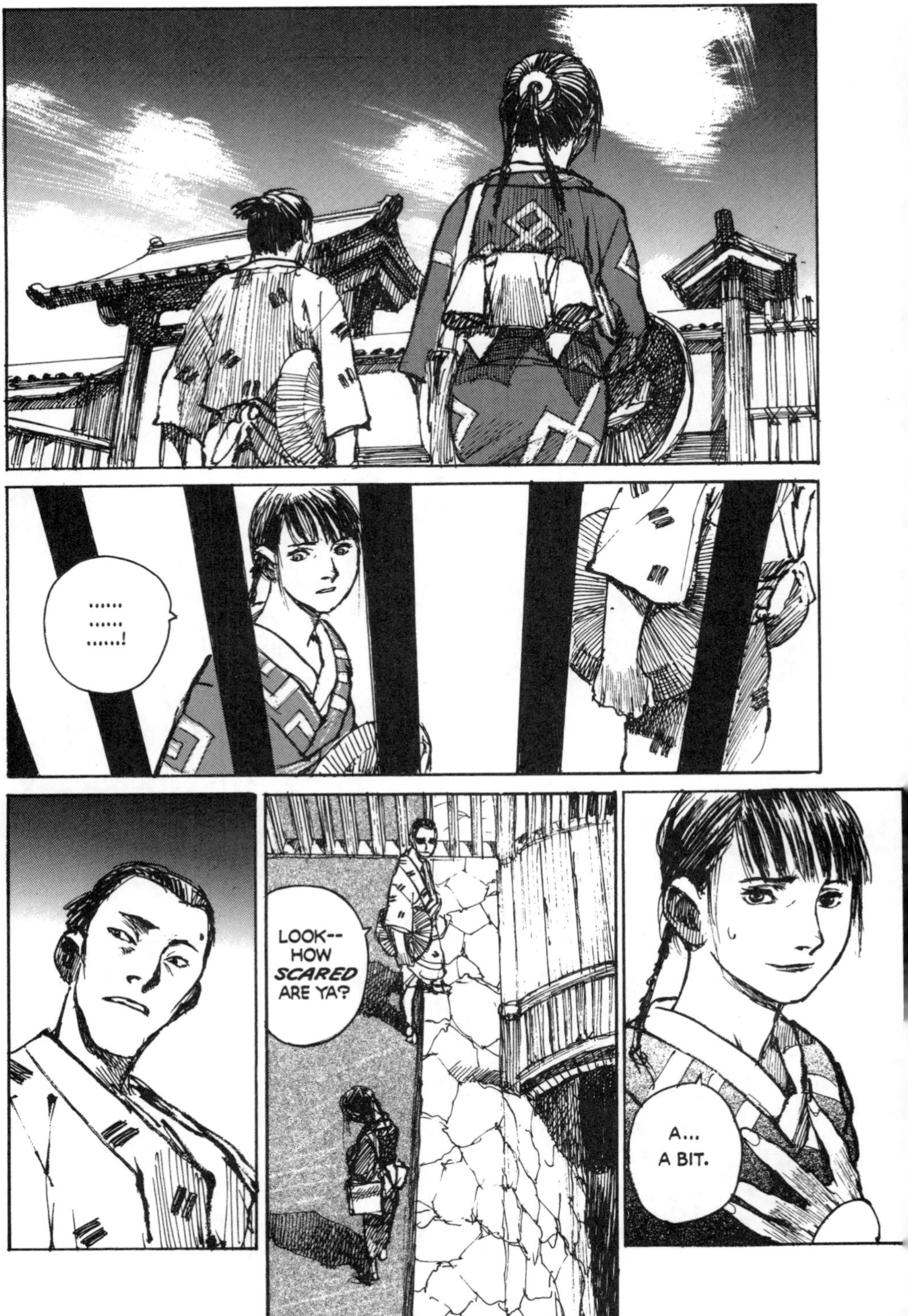
......
......
......!
LOOK--
HOW
SCARED
ARE YA?
A...
A BIT.

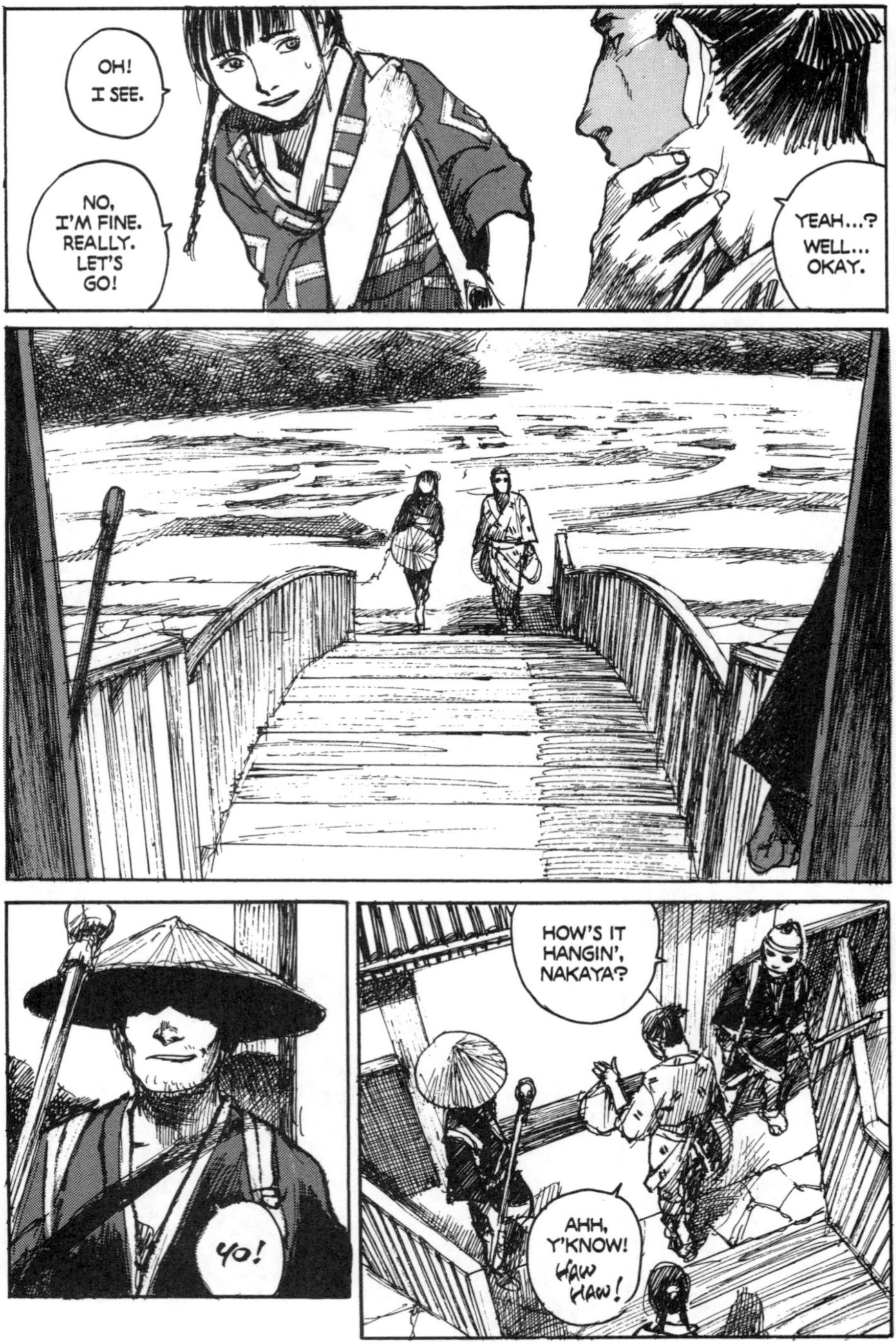
OH! I SEE.
NO, I'M FINE. REALLY. LET'S GO!
YEAH...? WELL... OKAY.
YO!
HOW'S IT HANGIN', NAKAYA?
AHH, Y'KNOW! HAW HAW!

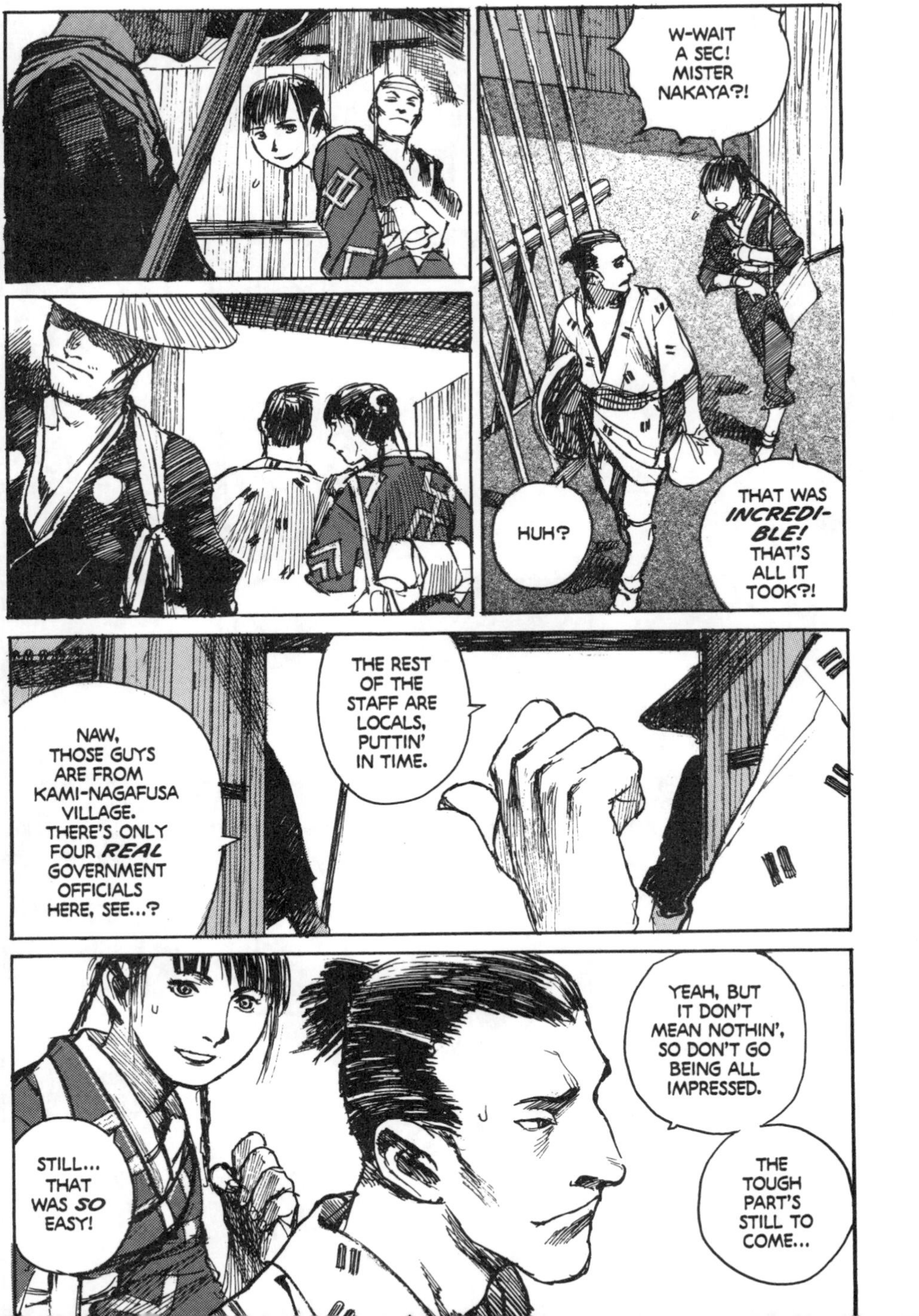
W-WAIT A SEC! MISTER NAKAYA?!
HUH?
THAT WAS *INCREDIBLE!* THAT'S ALL IT TOOK?!
NAW, THOSE GUYS ARE FROM KAMI-NAGAFUSA VILLAGE. THERE'S ONLY FOUR ***REAL*** GOVERNMENT OFFICIALS HERE, SEE...?
THE REST OF THE STAFF ARE LOCALS, PUTTIN' IN TIME.
STILL... THAT WAS ***SO*** EASY!
YEAH, BUT IT DON'T MEAN NOTHIN', SO DON'T GO BEING ALL IMPRESSED.
THE TOUGH PART'S STILL TO COME...

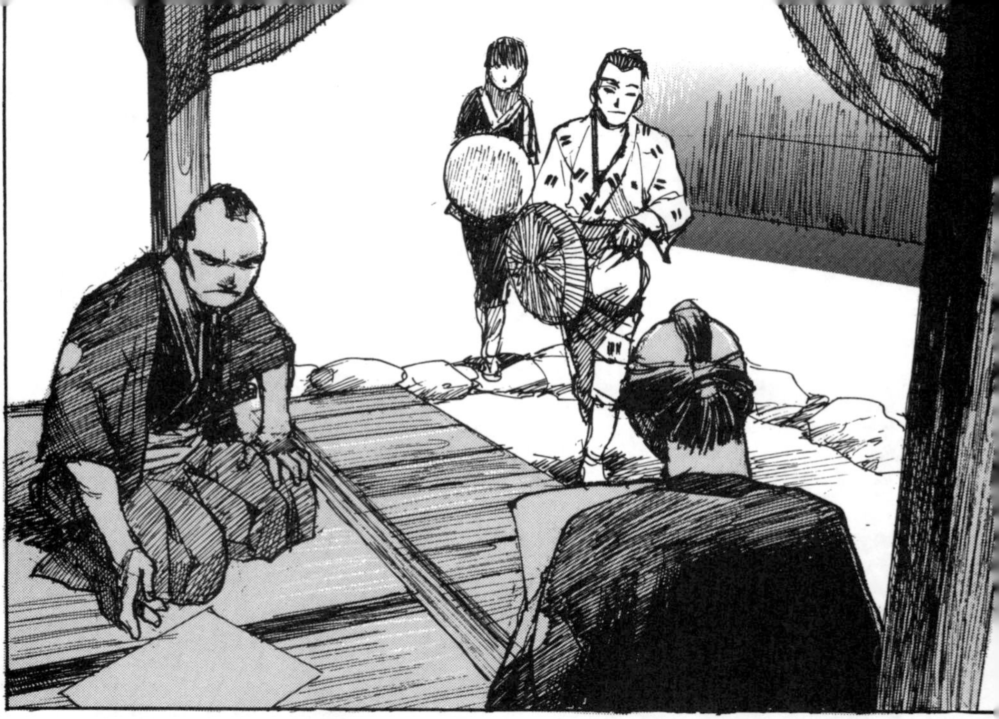

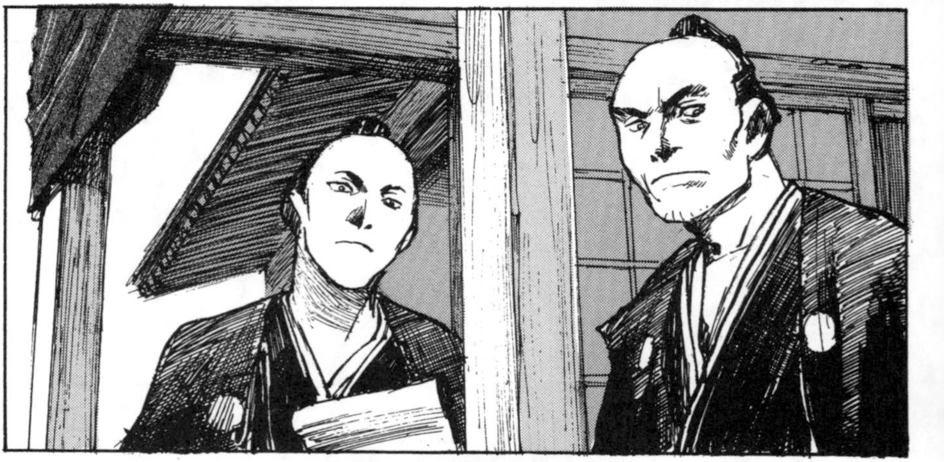

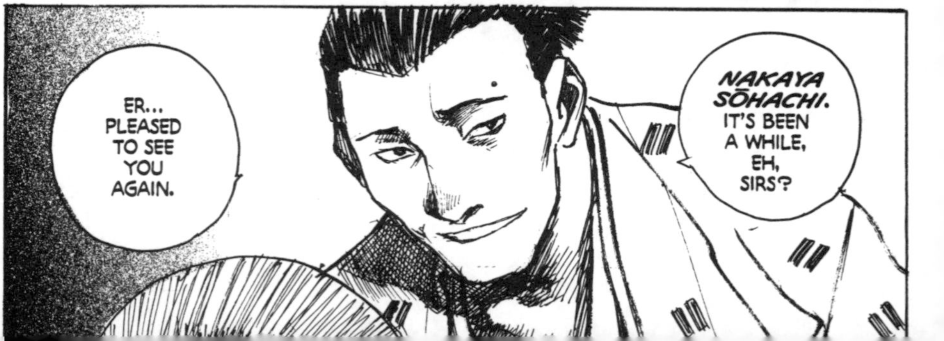
ER... PLEASED TO SEE YOU AGAIN.
NAKAYA SŌHACHI. IT'S BEEN A WHILE, EH, SIRS?

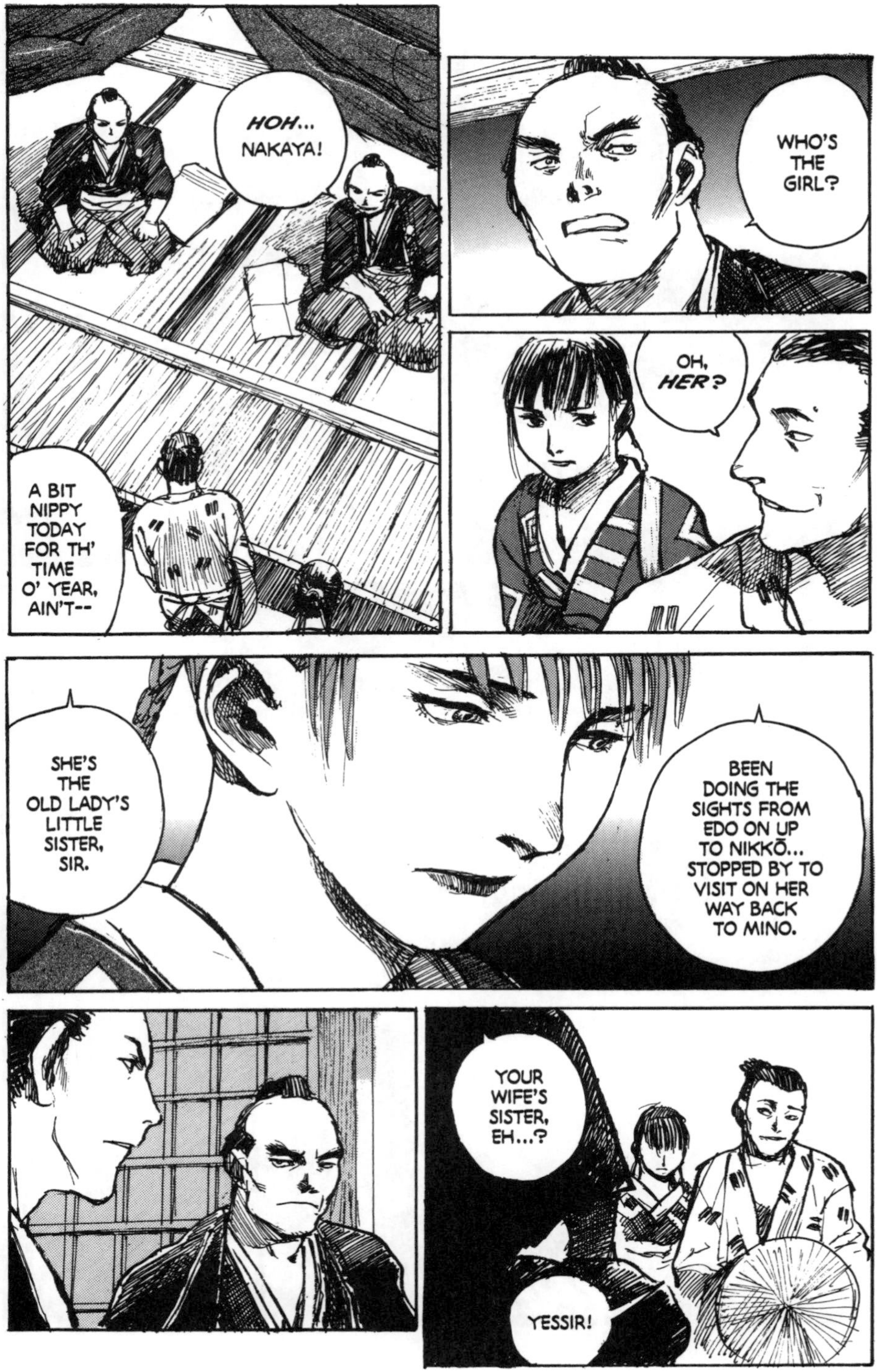
HOH... NAKAYA!
A BIT NIPPY TODAY FOR TH' TIME O' YEAR, AIN'T--
WHO'S THE GIRL?
OH, HER?
SHE'S THE OLD LADY'S LITTLE SISTER, SIR.
BEEN DOING THE SIGHTS FROM EDO ON UP TO NIKKŌ... STOPPED BY TO VISIT ON HER WAY BACK TO MINO.
YOUR WIFE'S SISTER, EH...?
YESSIR!

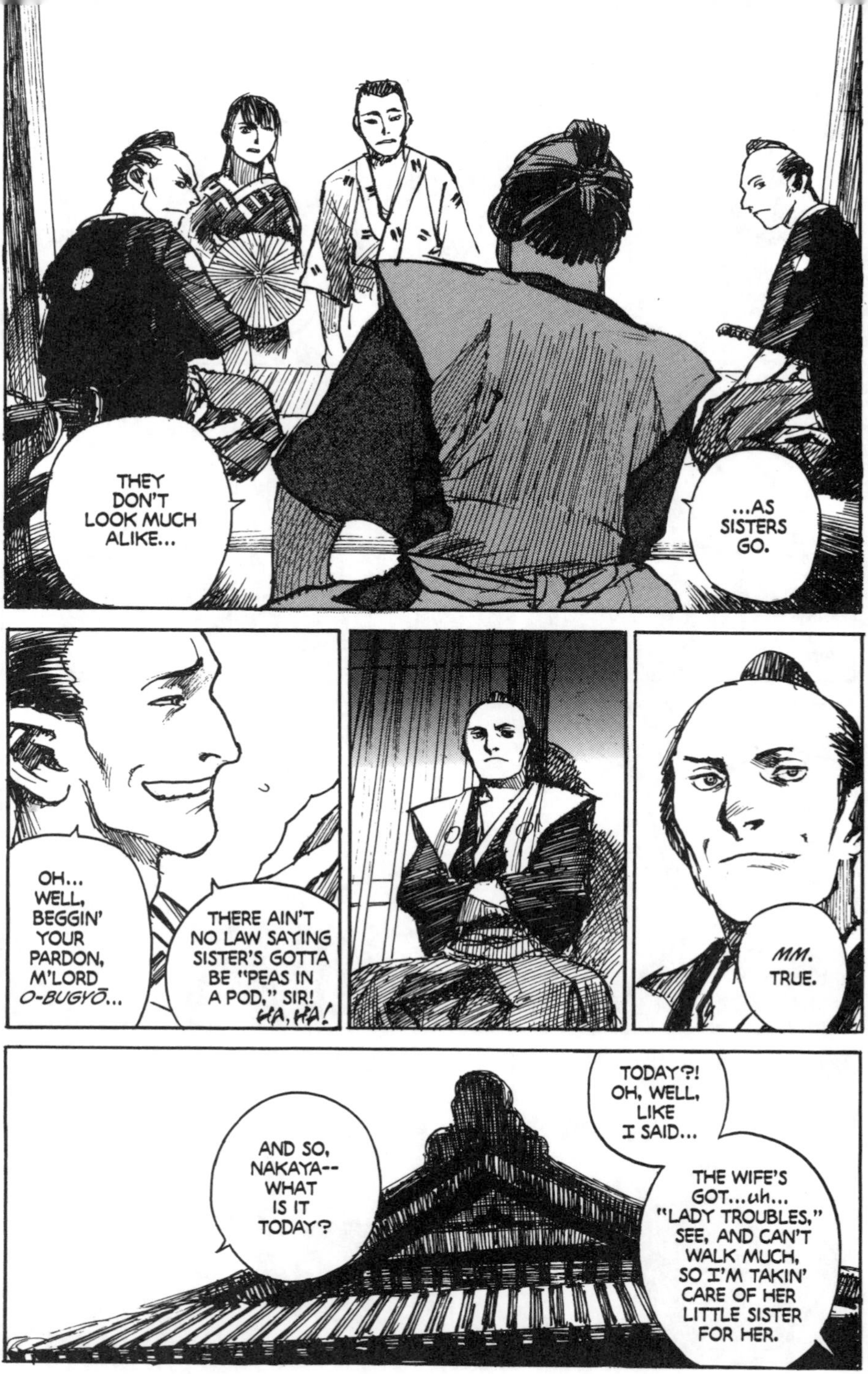
THEY DON'T LOOK MUCH ALIKE...
...AS SISTERS GO.
OH... WELL, BEGGIN' YOUR PARDON, M'LORD *O-BUGYŌ*...
THERE AIN'T NO LAW SAYING SISTER'S GOTTA BE "PEAS IN A POD," SIR!
HA, HA!
MM. TRUE.
AND SO, NAKAYA-- WHAT IS IT TODAY?
TODAY?! OH, WELL, LIKE I SAID...
THE WIFE'S GOT...*uh*... "LADY TROUBLES," SEE, AND CAN'T WALK MUCH, SO I'M TAKIN' CARE OF HER LITTLE SISTER FOR HER.

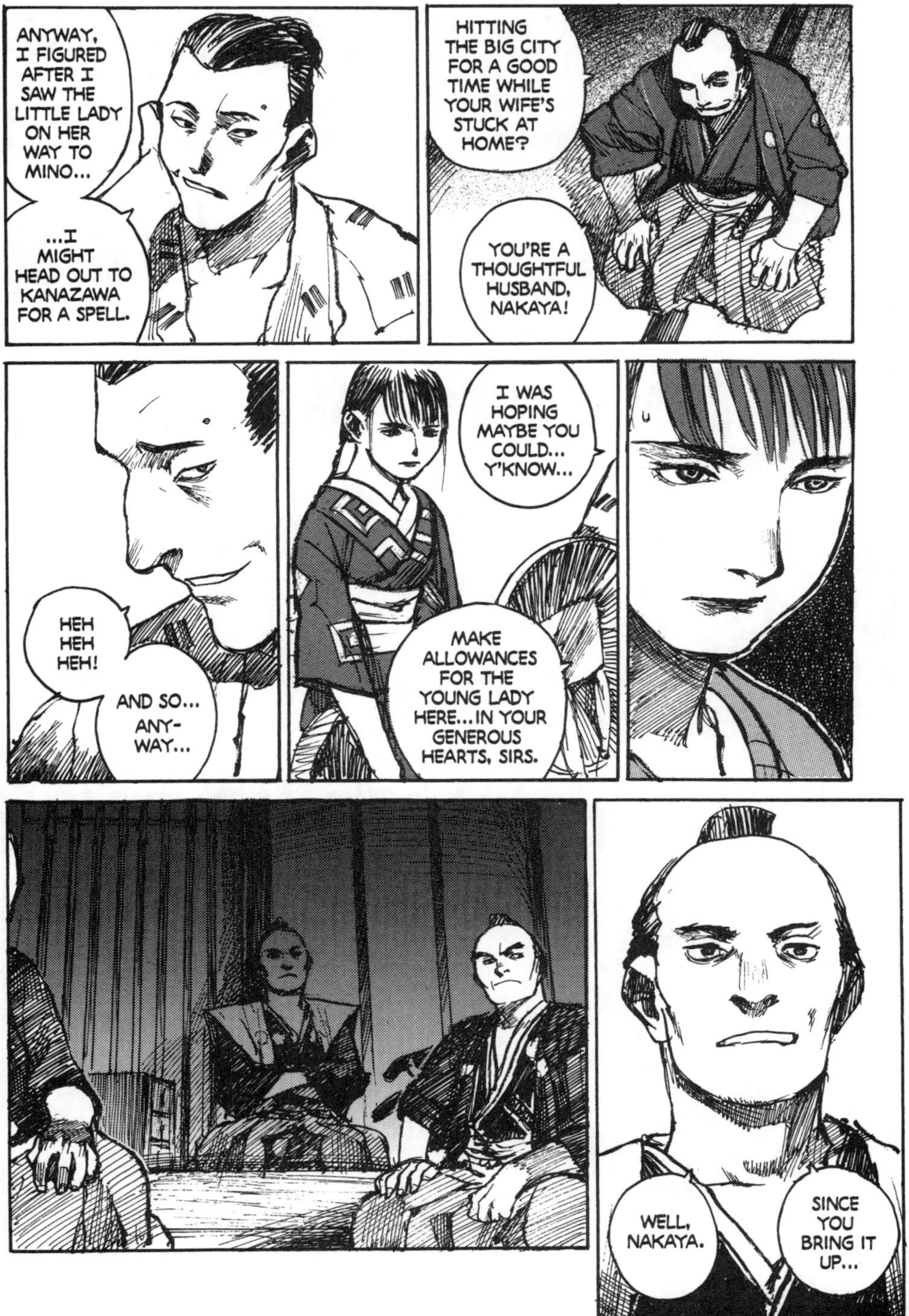
ANYWAY, I FIGURED AFTER I SAW THE LITTLE LADY ON HER WAY TO MINO...
...I MIGHT HEAD OUT TO KANAZAWA FOR A SPELL.
HITTING THE BIG CITY FOR A GOOD TIME WHILE YOUR WIFE'S STUCK AT HOME?
YOU'RE A THOUGHTFUL HUSBAND, NAKAYA!
HEH HEH HEH!
AND SO... ANY-WAY...
I WAS HOPING MAYBE YOU COULD... Y'KNOW...
MAKE ALLOWANCES FOR THE YOUNG LADY HERE...IN YOUR GENEROUS HEARTS, SIRS.
WELL, NAKAYA.
SINCE YOU BRING IT UP...

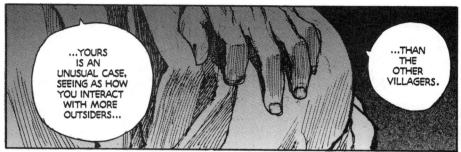

...YOURS IS AN UNUSUAL CASE, SEEING AS HOW YOU INTERACT WITH MORE OUTSIDERS...

...THAN THE OTHER VILLAGERS.

WE HAVE BEEN CONSIDERING IT, AND WE'VE COME TO THE DECISION...

...THAT YOU'LL HAVE TO APPLY FOR A *TEGATA* EVERY TIME YOU TRANSIT THIS *SEKISHO.*

H- HUH?!

ESPECIALLY IN LIGHT OF YOUR...

...*PAST RECORD.*

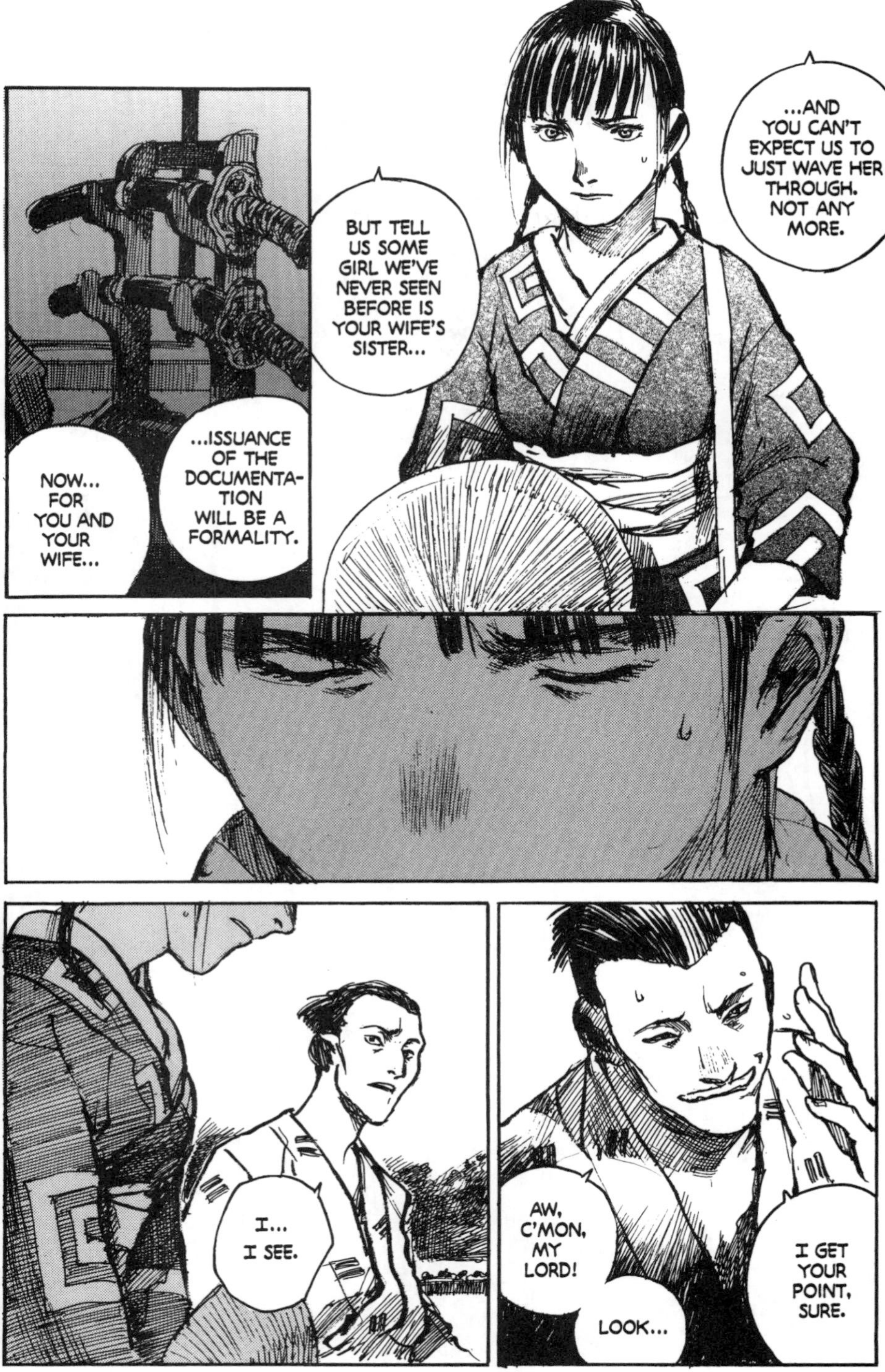
NOW... FOR YOU AND YOUR WIFE...
...ISSUANCE OF THE DOCUMENTATION WILL BE A FORMALITY.
BUT TELL US SOME GIRL WE'VE NEVER SEEN BEFORE IS YOUR WIFE'S SISTER...
...AND YOU CAN'T EXPECT US TO JUST WAVE HER THROUGH. NOT ANY MORE.
I... I SEE.
AW, C'MON, MY LORD!
LOOK...
I GET YOUR POINT, SURE.

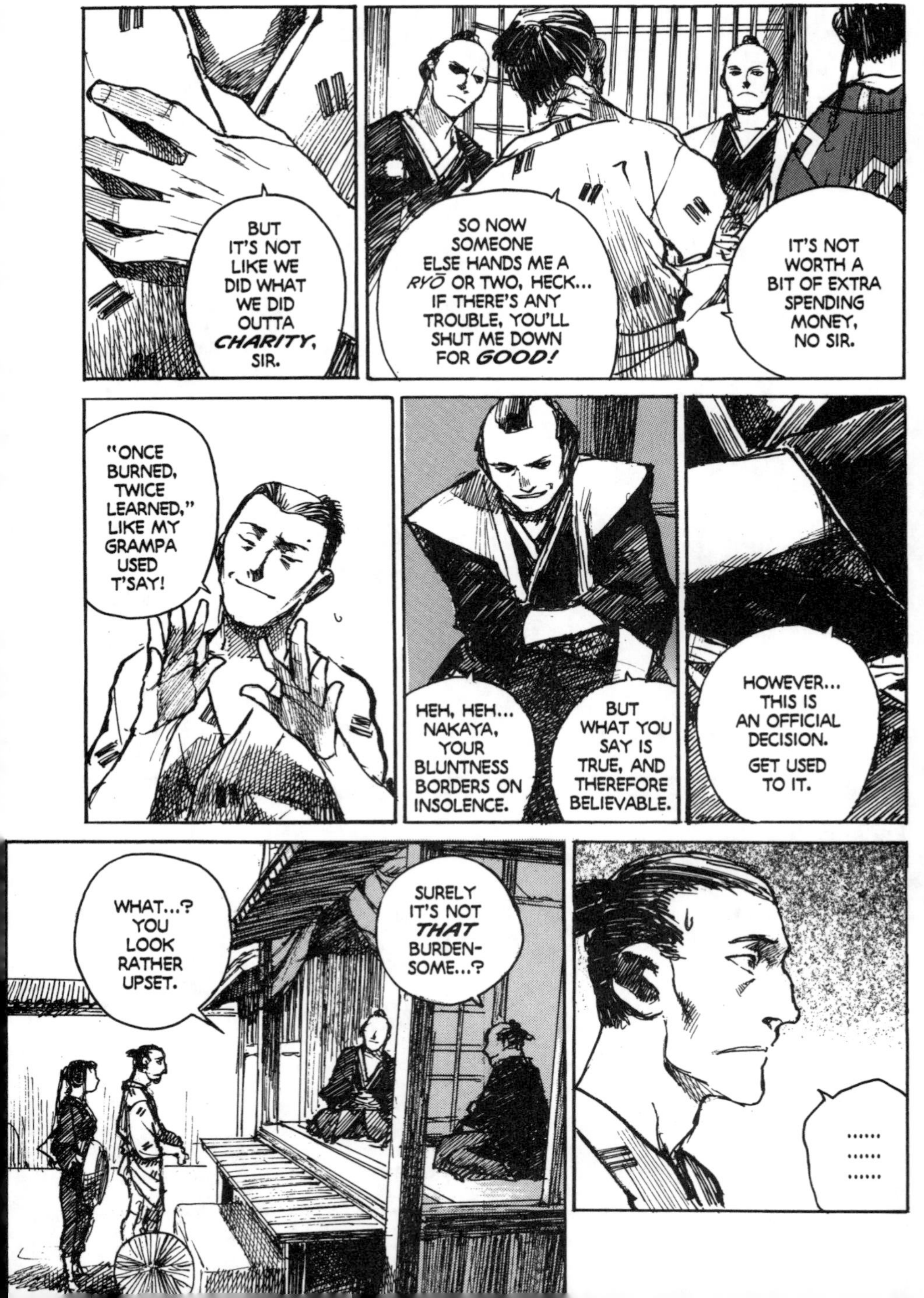
BUT IT'S NOT LIKE WE DID WHAT WE DID OUTTA CHARITY, SIR.
SO NOW SOMEONE ELSE HANDS ME A RYŌ OR TWO, HECK... IF THERE'S ANY TROUBLE, YOU'LL SHUT ME DOWN FOR GOOD!
IT'S NOT WORTH A BIT OF EXTRA SPENDING MONEY, NO SIR.
"ONCE BURNED, TWICE LEARNED," LIKE MY GRAMPA USED T'SAY!
HEH, HEH... NAKAYA, YOUR BLUNTNESS BORDERS ON INSOLENCE.
BUT WHAT YOU SAY IS TRUE, AND THEREFORE BELIEVABLE.
HOWEVER... THIS IS AN OFFICIAL DECISION.
GET USED TO IT.
WHAT...? YOU LOOK RATHER UPSET.
SURELY IT'S NOT THAT BURDEN-SOME...?
......
......
......

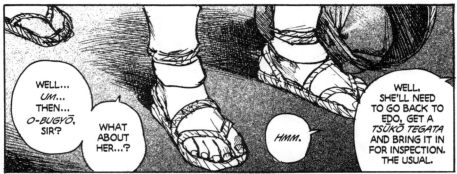

WELL...
UM...
THEN...
O-BUGYŌ,
SIR?

WHAT
ABOUT
HER...?

HMM.

WELL,
SHE'LL NEED
TO GO BACK TO
EDO, GET A
TSŪKŌ TEGATA
AND BRING IT IN
FOR INSPECTION.
THE USUAL.

BUT...
HOW-
EVER...

HAVING
SAID
THAT...

THERE'S
FAULT ON
OUR SIDE FOR
JUST SPRINGING
THIS ON YOU
WITHOUT PRIOR
NOTIFICA-
TION.

AND
IT WOULD
BE SOMEWHAT
UNFAIR FOR THE
YOUNG LADY
TO HAVE TO
TRAVEL ALL THAT
WAY AGAIN...
AND SO!

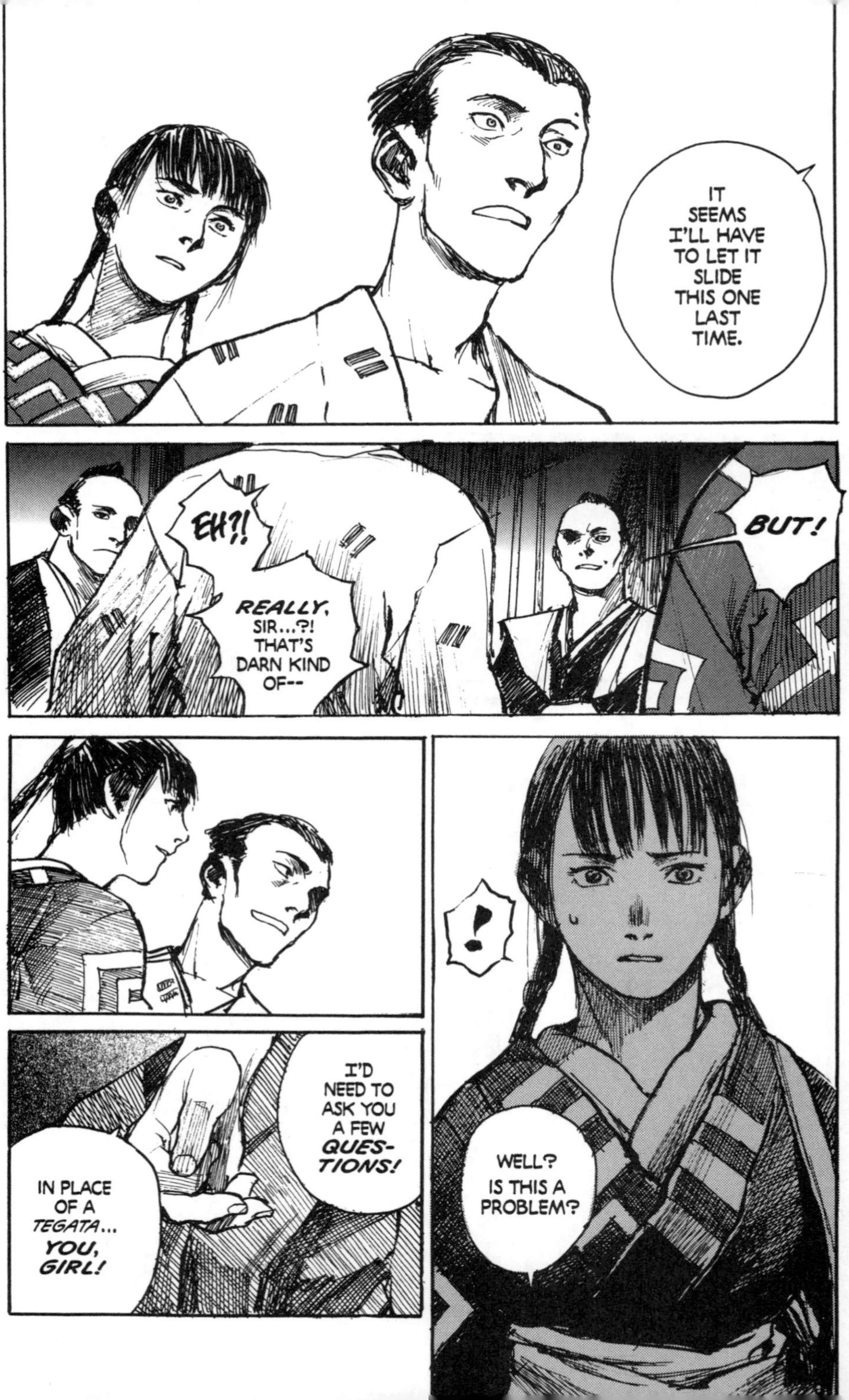
IT SEEMS I'LL HAVE TO LET IT SLIDE THIS ONE LAST TIME.
EH?!
REALLY, SIR...?! THAT'S DARN KIND OF--
BUT!
IN PLACE OF A TEGATA... YOU, GIRL!
I'D NEED TO ASK YOU A FEW QUES-TIONS!
!
WELL? IS THIS A PROBLEM?

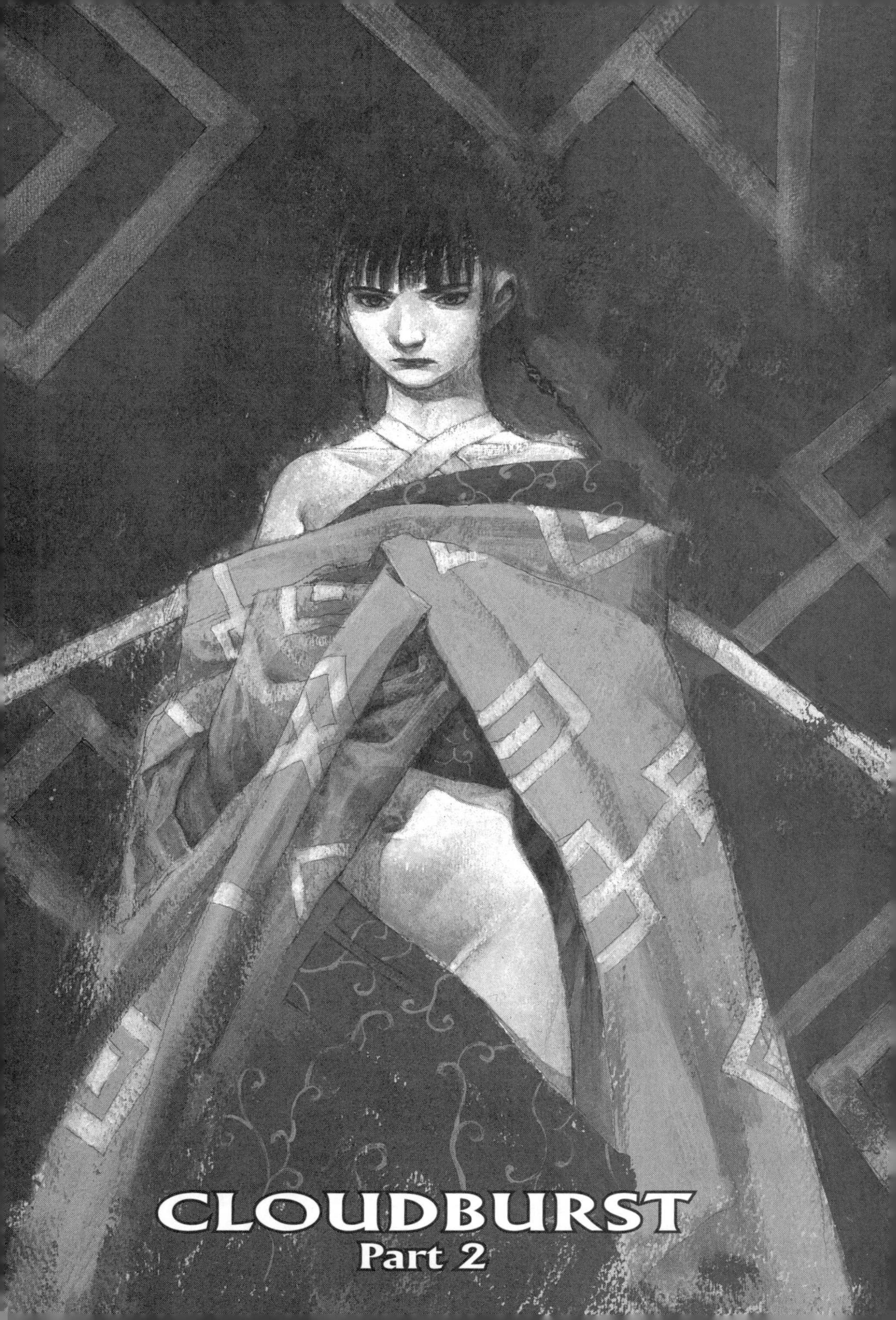

CLOUDBURST
Part 2

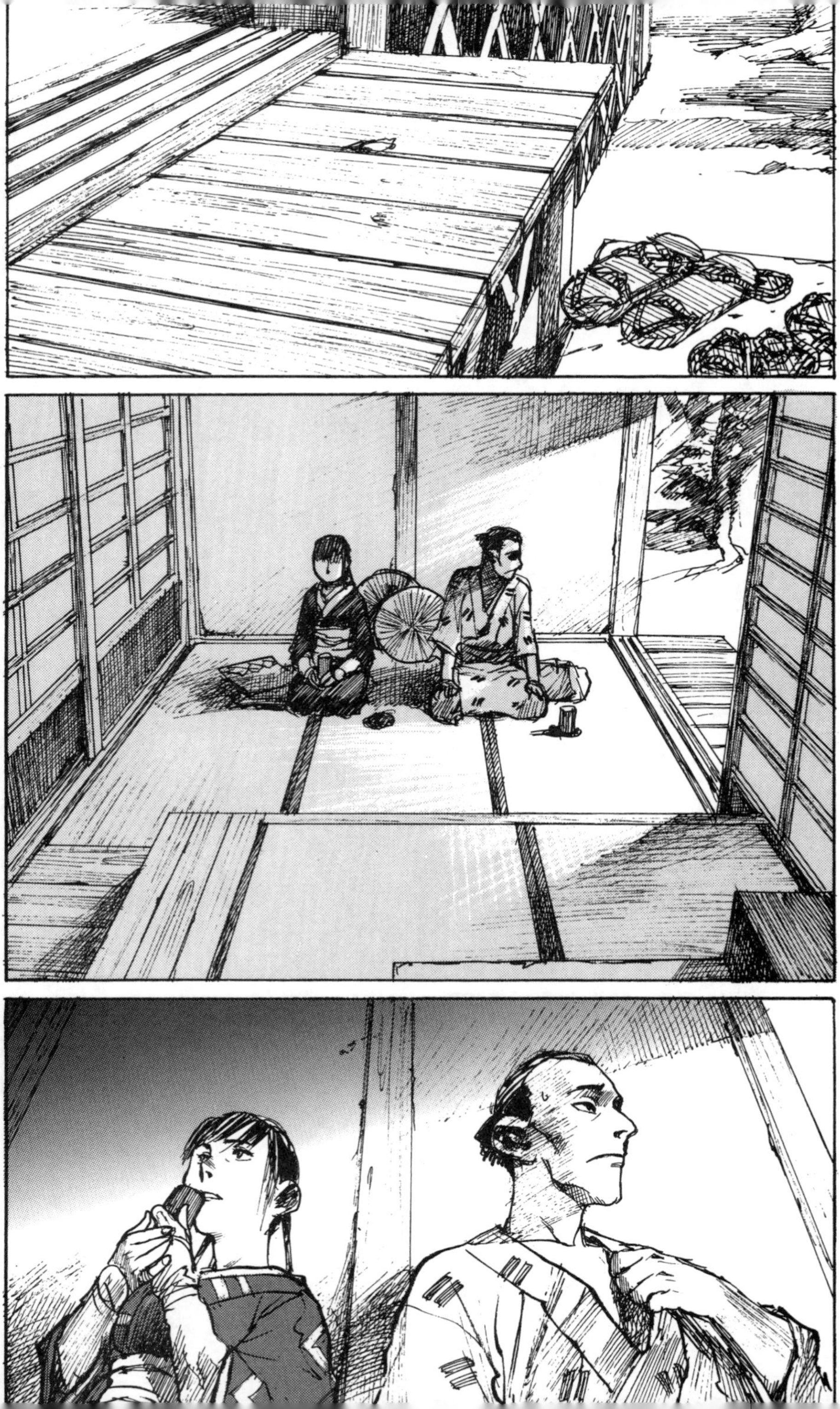

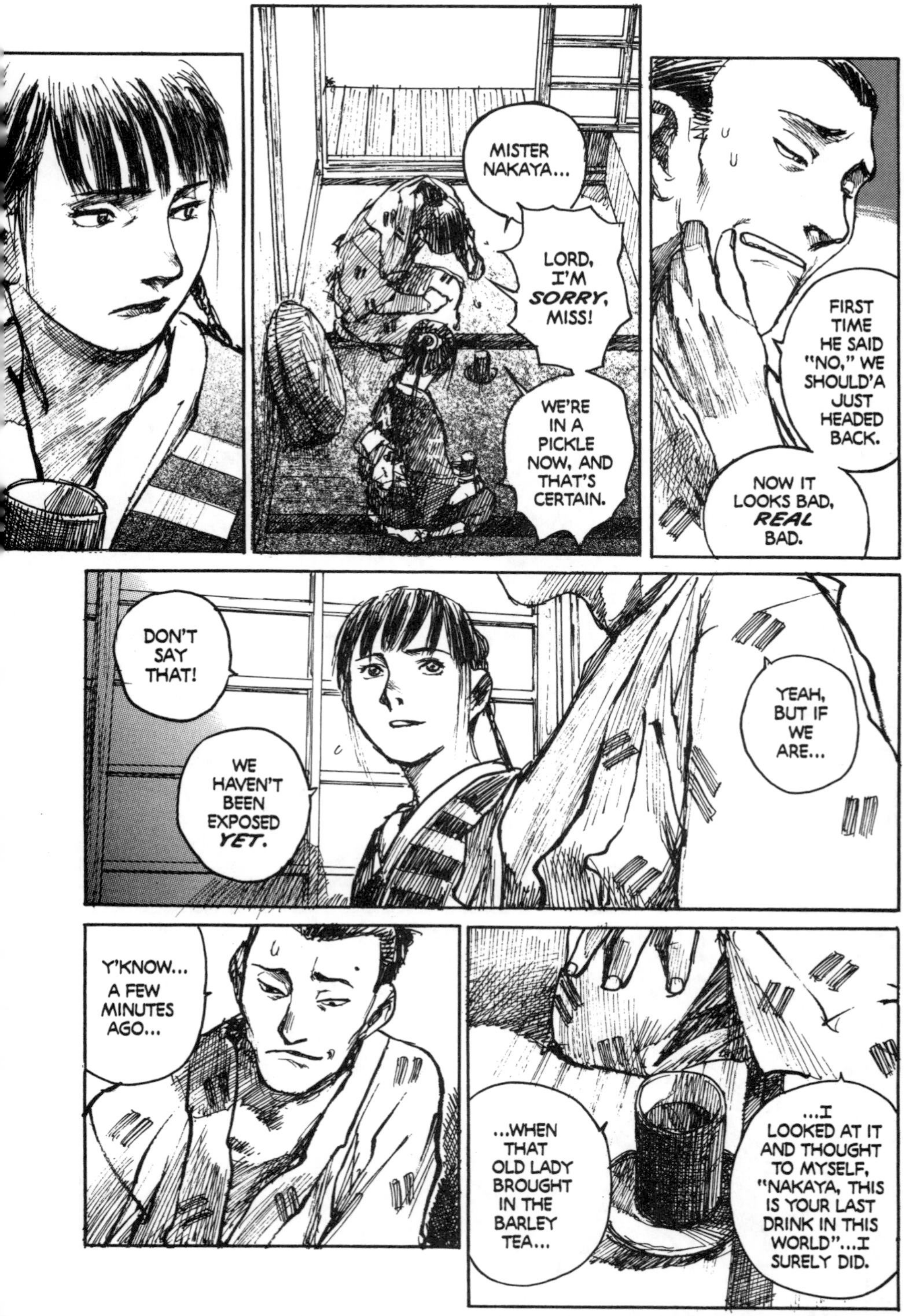
MISTER NAKAYA...
LORD, I'M *SORRY*, MISS!
WE'RE IN A PICKLE NOW, AND THAT'S CERTAIN.
FIRST TIME HE SAID "NO," WE SHOULD'A JUST HEADED BACK.
NOW IT LOOKS BAD, *REAL* BAD.
DON'T SAY THAT!
WE HAVEN'T BEEN EXPOSED *YET*.
YEAH, BUT IF WE ARE...
Y'KNOW... A FEW MINUTES AGO...
...WHEN THAT OLD LADY BROUGHT IN THE BARLEY TEA...
...I LOOKED AT IT AND THOUGHT TO MYSELF, "NAKAYA, THIS IS YOUR LAST DRINK IN THIS WORLD"...I SURELY DID.

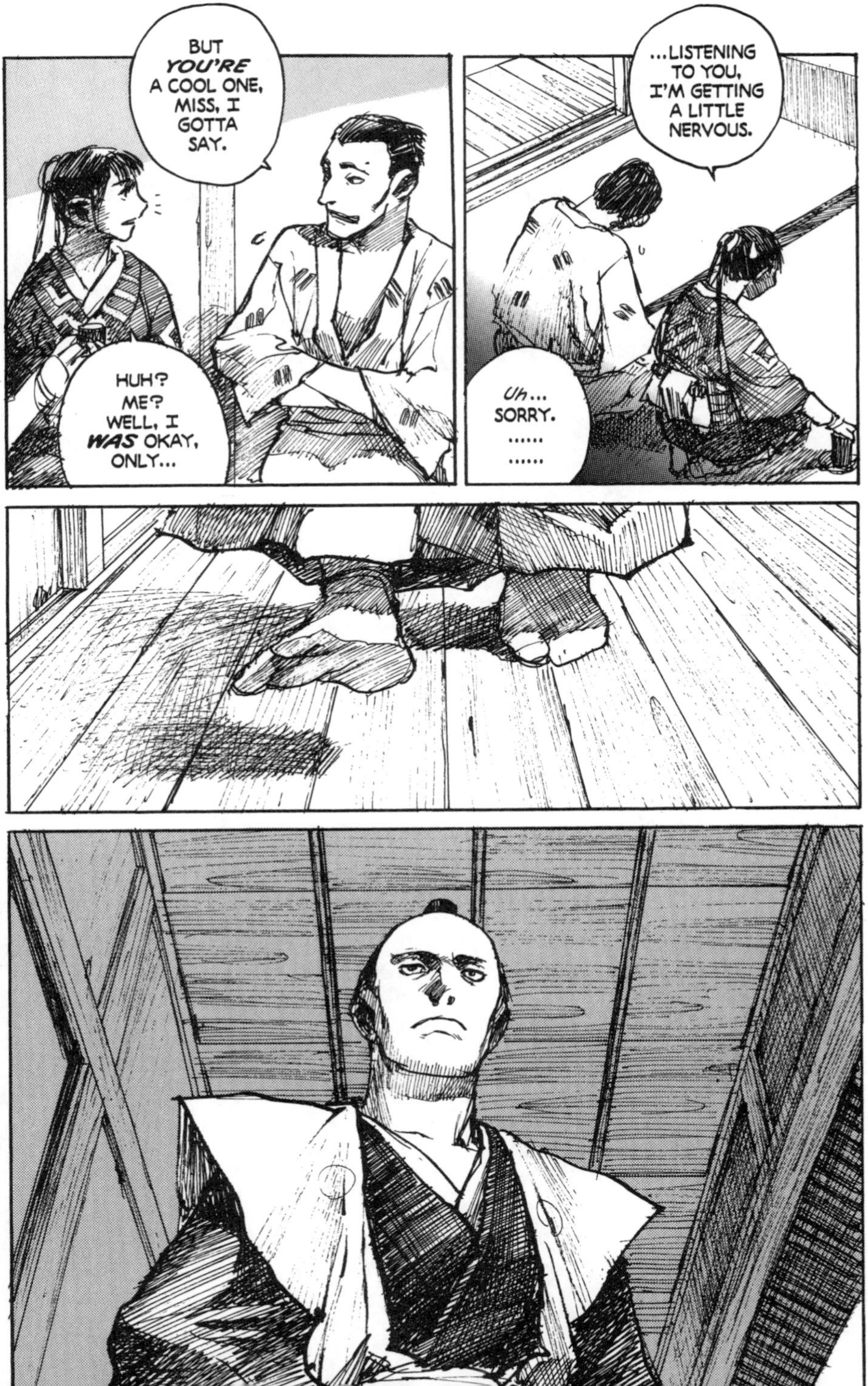
BUT YOU'RE A COOL ONE, MISS, I GOTTA SAY.
HUH? ME? WELL, I WAS OKAY, ONLY...
...LISTENING TO YOU, I'M GETTING A LITTLE NERVOUS.
Uh... SORRY. ....

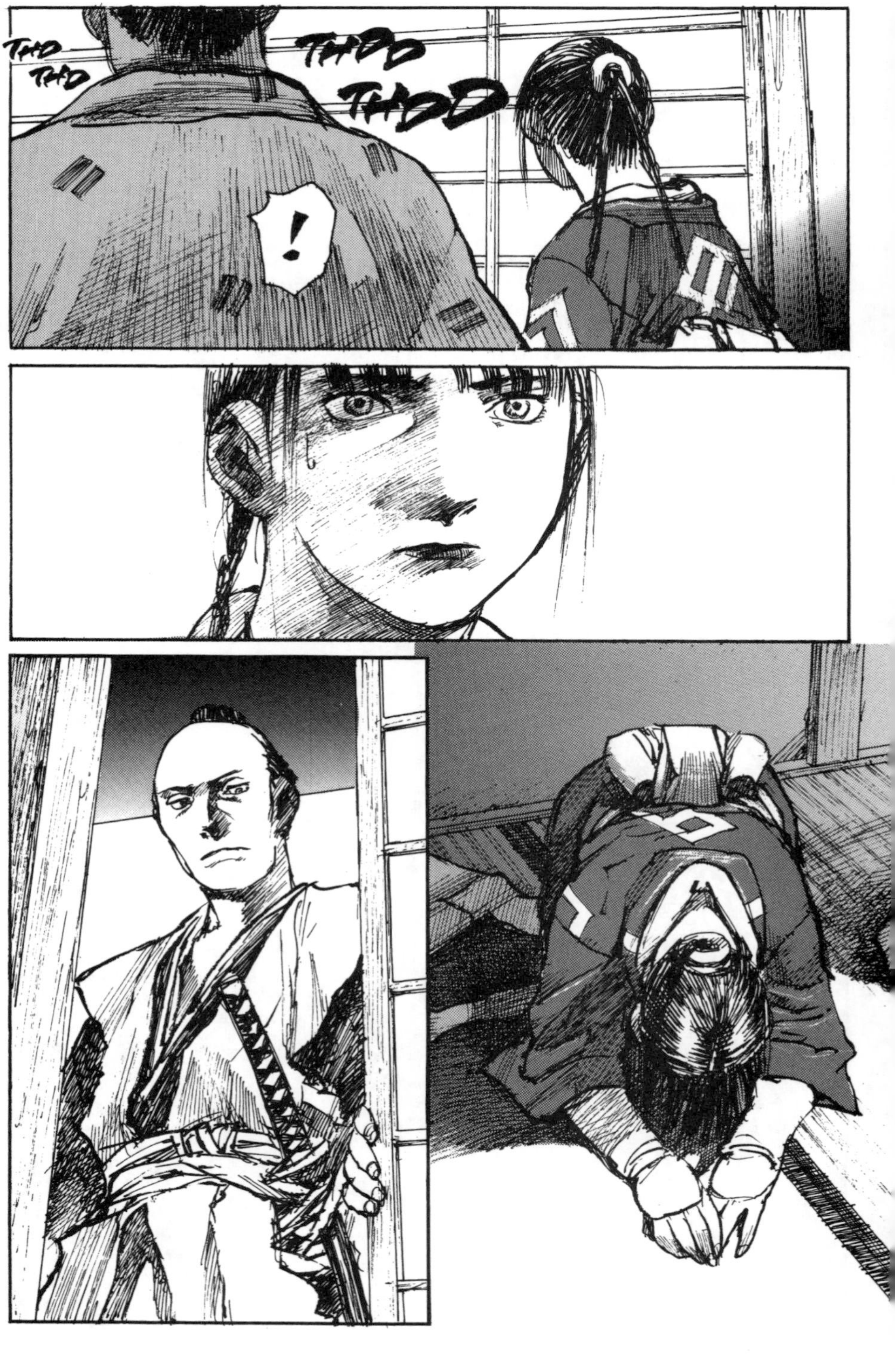
THD THD
THOD THOD
!

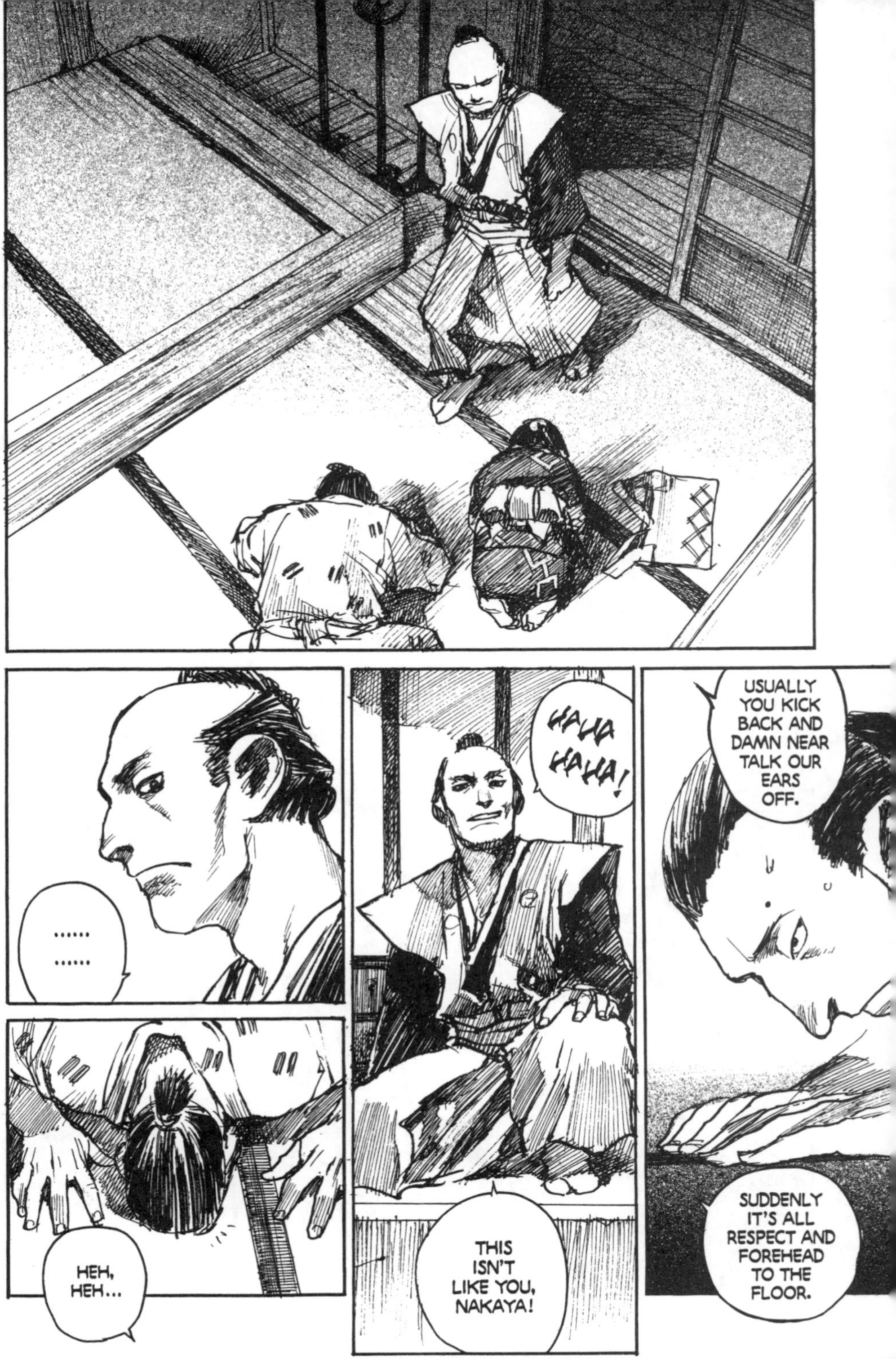
......
......
HEH, HEH...
HAHA HAHA!
THIS ISN'T LIKE YOU, NAKAYA!
USUALLY YOU KICK BACK AND DAMN NEAR TALK OUR EARS OFF.
SUDDENLY IT'S ALL RESPECT AND FOREHEAD TO THE FLOOR.

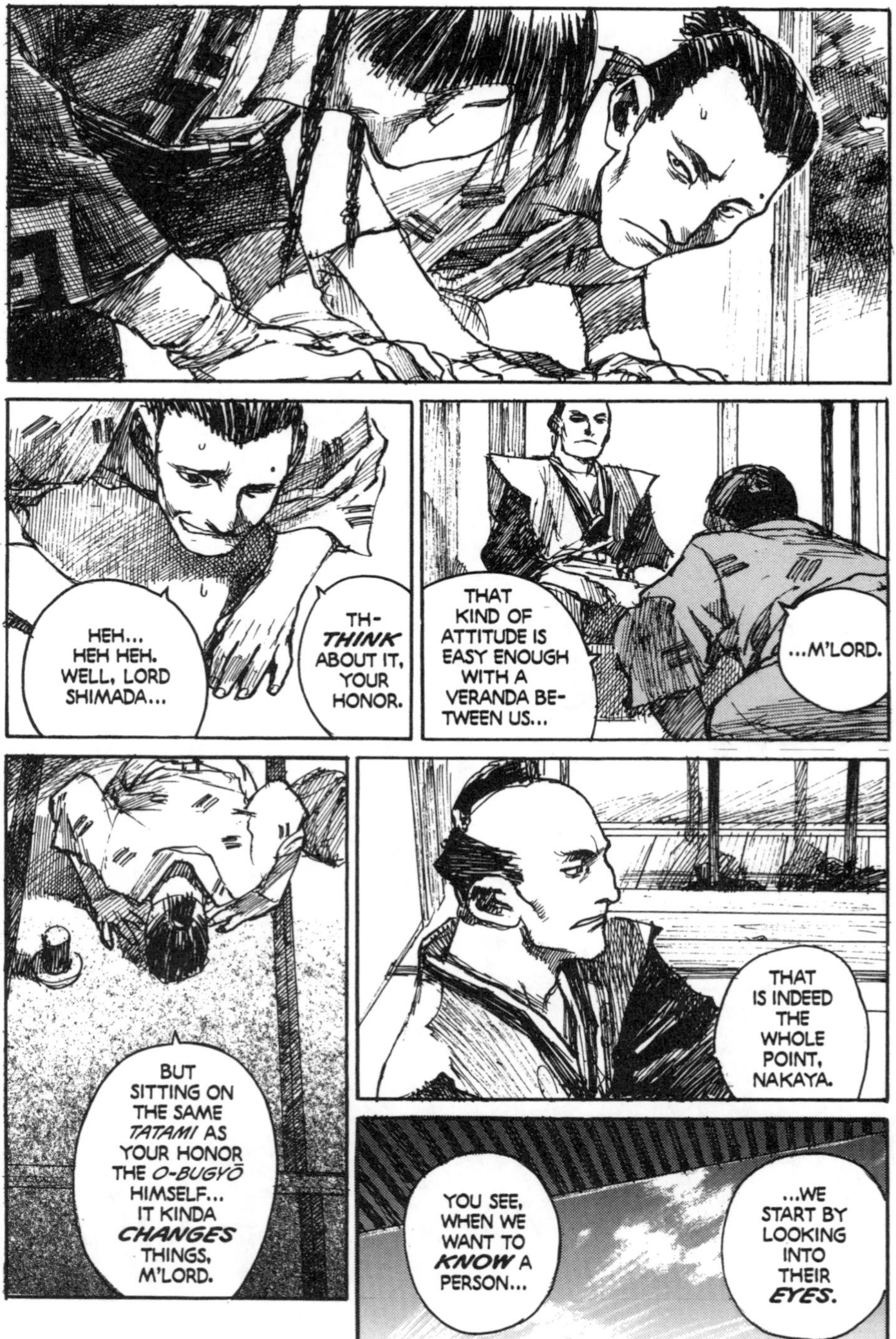
HEH... HEH HEH. WELL, LORD SHIMADA...
TH-*THINK* ABOUT IT, YOUR HONOR.
THAT KIND OF ATTITUDE IS EASY ENOUGH WITH A VERANDA BE-TWEEN US...
...M'LORD.
BUT SITTING ON THE SAME *TATAMI* AS YOUR HONOR THE *O-BUGYŌ* HIMSELF... IT KINDA ***CHANGES*** THINGS, M'LORD.
THAT IS INDEED THE WHOLE POINT, NAKAYA.
YOU SEE, WHEN WE WANT TO ***KNOW*** A PERSON...
...WE START BY LOOKING INTO THEIR ***EYES***.

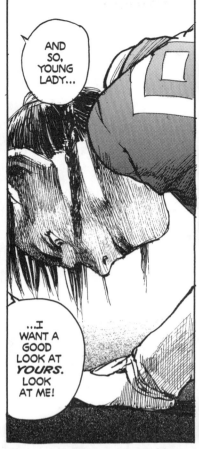

AND SO, YOUNG LADY...

...I WANT A GOOD LOOK AT *YOURS*. LOOK AT ME!

......
......

HMM. SEEING YOU UP CLOSE...

...YOU *DO* LOOK A BIT LIKE NAYAKA'S WIFE.

DON'T YOU...?

EH...?

OH... WELL, *UM*...

VERY CLEVER...

I BET HE DOESN'T THINK THAT AT ALL.

SO--YOU REMEMBER THE BIG FUSS A WHILE BACK, NAKAYA... EH?

HUH?

THE *MURDERS*-- THOSE DRUG SALESMEN, JUST DOWN THE ROAD.

UH... OH, YEAH... RIGHT.

WANTED POSTERS UP ALONG ALL THE ROADS...A MAN AND A WOMAN... NEVER DID CATCH THEM.

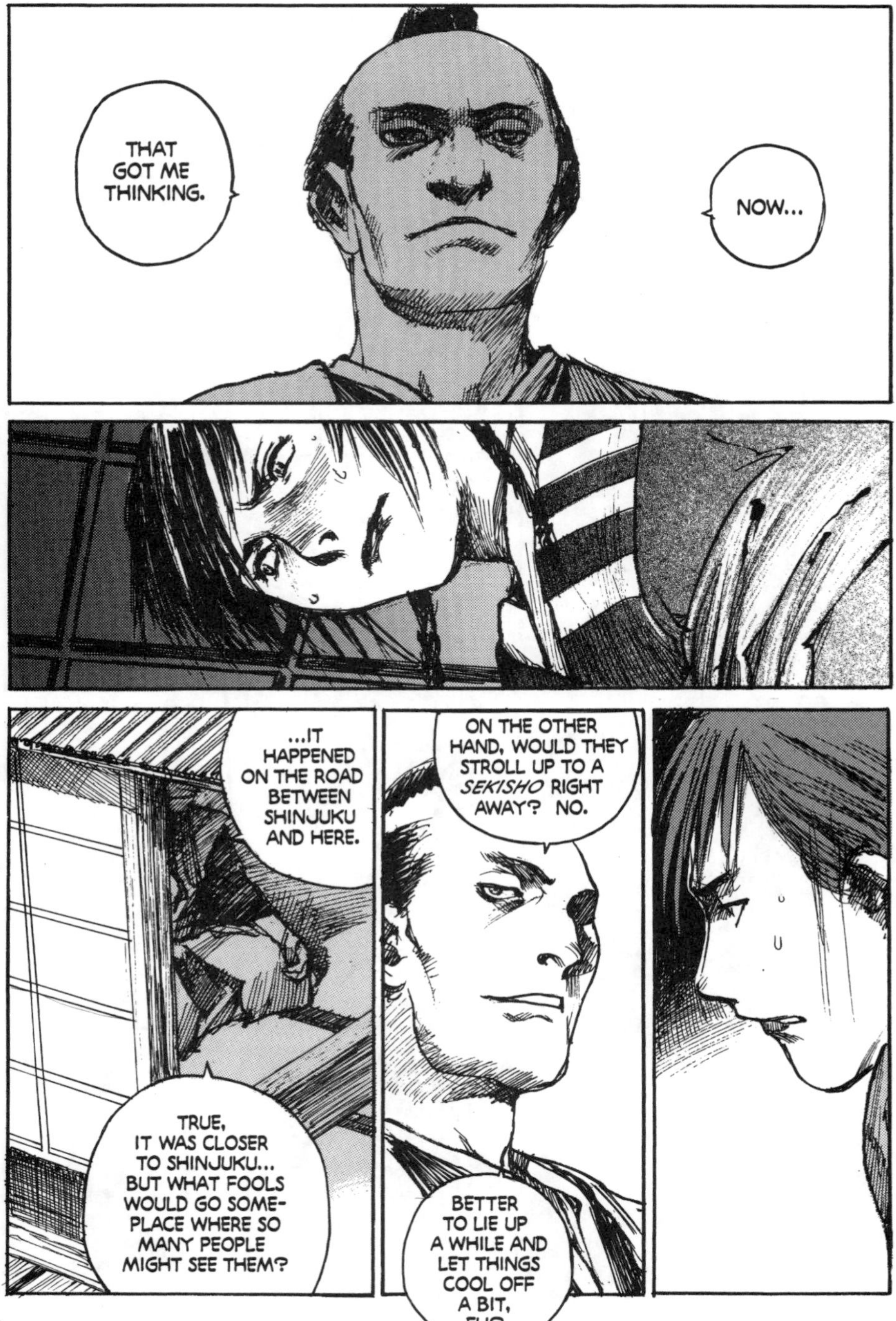
THAT GOT ME THINKING.
NOW...
...IT HAPPENED ON THE ROAD BETWEEN SHINJUKU AND HERE.
TRUE, IT WAS CLOSER TO SHINJUKU... BUT WHAT FOOLS WOULD GO SOME-PLACE WHERE SO MANY PEOPLE MIGHT SEE THEM?
ON THE OTHER HAND, WOULD THEY STROLL UP TO A *SEKISHO* RIGHT AWAY? NO.
BETTER TO LIE UP A WHILE AND LET THINGS COOL OFF A BIT, EH?

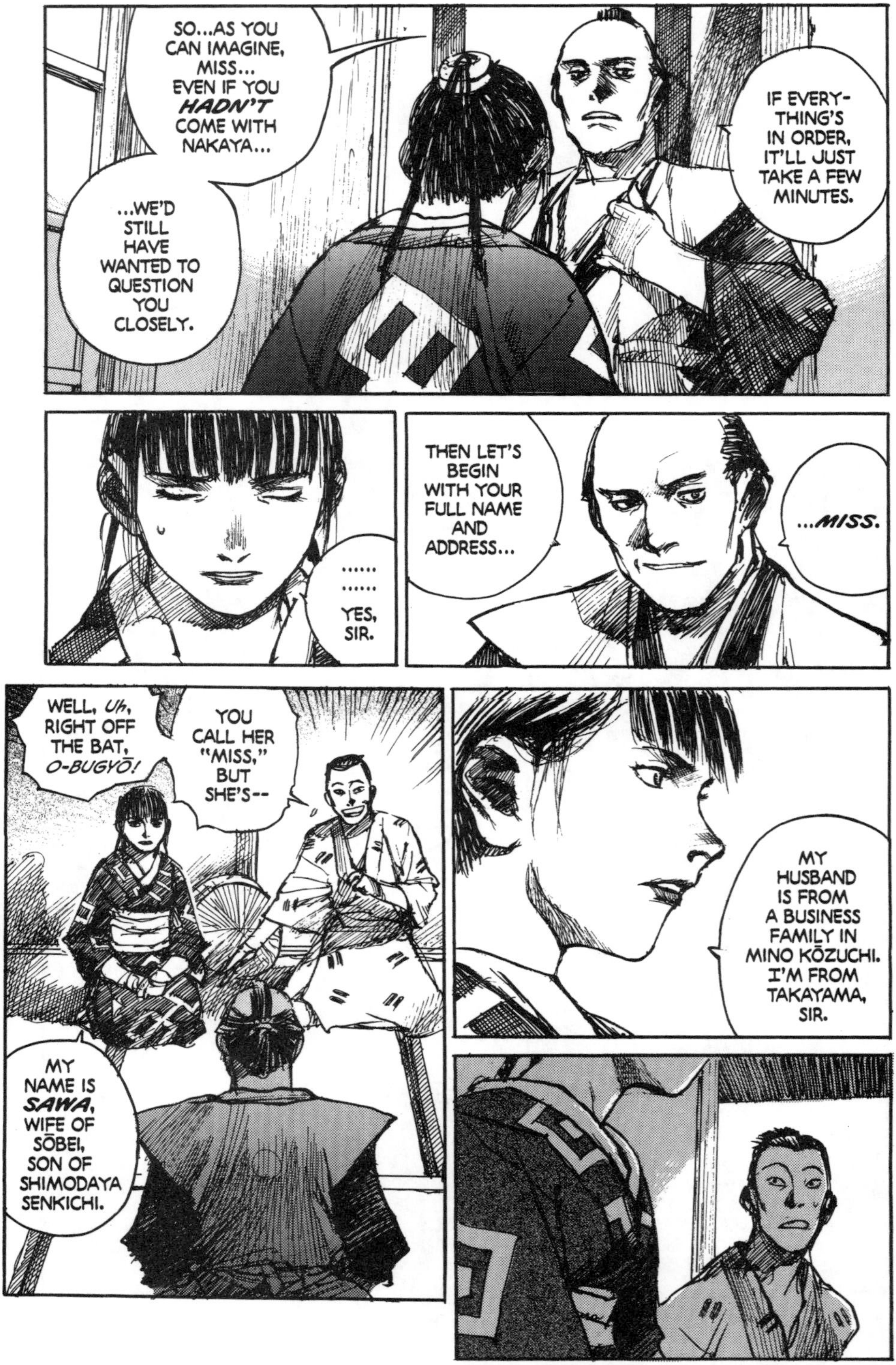
SO...AS YOU CAN IMAGINE, MISS... EVEN IF YOU HADN'T COME WITH NAKAYA...
...WE'D STILL HAVE WANTED TO QUESTION YOU CLOSELY.
IF EVERY-THING'S IN ORDER, IT'LL JUST TAKE A FEW MINUTES.
.... YES, SIR.
THEN LET'S BEGIN WITH YOUR FULL NAME AND ADDRESS...
...MISS.
WELL, Uh, RIGHT OFF THE BAT, O-BUGYŌ!
YOU CALL HER "MISS," BUT SHE'S--
MY NAME IS SAWA, WIFE OF SŌBEI, SON OF SHIMODAYA SENKICHI.
MY HUSBAND IS FROM A BUSINESS FAMILY IN MINO KŌZUCHI. I'M FROM TAKAYAMA, SIR.

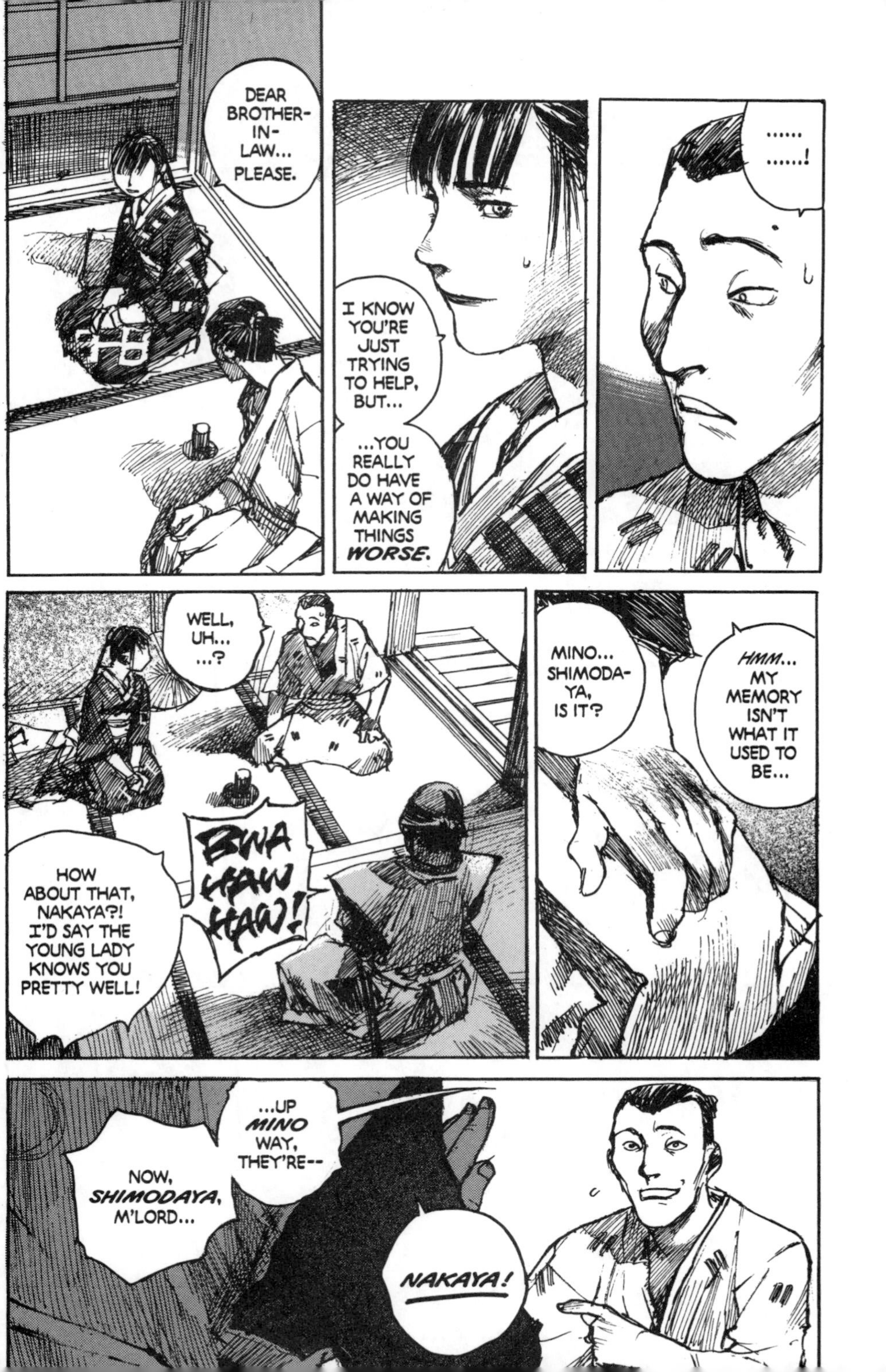
DEAR BROTHER-IN-LAW... PLEASE.
I KNOW YOU'RE JUST TRYING TO HELP, BUT...
...YOU REALLY DO HAVE A WAY OF MAKING THINGS *WORSE*.
......
......!
WELL, UH... ...?
HOW ABOUT THAT, NAKAYA?! I'D SAY THE YOUNG LADY KNOWS YOU PRETTY WELL!
BWA HAW HAW!
MINO... SHIMODA-YA, IS IT?
HMM... MY MEMORY ISN'T WHAT IT USED TO BE...
NOW, *SHIMODAYA*, M'LORD...
...UP *MINO* WAY, THEY'RE--
NAKAYA!

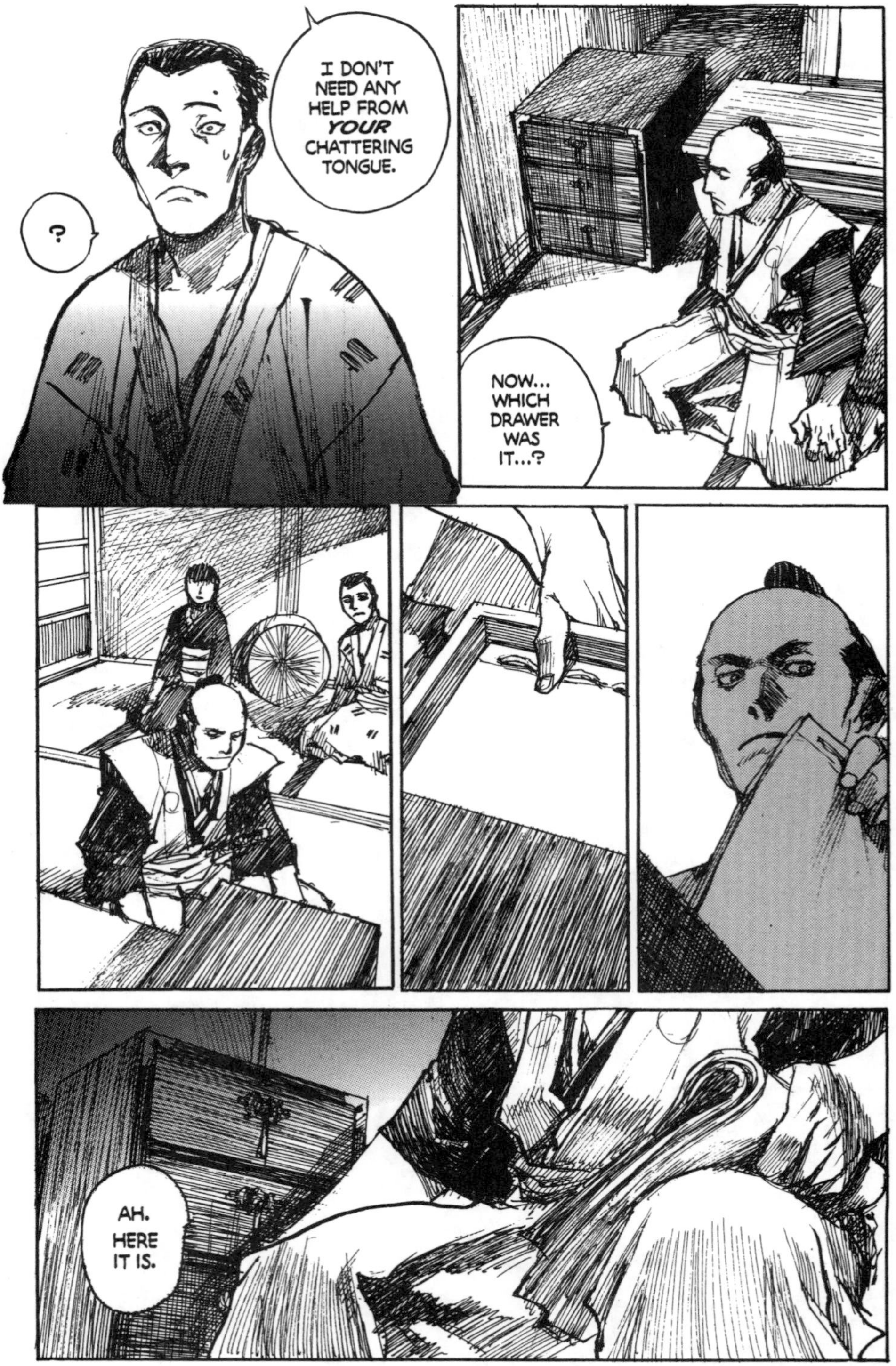
I DON'T NEED ANY HELP FROM *YOUR* CHATTERING TONGUE.
?
NOW... WHICH DRAWER WAS IT...?
AH. HERE IT IS.

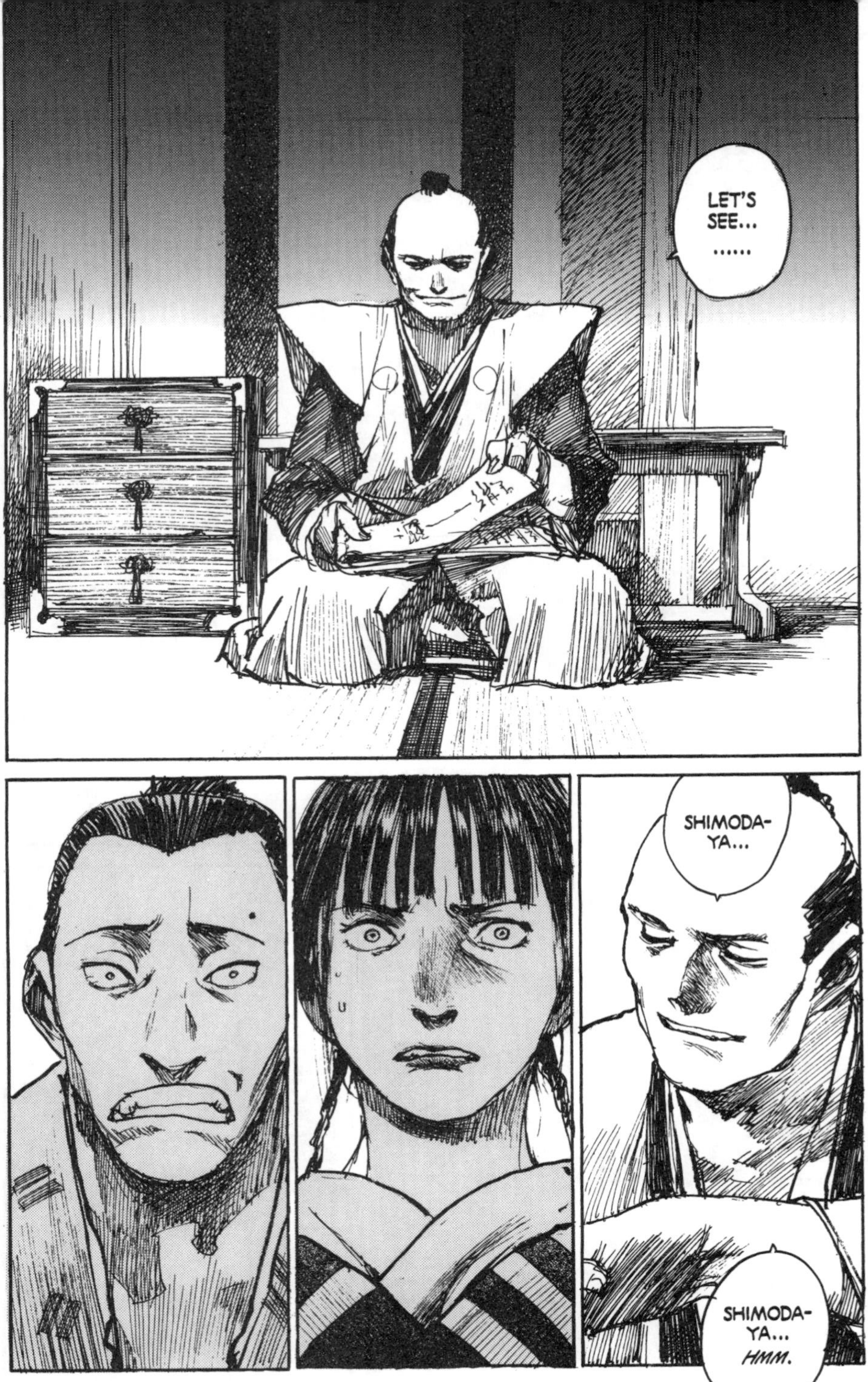
LET'S SEE... ......
SHIMODA-YA...
SHIMODA-YA... *HMM.*

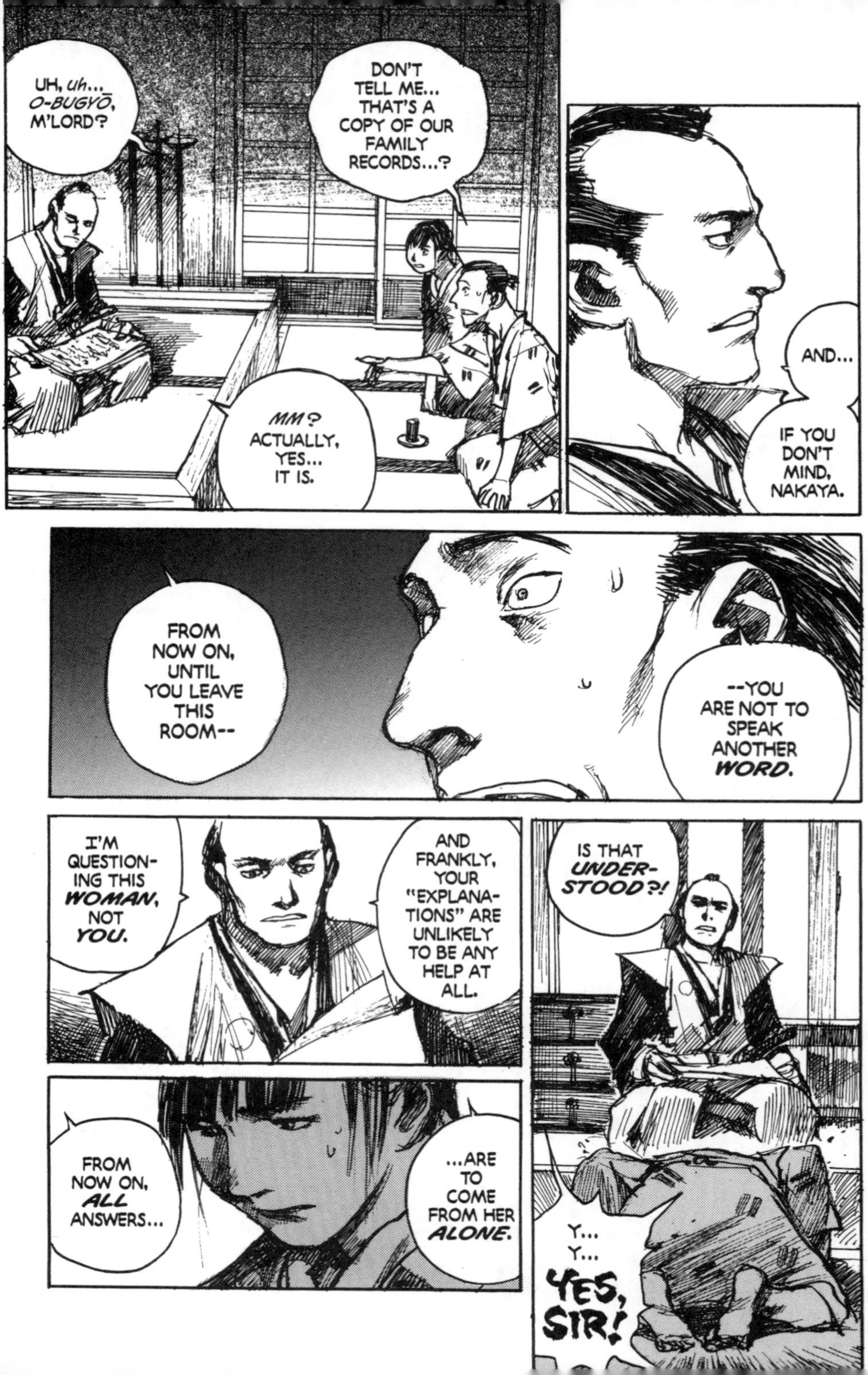
UH, *uh*... *O-BUGYŌ*, M'LORD?
DON'T TELL ME... THAT'S A COPY OF OUR FAMILY RECORDS...?
MM? ACTUALLY, YES... IT IS.
AND...
IF YOU DON'T MIND, NAKAYA.
FROM NOW ON, UNTIL YOU LEAVE THIS ROOM--
--YOU ARE NOT TO SPEAK ANOTHER ***WORD***.
I'M QUESTIONING THIS ***WOMAN***, NOT ***YOU***.
AND FRANKLY, YOUR "EXPLANATIONS" ARE UNLIKELY TO BE ANY HELP AT ALL.
FROM NOW ON, ***ALL*** ANSWERS...
...ARE TO COME FROM HER ***ALONE***.
IS THAT ***UNDERSTOOD***?!
Y... Y...
YES, SIR!

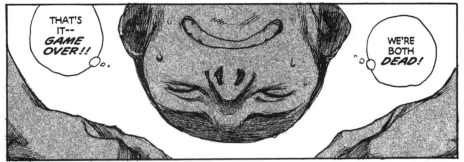

THAT'S IT-- *GAME OVER!!*

WE'RE BOTH *DEAD!*

SO.

MRS. SHIMODAYA SAWA.

ACCORDING TO THIS REPORT, YOUR HUSBAND, SŌBEI, IS THE SECOND-BORN SON OF THE OWNERS OF THE SHIMODAYA INN...

...AND THEY'VE BEEN IN BUSINESS IN MINO FOR THREE GENERATIONS.

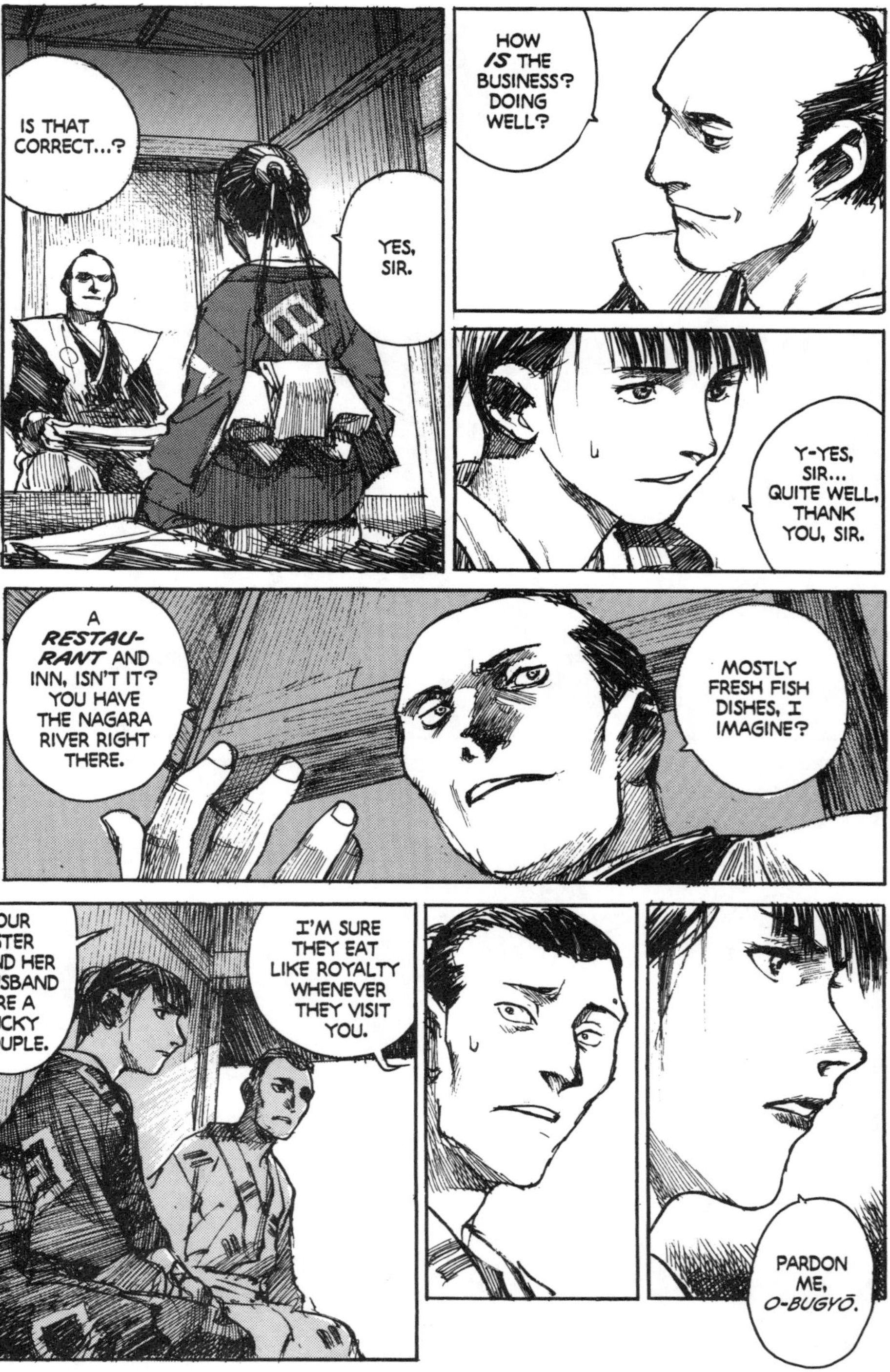
IS THAT CORRECT...?
YES, SIR.
HOW *IS* THE BUSINESS? DOING WELL?
Y-YES, SIR... QUITE WELL, THANK YOU, SIR.
A *RESTAU-RANT* AND INN, ISN'T IT? YOU HAVE THE NAGARA RIVER RIGHT THERE.
MOSTLY FRESH FISH DISHES, I IMAGINE?
YOUR SISTER AND HER HUSBAND ARE A LUCKY COUPLE.
I'M SURE THEY EAT LIKE ROYALTY WHENEVER THEY VISIT YOU.
PARDON ME, *O-BUGYŌ*.

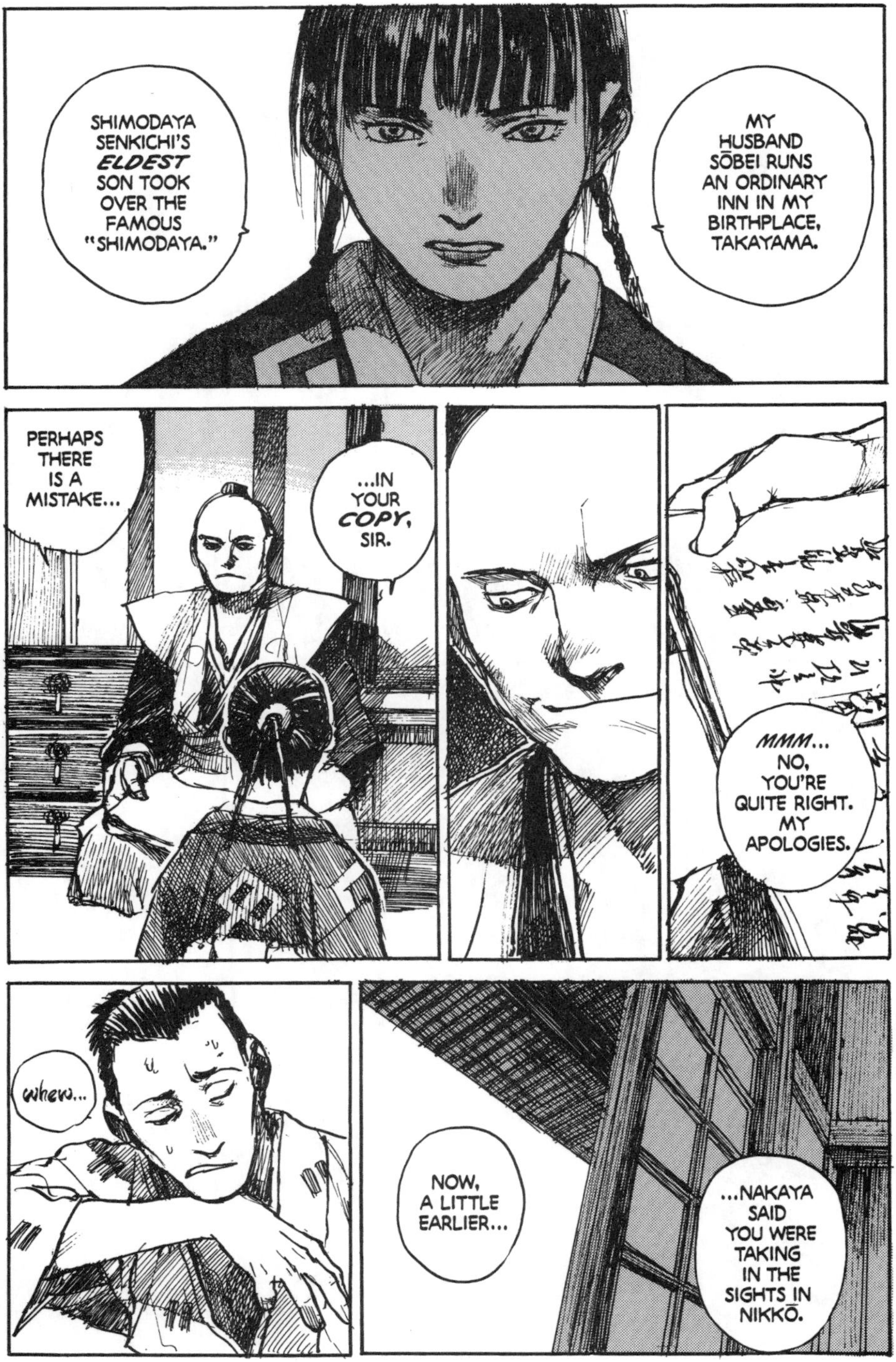

SHIMODAYA SENKICHI'S *ELDEST* SON TOOK OVER THE FAMOUS "SHIMODAYA."
MY HUSBAND SŌBEI RUNS AN ORDINARY INN IN MY BIRTHPLACE, TAKAYAMA.
PERHAPS THERE IS A MISTAKE...
...IN YOUR *COPY*, SIR.
MMM... NO, YOU'RE QUITE RIGHT. MY APOLOGIES.
whew...
NOW, A LITTLE EARLIER...
...NAKAYA SAID YOU WERE TAKING IN THE SIGHTS IN NIKKŌ.

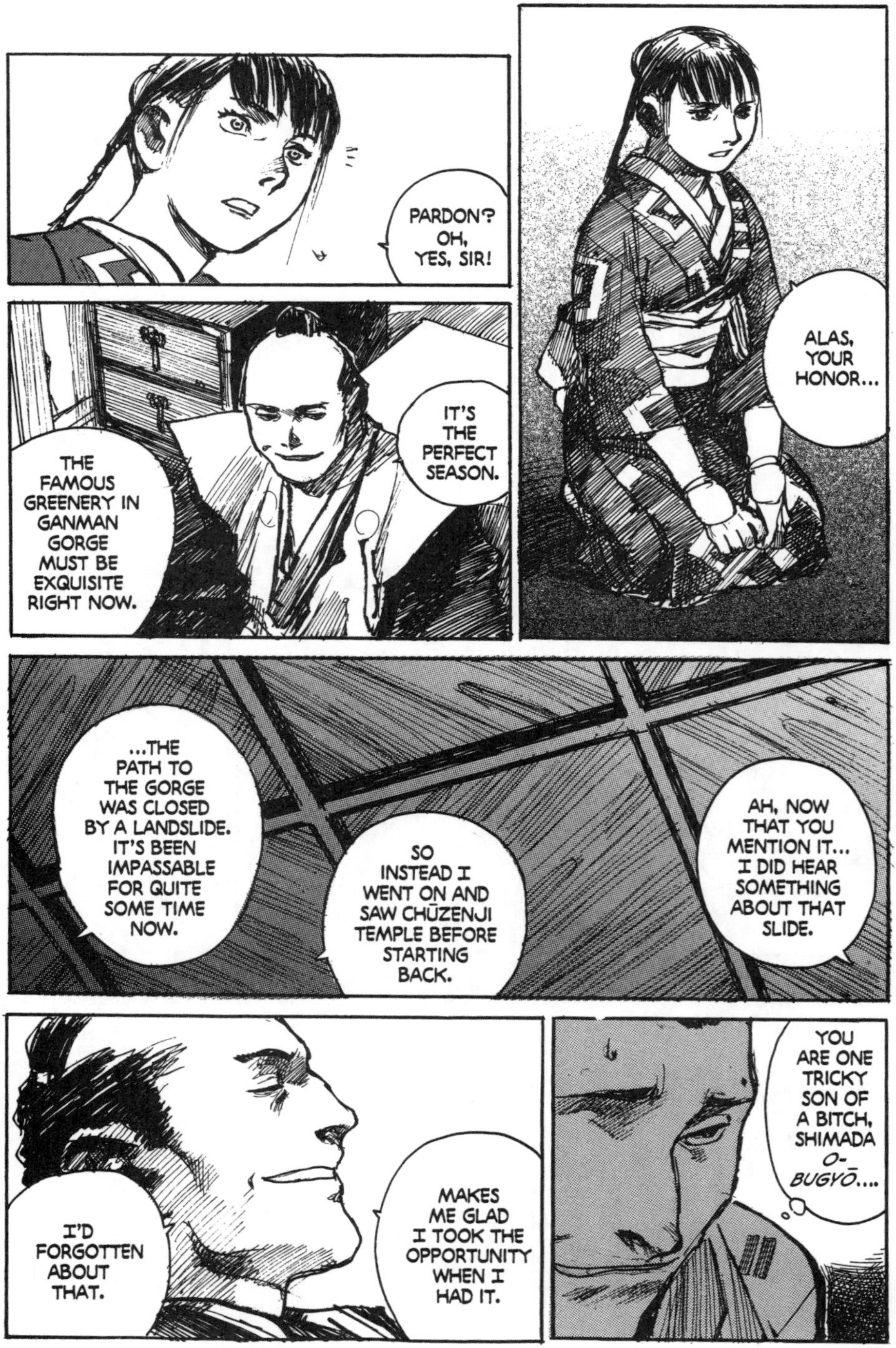
PARDON? OH, YES, SIR!
THE FAMOUS GREENERY IN GANMAN GORGE MUST BE EXQUISITE RIGHT NOW.
IT'S THE PERFECT SEASON.
ALAS, YOUR HONOR...
...THE PATH TO THE GORGE WAS CLOSED BY A LANDSLIDE. IT'S BEEN IMPASSABLE FOR QUITE SOME TIME NOW.
SO INSTEAD I WENT ON AND SAW CHŪZENJI TEMPLE BEFORE STARTING BACK.
AH, NOW THAT YOU MENTION IT... I DID HEAR SOMETHING ABOUT THAT SLIDE.
I'D FORGOTTEN ABOUT THAT.
MAKES ME GLAD I TOOK THE OPPORTUNITY WHEN I HAD IT.
YOU ARE ONE TRICKY SON OF A BITCH, SHIMADA *O-BUGYŌ*....

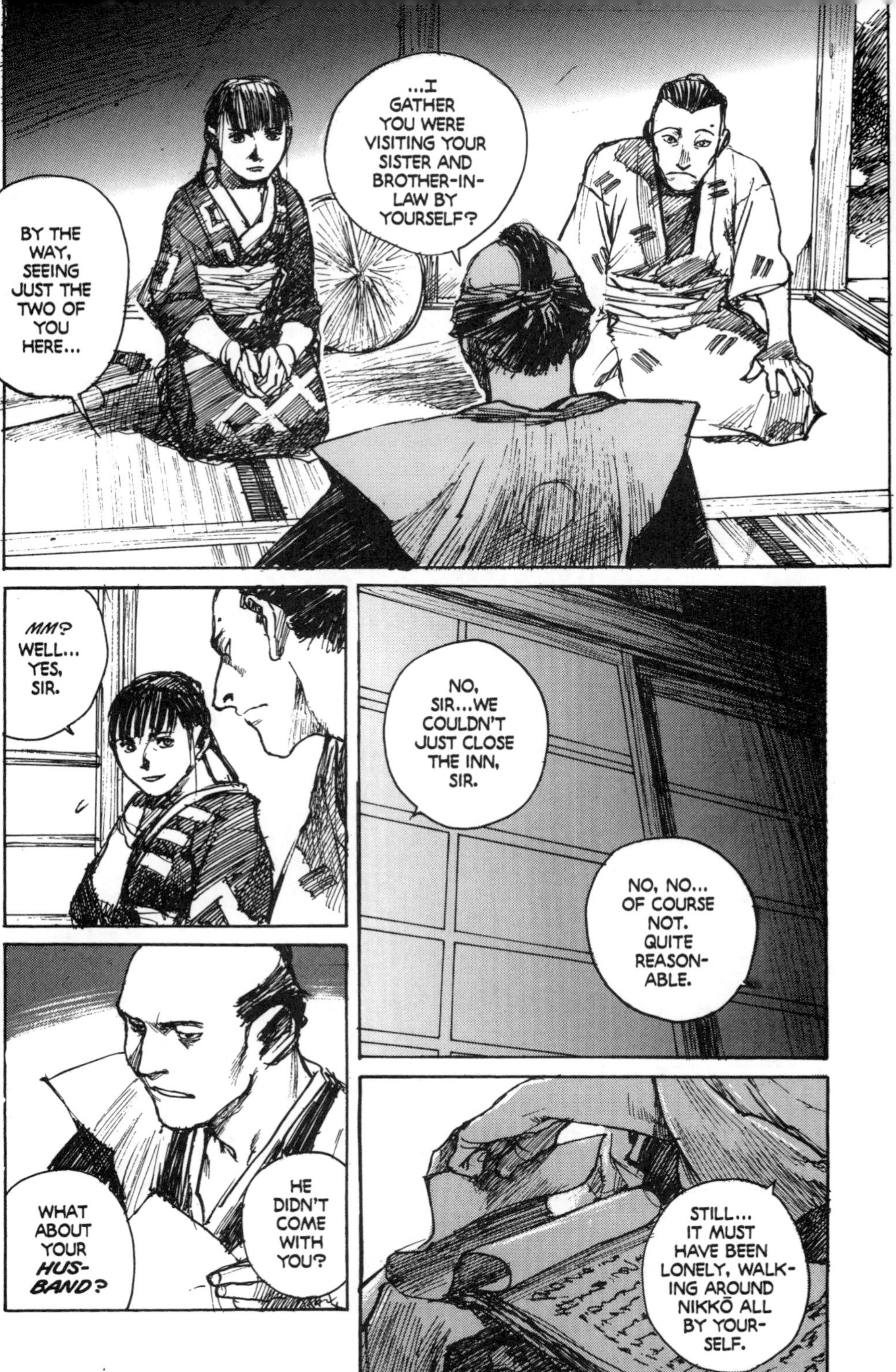
BY THE WAY, SEEING JUST THE TWO OF YOU HERE...
...I GATHER YOU WERE VISITING YOUR SISTER AND BROTHER-IN-LAW BY YOURSELF?
MM? WELL... YES, SIR.
NO, SIR...WE COULDN'T JUST CLOSE THE INN, SIR.
NO, NO... OF COURSE NOT. QUITE REASONABLE.
WHAT ABOUT YOUR HUSBAND?
HE DIDN'T COME WITH YOU?
STILL... IT MUST HAVE BEEN LONELY, WALKING AROUND NIKKŌ ALL BY YOURSELF.

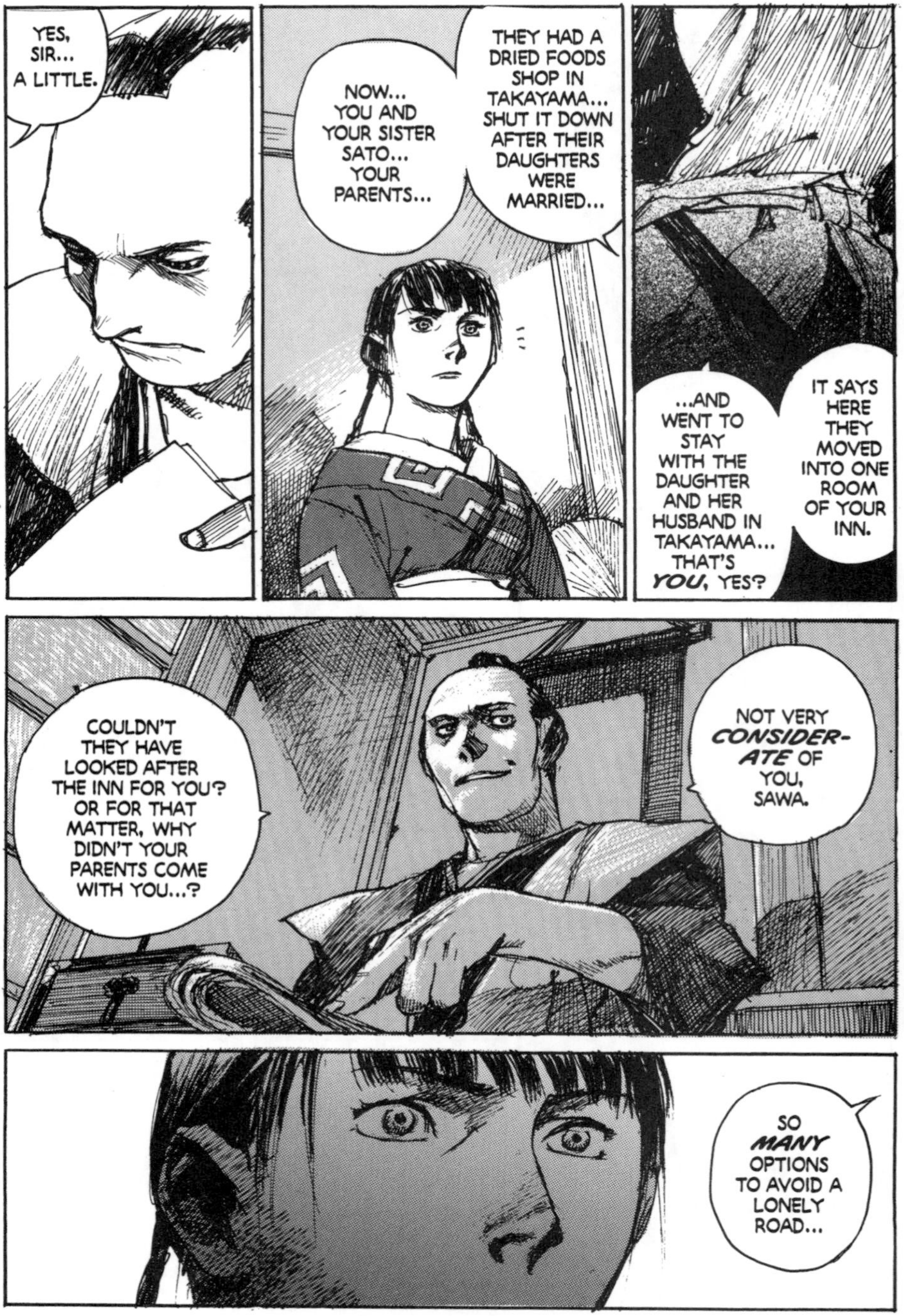
YES, SIR... A LITTLE.
NOW... YOU AND YOUR SISTER SATO... YOUR PARENTS...
THEY HAD A DRIED FOODS SHOP IN TAKAYAMA... SHUT IT DOWN AFTER THEIR DAUGHTERS WERE MARRIED...
...AND WENT TO STAY WITH THE DAUGHTER AND HER HUSBAND IN TAKAYAMA... THAT'S *YOU*, YES?
IT SAYS HERE THEY MOVED INTO ONE ROOM OF YOUR INN.
COULDN'T THEY HAVE LOOKED AFTER THE INN FOR YOU? OR FOR THAT MATTER, WHY DIDN'T YOUR PARENTS COME WITH YOU...?
NOT VERY *CONSIDER-ATE* OF YOU, SAWA.
SO *MANY* OPTIONS TO AVOID A LONELY ROAD...

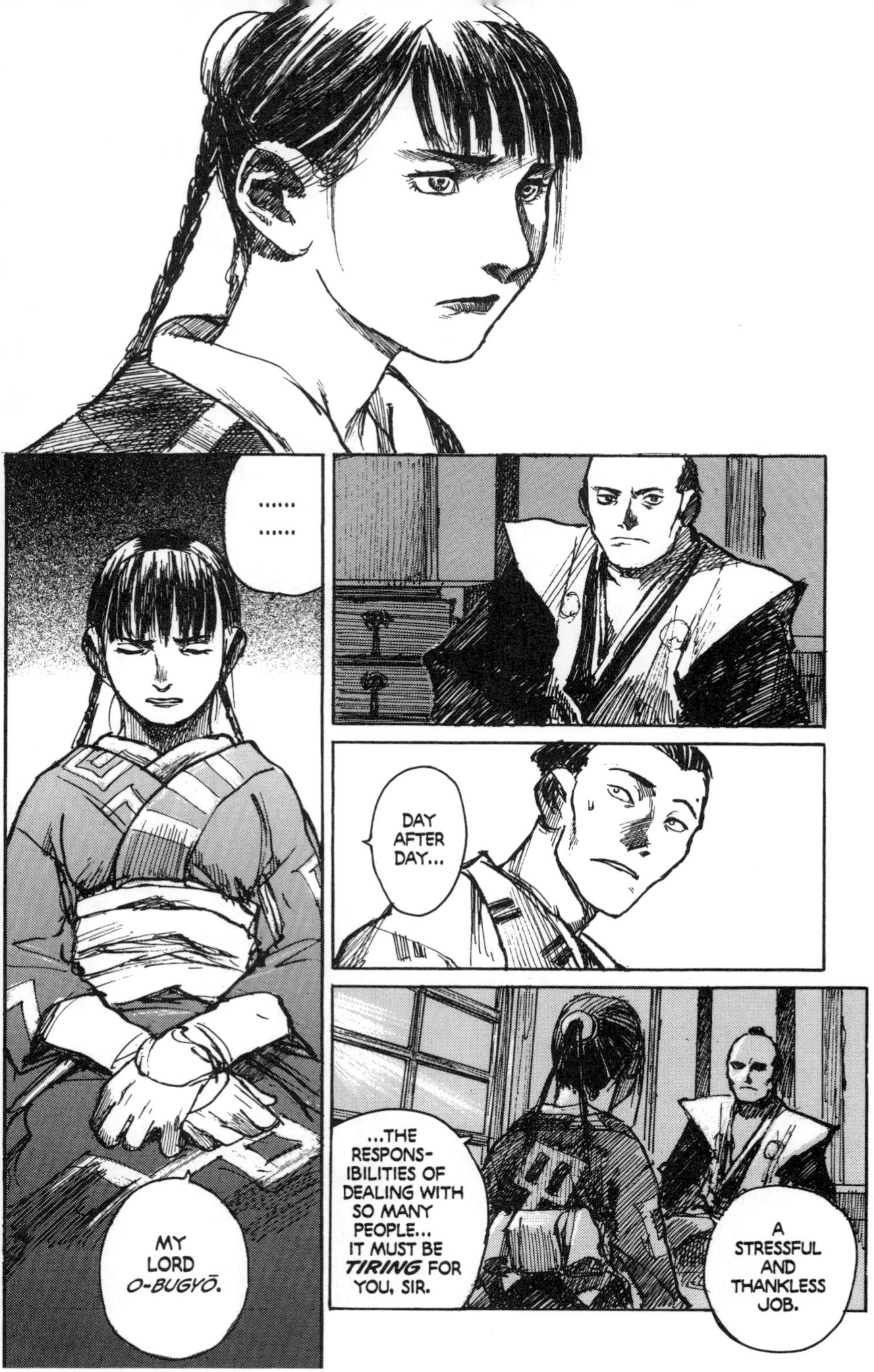

......
......
MY LORD *O-BUGYŌ*.
DAY AFTER DAY...
...THE RESPONS-IBILITIES OF DEALING WITH SO MANY PEOPLE... IT MUST BE ***TIRING*** FOR YOU, SIR.
A STRESSFUL AND THANKLESS JOB.

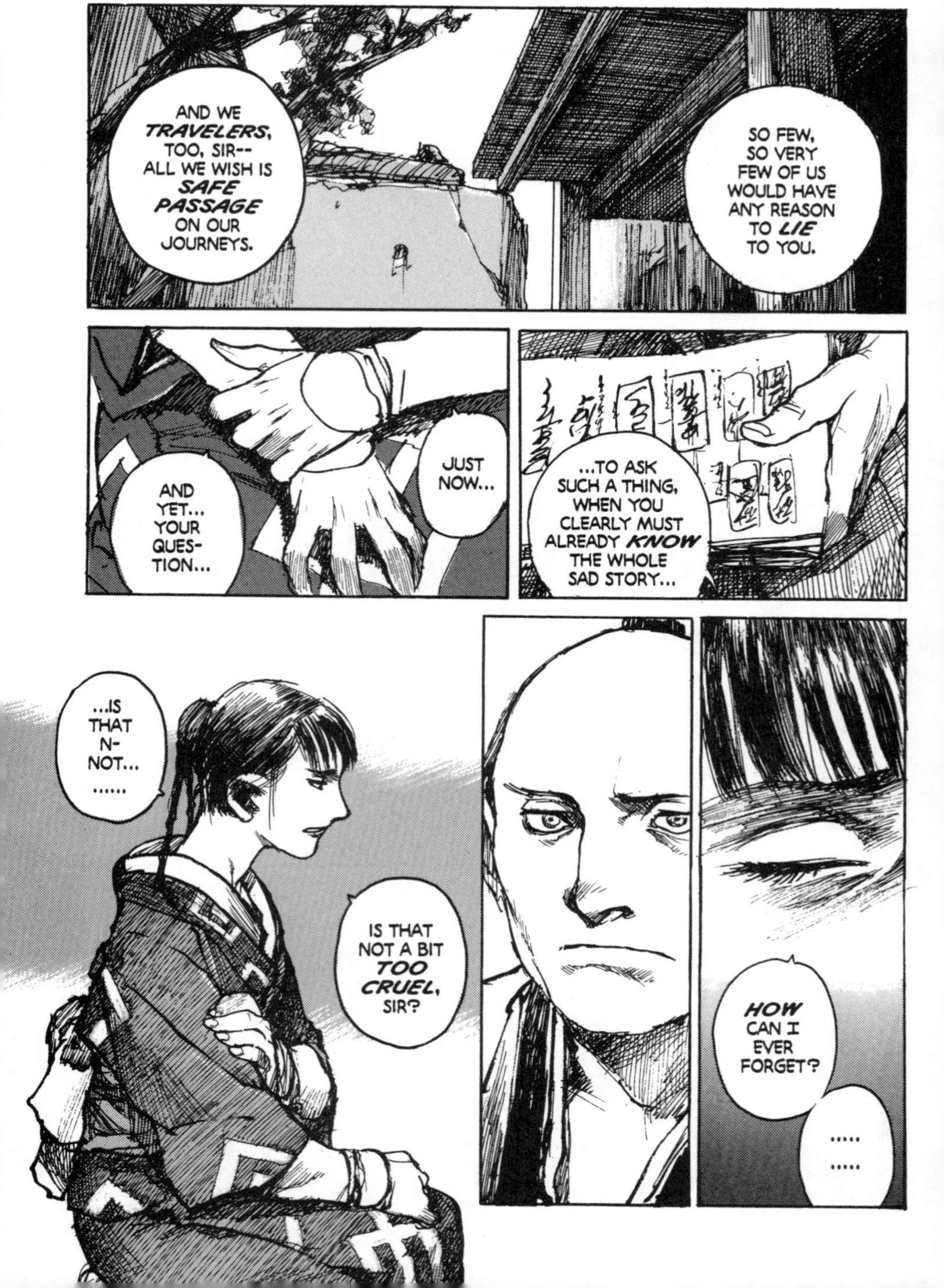
AND WE TRAVELERS, TOO, SIR-- ALL WE WISH IS SAFE PASSAGE ON OUR JOURNEYS.
SO FEW, SO VERY FEW OF US WOULD HAVE ANY REASON TO LIE TO YOU.
AND YET... YOUR QUES-TION...
JUST NOW...
...TO ASK SUCH A THING, WHEN YOU CLEARLY MUST ALREADY KNOW THE WHOLE SAD STORY...
...IS THAT N-NOT... ......
IS THAT NOT A BIT TOO CRUEL, SIR?
HOW CAN I EVER FORGET?
....

THE FIRST SUMMER AFTER MY MARRIAGE, I DID JUST AS YOU'VE SUGGESTED.

I LEFT THE INN TO MY HUSBAND, AND TOOK MY PARENTS TO SEE NIKKŌ.

THE HIKE FROM CHŪZENJI TO THE HOT SPRINGS WAS FINE.

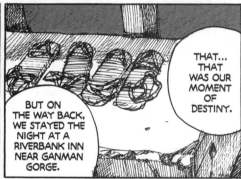

BUT ON THE WAY BACK, WE STAYED THE NIGHT AT A RIVERBANK INN NEAR GANMAN GORGE.

THAT... THAT WAS OUR MOMENT OF DESTINY.

THERE WAS A *CLOUDBURST*, A DOWNPOUR, TURNING THE ŌTANI RIVER INTO A RAGING TORRENT. WE WERE STUCK, TRAPPED IN THE MOUNTAINS FOR TWO WHOLE DAYS. AND ON THE THIRD DAY, *STILL* IT FELL...

...UNTIL THE LITTLE INN ITSELF WAS IN DANGER OF BEING SWEPT AWAY ON THE FLOOD. WE HAD TO CHANCE IT. THAT NIGHT, WE AND THE INNKEEPERS TOOK OUR LIVES INTO OUR HANDS...

...AND CROSSED THE LONG, NARROW, AND DANGEROUS BRIDGE TO THE TŌSHŌGŪ SHRINE, BLINDED BY THE DARK AND THE DRIVING RAIN.

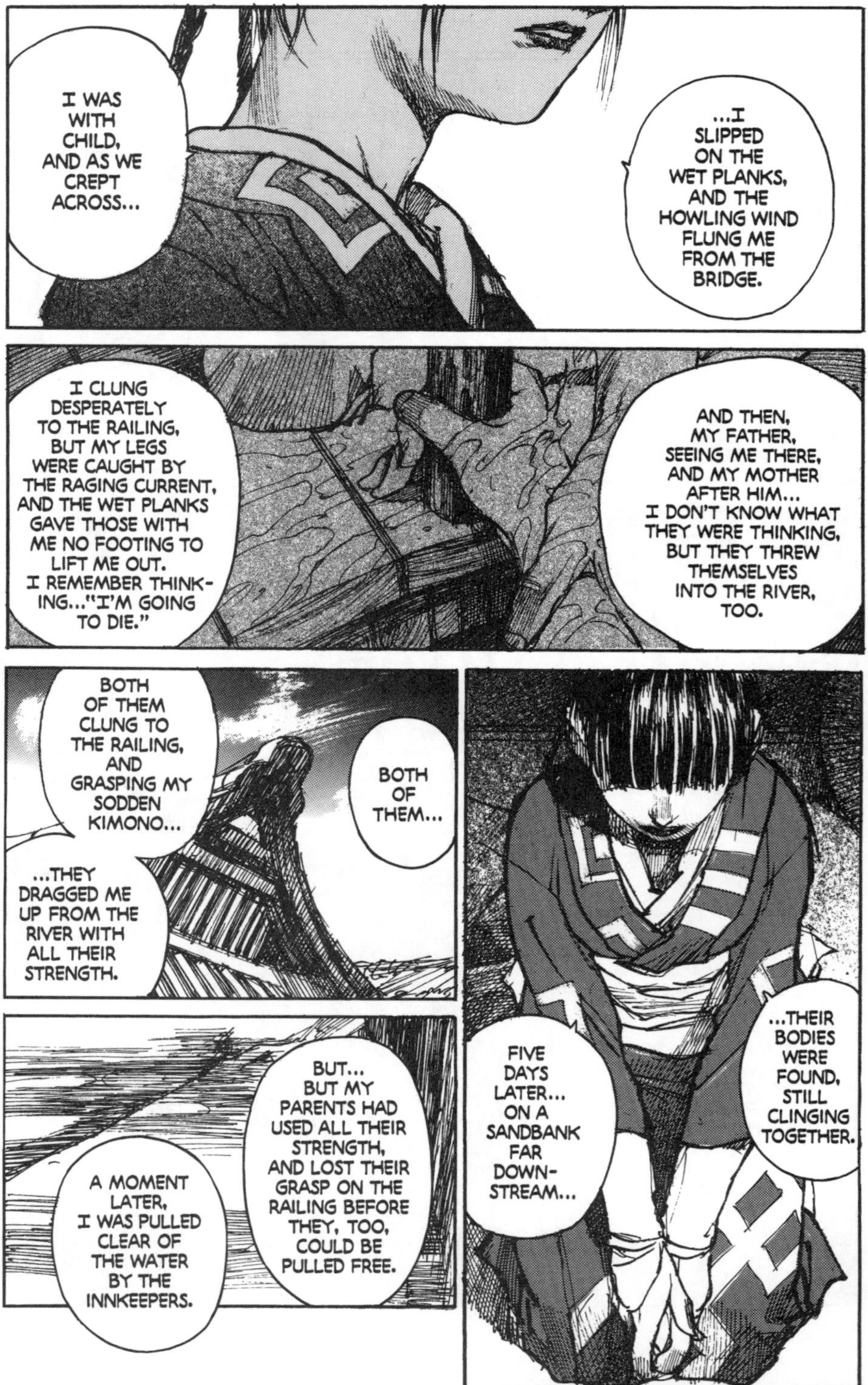
I WAS WITH CHILD, AND AS WE CREPT ACROSS...
...I SLIPPED ON THE WET PLANKS, AND THE HOWLING WIND FLUNG ME FROM THE BRIDGE.
I CLUNG DESPERATELY TO THE RAILING, BUT MY LEGS WERE CAUGHT BY THE RAGING CURRENT, AND THE WET PLANKS GAVE THOSE WITH ME NO FOOTING TO LIFT ME OUT. I REMEMBER THINKING..."I'M GOING TO DIE."
AND THEN, MY FATHER, SEEING ME THERE, AND MY MOTHER AFTER HIM... I DON'T KNOW WHAT THEY WERE THINKING, BUT THEY THREW THEMSELVES INTO THE RIVER, TOO.
BOTH OF THEM CLUNG TO THE RAILING, AND GRASPING MY SODDEN KIMONO...
BOTH OF THEM...
...THEY DRAGGED ME UP FROM THE RIVER WITH ALL THEIR STRENGTH.
A MOMENT LATER, I WAS PULLED CLEAR OF THE WATER BY THE INNKEEPERS.
BUT... BUT MY PARENTS HAD USED ALL THEIR STRENGTH, AND LOST THEIR GRASP ON THE RAILING BEFORE THEY, TOO, COULD BE PULLED FREE.
FIVE DAYS LATER... ON A SANDBANK FAR DOWN-STREAM...
...THEIR BODIES WERE FOUND, STILL CLINGING TOGETHER.

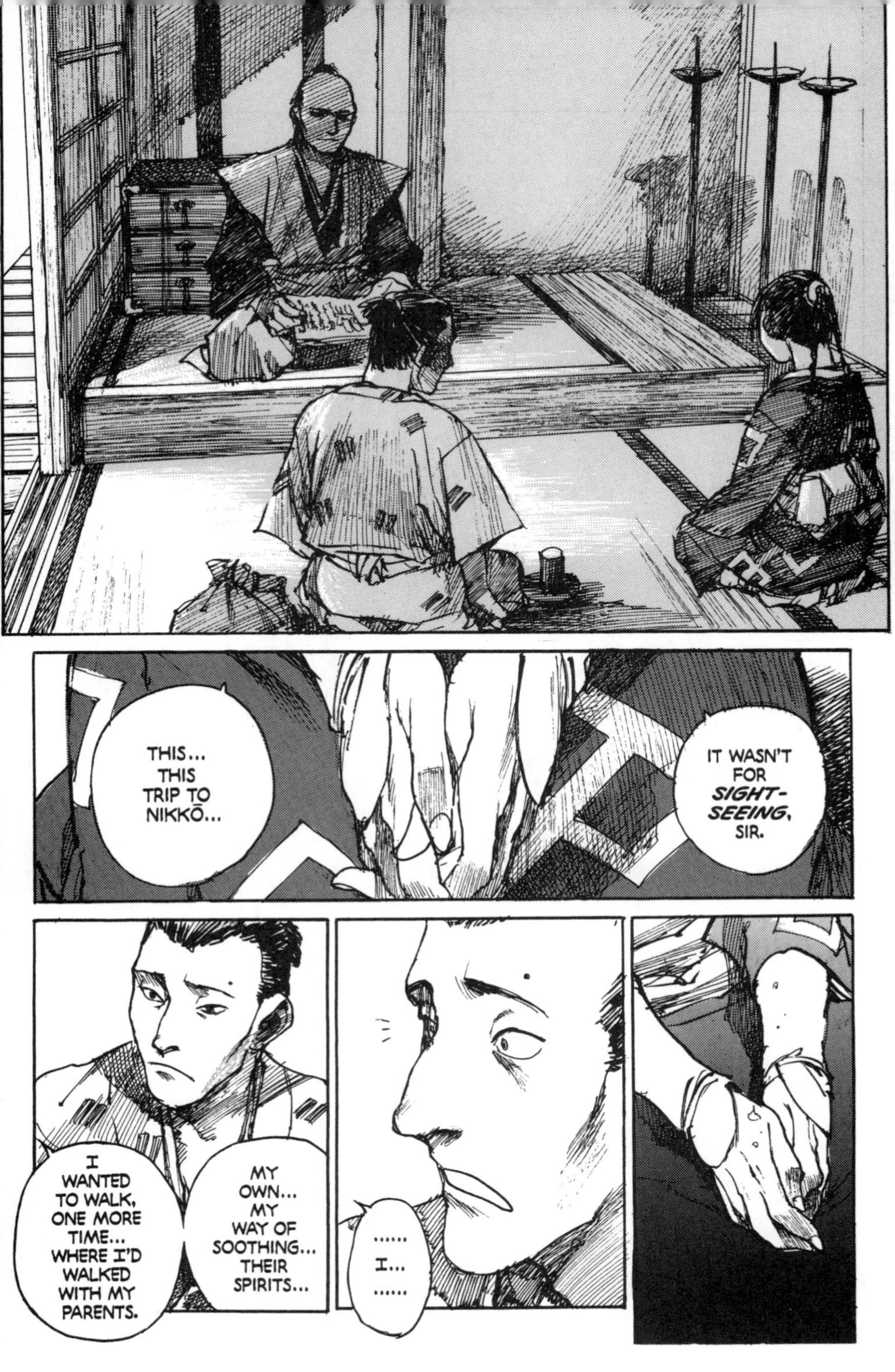
THIS... THIS TRIP TO NIKKŌ...
IT WASN'T FOR *SIGHT-SEEING*, SIR.
I WANTED TO WALK, ONE MORE TIME... WHERE I'D WALKED WITH MY PARENTS.
MY OWN... MY WAY OF SOOTHING... THEIR SPIRITS...
...... I... ......

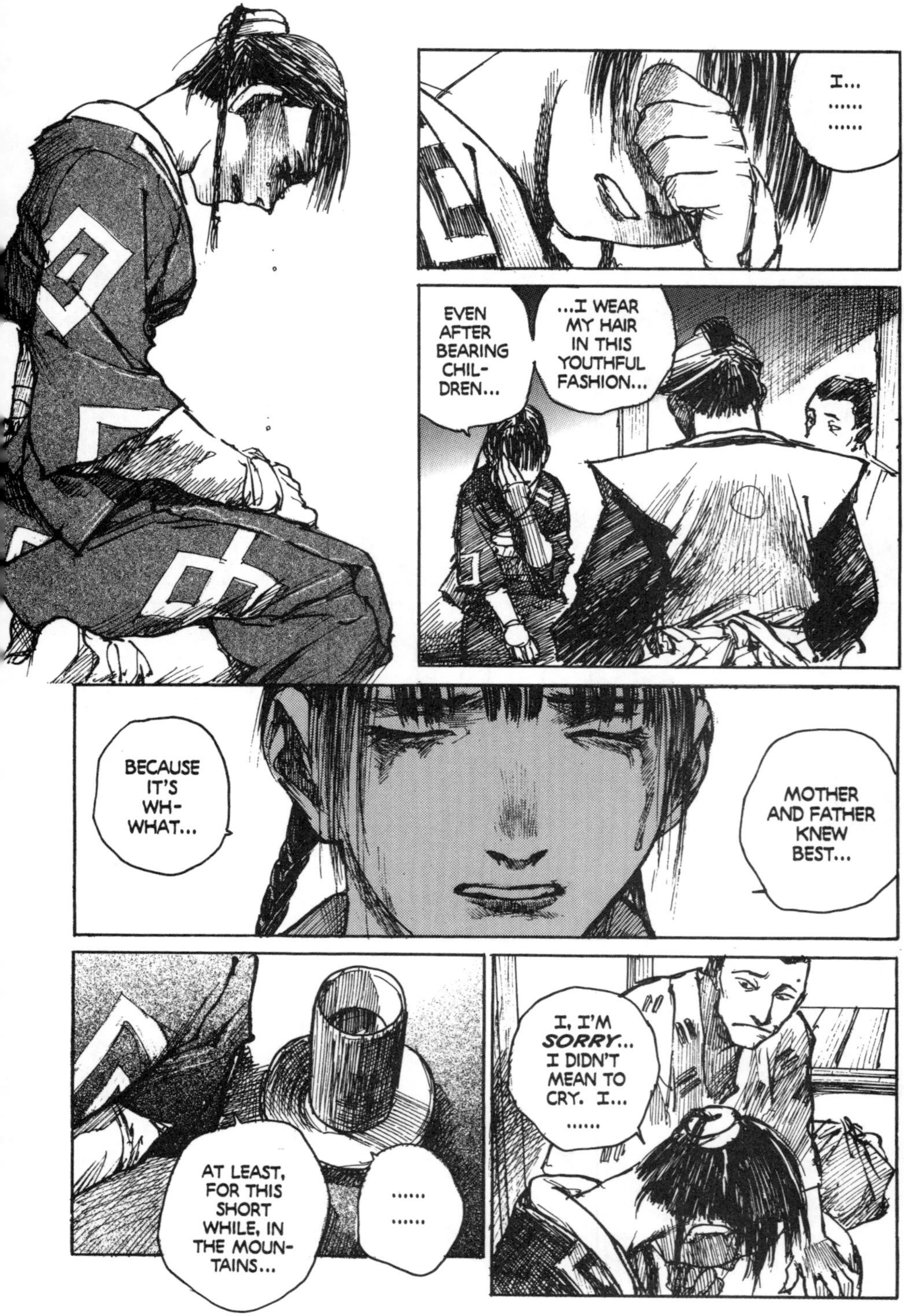
I...
......
......
EVEN AFTER BEARING CHIL- DREN...
...I WEAR MY HAIR IN THIS YOUTHFUL FASHION...
BECAUSE IT'S WH- WHAT...
MOTHER AND FATHER KNEW BEST...
AT LEAST, FOR THIS SHORT WHILE, IN THE MOUN- TAINS...
....
I, I'M SORRY... I DIDN'T MEAN TO CRY. I... ......

....

I UNDER-STAND.

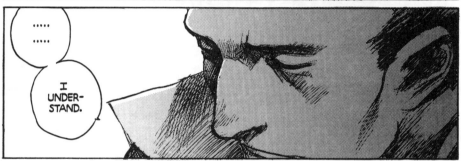

BUT-- YOU RESEMBLE THE DRAWING ON THE WANTED POSTER.

I HAD TO BE RUTHLESS.

THIS STORY YOU'VE TOLD...

IT'S STILL POSSIBLE YOU COULD SIMPLY HAVE *MEMORIZED IT*, BUT... ......

WELL... ENOUGH.

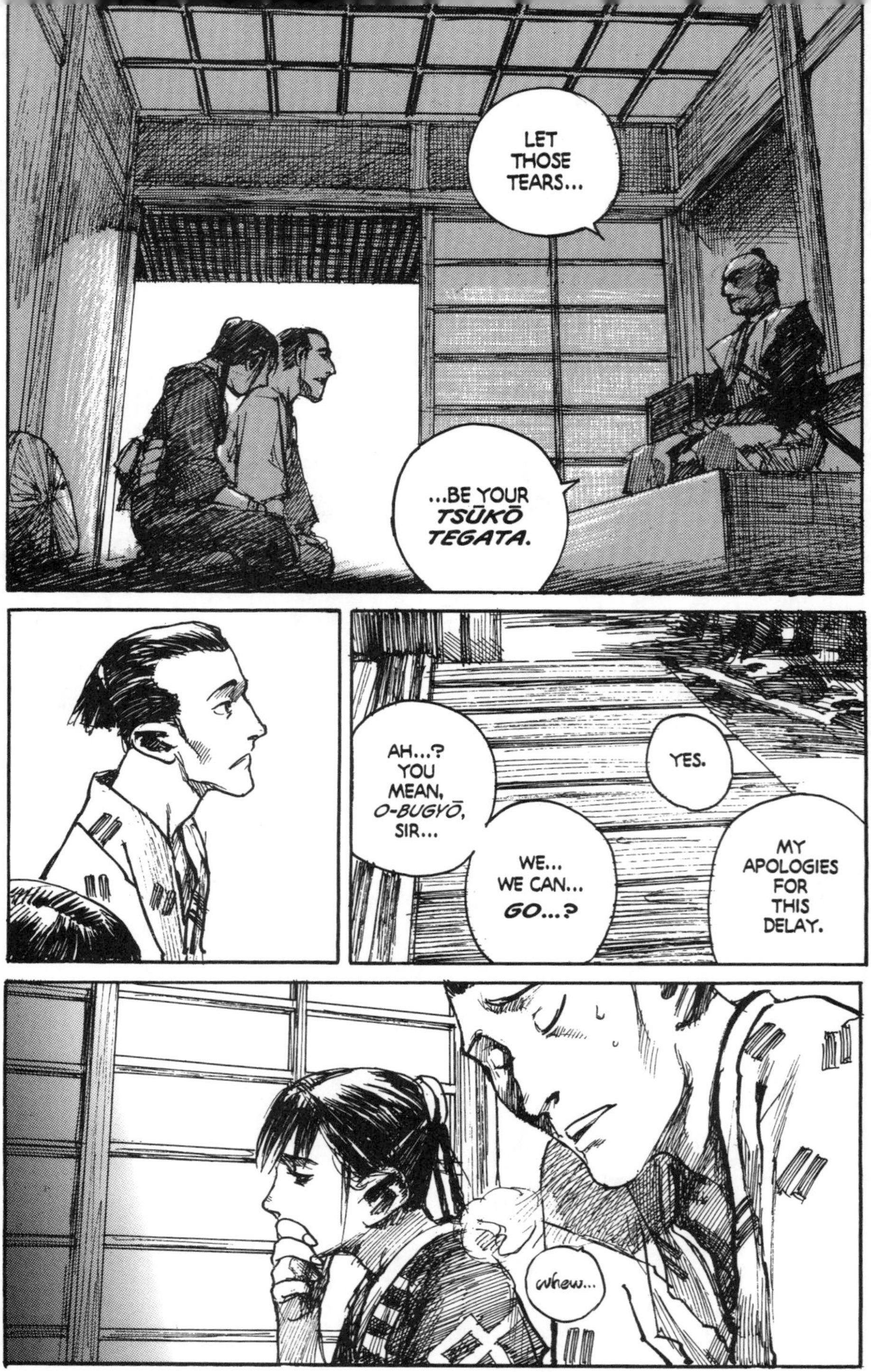
LET THOSE TEARS...
...BE YOUR *TSŪKŌ TEGATA*.
AH...? YOU MEAN, *O-BUGYŌ*, SIR...
WE... WE CAN... *GO...?*
YES.
MY APOLOGIES FOR THIS DELAY.
whew...

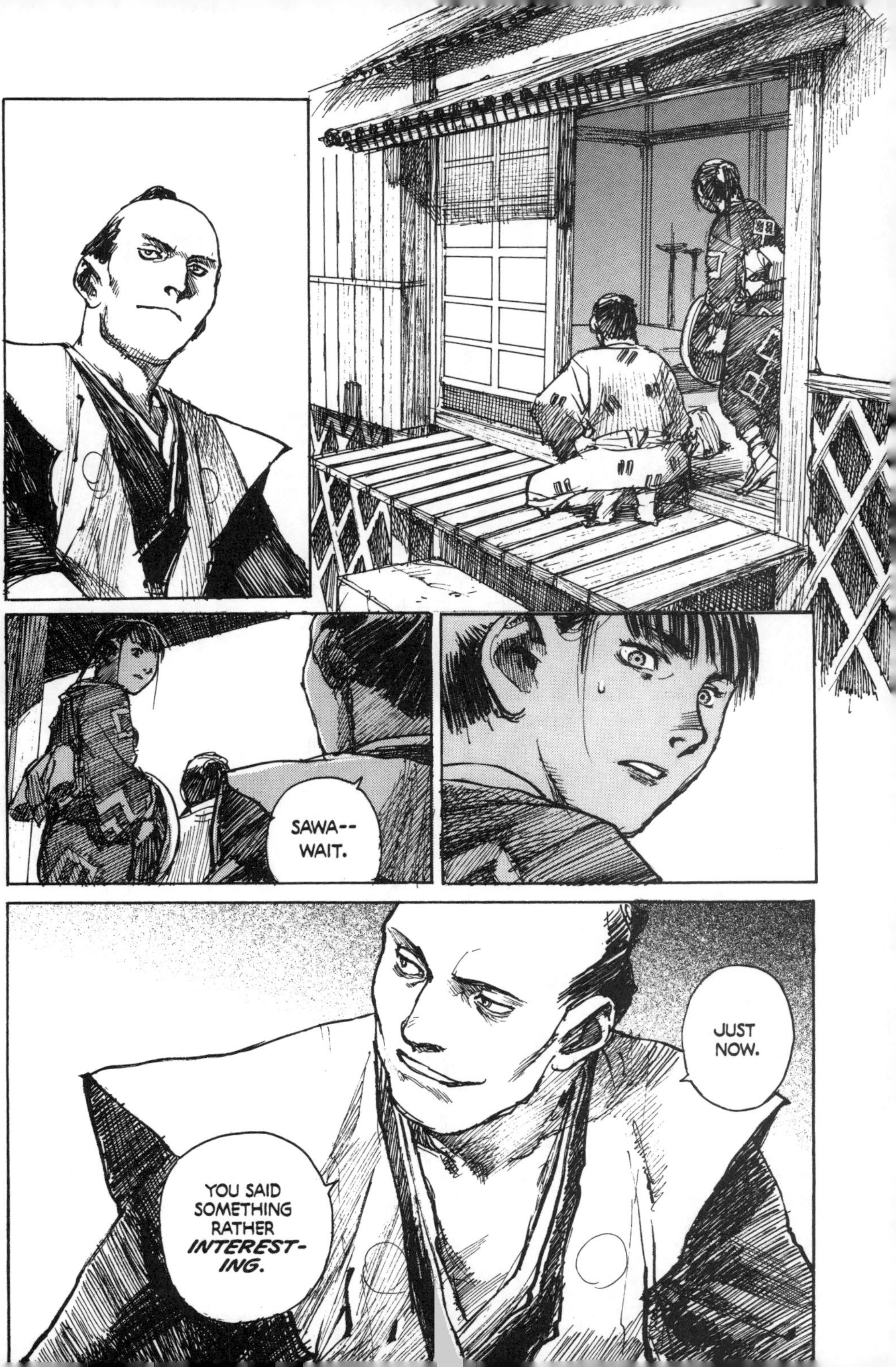
SAWA--
WAIT.
JUST NOW.
YOU SAID SOMETHING RATHER *INTERESTING.*

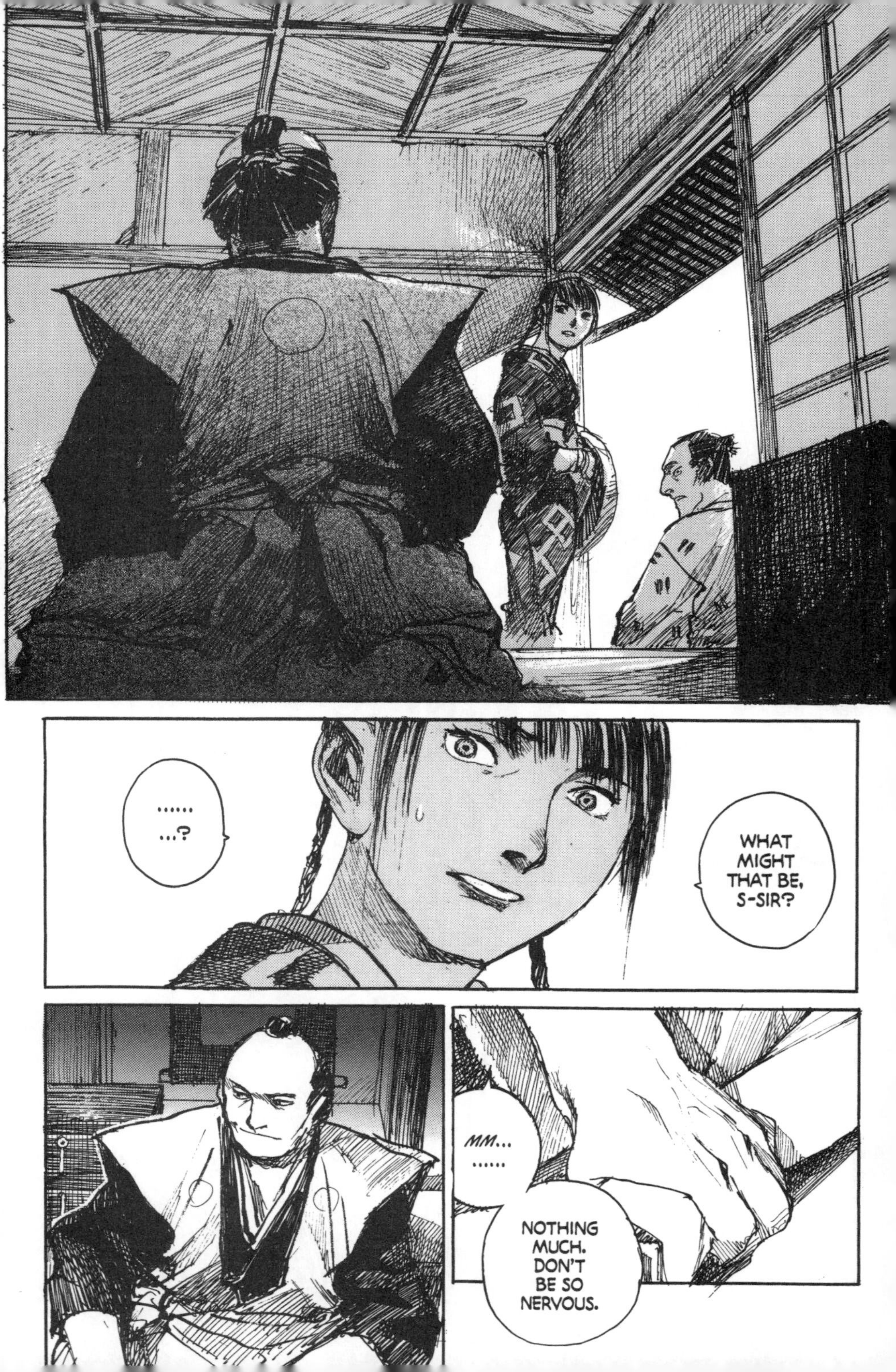
....?
WHAT MIGHT THAT BE, S-SIR?
MM... ......
NOTHING MUCH. DON'T BE SO NERVOUS.

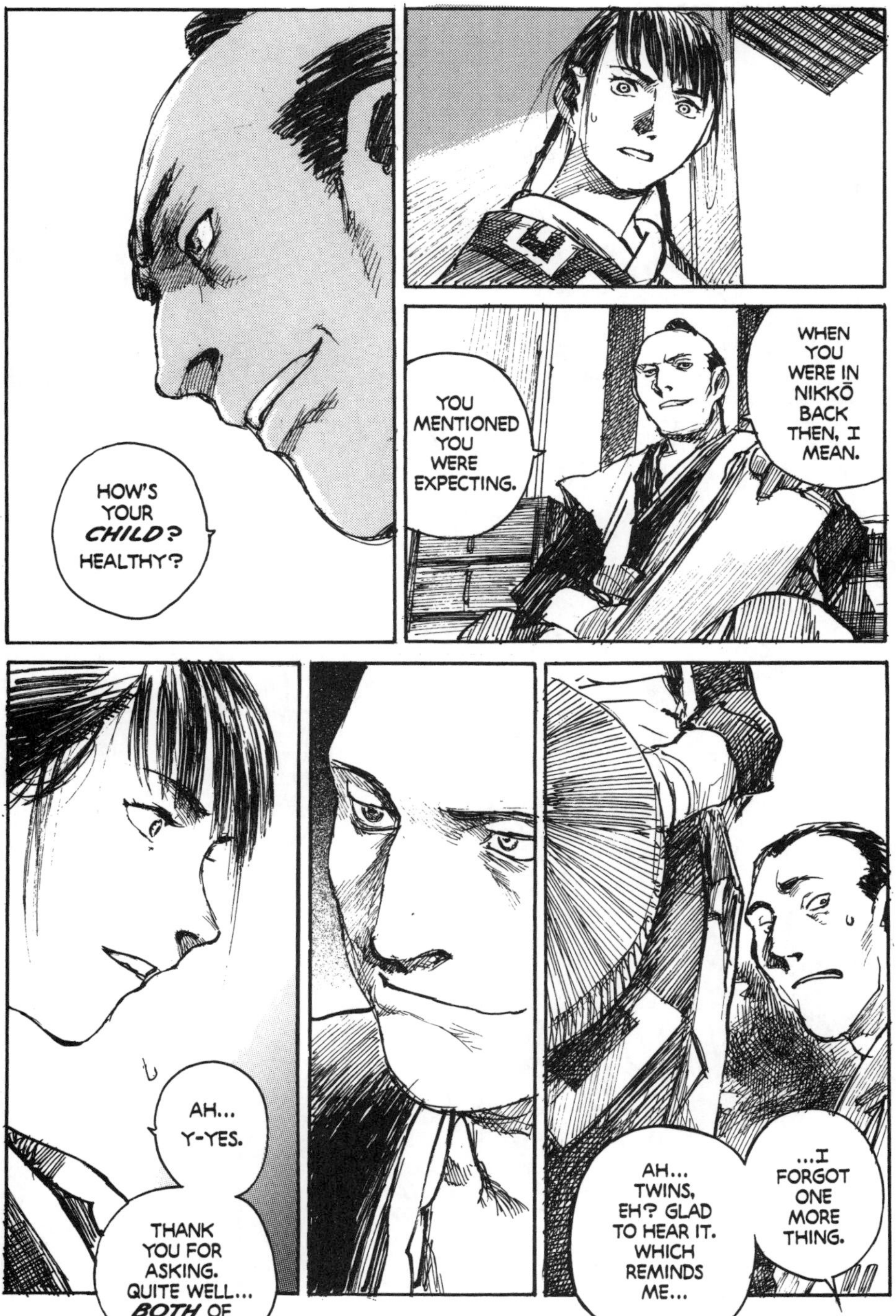
HOW'S YOUR CHILD? HEALTHY?
YOU MENTIONED YOU WERE EXPECTING.
WHEN YOU WERE IN NIKKŌ BACK THEN, I MEAN.
AH... Y-YES.
THANK YOU FOR ASKING. QUITE WELL... BOTH OF THEM.
AH... TWINS, EH? GLAD TO HEAR IT. WHICH REMINDS ME...
...I FORGOT ONE MORE THING.

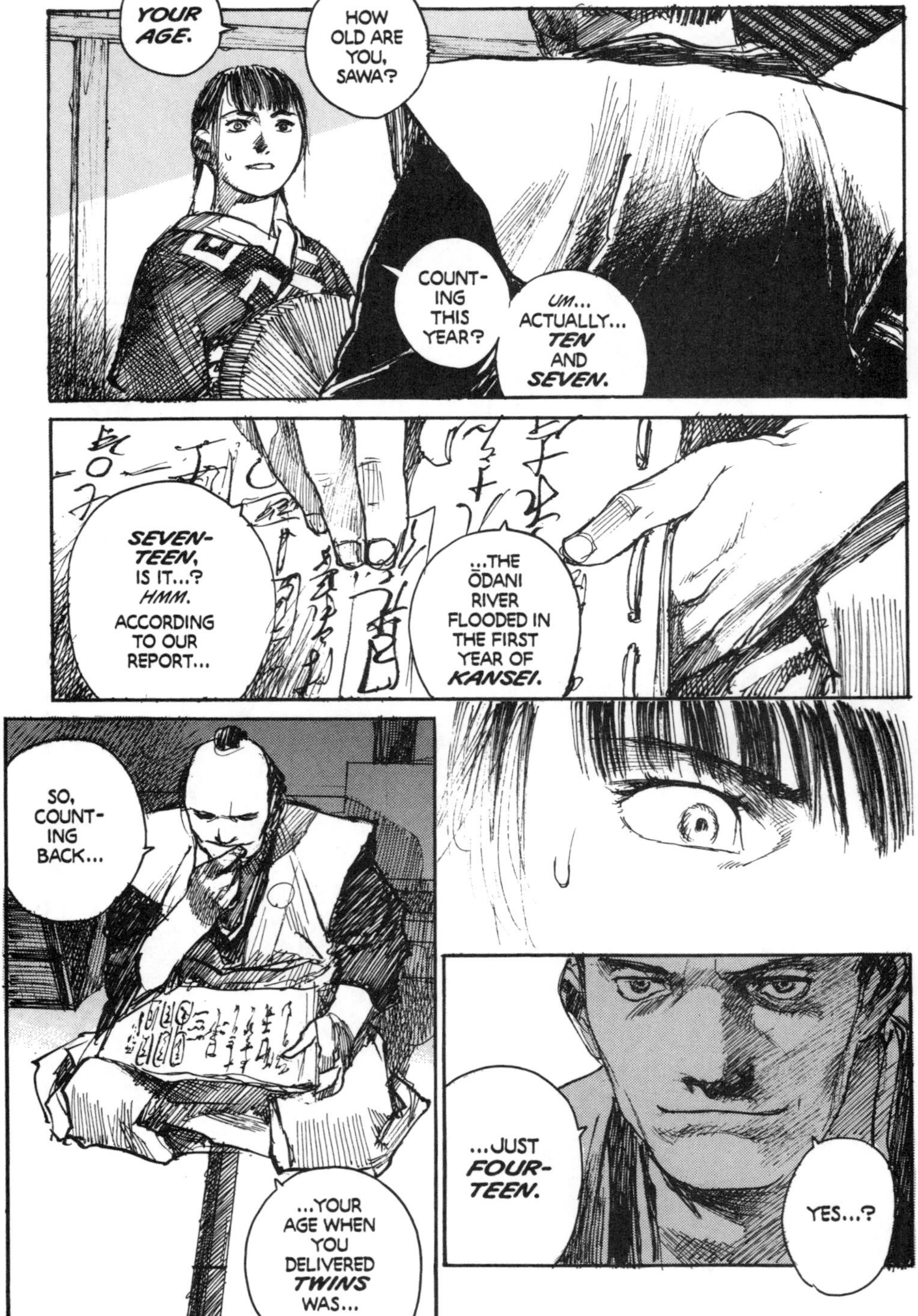
YOUR AGE.
HOW OLD ARE YOU, SAWA?
COUNTING THIS YEAR?
UM... ACTUALLY... TEN AND SEVEN.
SEVENTEEN, IS IT...? HMM. ACCORDING TO OUR REPORT...
...THE ŌDANI RIVER FLOODED IN THE FIRST YEAR OF KANSEI.
SO, COUNTING BACK...
...YOUR AGE WHEN YOU DELIVERED TWINS WAS...
...JUST FOURTEEN.
YES...?

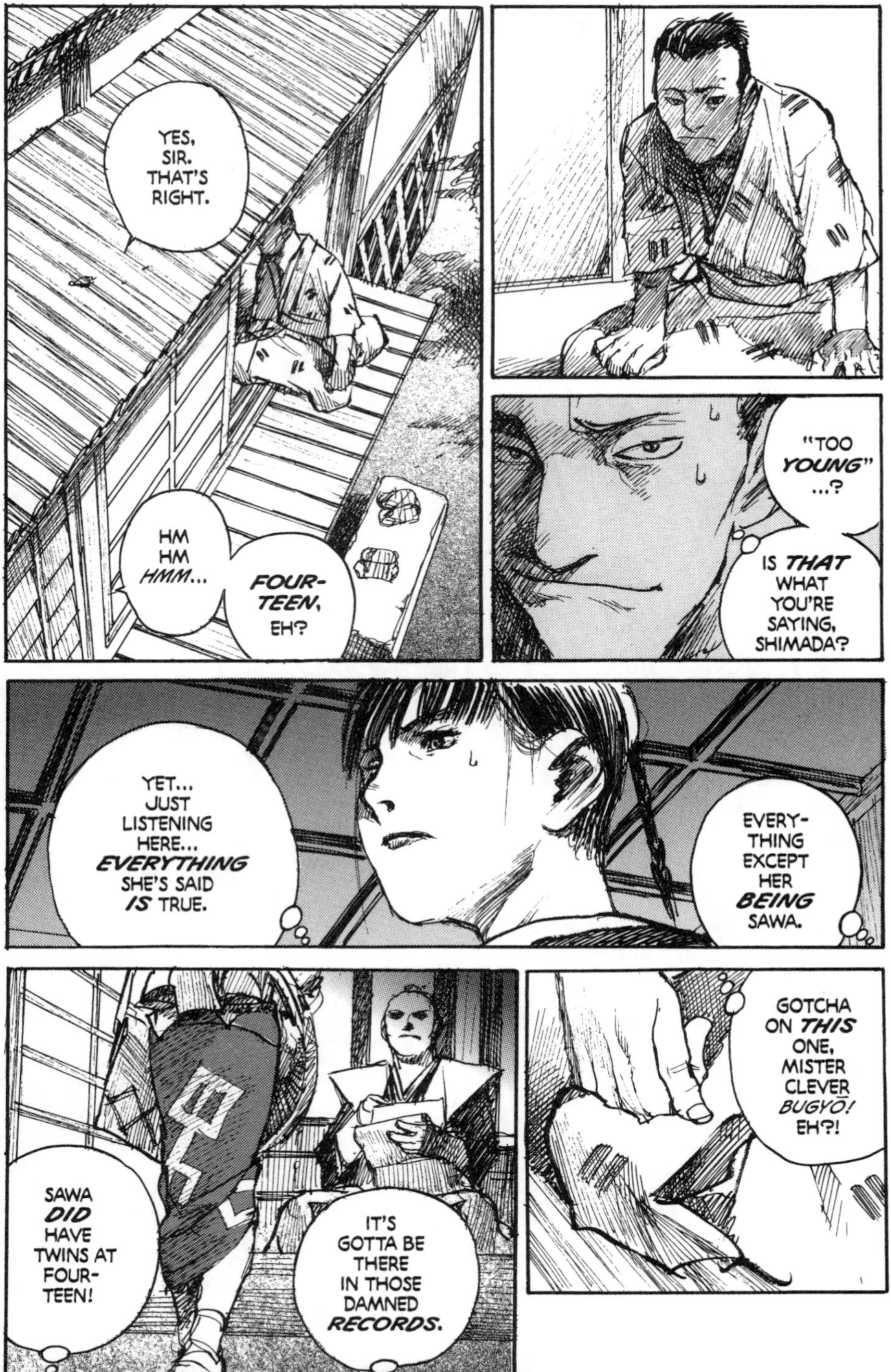
YES, SIR. THAT'S RIGHT.
HM HM *HMM*...
FOUR-TEEN, EH?
"TOO ***YOUNG***" ...?
IS ***THAT*** WHAT YOU'RE SAYING, SHIMADA?
YET... JUST LISTENING HERE... ***EVERYTHING*** SHE'S SAID ***IS*** TRUE.
EVERY-THING EXCEPT HER ***BEING*** SAWA.
SAWA ***DID*** HAVE TWINS AT FOUR-TEEN!
IT'S GOTTA BE THERE IN THOSE DAMNED ***RECORDS.***
GOTCHA ON ***THIS*** ONE, MISTER CLEVER *BUGYŌ!* EH?!

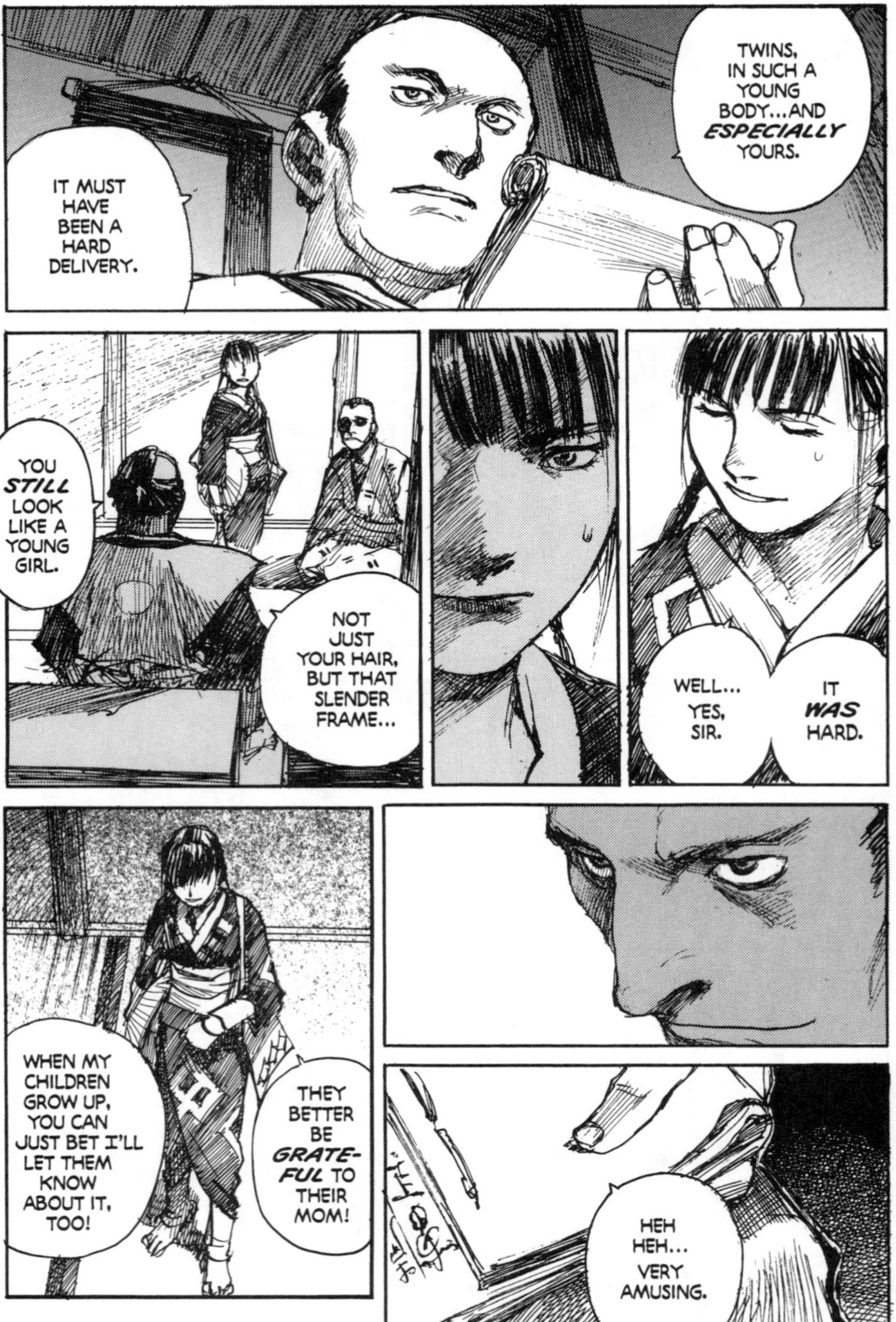
IT MUST HAVE BEEN A HARD DELIVERY.
TWINS, IN SUCH A YOUNG BODY...AND *ESPECIALLY* YOURS.
YOU *STILL* LOOK LIKE A YOUNG GIRL.
NOT JUST YOUR HAIR, BUT THAT SLENDER FRAME...
WELL... YES, SIR.
IT *WAS* HARD.
WHEN MY CHILDREN GROW UP, YOU CAN JUST BET I'LL LET THEM KNOW ABOUT IT, TOO!
THEY BETTER BE *GRATE-FUL* TO THEIR MOM!
HEH HEH... VERY AMUSING.

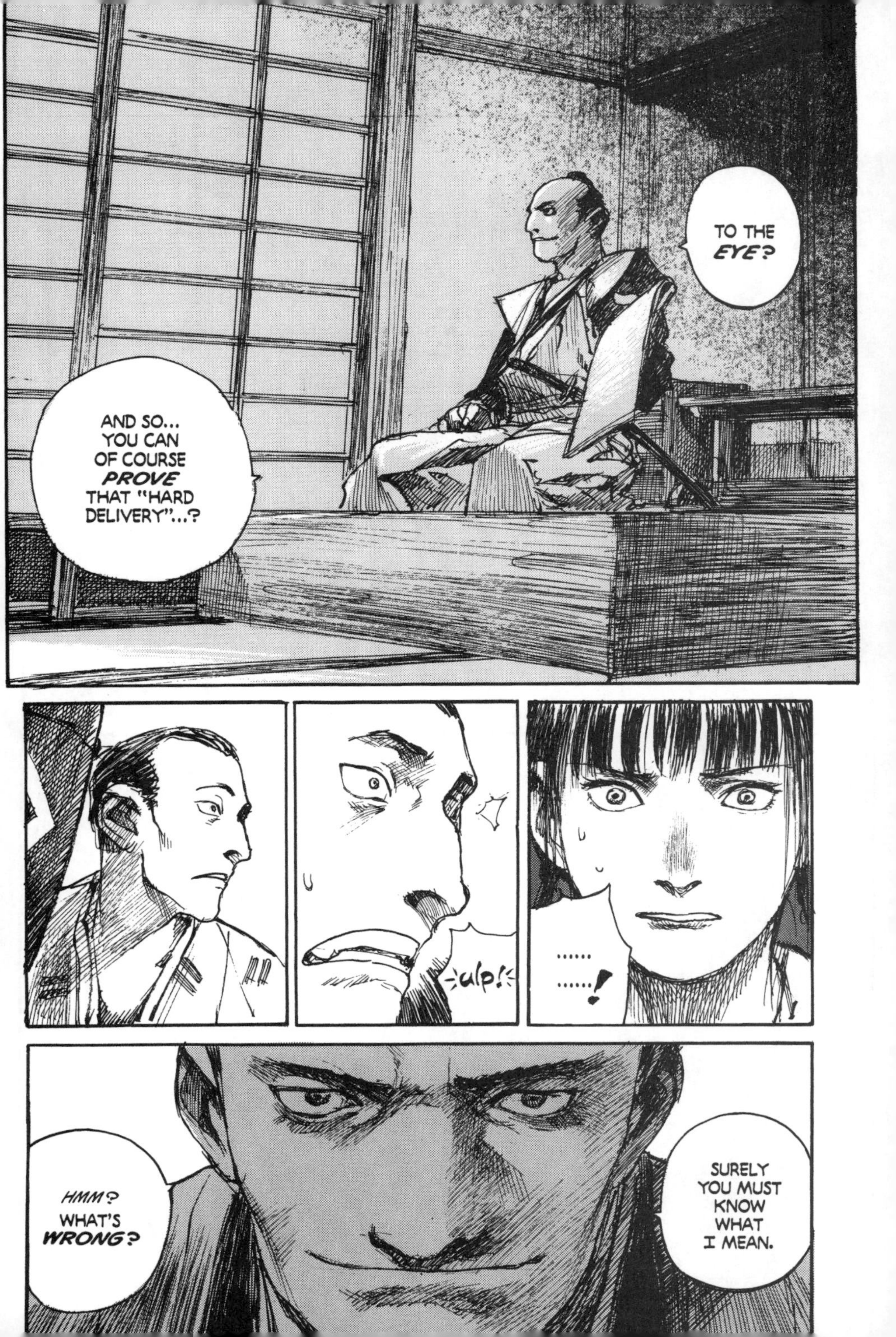
AND SO... YOU CAN OF COURSE PROVE THAT "HARD DELIVERY"...?
TO THE EYE?
ulp!
......
......!
HMM? WHAT'S WRONG?
SURELY YOU MUST KNOW WHAT I MEAN.

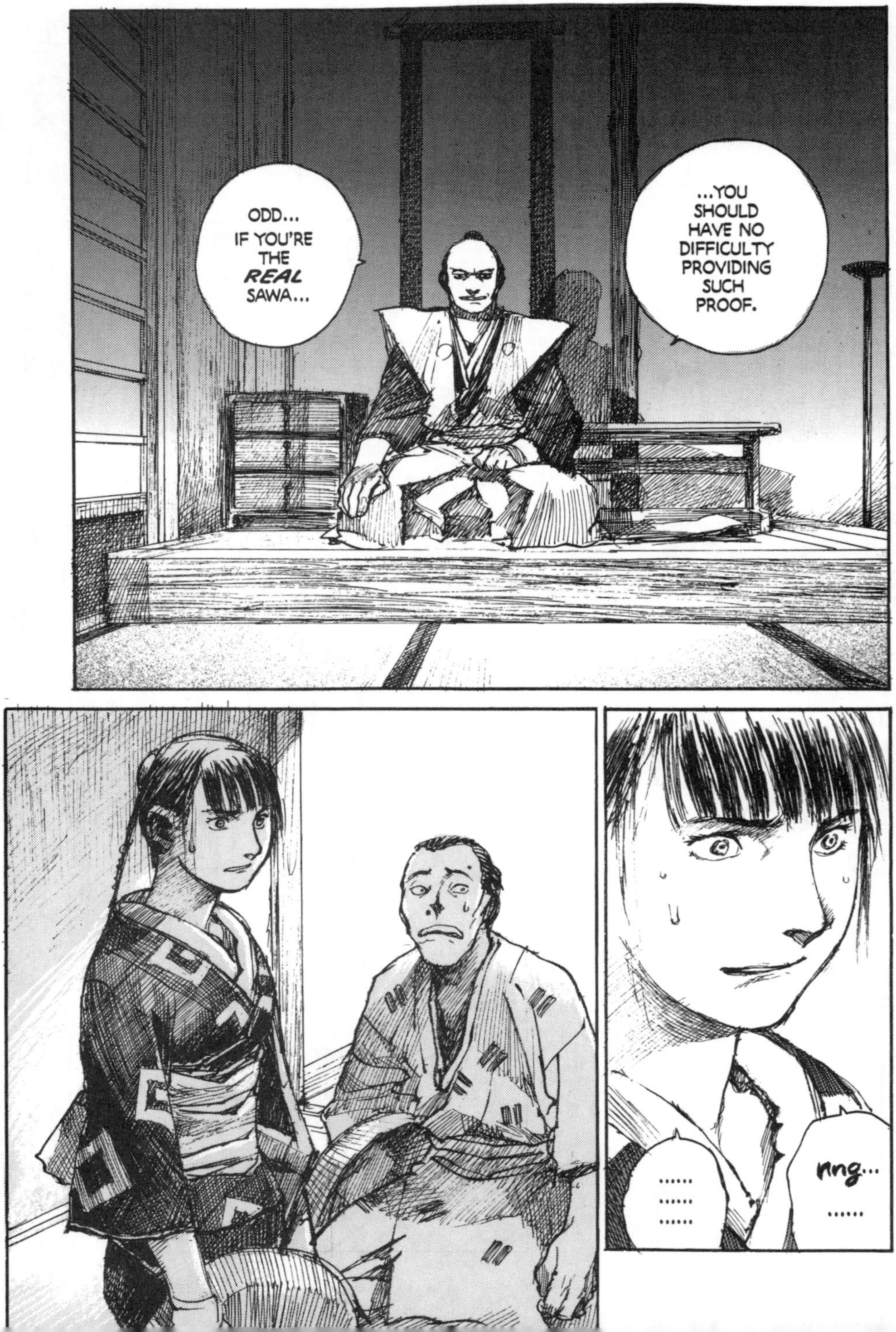
ODD... IF YOU'RE THE *REAL* SAWA...
...YOU SHOULD HAVE NO DIFFICULTY PROVIDING SUCH PROOF.
....
nng... ......

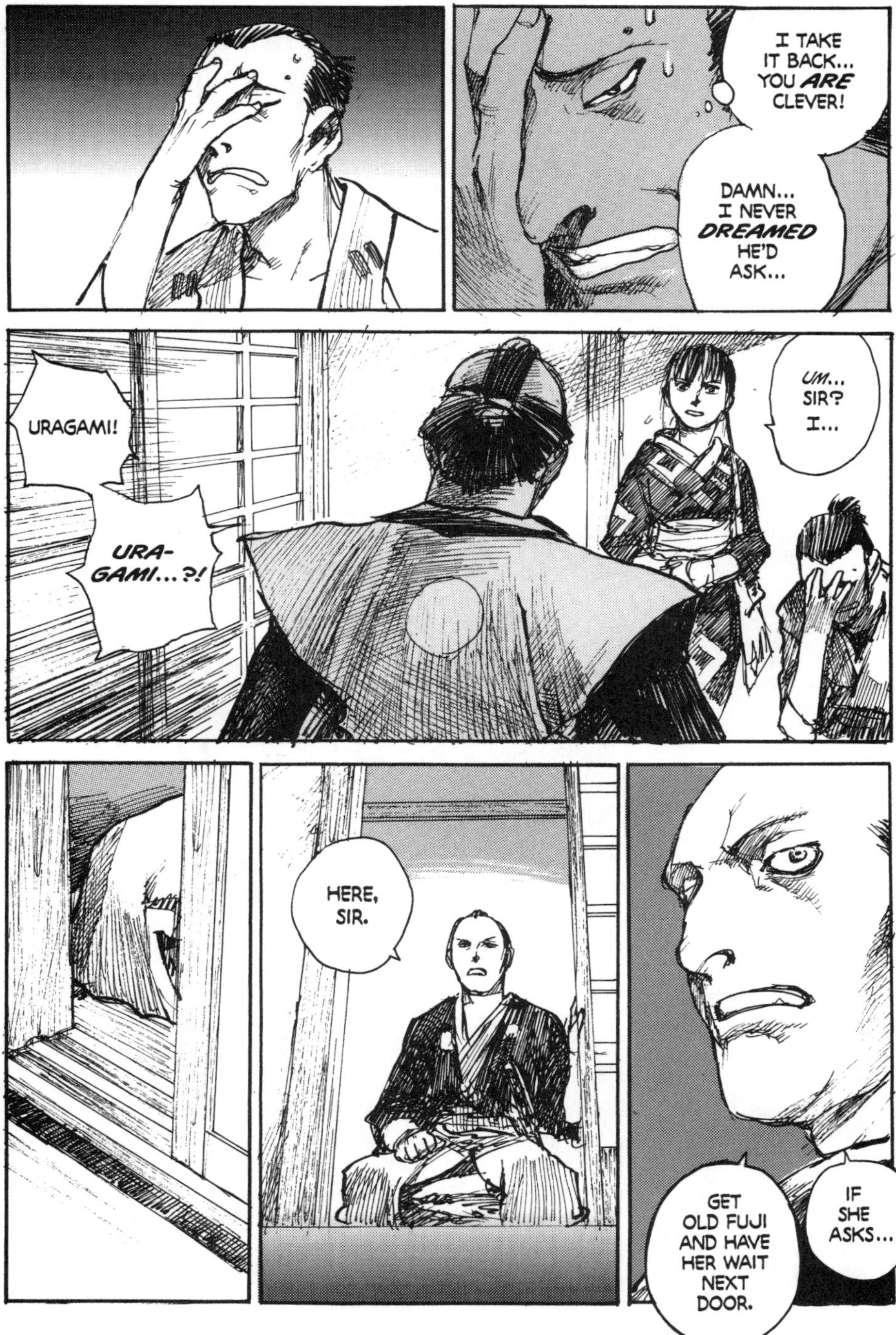
I TAKE IT BACK... YOU *ARE* CLEVER!
DAMN... I NEVER *DREAMED* HE'D ASK...
URAGAMI!
URA-GAMI...?!
UM... SIR? I...
HERE, SIR.
GET OLD FUJI AND HAVE HER WAIT NEXT DOOR.
IF SHE ASKS...

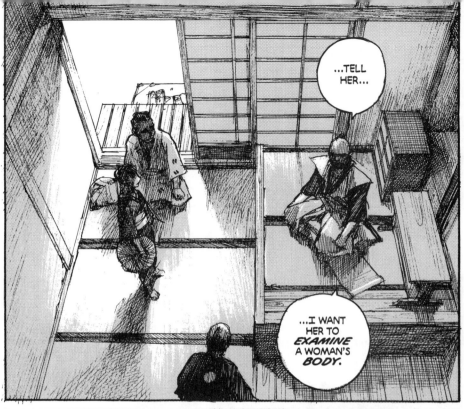

...TELL HER...

...I WANT HER TO *EXAMINE* A WOMAN'S *BODY.*

B-BUT, *SIR!*

JUST HOLD *ON* THERE! SAWA IS A *MARRIED WOMAN!* YOU CAN'T JUST--

O-BUGYŌ-SAMA!!

....

I... I AM...

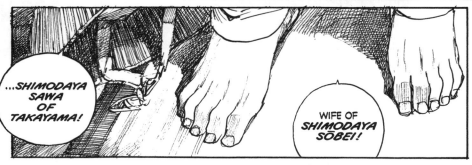

...SHIMODAYA SAWA OF TAKAYAMA!

WIFE OF SHIMODAYA SŌBEI!

AND SO, THESE MYSTERIOUS WORDS YOU SPEAK?

I UNDERSTAND THEM PERFECTLY.

IF YOU DISTRUST ME SO MUCH, YOU DON'T NEED TO CALL THE OLD WOMAN.

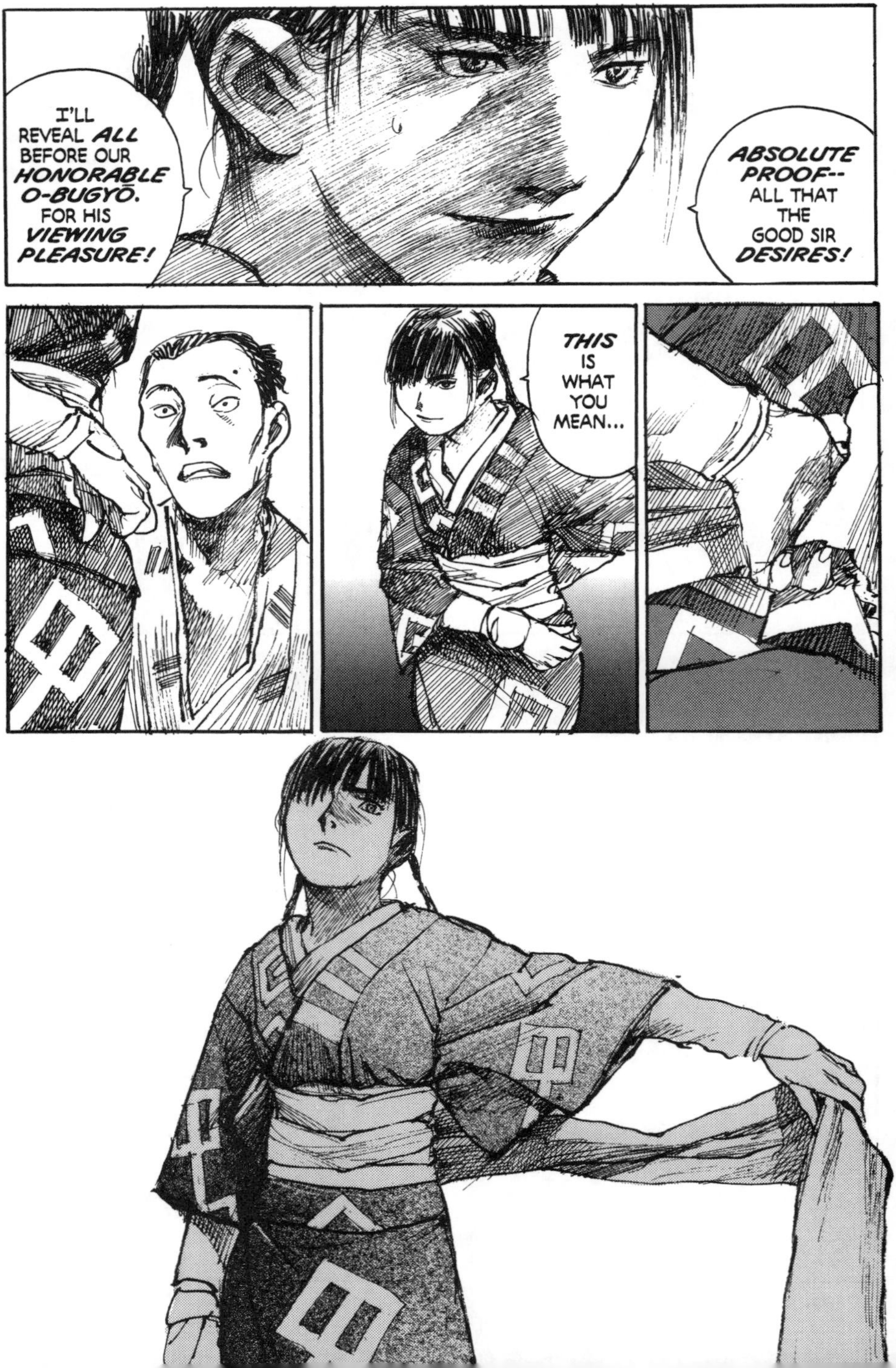
I'LL REVEAL ALL BEFORE OUR HONORABLE O-BUGYŌ. FOR HIS VIEWING PLEASURE!
ABSOLUTE PROOF-- ALL THAT THE GOOD SIR DESIRES!
THIS IS WHAT YOU MEAN...

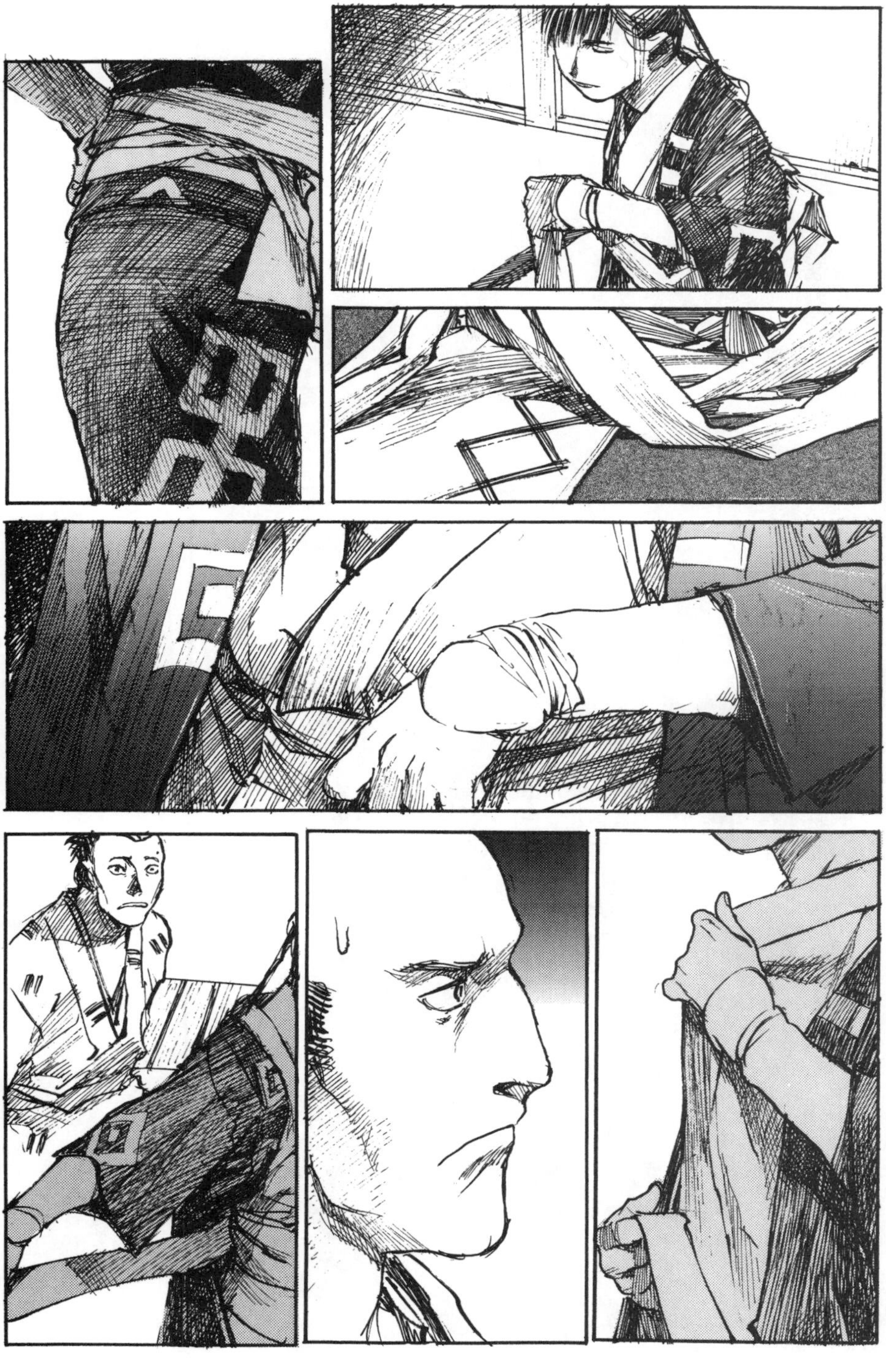

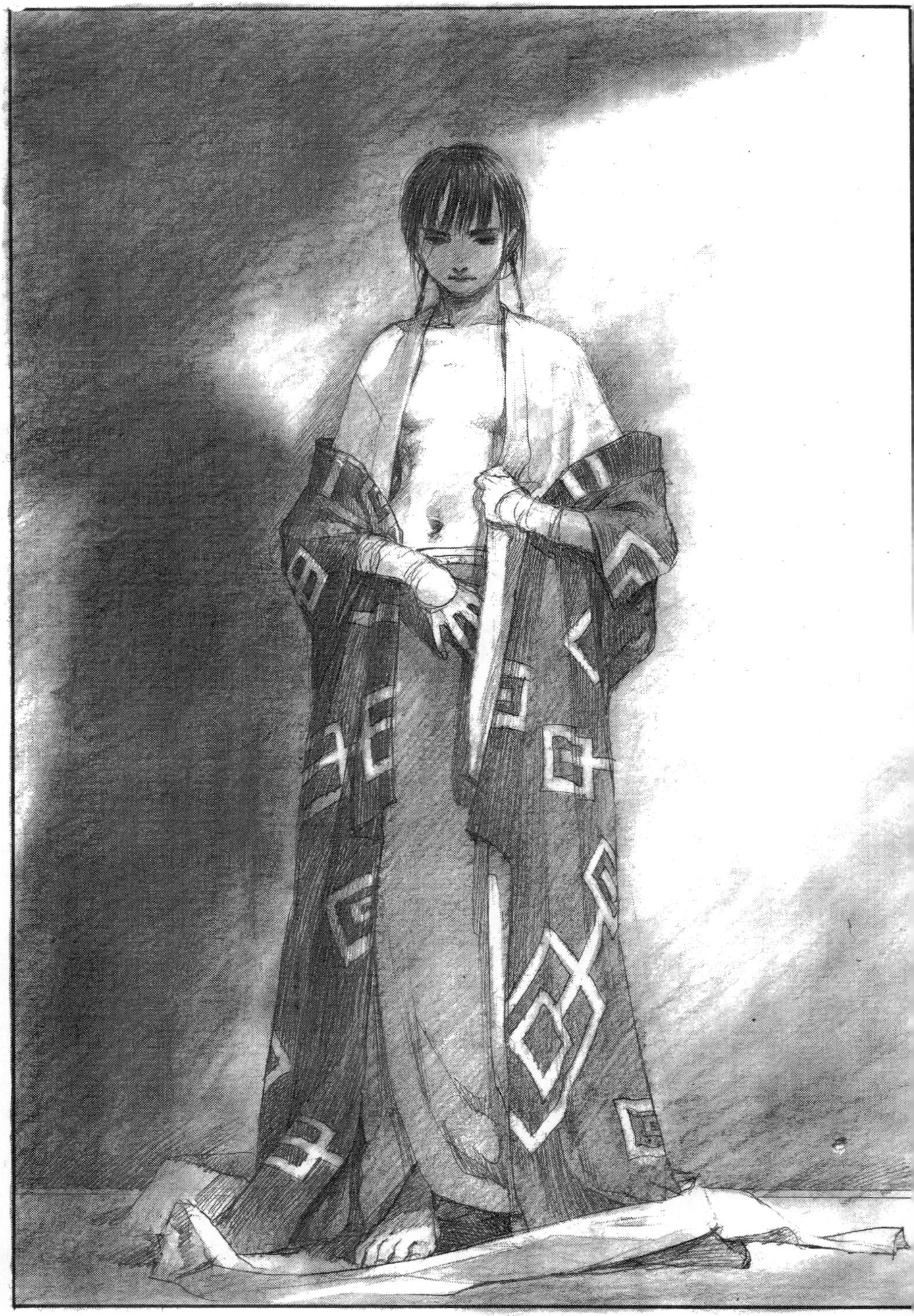

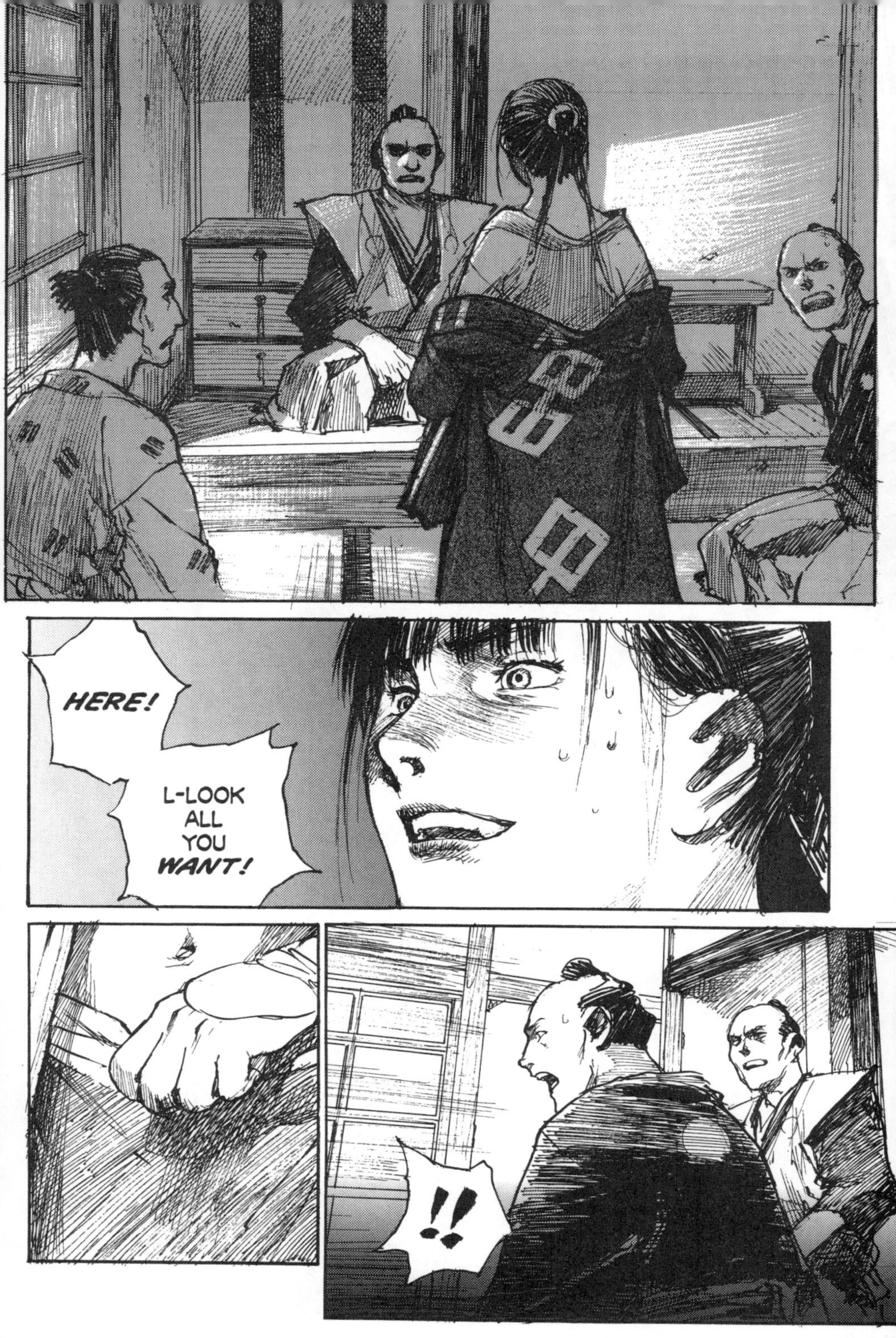
HERE!
L-LOOK ALL YOU WANT!
!!

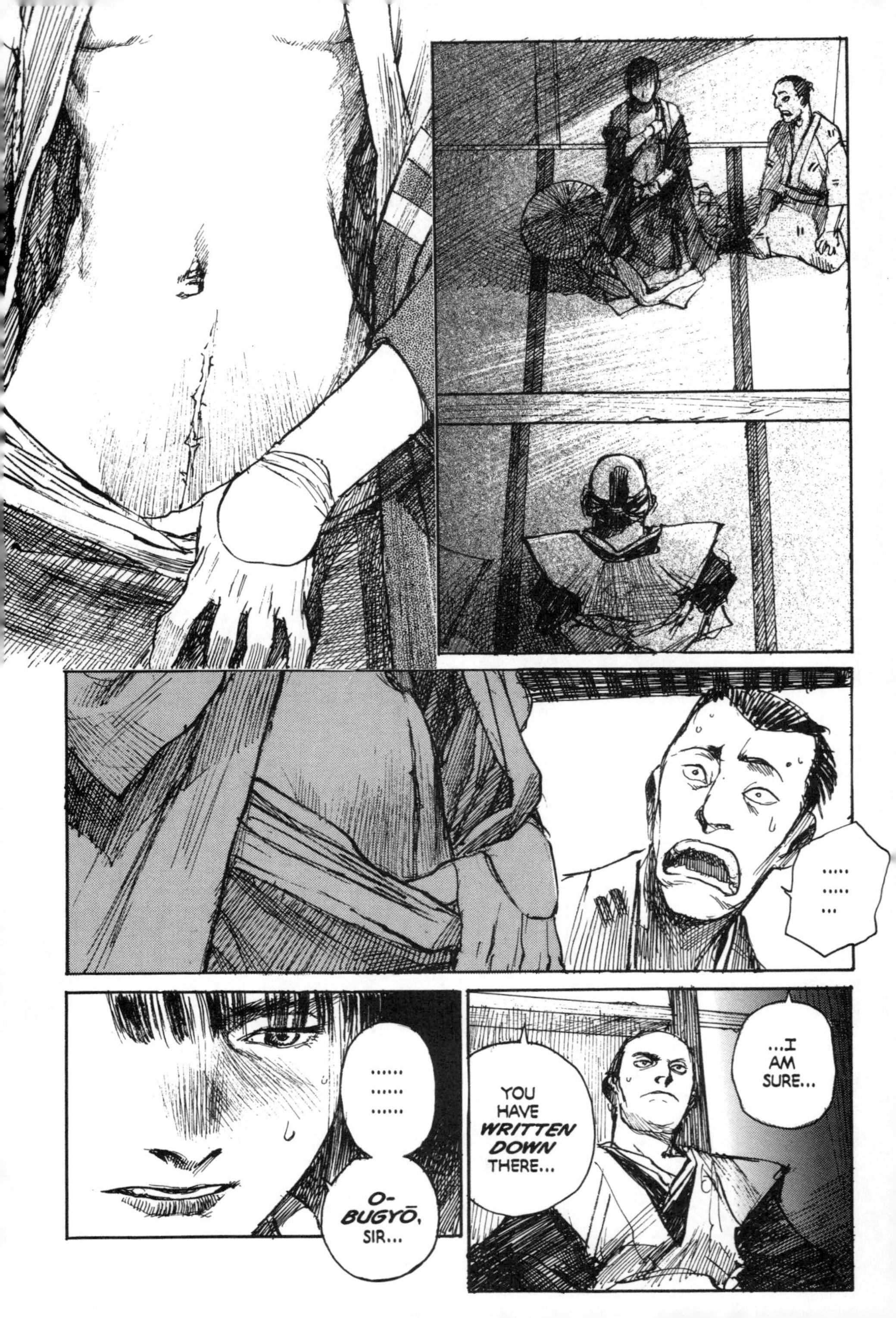

......
......
...
......
......
......
O-BUGYŌ, SIR...
...I AM SURE...
YOU HAVE *WRITTEN DOWN* THERE...

...THAT THE EFFECTS OF THOSE TERRIBLE EVENTS IN GANMAN GORGE...

...TOUCHED EVEN MY UNBORN BABIES.

THE SHOCK THREW ME INTO LABOR--AND MY YOUNG BODY WAS NOT MADE TO DELIVER *TWO* CHILDREN.

EVEN MORE SO WHEN THEY WERE A BREECH BIRTH.

THE TWO SONS I HAVE TODAY LIVE ONLY BECAUSE...

...ON THE JUDGMENT OF THE MIDWIFE AND MY HUSBAND...

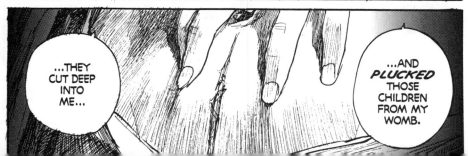

...THEY CUT DEEP INTO ME...

...AND *PLUCKED* THOSE CHILDREN FROM MY WOMB.

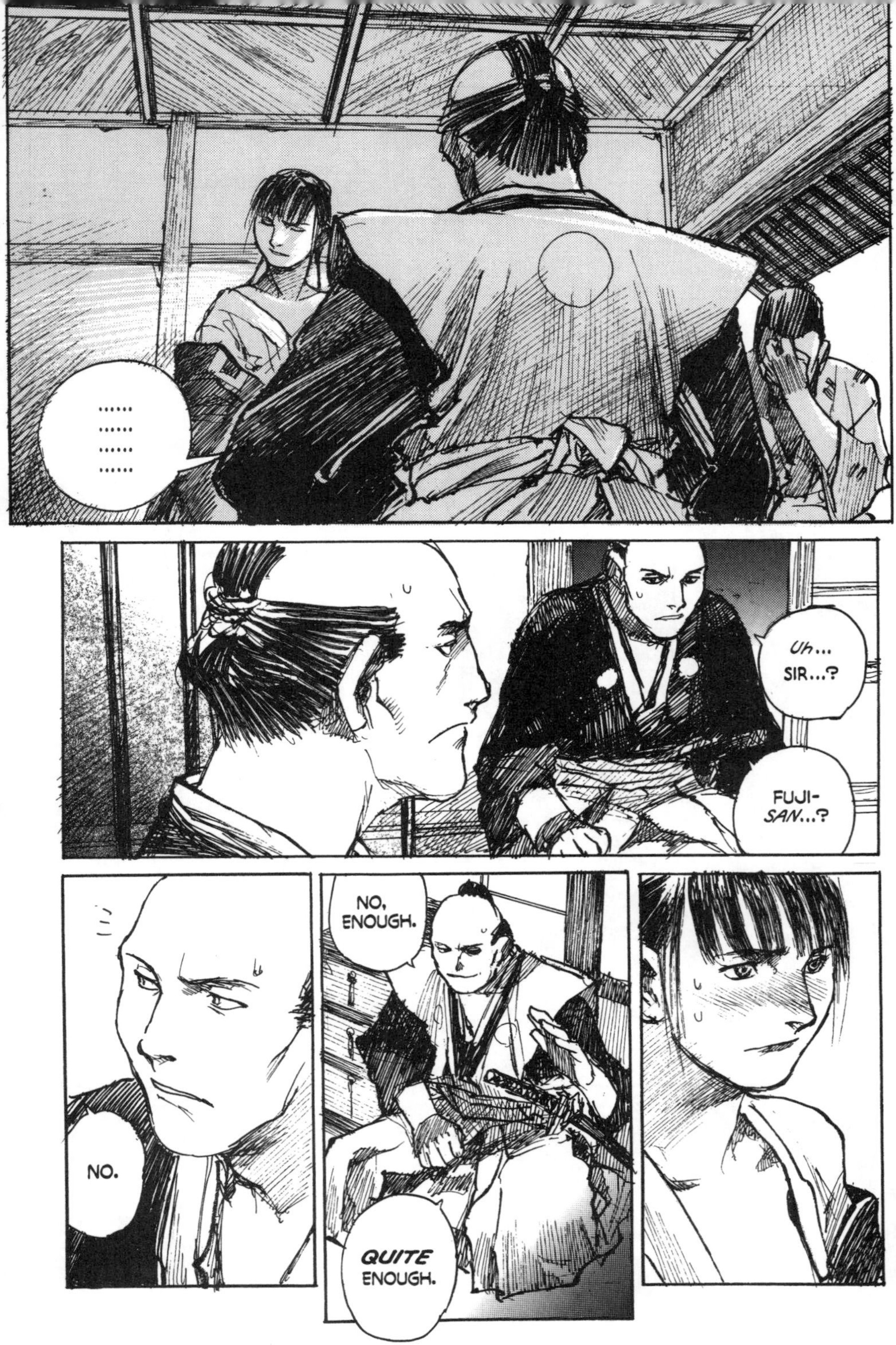
......
......
......
......
Uh... SIR...?
FUJI-SAN...?
NO.
NO, ENOUGH.
QUITE ENOUGH.

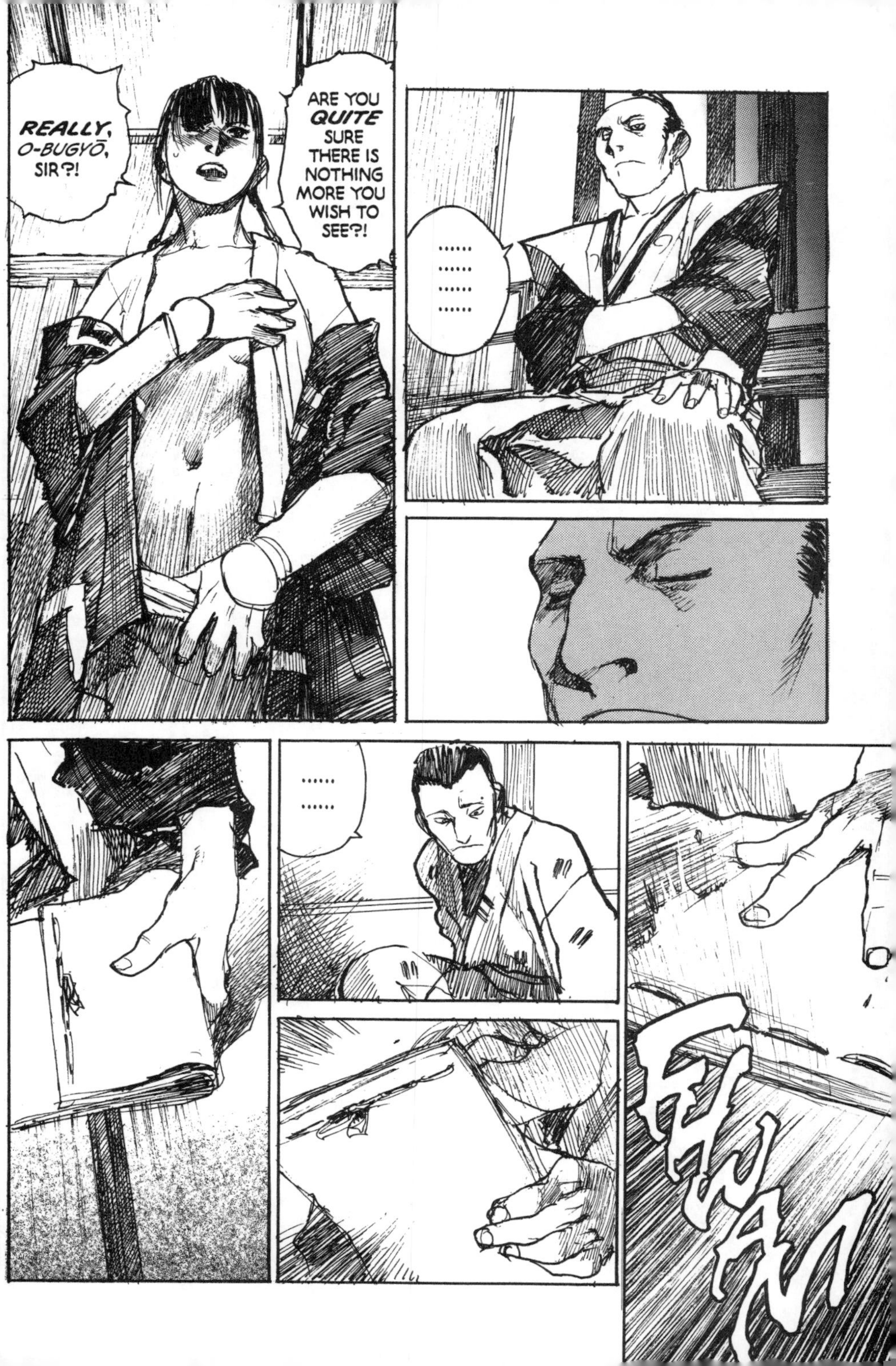
REALLY, O-BUGYŌ, SIR?!
ARE YOU QUITE SURE THERE IS NOTHING MORE YOU WISH TO SEE?!
....
....

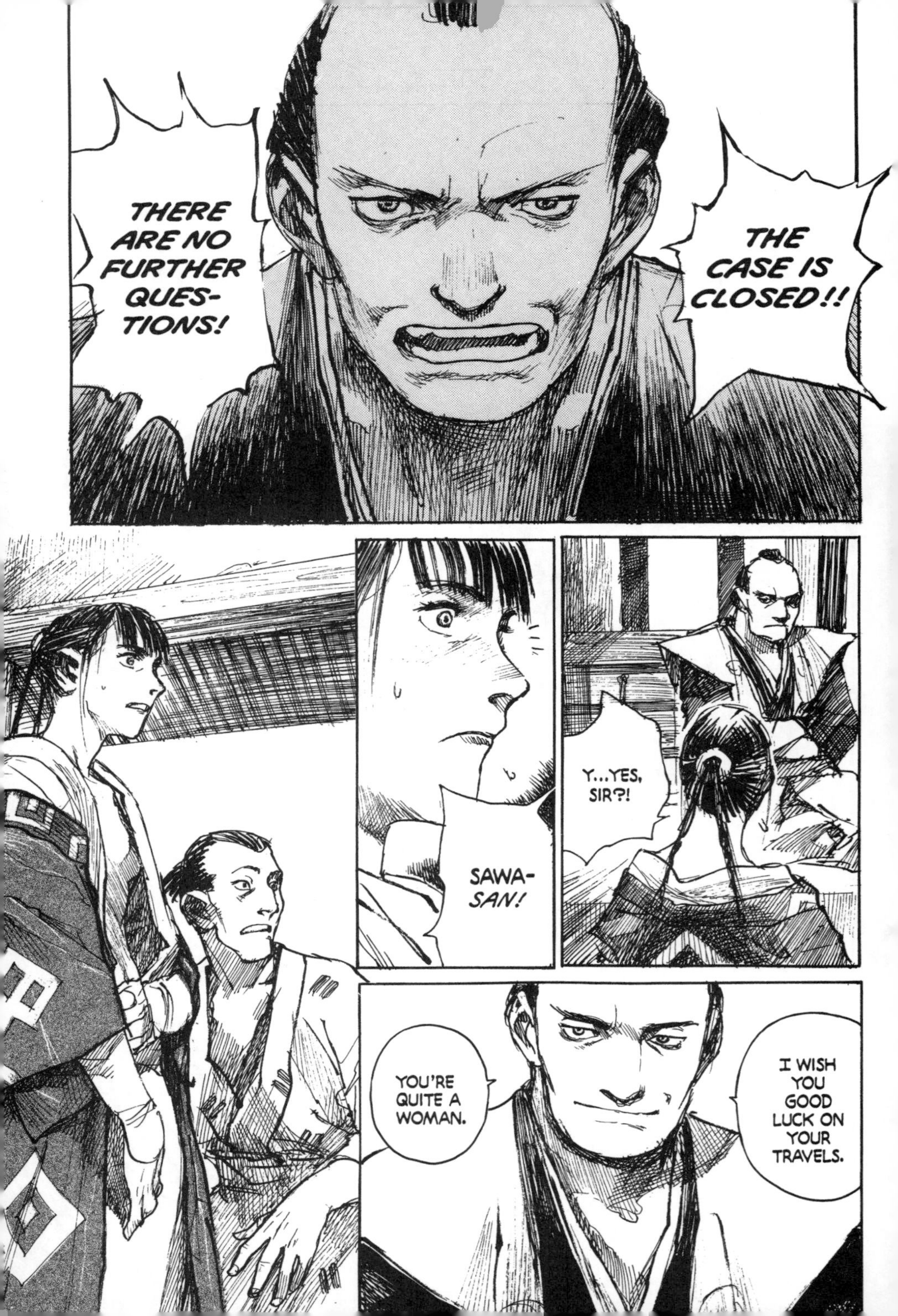
THERE ARE NO FURTHER QUES-TIONS!
THE CASE IS CLOSED!!
SAWA-SAN!
Y...YES, SIR?!
YOU'RE QUITE A WOMAN.
I WISH YOU GOOD LUCK ON YOUR TRAVELS.

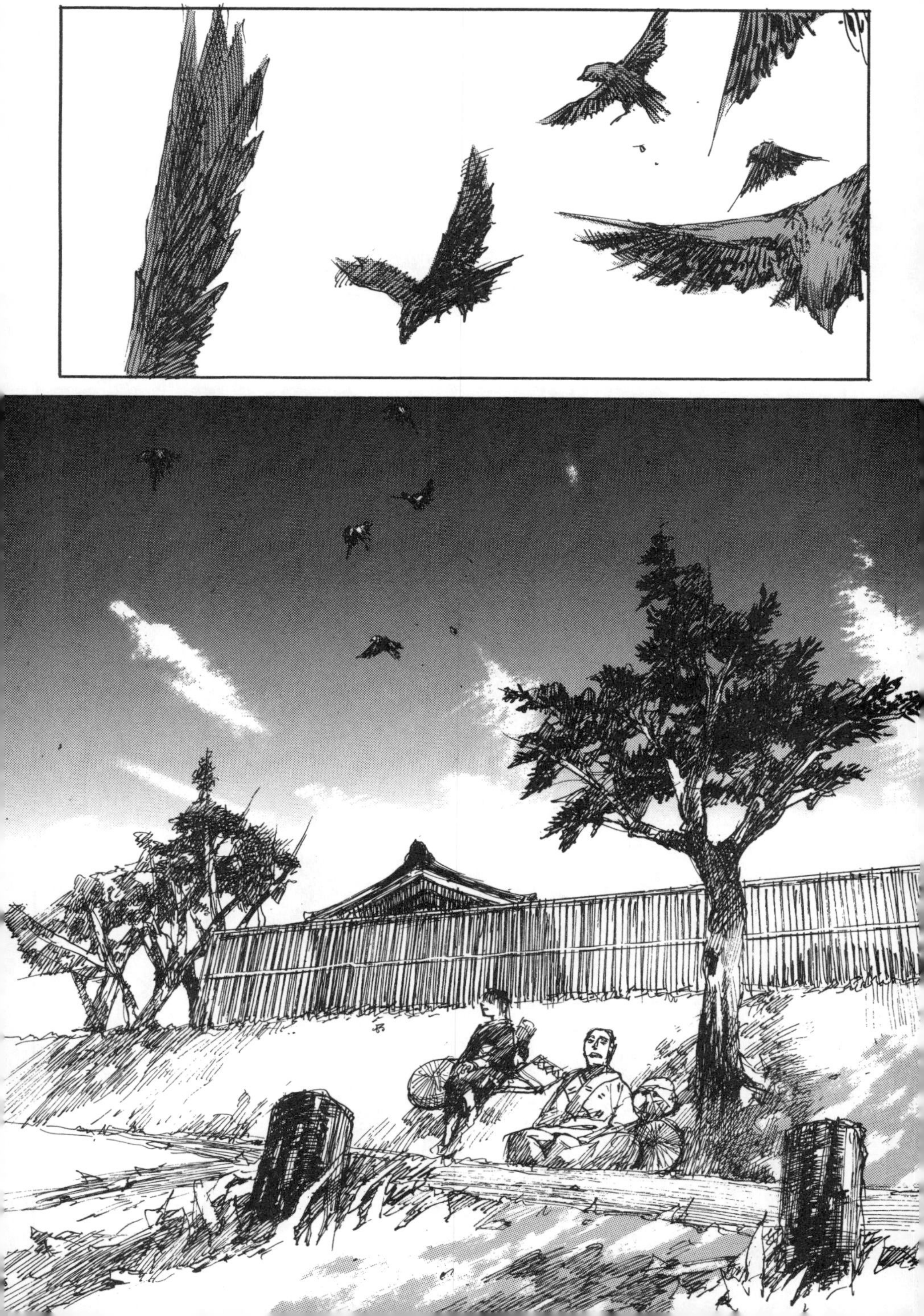

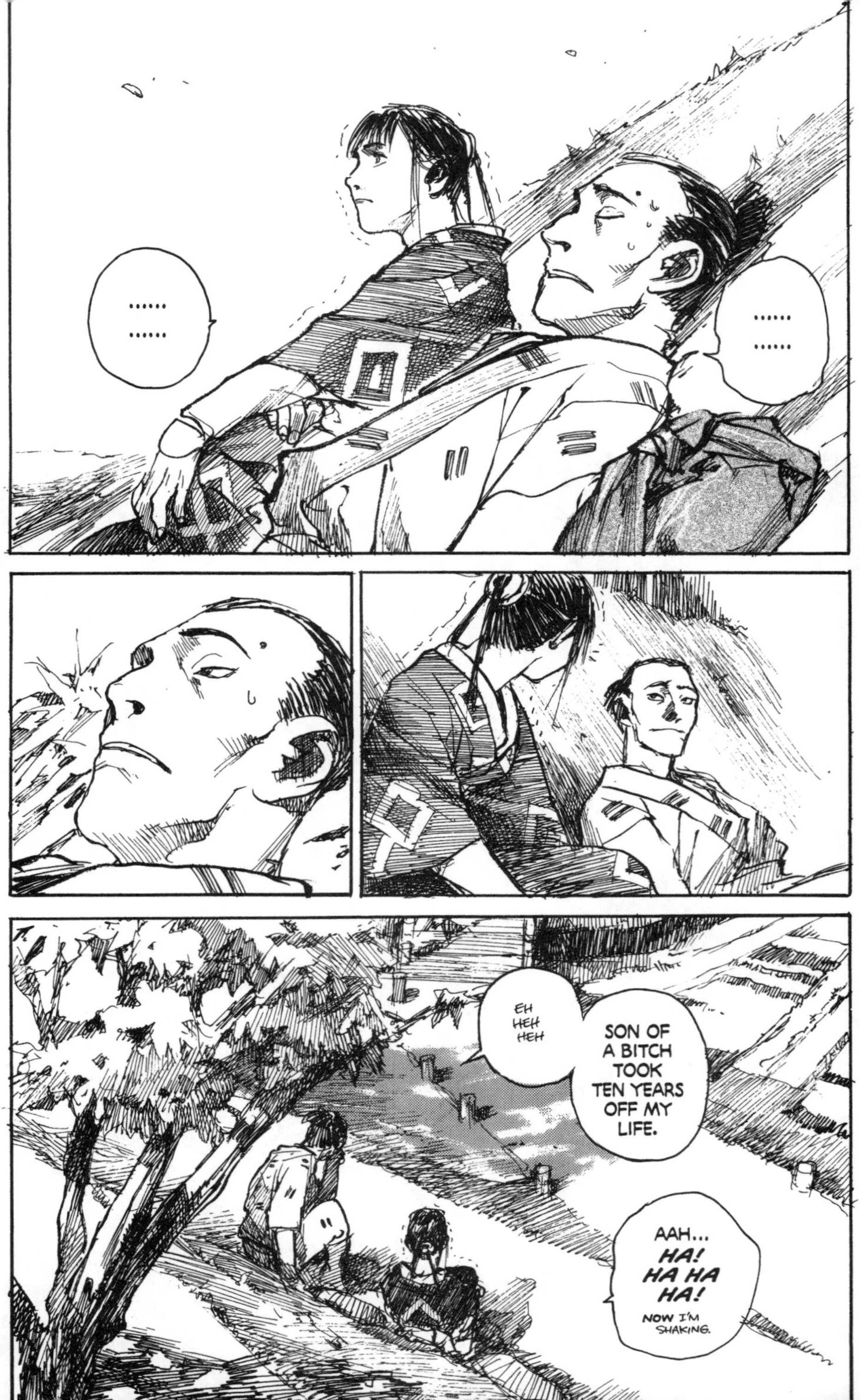
......
......
......
......
EH HEH HEH
SON OF A BITCH TOOK TEN YEARS OFF MY LIFE.
AAH... HA! HA HA HA!
NOW I'M SHAKING.

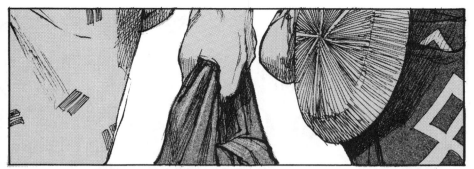

CAN'T HARDLY LOOK YOU IN THE FACE, MISS.

?? PARDON...?

AFTER EVERYTHING I TOLD YOU... HEH.

I COULDN'T LIFT A FINGER TO HELP YOU.

BUT IF I HADN'T BEEN WITH *YOU*, MISTER NAKAYA...

...I'D NEVER HAVE MADE IT AS FAR AS THE INTERROGATION.

YEAH, WELL... TRUE ENOUGH.

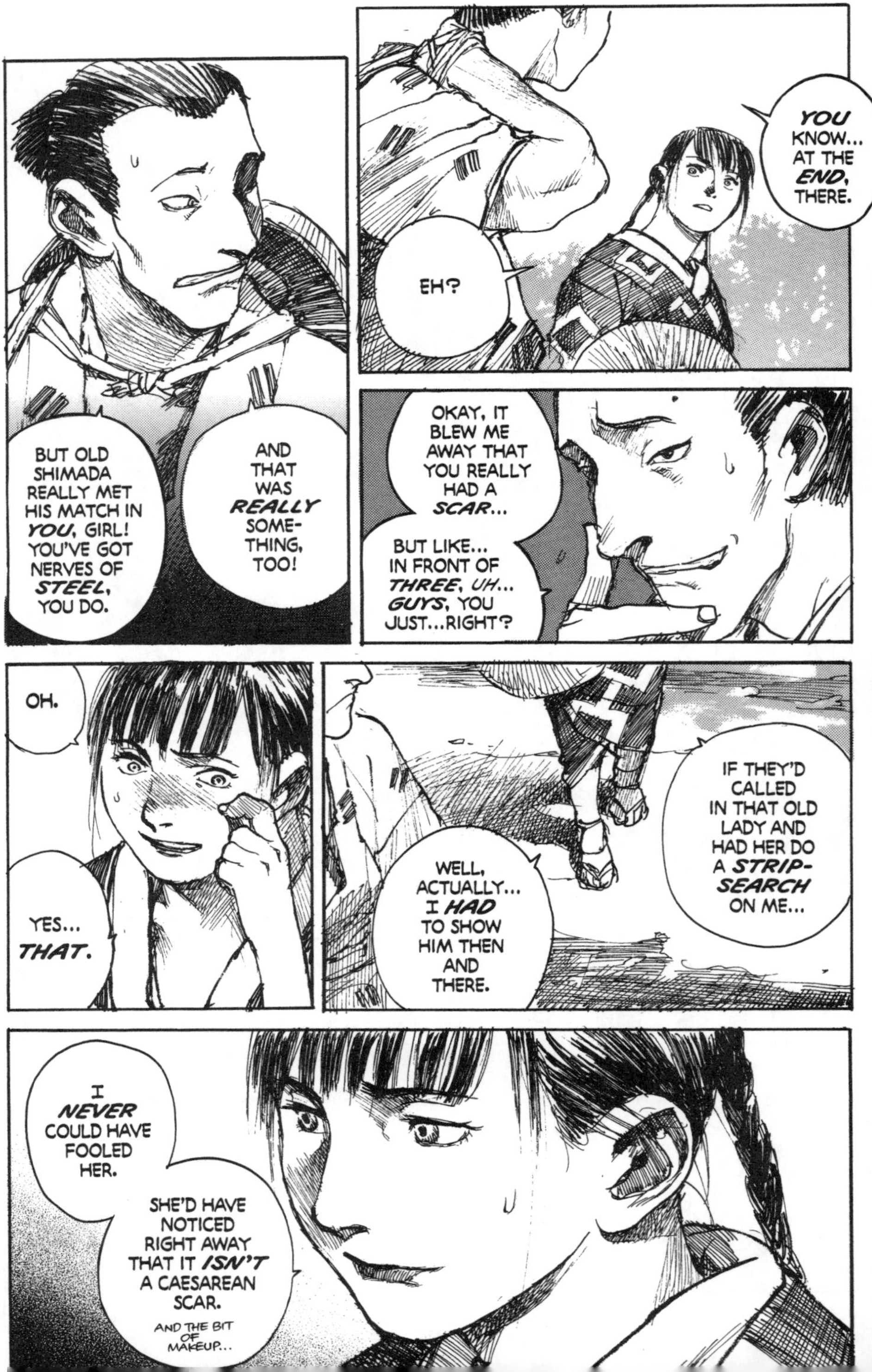
BUT OLD SHIMADA REALLY MET HIS MATCH IN *YOU*, GIRL! YOU'VE GOT NERVES OF *STEEL*, YOU DO.
AND THAT WAS *REALLY* SOME-THING, TOO!
YOU KNOW... AT THE *END*, THERE.
EH?
OKAY, IT BLEW ME AWAY THAT YOU REALLY HAD A *SCAR*...
BUT LIKE... IN FRONT OF *THREE*, *UH*... *GUYS*, YOU JUST...RIGHT?
OH.
YES... *THAT*.
WELL, ACTUALLY... I *HAD* TO SHOW HIM THEN AND THERE.
IF THEY'D CALLED IN THAT OLD LADY AND HAD HER DO A *STRIP-SEARCH* ON ME...
I *NEVER* COULD HAVE FOOLED HER.
SHE'D HAVE NOTICED RIGHT AWAY THAT IT *ISN'T* A CAESAREAN SCAR.
AND THE BIT OF MAKEUP...

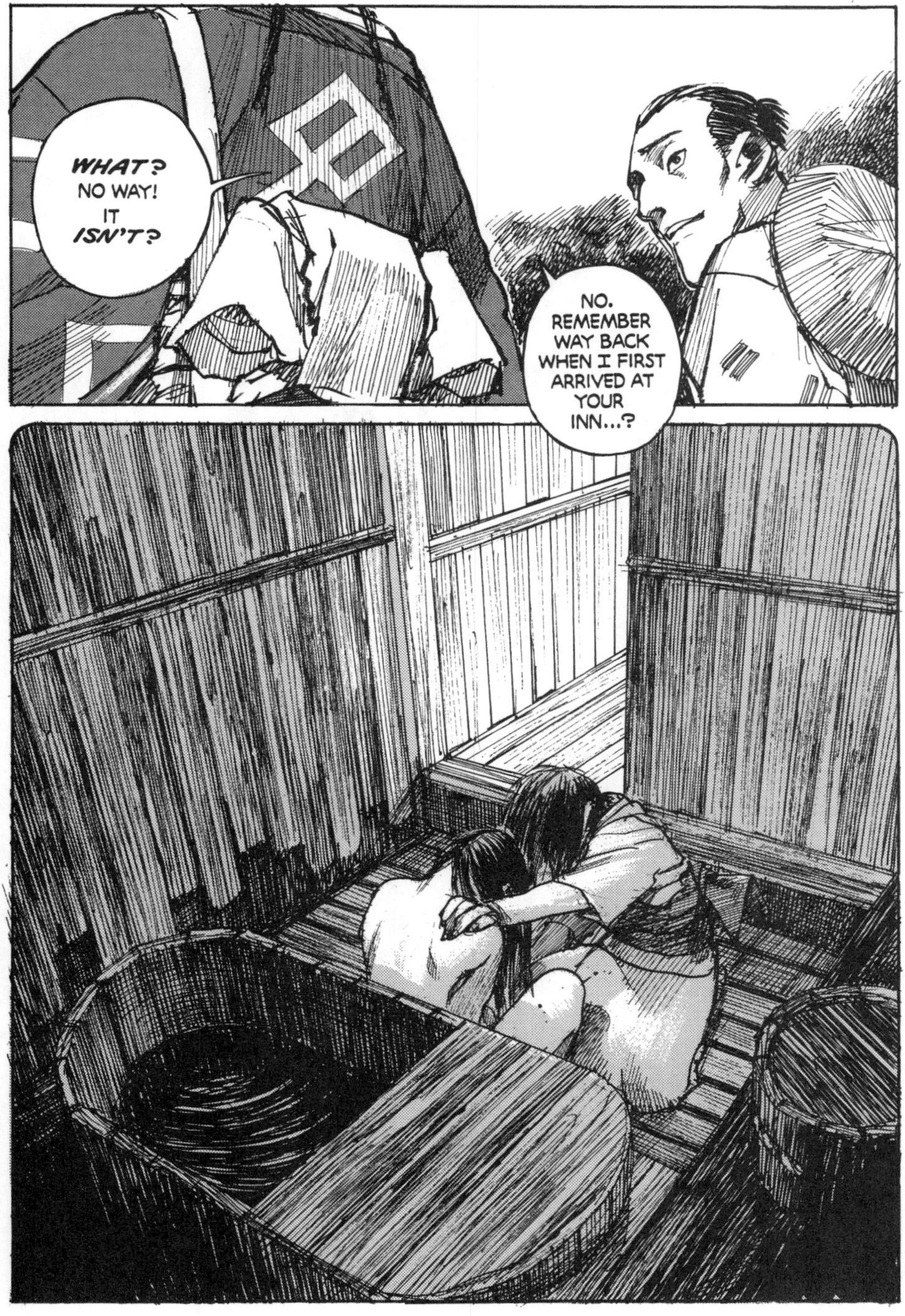
WHAT? NO WAY! IT ISN'T?
NO. REMEMBER WAY BACK WHEN I FIRST ARRIVED AT YOUR INN...?

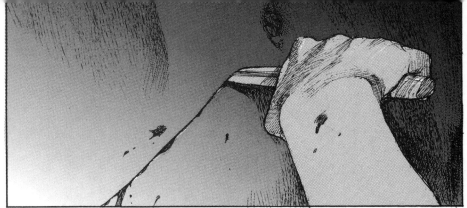

HURTS?

I'M ALMOST DONE... *BEAR* IT.

....! nnk!

NOW... PRESS DOWN UNTIL THE BLEEDING STOPS.

I DIDN'T CUT VERY DEEP.

A YEAR FROM NOW IT'LL HARDLY BE VISIBLE.

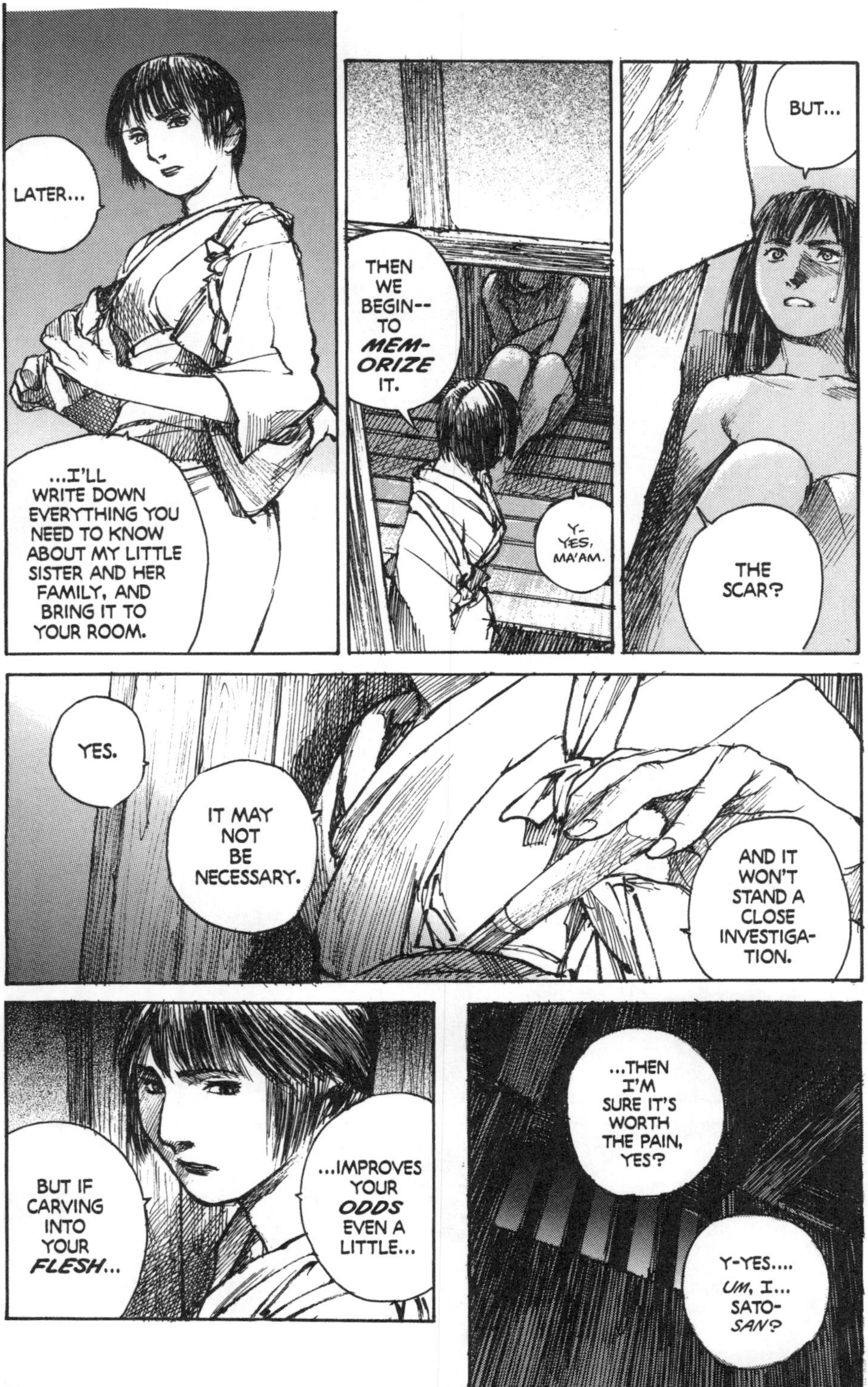
LATER...
...I'LL WRITE DOWN EVERYTHING YOU NEED TO KNOW ABOUT MY LITTLE SISTER AND HER FAMILY, AND BRING IT TO YOUR ROOM.
THEN WE BEGIN-- TO *MEMORIZE* IT.
Y-YES, MA'AM.
BUT...
THE SCAR?
YES.
IT MAY NOT BE NECESSARY.
AND IT WON'T STAND A CLOSE INVESTIGATION.
BUT IF CARVING INTO YOUR ***FLESH***...
...IMPROVES YOUR ***ODDS*** EVEN A LITTLE...
...THEN I'M SURE IT'S WORTH THE PAIN, YES?
Y-YES.... *UM,* I... SATO-*SAN?*

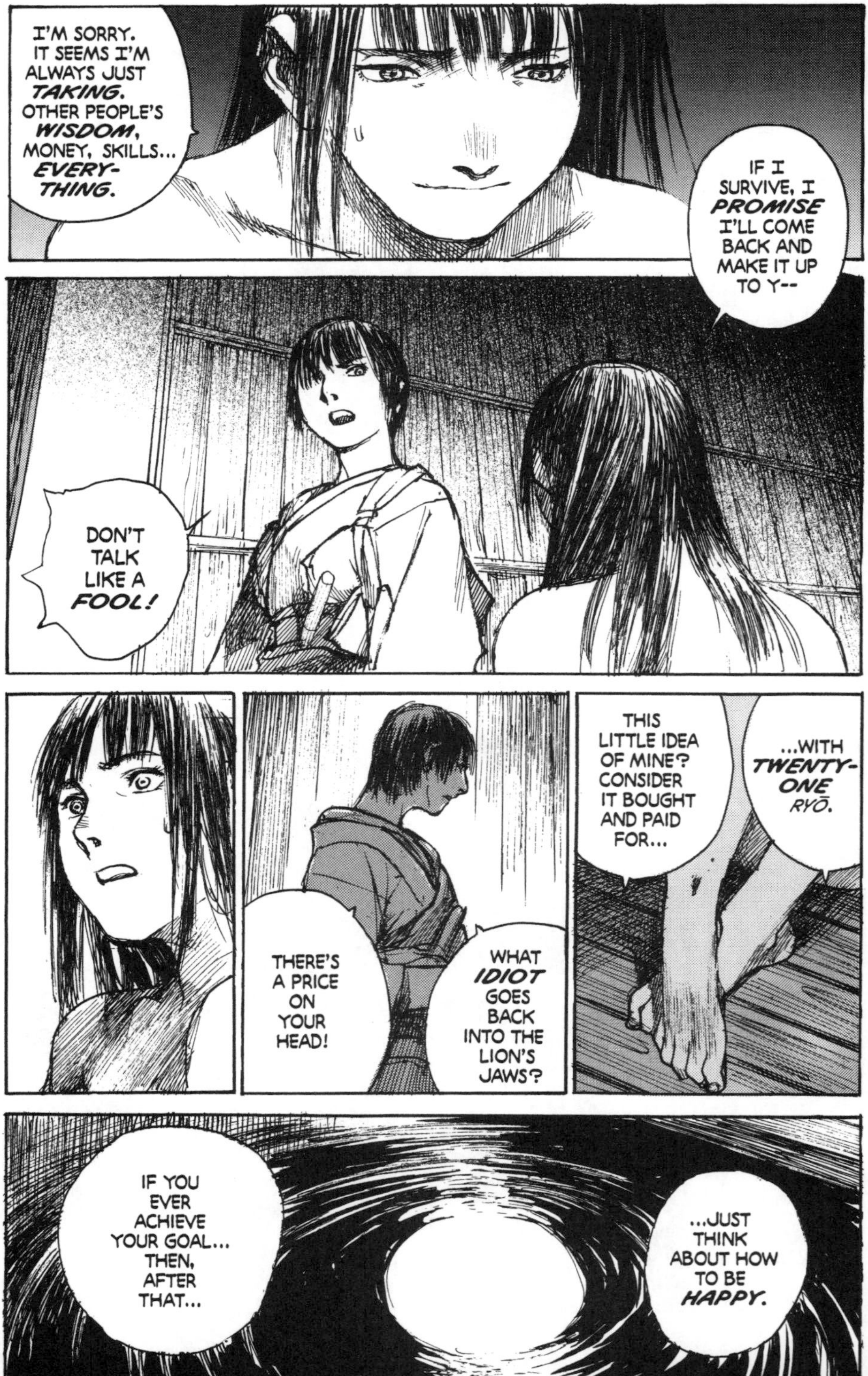
I'M SORRY. IT SEEMS I'M ALWAYS JUST TAKING. OTHER PEOPLE'S WISDOM, MONEY, SKILLS... EVERY-THING.
IF I SURVIVE, I PROMISE I'LL COME BACK AND MAKE IT UP TO Y--
DON'T TALK LIKE A FOOL!
THERE'S A PRICE ON YOUR HEAD!
WHAT IDIOT GOES BACK INTO THE LION'S JAWS?
THIS LITTLE IDEA OF MINE? CONSIDER IT BOUGHT AND PAID FOR...
...WITH TWENTY-ONE RYŌ.
IF YOU EVER ACHIEVE YOUR GOAL... THEN, AFTER THAT...
...JUST THINK ABOUT HOW TO BE HAPPY.

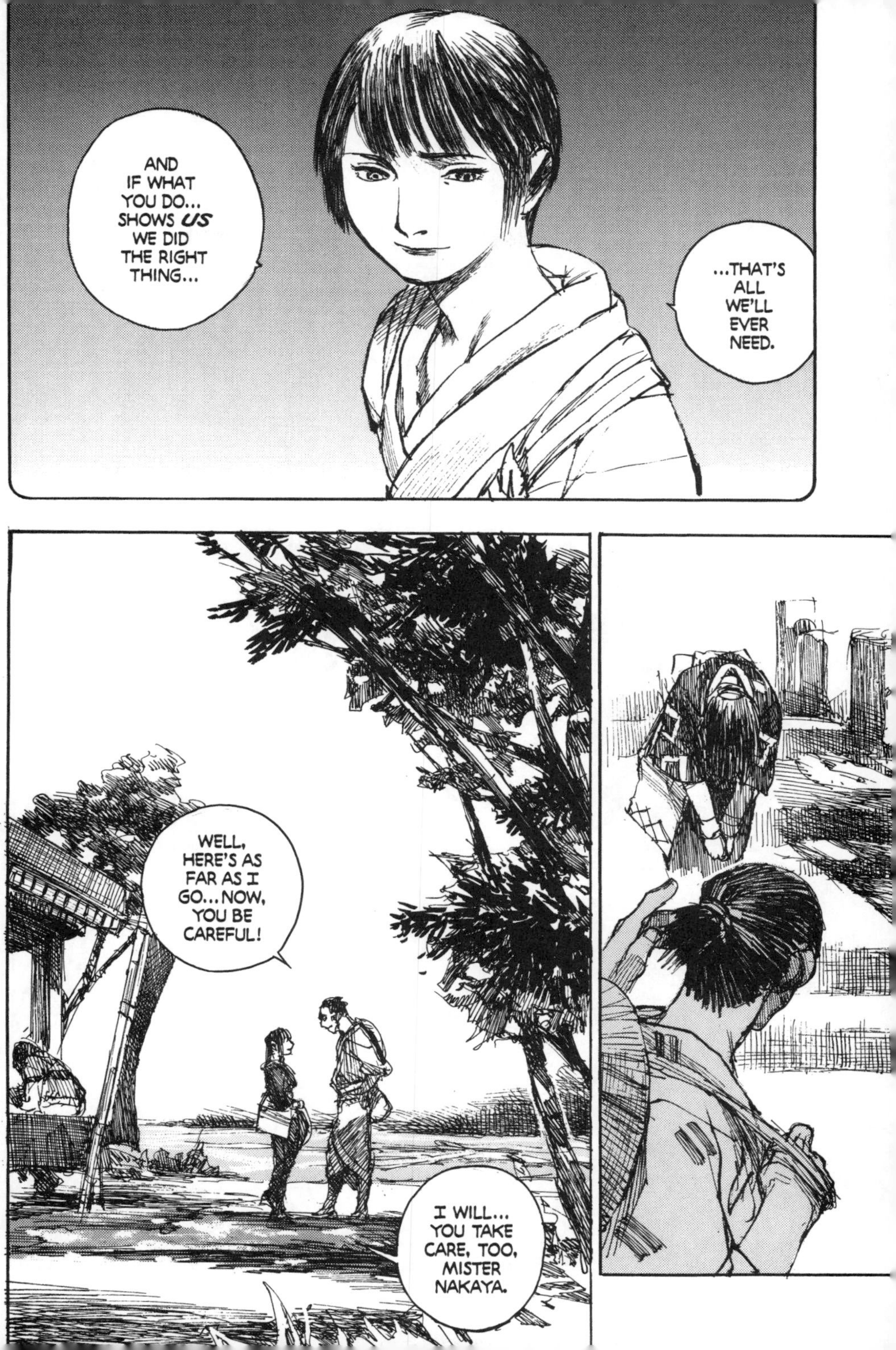
AND IF WHAT YOU DO... SHOWS *US* WE DID THE RIGHT THING...
...THAT'S ALL WE'LL EVER NEED.
WELL, HERE'S AS FAR AS I GO...NOW, YOU BE CAREFUL!
I WILL... YOU TAKE CARE, TOO, MISTER NAKAYA.

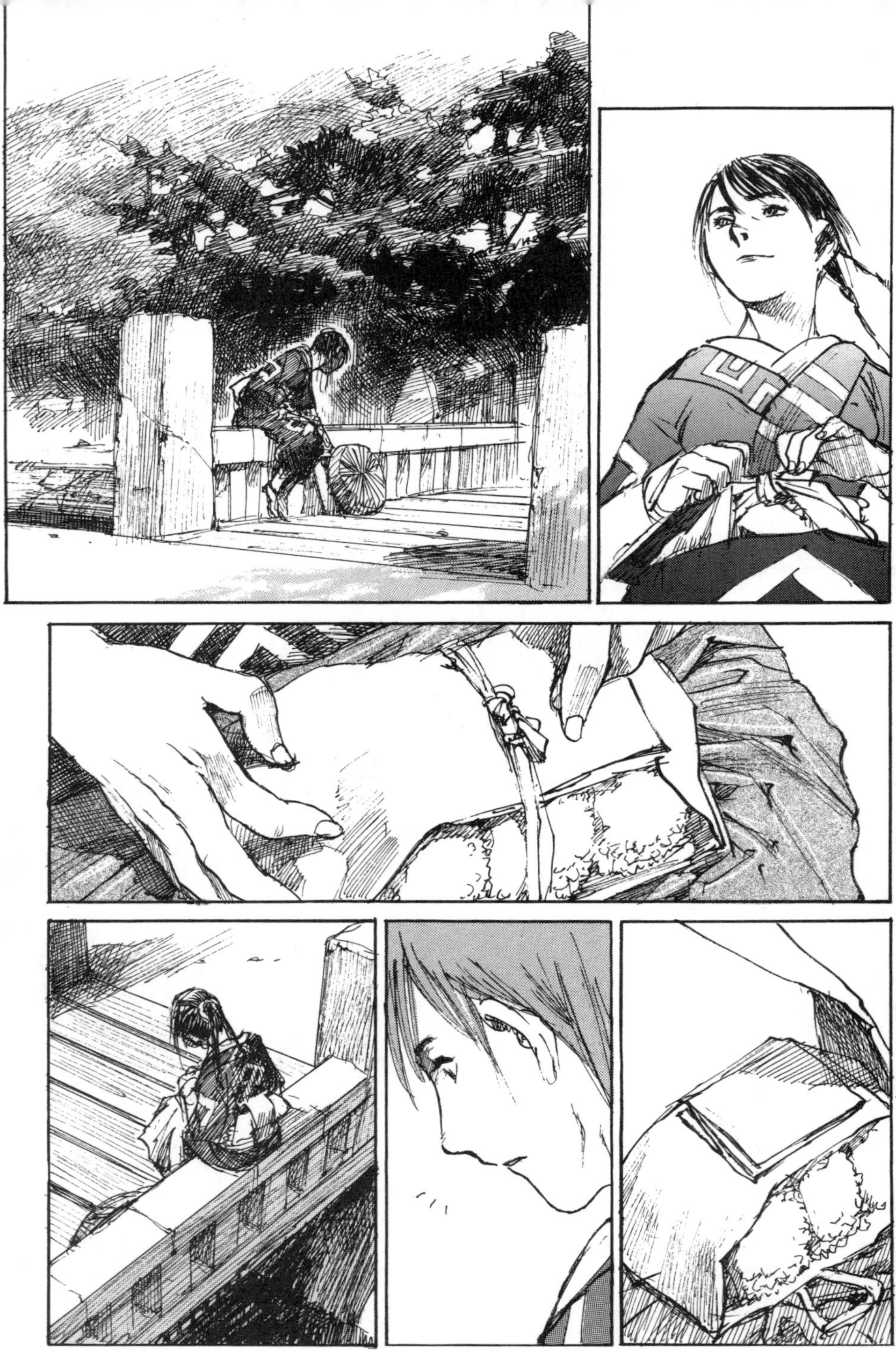

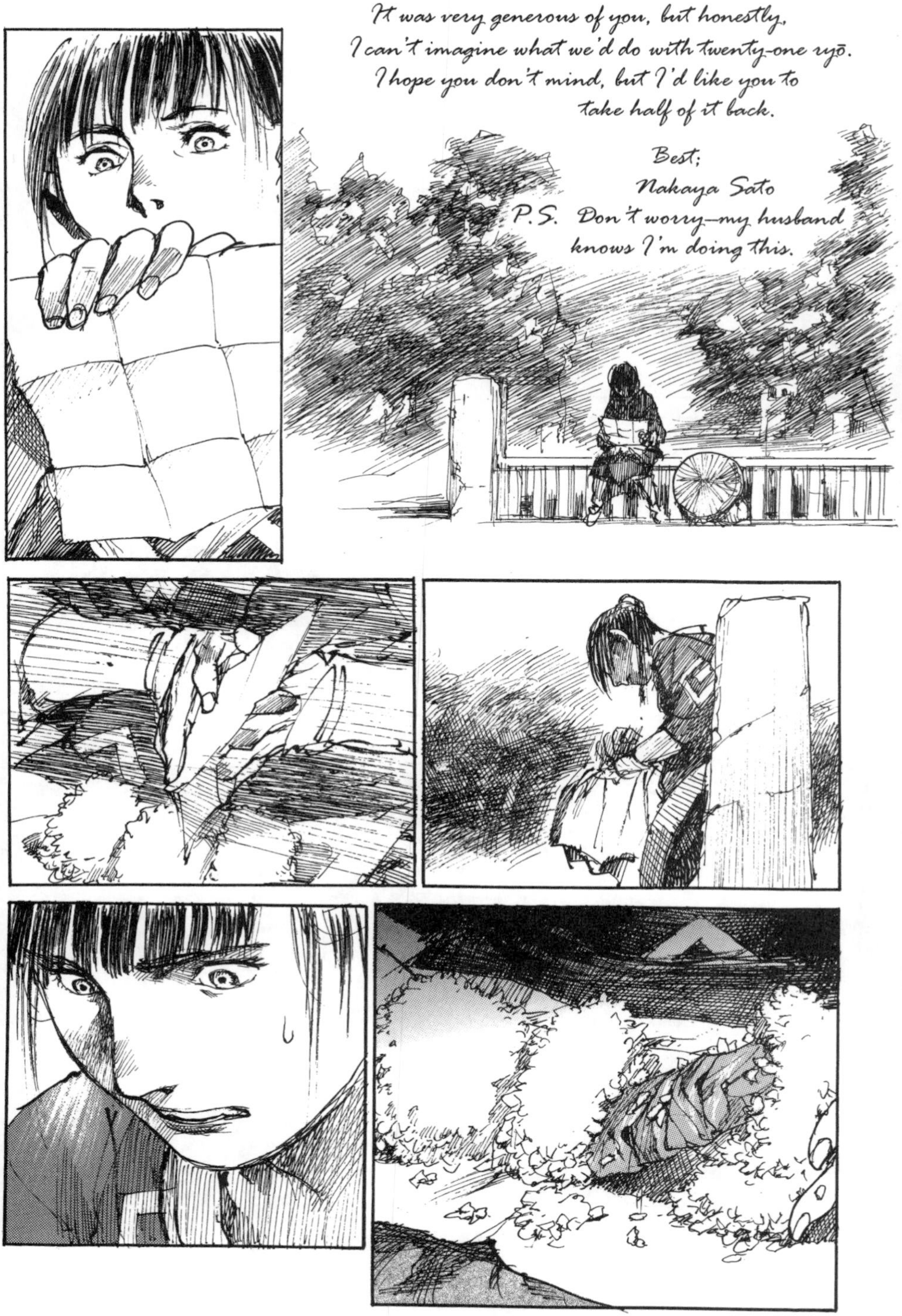
It was very generous of you, but honestly, I can't imagine what we'd do with twenty-one ryō. I hope you don't mind, but I'd like you to take half of it back.
Best;
Nakaya Sato
P.S. Don't worry—my husband knows I'm doing this.

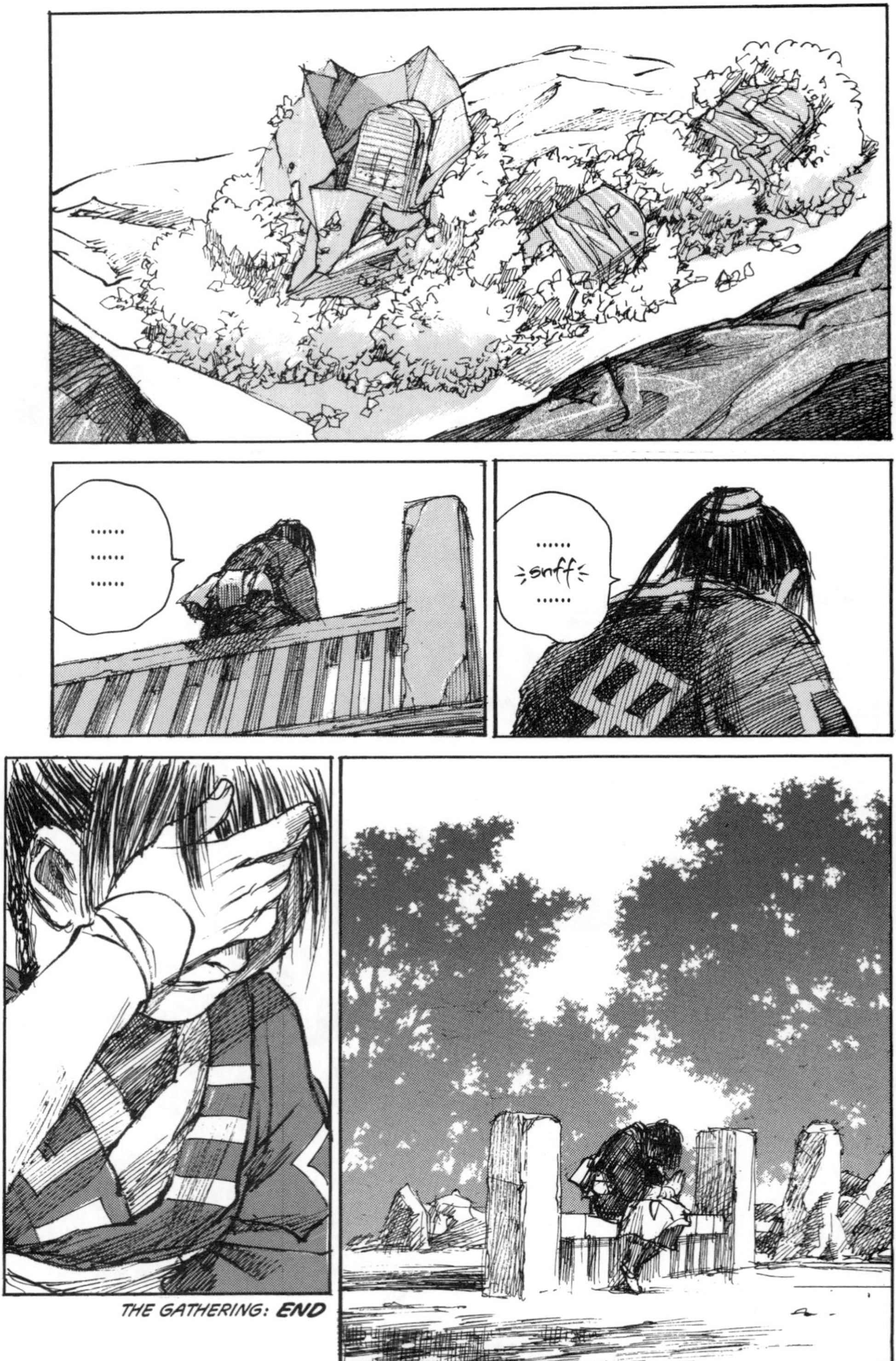
......
......
......
......
snff
......
THE GATHERING: END

GLOSSARY

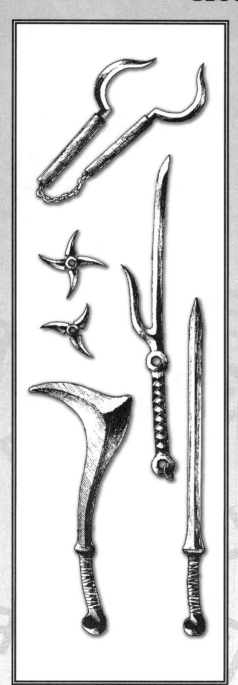

banshi: samurai manning a *sekisho* (checkpoint)

bugyō: a high-ranked samurai in charge of keeping the peace, with the help of the men under his command and volunteer "posse" members

Koshū Byway: one of the main roads out of Edo to the western provinces

ryō: a gold piece (note: the money Rin gives Nakaya and Sato in this story would probably amount to several years' worth of normal income for the innkeepers)

sekisho: checkpoint regulating travel from Edo to other *han* (feudal domains). All travelers had to submit papers at official checkpoints along the main highways into and out of Edo.

tatami: a thick, rice straw mat used as flooring in traditional Japanese households, still commonly found in at least one room of a residence even today

tegata (tsūkō tegata): official travel pass for transiting *sekisho*

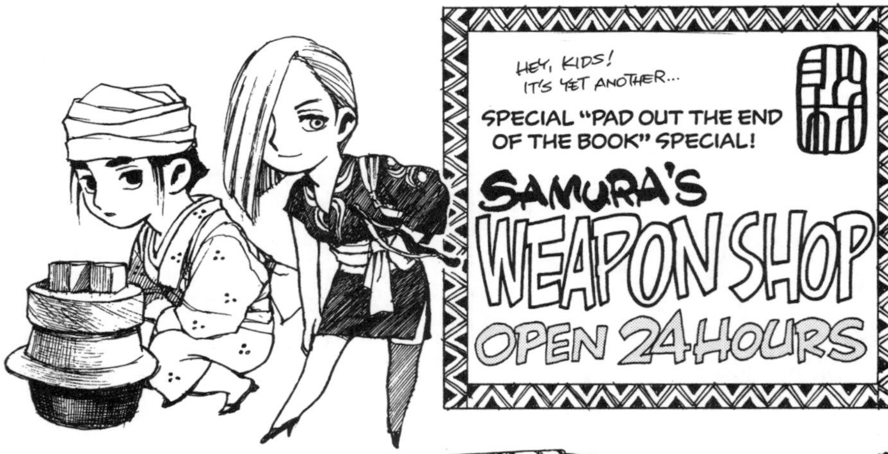
HEY, KIDS!
IT'S YET ANOTHER...
SPECIAL "PAD OUT THE END OF THE BOOK" SPECIAL!
SAMURA'S
WEAPON SHOP
OPEN 24 HOURS

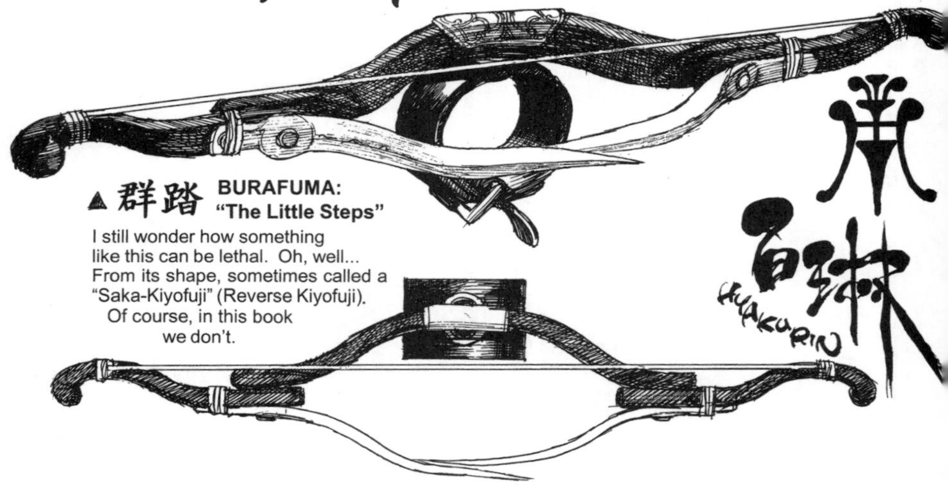
HYAKURIN

▲ 群踏 **BURAFUMA:**
"The Little Steps"

I still wonder how something like this can be lethal. Oh, well... From its shape, sometimes called a "Saka-Kiyofuji" (Reverse Kiyofuji). Of course, in this book we don't.

—— HOW TO CONCEAL YOUR BURAFUMA IN THREE EASY STEPS ——

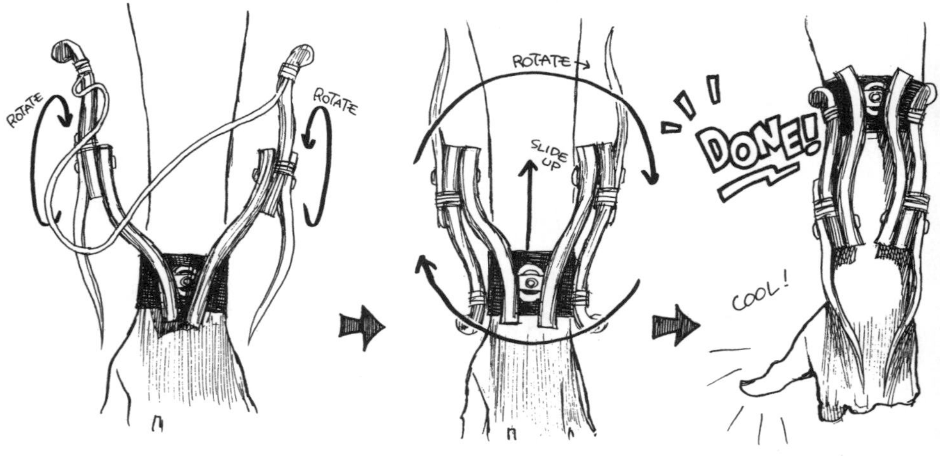
ROTATE
ROTATE
ROTATE
SLIDE UP
DONE!
COOL!

GIICHI

錦連・三途ノ守　KANETSURA'S MITO-NO-KAMI:
"Guardian of the Three Paths"

Forged by the mystery swordsmith, Kanetsura, this weapon is constructed like a handcuff. The main blade is sharpened on both sides, while the moving blade is sharpened only on the inside.

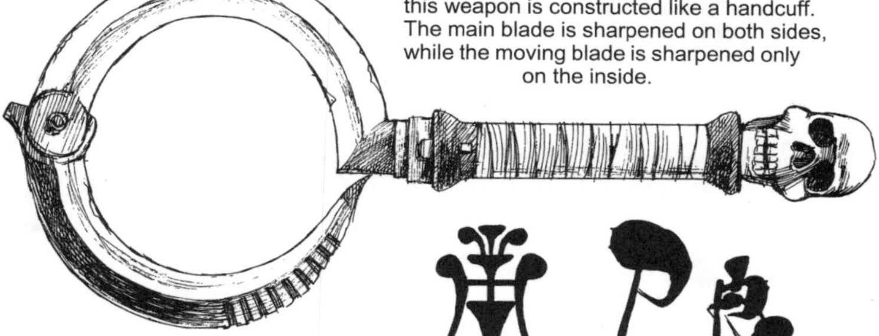

SHIRA

OUT OF THE TRIO OF HYAKURIN, SHIRA, AND GIICHI, ONLY SHIRA CAN REALLY BE CALLED A **SWORD**SMAN...

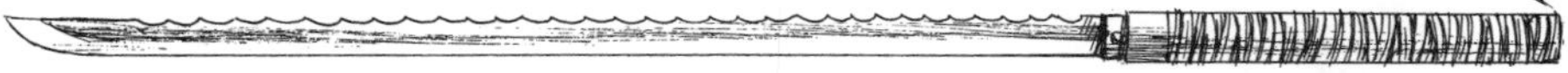

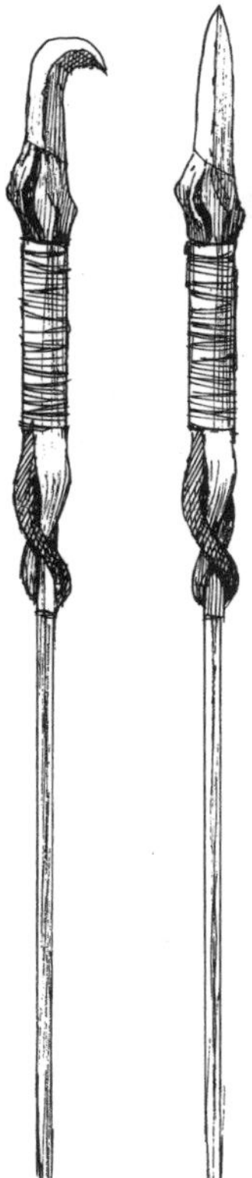

◀燕誅丸
ENCHŪ-MARU:
"Swallows of Death"

To be perfectly honest, I wonder why he doesn't just use a normal sword. You can't kill anyone with these things unless you precisely strike a lethal point.

鬼太鼓桴▶
ONDEKO-BACHI:
"Devil's Drumstick"

Uruma swings this thing around like some college baseball star.

By the way, Hanada was supposed to look like John Lennon, but when I was finished he was just another *otaku* dude. Where did I go wrong...?

▲ホトソギ（女陰削ぎ）
HOTOSOGI:

The *kanji* for writing the name of this weapon have a very unpleasant second meaning. The sawlike edge of the blade has only one purpose— to inflict maximum pain.
It's a heretical sword that seems to crystallize Shira's own warped personality.

HANADA

URUMA

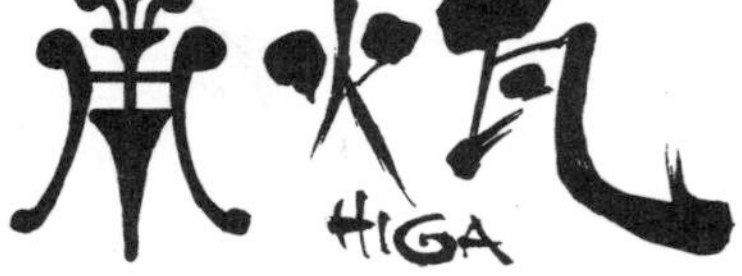

HIGA

▼神刀 **KAMUJIN: "Godblade"**

Out of all the countries Japan was trading with at the time, who would have exported this vaguely Southeast Asian sword? Putting that aside for now, this is another piece that, depending on the skill of the wielder, is weighty enough to shatter an opponent's blade.

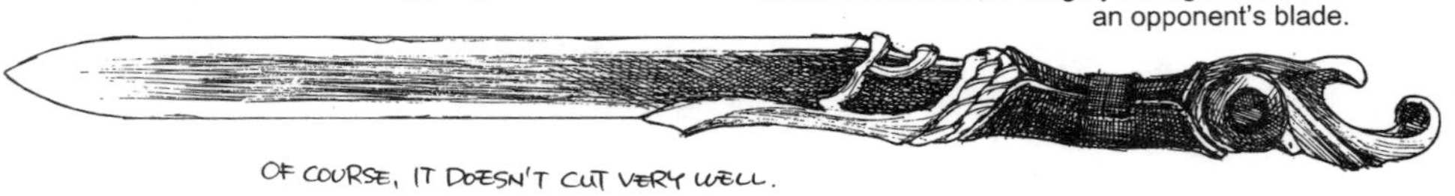

OF COURSE, IT DOESN'T CUT VERY WELL.

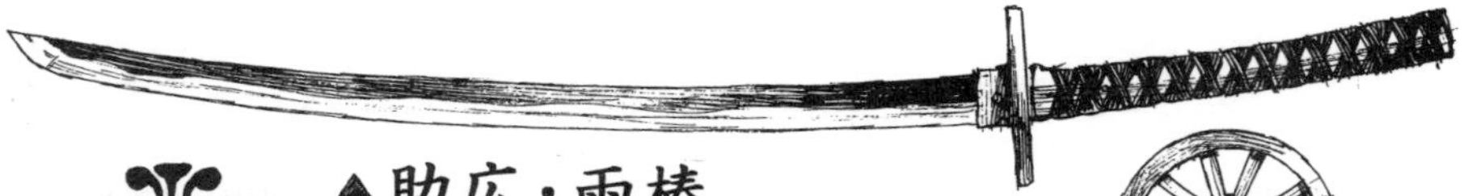

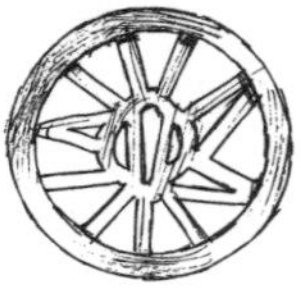

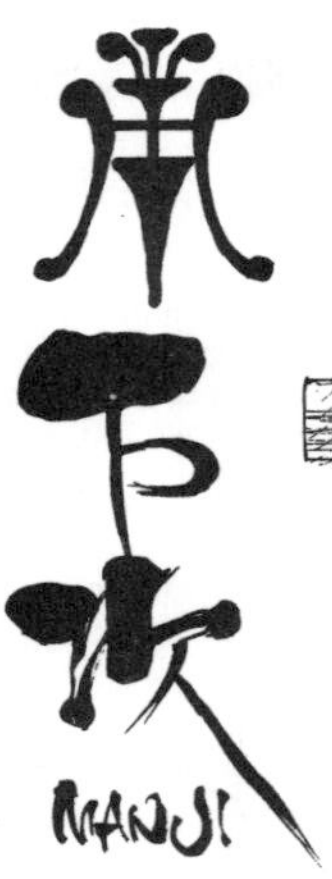

MANJI

▲助広・雨椿

SUKEHIRO AMATSUBAKI: "Rain Camellia"

This is a regular *nihon-to* (Japanese sword), but a famous one, made by the master swordsmith Sukehiro.

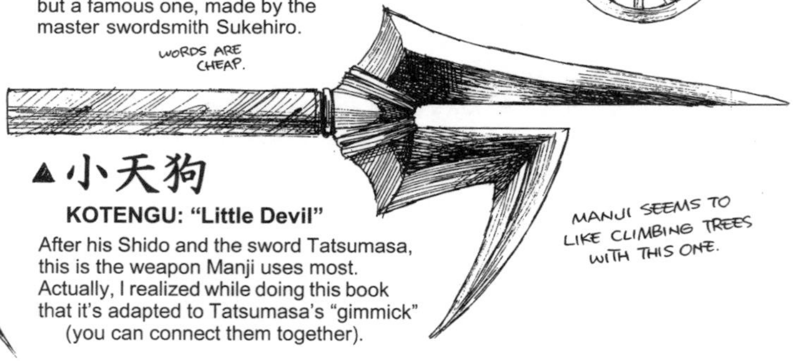

WORDS ARE CHEAP.
MANJI SEEMS TO LIKE CLIMBING TREES WITH THIS ONE.

▲小天狗

KOTENGU: "Little Devil"

After his Shido and the sword Tatsumasa, this is the weapon Manji uses most. Actually, I realized while doing this book that it's adapted to Tatsumasa's "gimmick" (you can connect them together).

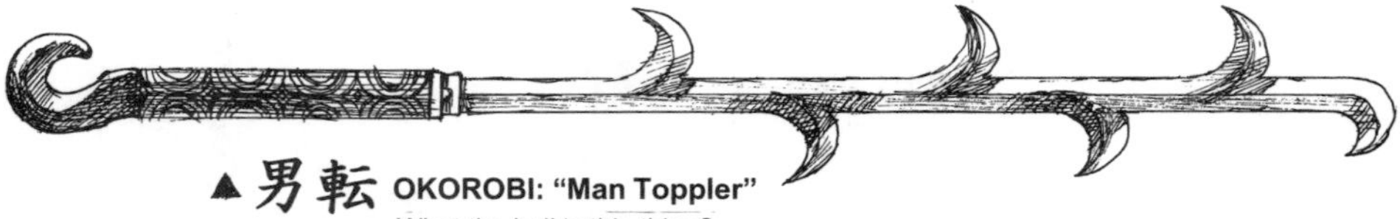

▲男転 **OKOROBI: "Man Toppler"**

What the hell is this thing? Don't ask me.

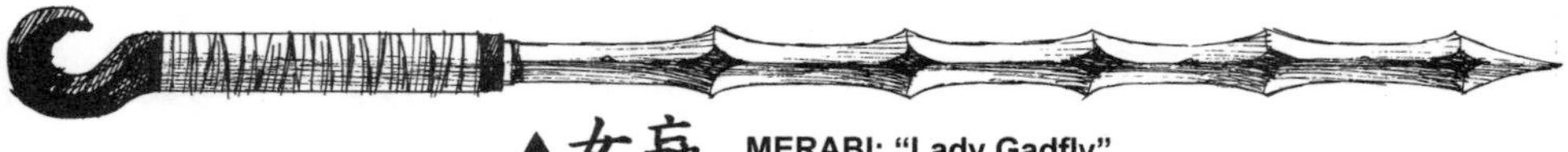

▲女蝱 **MERABI: "Lady Gadfly"**

By the time you get to this, it's hard to tell if it's a sword at all. Maybe it started out as a carpenter's tool, or surveyor's gear or something...? He's never given either of them a real workout in the story so far (...although he does use them a little bit in *Dreamsong*). I guess I'll use them again at least once before the series ends.

HIROAKI SAMURA

OF THE IMMORTAL

BLOOD OF A THOUSAND
ISBN: 1-56971-239-5 / $14.95

CRY OF THE WORM
ISBN: 1-56971-300-6 / $14.95

DREAMSONG
ISBN: 1-56971-357-X / $14.95

ON SILENT WINGS
ISBN: 1-56971-412-6 / $14.95

ON SILENT WINGS II
ISBN: 1-56971-444-4 / $14.95

DARK SHADOWS
ISBN: 1-56971-469-X / $14.95

HEART OF DARKNESS
ISBN: 1-56971-531-9 / $16.95

THE GATHERING
ISBN: 1-56971-546-7 / $15.95

THE GATHERING II
ISBN: 1-56971-560-2 / $15.95

SECRETS
ISBN: 1-56971-746-X / $16.95

BEASTS
ISBN: 1-56971-741-9 / $14.95

AUTUMN FROST
ISBN: 1-56971-991-8 / $16.95

MIRROR OF THE SOUL
ISBN: 1-56971-218-X / $17.95

AVAILABLE AT YOUR LOCAL COMICS SHOP OR BOOKSTORE • TO FIND A COMICS SHOP IN YOUR AREA, CALL 1-888-266-4226
For more information or to order direct visit darkhorse.com or call 1-800-862-0052 Mon.-Sat. 9 A.M. to 5 P.M. Pacific Time
*Prices and availability subject to change without notice